THOMAS MANN'S WAR

THOMAS MANN'S WAR

LITERATURE, POLITICS, AND THE
WORLD REPUBLIC OF LETTERS

TOBIAS BOES

CORNELL UNIVERSITY PRESS
Ithaca and London

First published 2019 by Cornell University Press

Printed in the United States of America

Library of Congress Cataloging-in-Publication Data

Names: Boes, Tobias, 1976– author.
Title: Thomas Mann's war : literature, politics, and the world republic of letters / Tobias Boes.
Description: Ithaca : Cornell University Press, 2019. | Includes bibliographical references and index.
Identifiers: LCCN 2019019611 (print) | LCCN 2019020253 (ebook) | ISBN 9781501745010 (epub/mobi) | ISBN 9781501745003 (pdf) | ISBN 9781501744990 | ISBN 9781501744990 (cloth ; alk. paper)
Subjects: LCSH: Mann, Thomas, 1875–1955—Political activity. | Authors, German—20th century—Political and social views. | Authors, Exiled—Political activity—United States. | Politics and literature—Germany—History—20th century. | World War, 1939–1945—Literature and the war. | World War, 1939–1945—Public opinion.
Classification: LCC PT2625.A44 (ebook) | LCC PT2625. A44 Z54256 2019 (print) | DDC 833/.912—dc23
LC record available at https://lccn.loc.gov/2019019611

For Luisa—and for Richard

Contents

Illustrations

ACKNOWLEDGMENTS

This book has been a long time in the making, and I accrued a lot of debts during the years in which I was writing it. I conducted initial research for the project during a fellowship year sponsored by the National Endowment for the Humanities in 2015. I was able to complete the manuscript thanks to an Alexander von Humboldt Fellowship for Experienced Researchers that took me to the Georg-August-Universität Göttingen in the spring and summer of 2018. I owe special thanks to my initial sponsor, Gerhard Lauer, and to my host at Göttingen, Heinrich Detering. The Institute for Scholarship in the Liberal Arts (ISLA) and the Nanovic Institute for European Studies, both at the University of Notre Dame, supported my visits to archives in the United States and in Germany. ISLA also provided a publishing subvention that helped defray the cost of producing this book.

My archival forays would not have been nearly as productive without the help of several experienced librarians and archivists: Katrin Bedenig at the Thomas-Mann-Archive of the Eidgenössische Technische Hochschule in Zurich, Rick Watson at the Harry Ransom Humanities Center at the University of Texas at Austin, Ned Comstock at the USC Cinematic Arts Library, and Maren Roth at the Melvin J. Lasky Center for Transatlantic Studies, University of Munich. Sara Judy, at the time a graduate student at the University of Vermont, conducted remote research for me in the Dorothy Canfield Fisher Papers, while Nikita Allgire, a graduate student at the University of Southern California, scouted the way at USC. I'd also like to thank the staff of the Library of Congress, the New York Public Library, and the Harvard and Princeton University archives.

My manuscript improved considerably as a result of feedback that I received at several invited lectures and public discussions. I'd like to thank the following personal and institutional hosts: Rebecca Johnson and Christopher Bush at Northwestern University; Benedict Schofield and Erica Carter at King's College, London; Rüdiger Görner at Queen Mary University, London; Helen Finch and Stuart Taberner at the University of Leeds; Julia Faisst at the Katholische Universität Eichstätt-Ingolstadt; Chris van den Berg at

Amherst College; Katra Byram and Robert Holub at The Ohio State University; Caroline Kita and Jennifer Kapczynski at Washington University in St. Louis; Frank Wolff and Laura Roos at the Centre Marc Bloch, Berlin; Anna Kinder at the Deutsches Literaturarchiv Marbach. I also gave presentations on my manuscript at the German Studies Association, the Modernist Studies Association, the American Comparative Literature Association, the Internationale Vereinigung für Germanistik, and the Biannual Jewish-German Workshop at the University of Notre Dame.

Fellow Thomas Mann scholars Hans Rudolf Vaget, Tim Lörke, and Kai Sina kindly read parts of the manuscript and shared their expertise with me. Todd Kontje and Lynne Tatlock have also followed this project from the very beginning, and served as an inspiration for my thinking about transatlantic cultural exchange. The members of the Cultural Transformations in Modern Europe working group at Notre Dame provided feedback on virtually the entire manuscript as I was developing it. I am deeply grateful to the group's members: Christopher Chowrimootoo, John Deak, Julia Douthwaite, Perin Gurel, Katie Jarvis, Tom Kselman, Alex Martin, Vittorio Montemaggi, Ian Newman, Joseph Rosenberg, and Yasmin Solomonescu.

A long list of people provided additional help and encouragement, or just asked provocative questions. Among them were Jessica Berman, Rebecca Braun, William Coker, Erika Doss, Sean Franzel, Laurie Johnson, Yuliya Komska, Robert Leucht, Eric Lindstrom, Kate Marshall, Jim McAdams, Barry McCrea, Andree Michaelis, Michael Valdez Moses, Carl Niekerk, Anna Parkinson, Thomas Pfau, Daniel Purdy, Paul Saint-Amour, Emily Spiers, Susanne Vees-Gulani, and Johannes von Moltke.

Melissa Dinsman, in her outstanding dissertation on modernist radio culture, asked methodological questions that would come to haunt me as well— and did excellent work on Thomas Mann's BBC broadcasts. Jade Panlener, an undergraduate at Notre Dame, tracked down numerous page references from American works for me while I was on research leave in Germany.

A very early version of chapter 2 was published in *Modernism/modernity*; an early version of interlude II, in *Kongressakten der Konferenz der Internationalen Vereinigung für Germanistik in Tongji*. I thank these venues for the permission to reproduce this material.

ABBREVIATIONS

Quotations from the works of Thomas Mann are given in English throughout the text and are followed by parenthetical references to both English- and German-language editions. I have mostly cited the first American publications, though in some cases I have given preference to later editions if they achieved a much wider circulation during Thomas Mann's lifetime or if doing so could help impose some consistency. The German references are to the most up-to-date critical editions available, as explained below. For texts that have as yet not been published in English, only a German citation appears, and the translation is my own. Similarly, on the rare occasion that an English text by Thomas Mann has never been translated into German, only the English citation appears.

English-language works of Thomas Mann

ADH   *Addresses at the Dinner in Honor of Dr. Thomas Mann, on the Occasion of His Seventieth Birthday, New York, June 25, 1945.* New York: Nation Associates, 1945.

AGP   "Address to the German People." *Nation*, May 12, 1945, 535.

BR   *The Beloved Returns: Lotte in Weimar.* Translated by H. T. Lowe-Porter. New York: Alfred A. Knopf, 1940.

D   *Thomas Mann: Diaries 1918–1939.* Edited by Hermann Kesten. Translated by Richard and Clara Winston. London: Robin Clark, 1984.

DF   *Doctor Faustus: The Life of the German Composer, Adrian Leverkühn, as Told by a Friend.* Translated by H. T. Lowe-Porter. New York: Alfred A. Knopf, 1948.

ED   *Essays of Three Decades.* Translated by H. T. Lowe-Porter. New York: Alfred A. Knopf, 1947.

EF   *An Exceptional Friendship: The Correspondence of Erich Kahler and Thomas Mann.* Translated by Richard and Clara Winston. Ithaca, NY: Cornell University Press, 1975.

EL   *An Exchange of Letters.* Translated by H. T. Lowe-Porter. New York: Alfred A. Knopf, 1937.

EW   "The Exiled Writer's Relation to His Homeland." In *Writers' Congress: The Proceedings of the Conference Held in October 1943 under the Sponsorship of the Hollywood Writers' Mobilization and the University of California Berkeley.* Los Angeles: University of California Press, 1944.

GL   "German Letter." *Dial,* December 1922, 645–54.

GM   "Germany's Guilt and Mission." Translated by Heinz and Ruth Norden. *Decision* 2, no. 1 (July 1941): 9–14.

GR   "On the German Republic." Translated by Lawrence S. Rainey. *Modernism/modernity* 14, no. 2 (January 2007): 109-32.

GT   "Germany Today." *New York Times Magazine,* September 25, 1949, 14, 16, 28, 32–34.

HM   *The Correspondence of Hermann Hesse and Thomas Mann, 1910–1955.* Edited by Anni Carlsson and Volker Michels. Translated by Ralph Mannheim. New York: Harper & Row, 1975.

IMD   "In My Defense." *Atlantic Monthly,* October 1944, 100–102.

J   *Joseph and His Brothers.* Translated by H. T. Lowe-Porter. New York: Knopf, 1948.

L   *The Letters of Thomas Mann, 1889–1955.* Selected and translated from the German by Richard and Clara Winston. New York: Alfred A. Knopf, 1970.

LC   *Addresses Delivered at the Library of Congress.* Washington, DC: Library of Congress, 1963.

LG   *Listen, Germany! Twenty-Five Radio Messages to the German People over BBC.* New York: Alfred A. Knopf, 1943.

LS   "The Living Spirit." *Social Research* 4, no. 3 (1937): 265–72.

MH   *Mythology and Humanism: The Correspondence of Thomas Mann and Karl Kerényi.* Translated by Alexander Gelley. Ithaca, NY: Cornell University Press, 1975.

MM   *The Magic Mountain.* Edition in one volume. Translated by H. T. Lowe-Porter. New York: Alfred A. Knopf, 1928.

MoM   "The Making of *The Magic Mountain.*" Translated by H. T. Lowe-Porter. *Atlantic Monthly,* January 1953, 41–45.

MSL   "Mediators between the Spirit and Life." Translator unknown. *Publisher's Weekly,* May 27, 1939, 1886–88.

OD   *Order of the Day.* Translated by H. T. Lowe-Porter, Agnes E. Meyer, and Eric Sutton. New York: Alfred A. Knopf, 1942.

R   *Reflections of a Nonpolitical Man.* Translated by Walter D. Morris. New York: Frederick Ungar, 1983.

SD   *Stories of Three Decades.* Translated by H. T. Lowe-Porter. New York: Alfred A. Knopf, 1936.

SN   *The Story of a Novel: The Genesis of "Doctor Faustus."* Translated by Richard and Clara Winston. New York: Alfred A. Knopf, 1961.

SP   "Seeking to Preserve German Cultural Freedom." Letter to the editor. *New York Times*, December 12, 1936, 18.

SS   *Selected Short Stories of Thomas Mann.* Translated by H. T. Lowe-Porter. [New York]: Editions for the Armed Services by arrangement with Alfred A. Knopf, 1944.

TC   *Thou Shalt Have No Other Gods before Me.* Translated by George R. Marek. In *The Ten Commandments: Ten Short Novels of Hitler's War against the Moral Code*, edited by Armin L. Robinson, 1–70. New York: Simon and Schuster, 1943.

German-language works of Thomas Mann

Major critical editions

GKFA   *Große kommentierte Frankfurter Ausgabe—Werke, Briefe, Tagebücher.* Edited by Heinrich Detering, Eckhard Heftrich, Hermann Kurzke, Terence J. Reed, Thomas Sprecher, Hans Rudolf Vaget, and Ruprecht Wimmer in collaboration with the Thomas-Mann-Archive of the ETH, Zurich. 17 vols. Frankfurt am Main: S. Fischer Verlag, 2002–. Text citations give volume, book, and page number (i.e., *GKFA*, 5.1:445). This edition will comprise thirty-eight volumes when complete.

GW   *Gesammelte Werke in dreizehn Bänden.* Edited by Peter de Mendelssohn. 13 vols. Frankfurt am Main: S. Fischer Verlag, 1974.

All other references to German works

Br.   *Briefe.* Edited by Erika Mann. 3 vols. Frankfurt am Main: S. Fischer Verlag, 1961–65.

Br. AJ   *Thomas Mann, Katia Mann—Anna Jacobson: Ein Briefwechsel.* Edited by Werner Frizen and Friedhelm Marx. Frankfurt am Main: Vittorio Klostermann, 2005.

Br. AM   *Thomas Mann und Agnes E. Meyer: Briefwechsel 1937–1955.* Edited by Hans Rudolf Vaget. Frankfurt am Main: S. Fischer Verlag, 1992.

Br. Au.   *Briefwechsel mit Autoren.* Edited by Hans Wysling. Frankfurt am Main: S. Fischer Verlag, 1988.

Br. EK   *Thomas Mann und Erich von Kahler: Briefwechsel 1931–1955.* Edited by Michael Assmann. 2 vols. Hamburg: Luchterhand Literaturverlag, 1993.

Br. GBF   *Briefwechsel mit seinem Verleger Gottfried Bermann Fischer, 1932–1955.* Edited by Peter de Mendelssohn. Frankfurt am Main: S. Fischer Verlag, 1973.

Br. HH   *Hermann Hesse—Thomas Mann: Briefwechsel.* Edited by Anni Carlsson and Volker Michels. Frankfurt am Main: Suhrkamp Verlag, 1968.

Br. HW   "Thomas Mann, Hermann J. Weigand und die Yale University. Versuch einer Dokumentation." Edited by Klaus W. Jonas. *Philobiblon* 38 (June 1994): 97–147.

Br. KK   *Thomas Mann/Karl Kerényi: Gespräch in Briefen.* Munich: Deutscher Taschenbuch Verlag, 1967.

Br. LF   *Ludwig Fulda: Briefwechsel 1882–1939.* Edited by Bernhard Gajek and Wolfgang von Ungern-Sternberg. Frankfurt am Main: S. Fischer Verlag, 1988.

Br. RS   *Jahre des Unmuts: Thomas Manns Briefwechsel mit René Schickele 1930–1940.* Edited by Hans Wysling. Frankfurt am Main: Vittorio Klostermann, 1992.

DüD   *Dichter über ihre Dichtungen: Thomas Mann.* Edited by Hans Wysling and Marianne Fischer. 3 vols. Frankfurt am Main: S. Fischer Verlag, 1975–81.

E   *Essays.* Edited by Hermann Kurzke and Stephan Stachorski. 6 vols. Frankfurt am Main: S. Fischer Verlag, 1993–97.

GG   "Goethe: Gespräche mit Friedrich Wilhelm Riemer." *Frankfurter Hefte* 1, no. 2 (1946): 70.

GuK   "'Geist und Kunst.' Thomas Manns Notizen zu einem 'Literatur-Essay.'" Edited by Hans Wysling. In *Quellenkritische Studien zum Werk Thomas Manns,* edited by Paul Scherrer and Hans Wysling, 123–233. Bern: Francke Verlag, 1967.

Nb.   *Notizbücher.* Edited by Hans Wysling and Yvonne Schmidlin. 2 vols. Frankfurt am Main: S. Fischer Verlag, 1991–92.

Reg.   *Die Briefe Thomas Manns, Regesten und Register.* Edited by Hans Bürgin and Hans-Otto Mayer, with the assistance of Gert Heine and Yvonne Schmidlin. 6 vols. Frankfurt am Main: S. Fischer Verlag, 1976–1987.

Tb.   *Tagebücher 1918–21 und 1933–1943.* Edited by Peter de Mendelssohn. *Tagebücher 1944–55.* Edited by Inge Jens. 10 vols. Frankfurt am Main: S. Fischer Verlag, 1977–1995.

Archives

GRI   The Getty Research Institute, Los Angeles

HRC   Harry Ransom Humanities Research Center, University of Texas at Austin

HUA   Harvard University Archives, Cambridge, MA

LoC   Manuscript Division, Library of Congress, Washington, DC

NYPL   New York Public Library Rare Books Division, New York City

PUA   Princeton University Archives, Princeton, NJ

TMA   Thomas-Mann-Archiv, Eidgenössische Technische Hochschule, Zurich

UCL   University of Chicago Library, Chicago

USC   Cinematic Arts Library, University of Southern California, Los Angeles

THOMAS MANN'S WAR

.

Introduction
The German Envoy to America

The ambassadors of the Third Reich, Hitler's dangerously industrious agents, may well claim to speak for Germany, but nobody listens to them. . . . The true German in America, the representative of all things German in the United States, is Thomas Mann, no matter how much this may displease certain people.

—Bodo Uhse, "The German Envoy to America," July 23 / 24, 1939

Only the timeless verdict of the German nation itself can decide what counts as German culture and what doesn't. For our time, that judgment has been made. The opinions of certain foreign circles, who believe that they can act as judges in this matter, will not change it.

—*Völkischer Beobachter* (official newspaper of the Nazi Party), October 25, 1935

In the morning hours of February 21, 1938, the ocean liner *Queen Mary* pulled into New York harbor, completing its transatlantic journey from Cherbourg, France. On board was one of the most famous writers of the day, the German novelist Thomas Mann, who had won the Nobel Prize in Literature in 1929 and become the first non-Anglophone author to grace the cover of *Time* magazine in 1934. Now he was regularly celebrated in the US press as the "greatest living man of letters."

This was Mann's fourth trip to the United States in as many years, and New York's journalists might have been forgiven had they chosen to relegate his arrival to a small note in the society columns (figure 0.1). The opposite was the case, however. The author was greeted by a throng of reporters that included representatives of all the major city papers, along with a film crew from the Paramount News Corporation, which recorded his impromptu press conference on the main deck of the *Queen Mary* for

FIGURE 0.1. Thomas Mann, his wife Katia, and their oldest daughter, Erika, who frequently served as his translator, en route to America on board the steamer *Île-de-France* in 1937. No images survive of their 1938 passage on the *Queen Mary*. Thomas-Mann-Archive, ETH Zurich.

later use in a newsreel.[1] As the title of this newsreel—"U.S. Reacts to European Crisis"—indicates, literary considerations were of decidedly secondary importance for the commotion. The reporters were there because of recent political developments. Roughly a week earlier, Adolf Hitler had forced the Austrian chancellor, Kurt von Schuschnigg, to include members of the Austrian Nazi Party in his government, thereby effectively staging a coup in the neighboring country. Many observers predicted that this would mark the end of an independent Austria, and indeed by mid-March German tanks made an unopposed entrance into Vienna. The American public followed the developments in Europe with bated breath, and the reporters were thus eager to hear what Mann, who had been living in exile in Switzerland ever since Hitler had come to power, might have to say about the situation.

The famous author gladly obliged. In a pointed address, he correctly predicted the annexation of Austria and compared it to Benito Mussolini's invasion of Ethiopia two and a half years earlier. He also condemned the appeasement policy pursued by the British prime minister, Neville Chamberlain (*E*, 4:246). The remarks that Mann delivered aboard the *Queen Mary* were exclusively political in nature, but during a second press conference later that

day, he did add a few words about the contentious relationship between the
official culture of fascism and his personal creative work. Asked whether he
did not find exile to be a rather lonely occasion, Mann defiantly replied, "It is
hard to bear. But what makes it easier is the realization of the poisoned atmosphere in Germany. That makes it easier because it's actually no loss. Where
I am, there is Germany. I carry my German culture in me. I have contact with
the world and I do not consider myself fallen."[2]

This was not the first time that Mann had publicly identified himself with
German culture and used this claim to position himself in opposition to the
Nazi regime. Roughly a year earlier, in an open letter to the dean of the
philosophical faculty of the University of Bonn, which had just stripped him
of an honorary doctorate that had been conferred in 1919, Mann had written, "Justly or not, my name [has] once and for all become connected for
the world with the conception of a Germany which it loved and honoured.
The disquieting challenge [rings] in my cars: that I and no other must in
clear terms contradict the ugly falsification which this conception of Germany [is] now suffering" (EL, 7; GW, 12:788). The leading liberal weekly the
Nation published an English translation of Mann's letter under the attention-
grabbing headline "I Accuse the Hitler Regime," and Reader's Digest carried
a condensed version of it into millions of American homes.[3] A few months
later, Mann's US publisher, Alfred A. Knopf, reissued the entire document as
An Exchange of Letters, just in time for the book signings during Mann's first
American lecture tour.

From this point on, and especially after he took up permanent residency
in the United States in September of 1938, Mann, who had once described
himself in the title of one of his books as a "nonpolitical man," acquired
a new role in the eyes of his US audience. For the hundreds of thousands
of American readers who purchased his books, flocked to his lectures, or
followed his endeavors by means of the frequently breathless news coverage, Mann became an embodiment of German culture as well as a personal
antagonist to Hitler, Joseph Goebbels, and the Nazi regime. Through his
words and actions, he seemed to personify a great cultural tradition now in
danger of being irreversibly corrupted or even eradicated by fascism. Mann
himself took great satisfaction in this development and fully understood its
implications. As he commented in a 1941 letter to his American patron Agnes
E. Meyer, "I am waging a war" (L, 354; Br. AM, 253; Je fais la guerre).

My aim in this book is to explore the circumstances that made this remarkable development possible, as well as to chart its significance for literary history more generally. Writers have certainly served as a thorn in the side of
the powerful almost since the beginnings of recorded history. But Mann's

case was nevertheless novel. He became famous in America not because of his personal criticism of Hitler nor even because he found powerful words to attack governmental injustice, as his nineteenth-century predecessors Heinrich Heine and Émile Zola had done. His fame instead rested on the quietly dignified aura of culture and tradition with which he surrounded himself and that seemed to emanate from every page that he wrote.

The story of Mann's life seems tailor-made to support such an impression. The son of a merchant and senator from the small north German town of Lübeck, Mann had grown up wealthy and had learned from an early age what it meant to assume a representative function in the eyes of the public. In 1894, when he was nineteen years old, Mann moved to Munich to begin a career as a writer, following in the footsteps of his older brother, Heinrich, a highly regarded novelist. Success and financial independence came with the publication of his first novel, *Buddenbrooks*, in 1901, and with the novella *Tonio Kröger* in 1903. Although Mann was gay, he shortly thereafter married Katia Pringsheim, the daughter of a prominent mathematics professor. The couple had six children, the two oldest of which, Erika and Klaus, had embarked upon promising literary careers of their own by the time that the Manns arrived in the United States. The Pringsheims were one of the wealthiest and most influential families in Munich, and from 1905 to 1933, the author and his ever-expanding household lived a life of affluence and social distinction. During this time Mann wrote what are now his most famous works, the novella *Death in Venice* (1912), and the novel *The Magic Mountain* (1924). He also penned numerous works of cultural criticism, with which he cemented the public impression that he was a writer in the great German lineage of Johann Wolfgang von Goethe, Friedrich Schiller, and Theodor Fontane, rather than an avant-garde revolutionary. By the time that he stepped foot off the *Queen Mary*, Mann was about halfway finished with a four-volume novel cycle recounting the biblical story of Joseph and his brothers. It was a "big" project in all senses of that term, a self-conscious attempt to cement a posthumous legacy.

Mann was, in other words, a writer unlike any of his contemporaries who continue to enjoy a similar level of fame in literary history: famous, rather than toiling in obscurity like Franz Kafka; wealthy, rather than penniless like James Joyce; well-traveled and outgoing, rather than reclusive like Marcel Proust; supremely self-confident, rather than clinically depressed like Virginia Woolf. It was precisely this studiously cultivated air of authority and dignity that made Mann a particularly potent actor in an age of totalitarian domination. The Nazi government based its representative claims on the notion of the *Volkswille*, a collective will that supposedly permeated every aspect of the German nation's identity. Under this totalitarian logic, Mann became a political threat precisely because of his pretensions toward cultural autonomy, not despite of them. In his letter to the dean of the philosophical faculty at Bonn, Mann had noted that "from the beginning of my intellectual life I [have] felt myself in happiest accord with the temper of my nation and at home in its intellectual traditions. I am better suited to represent those traditions than to become a martyr for them" (*EL*, 6; *GW*, 12:786). The complaint was justified, but also a bit beside the point. It was precisely because Mann was so well-equipped to represent the intellectual traditions of his nation that he was in danger of becoming a martyr at the hands of the Nazis.

There was a second novel quality to Thomas Mann's case as well. As both his interview with the *New York Times* and his letter to the dean note, Mann's representative authority was rooted not in the assent of the German *Volk*, but rather in that of the "world," or in what we might now call the global literary community. And indeed, translations of *An Exchange of Letters* quickly appeared not only in the United States but also in England, France, Denmark, Sweden, the Netherlands, Poland, Hungary, Czechoslovakia, the Soviet Union, Bulgaria, Argentina, and Japan. This was hardly surprising, for Mann had made a triumphant entrance into world literature at an early stage of his career, seeing his works widely translated throughout Europe and beyond. This development was greatly aided by the birth of stable copyright regimes and the growth of international publishing during the closing years of the nineteenth century. As a result of these larger developments, "German culture" became an entity that no longer assumed a coherent form in the eyes of Germans alone. It now was an export commodity and, like all such commodities, became a vehicle for fetishistic projections by international consumers. Regardless of how much they consolidated their territorial and cultural control over German-speaking Europe (excepting tiny Switzerland), the Nazis therefore could not prevent Mann's self-stylization as a representative German in the eyes of the world.

It's true that once the Second World War broke out, this "world" largely became confined to the North American continent. But this restriction was of little consequence, for once the war was over, US military and industrial might completely reshaped the literary world—especially in Europe, where entire publishing industries lay in ruins. As the United States rose to the status of a global hegemon, American tastes profoundly altered what the world read. This fact was not lost on other German writers, one of whom jealously described Thomas Mann as a "loyal American subject."[4]

These two factors that characterize Mann's case—the battle of cultural autonomy against totalitarian dependence and the struggle between international and national sources of literary esteem—continue to have a clear relevance for literary production into the present day. Here we need to think only of the Turkish writer Orhan Pamuk (perhaps not coincidentally a great admirer of Thomas Mann), who was recently accused by the progovernment media in his own country of being the "project" of an "international literature lobby" eager to destroy Turkish culture.[5] What Pamuk's case shares with Mann's is not only the constellation pitting an author against his own government, but also the fact that Pamuk's enemies claim that his representative authority derives from the opinions of the global literary community rather than from readers in his native country. Or we could think of the Israeli novelist Dorit Rabinyan, whose novel *All the Rivers*, a Jewish-Palestinian love story, received a wide international release even as it was banned from Israel's school curricula on the grounds that it threatened the "national-ethnic identity of the people" by downplaying the "significance of miscegenation."[6] Thomas Mann's story in the 1930s and 1940s is thus of clearly more than antiquarian interest. It instead marks the starting point of a historical situation that persists well into the twenty-first century.

The World Republic of Letters

An honorary doctoral diploma that Thomas Mann received from Harvard University in 1935 neatly illustrates the complex relationship connecting his battle for cultural autonomy to his struggle for international recognition. In *An Exchange of Letters*, Mann proudly invokes the Latin text of this diploma, which praises him as a "famous author who . . . together with a very few contemporaries sustains the high dignity of German culture" (*EL*, 4; *GW*, 12:786). For Mann, the diploma signified the existence of an autonomous cultural sphere that cut across national borders and could not be circumscribed by merely local actors, even ones as powerful as the *Reichsschrifttumskammer*, the Nazi agency in charge of literature and the book trade. A second doctoral diploma that he received four years later from Hobart College even gave a name to this autonomous sphere: the "international republic of letters."[7] During the summer of 1938, Mann also reread the *Conversations with Eckermann*, a transcript of a series of conversations between the poet Johann Wolfgang von Goethe and his assistant Johann Peter Eckermann in the 1820s and 1830s (*Tb.*, June 2, 1938). Mann made careful note of the famous passage in which Goethe predicts that the nation-state would become an increasingly unimportant arbiter of what constitutes literary greatness and that "the epoch of world literature is at hand."[8] References to it are scattered throughout several of his essays from the war years.

For Mann, the "international republic of letters" was by no means an apolitical realm. This is a crucial difference between his understanding of global literary circulation, developed during an age of unprecedented military conflict, and the twenty-first century notion of a "world republic of letters" proposed by the influential literary critic Pascale Casanova. Whereas Casanova regards the republic of letters as an aesthetic realm in which writers are freed of all "arbitrary political and national power," Mann believed that it was truly a *republic* in the original sense of that term: a space whose members acted as representatives or emissaries of their individual nations.[9] As early as 1922, Mann had asserted (in his essay "On National and International Art") that "there is no such thing as a pure, an absolute cosmopolitanism" in the realm of literature. Instead, "greatness and national character in a paradigmatic sense are related to one another in a causal and organic fashion, and while a great German, a great Frenchman, a great Russian do indeed 'belong to humanity,' they would not be great, and would thus also not 'belong to humanity' if they weren't first to a large degree German, French, or Russian" (*GKFA*, 15.1:506). He therefore saw his own place in world literature as a direct consequence of his ability to embody, rather than transcend, Germanic culture in the eyes of the world.

This belief, in turn, was shared was shared by a large number of other European intellectuals who had witnessed the devastation of 1914–18, when ideas, no less than soldiers, went to war with one another. In reaction to these experiences there arose a clear conviction among the European intelligentsia during the 1920s that artists and scholars had a duty to seek international dialogue not just out of a shared commitment to beauty or to the life of the mind, but rather in order to keep open conversations that were all too easily abandoned by power-hungry politicians. Thomas Mann took this conviction with him to America.

The *Nation*, when it retitled Mann's open letter "I Accuse the Hitler Regime," clearly intended to draw a connection to earlier expressions of protest by writers against their own governments, specifically to Émile Zola's famous manifesto "J'accuse."[10] As the concept of an "international republic of letters" illustrates, however, there was a decisive difference between Mann's self-positioning and that of nineteenth-century authors such as Zola or Heinrich Heine. Both Heine and Zola had remained firmly wedded to the literary systems of their countries of origin even in exile; they had no international cultural sphere such as the one Mann discerned in his Harvard diploma to fall back upon. Heine, for instance, had published many essays on German culture in French intellectual papers, but when it came time to combine these writings into a book that he decided to call *The Romantic*

School (1836), he returned to the German publisher Hoffmann & Campe, despite the fact that he there had to submit to heavy interference from government censors.[11] Zola, during his brief sojourn in London, never bothered to engage with the country that hosted him on any deeper level. He continued to publish in French and for a French market. His fame throughout the world came at second remove, through translations of his courageous interventions in his country's public sphere, not because he directly addressed himself to an international audience.

By the time that he arrived in America, Thomas Mann, on the other hand, had come to understand that the Nazi regime had irrevocably severed him from his audience in Germany. In a 1943 address, "The Exiled Writer's Relationship to His Homeland," he lamented,

> The exile of Victor Hugo, for example, was child's play compared with ours. To be sure, he sat as an outcast far from Paris on his island in the ocean, but the spiritual link between him and France was never broken. What he wrote was printed in the French press; his books could be bought and read at home. Today exile is a total exile, just as war, politics, world, and life have become total. We are not only physically far from our country but we have been radically expelled from its life both in the purpose and, at least for the present, in the effects of our exile. (EW, 342; GW, 13:195)

Of course, hundreds of other literary émigrés shared in the condition that Mann here describes. The lessons that the famous author drew from his analysis were starkly different from those of his contemporaries, however. A common hope within the émigré community was that German cultural institutions might simply be reconstructed in America, beyond the reach of the Nazis. To name but one example, Prince Hubertus zu Löwenstein, a scribbler of limited talent but immense ambitions and substantial means, spent the latter half of the 1930s building up his German Academy in Exile. Volkmar von Zühlsdorff, its managing director, later avowed that this academy was "intended to be an entirely German institution. It would have German roots, membership and aims; it was to be set up in exile only because its members had been driven from their homeland by the Nazi tyranny. It was to be a cultural equivalent to what, in politics, would be termed a government in exile."[12]

Thomas Mann was a founding member of the German Academy in Exile and even served as the president of its literary division. He had been extremely active in literary academies, guilds, and protective associations during the 1920s, and well understood their importance in fostering international solidarity. He also quickly came to realize, however, that projects such as the one pursued by Löwenstein, or by Alfred Kantorowicz, the general secretary of the League of German Writers in Exile, rested on a fundamentally flawed premise. Kantorowicz's motto, to which Löwenstein would have also subscribed, was "Germany is in our camp."[13] He assumed, in other words, that the cancer of fascism was only superficial and that German culture as such would survive association with the Nazis unscathed.

Mann's own perception was very different. In his most important political address, the lecture "Germany and the Germans" of 1945, he said, "there are *not* two Germanys, a good one and a bad one, but only one, whose best turned into evil through devilish cunning. Wicked Germany is merely good Germany gone astray, good Germany in misfortune, in guilt, and ruin. For that reason it is quite impossible for one born there simply to renounce the wicked guilty Germany and to declare: 'I am the good, the noble, the just Germany in the white robe; I leave it to you to exterminate the wicked one" (LC, 64; GW, 11:1146). Mann proposed, in other words, that the Nazi domination arose from structural conditions that were endemic to the German cultural tradition itself, inhering even in its very best elements. To simply carry this tradition across the Atlantic and start afresh with a new set of academies, publishing houses, and literary papers would mean to court disaster. Indeed, by the spring of 1940 (at a time when Nazi military might seemed insurmountable anywhere in Europe), Prince Löwenstein took to publicly complaining about the supposed "policy of annihilation directed against Germany," a pronouncement that resulted in an irreconcilable breach with the Mann family and ultimately to Löwenstein's resignation from his offices.[14]

In a 1936 letter to the editor of the *New York Times*, Mann spelled out a rather different worldview when he asserted, "The task of affirming [that there remains alive a tradition of German culture outside of the sphere of dictatorship] does not belong to us emigrants. It is the task of the world to proclaim this—of that world which cannot forget the sympathy and gratitude with which it time and again welcomed the questing and creative German spirit" (SP, 18; GW, 13:638). Mann believed, in other words, that in times of totalitarian terror, the continued care for German culture was no longer the responsibility of Germans alone, not even that of the politically unburdened Germans who had fled into exile. The global community would have to shoulder this task instead. In this context, the quotation from Bodo Uhse that serves as one of the epigraphs to this chapter is telling. Uhse speaks of Thomas Mann as a "delegate," that is, as someone who has been "sent" (ein Entsandter). Mann would no doubt have preferred another term that Uhse discusses but ultimately discards: someone who "has been called" (ein Berufener).

Cosmopolitan Germanness

In his 1940 essay "The War and the Future," Mann summarized his theory of exile as follows: "Emigration is no longer, as it once was, a search for temporary shelter, a hopeful and impatient waiting for the time when we can return. We are not waiting to return, we long ago gave up the idea. We are waiting for the future—and the future belongs to the new idea of world community, to the restriction of national sovereignties and autonomies. To this new state our emigration and the diaspora of our various cultures are merely the prelude" (OD, 244). Five years later, in a radio address to the newly liberated Germany, he revived this sentiment, adding to it the plea, "do not begrudge me my cosmopolitan Germanness [Weltdeutschtum]!" (GW, 13:747).[15]

To many of Mann's German contemporaries, these aspirations toward "cosmopolitan Germanness" reeked of a Jewish conspiracy.[16] Indeed, the author's break with the Nazi regime had been set into motion when Mann, in January 1936, issued a sharp rebuke to the Swiss journalist Eduard Korrodi, who had sought to drive a wedge between Jewish and German literature. Mann reminded Korrodi of the profoundly beneficial influence that Jewish writers had exerted on German letters, stressing that the " 'international' component of the Jew, at any rate, is his middle-European component, which is at the same time German, and without it German character wouldn't be German character" (GW, 11:792). The German ambassador to Switzerland reported Mann's pronouncements to his superiors; by the end of the year, Mann had been stripped of his citizenship, and his books were banned throughout the Reich.[17]

It would be perverse, of course, to compare the deprivations that Mann experienced over the next ten years to the collective suffering of the European Jews. Mann was forced into exile, his monetary assets were confiscated, and he saw both friends and family members perish or be taken off to concentration camps. But he never experienced genuine material hardship, he was not tortured, and his life was never in danger. Yet Mann's denaturalization and the persecution of the Jews were nevertheless governed by a similar political logic. In both cases, the Nazi state attempted to affirm the authority of its representative claims by establishing an excluded other. By depriving the Jews of even symbolic recognition of their membership in the national community, the Nazis could assert that their movement expressed the collective will of the entire German people. By casting Thomas Mann into exile and banning his books, they could advance the claim that German culture and tradition were entirely on their side.

This process of systematic exclusion from a cultural community brings us to the effect that translation had on Thomas Mann's self-understanding during the 1930s and 1940s. The fact that his stories could not legally be sold in Germany between December 1936 and May 1945 meant that the audience for his German books was essentially confined to neutral Switzerland, as well as a few pockets of refugees scattered all over the world, from Stockholm to São Paulo. In terms of both monetary gain and cultural prestige, the American editions published by Alfred A. Knopf thus acquired an outsized importance. In July 1938 Mann ruefully told his German publisher, Gottfried Bermann Fischer, that he was "frequently depressed by the fact that the German editions of my books are of so little importance in comparison to the English and American ones. Especially in regards to the economic point of view one gets the impression that the originals have more or less been lost, and only the translations remain in the world" (*Br. GBF*, 175).

Thomas Mann's attitude toward his reception in translation was never exclusively—or even primarily—mournful, however. In *An Exchange of Letters*, for example, he had still claimed that "my books . . . are written for Germans, for them above all; the outside world and its sympathy have always been for me only a happy accident. They are—these books of mine—the product of a mutually nourishing bond between nation and author" (*EL*, 6; *GW*, 12:787–88). But as the center of his life moved to the United States, Thomas Mann's attitude changed. By 1939 he was willing to grant his US publisher that "the American public in recent years has stepped into the place that the German public once occupied for me, now that politics—and what politics at that!—have separated me from it."[18]

Mann's correspondence also shows how he used his excellent reputation in the United States as leverage during negotiations with Bermann Fischer. When Bermann Fischer resisted Mann's idea of opening a German-language publishing house in the United States, for example, Mann insinuated that "an established American publisher with a wide distribution network and significant means might be a better [partner], and of course I'm thinking first and foremost of my friend Alfred Knopf" (*Br. GBF*, 144). On another occasion, the famous author openly reprimanded his German publisher when the latter wanted to assert copyright over a series of lectures that had been written specifically for the American market, reminding Bermann Fischer that "the original publication is, after all, the handiwork of Alfred A. Knopf in New York" (*Br. GBF*, 171).

Put slightly differently, while Mann never entirely reconciled himself to the thought that his cherished creations would be consumed primarily in translation, he was eminently pragmatic about the ways in which this fact affected his status as a writer. He had become perhaps the world's first author of what the literary critic Rebecca Walkowitz has called "born translated fiction."[19] And he intuitively understood that the advent of this condition would have transformative effects also on book publishing in the original language. Henceforth, even works written by a German for other Germans would in some small way be marked by the fact that they were part of a larger global literary system. A curious anecdote from 1947 illustrates this well. With the Nazi government finally toppled, the way was clear for Bermann Fischer to publish Mann's latest works in his home country again. But because Mann had by then become a US citizen, his books were legally vulnerable to piracy in America unless a copy that had been printed in the United States was submitted for copyright protection in Washington, DC, prior to publication. When Bermann Fischer wanted to sell the recently completed *Doktor Faustus* in Germany, he thus first had to produce a limited-edition German-language print run in America.[20] Mann accepted this necessity without so much as a jocular remark about its underlying absurdity (*Br.*, 2:561). He understood that the removal of the conditions that had necessitated his exile did not simultaneously dissolve his status as a "cosmopolitan German" writer.

The Function of an Author

Over the course of the seven years that he spent in involuntary exile while the Nazis were in power, Thomas Mann developed increasingly complicated and increasingly varied strategies to exploit his status as the "German envoy to America" and conduct a cultural war against Hitler and his propaganda ministry. Press conferences and lecture tours were only the beginning, later to be joined by radio broadcasts, congressional testimony, political action committees—and, of course, allegorical novels intended to, as Mann himself put it, "repurpose" the emotional allure of fascism and put it in the service of democracy (*GW*, 11:658). One ambition of this book is to tell the story of this struggle.

Ultimately, however, Mann's unique status in the United States during the 1930s and 1940s owed less to his personal actions than it did to the expectations that American audiences projected upon him. The true antagonist of Hitler in the United States was not Thomas Mann, the aging writer who had made a home for himself in exile, but rather "Thomas Mann": a name that adorned book covers and marquees at lecture halls throughout the nation and was eagerly discussed in both middlebrow magazines and intellectual journals. This idea of Thomas Mann corresponded not so much to a flesh-and-blood individual as it did to a networked entity, created through the labors of literary agents, translators, editors, publishers, journalists, literary critics, and, of course, ordinary readers. Thomas Mann became a cipher in which America could see itself.

To examine how such a networked construct was created, and how this construction irrevocably changed the place of authors in society, is my second main purpose here. This book is thus not a biography, and indeed, Mann himself will practically vanish from the narrative at certain points. Instead, those pages will offer detailed reconstructions of forces in US cultural history (for example, the rise of middlebrow publishing in the 1920s, or of the Popular Front in the mid-1930s) that changed the ways in which ordinary Americans thought about the relationship between literature and the world. Then as now, readers did not pick up books merely to be entertained, but also to find a mooring amid trying times and to see their hopes, fears, and anxieties validated in the palpable form of bestselling fiction.[21] Mann never set foot in a living room in rural Iowa, a Lower East Side tenement apartment, or a German prisoner-of-war camp in the swamps of Mississippi. And yet his books circulated in all these places, where they arrived framed in a certain fashion and became the subject of both rational discussions and inchoate longings that Mann himself could scarcely have anticipated. The results of these discussions redounded upon the author: they contributed to the creation of an American "Thomas Mann" that was only partially connected to the actual person by that name.

Thomas Mann made an especially suitable target for such projections because of his bold equation of himself with the broader construct of German cultural history. When the term "culture" first acquired widespread currency in German and French intellectual discourse during the mid-eighteenth century, it referred to the collective characteristics—frequently thought to be the product not of arbitrary traditions but rather of natural environments—of people living together in the same place and speaking the same language. In the late eighteenth and early nineteenth centuries, as nation-states sprung up all over Europe from the ashes of absolutist realms, the concepts of "nation" and "culture" became inextricably intertwined. Nowhere was this truer than in Germany, where political unity long proved elusive and where patriots thus had to seek refuge in the compensatory idea that they possessed an especially noble unifying culture.[22]

Over the course of the nineteenth century, as once-agricultural societies became urban and modern, and as literacy rates rose, this notion of "culture" as something inborn and environmentally determined gradually gave way to the realization that culture is instead a dynamic battlefield contested by specialists working in what the sociologist Pierre Bourdieu has called the "field of cultural production."[23] By the end of the century, this field of cultural production had acquired its own rules (such as the painterly conventions codified by academic art), its own accreditation standards (such as membership in prestigious salons or in national academies), and even its own behavioral expectations (as expressed, for example, by the bohémien).[24]

Born in 1875, Thomas Mann belonged to the first generation of European artists who were able to take the notion of autonomous cultural production entirely for granted and to reflect on its implications for their careers. Most of Mann's artistic contemporaries arrived at the conclusion that wealth and social prestige were to a large extent mutually exclusive accomplishments (fame, on the other hand, could accrue to either the wealthy or the prestigious). Wealth could most easily be obtained via a compromise with the demands of the market; prestige, by contrast, came most readily to those who developed a unique and uncompromising style. There thus arose a type of artist who, in the words of literary scholar Aaron Jaffe, strove to develop a stylistic signature or "imprimatur" that might "sanction elite, high cultural consumption in times when mass cultural values predominate[d]."[25] This hunt for a unique style by definition negated any claims to representativeness; to be a "modernist," as we now call such artists in English, meant to stand apart from the crowd—to reject the ambition, implicit in the original eighteenth-century understanding of culture, to speak for a social collective. Thomas Mann pursued a different strategy, however. From an early age, he was determined not only to acquire wealth, fame, and prestige all at the same time but also to be perceived as the foremost artist of his nation.[26] To some extent this ambition to be simultaneously autonomous and representative was internally contradictory, as Mann discovered during the time of the First World War, when his desire to be perceived as a quintessentially "German" artist drove him to ever more convoluted intellectual rear-guard actions. But when the time came to break with the Nazi regime, his struggle turned out to have been dialectical rather than merely oppositional. By simultaneously advancing his ambition of artistic autonomy and the claim to thereby speak for a crowd, Mann was able to give an intellectually coherent grounding to his defiance of the German government.

By crossing the Atlantic to America, however, Mann also entered into a part of the world in which the term "culture" carried a very different conceptual baggage than it did on the European continent. The United States was a country founded by immigrants; the notion that culture somehow is an expression of characteristics inherent in blood and soil had far weaker purchase there. Nor, given the country's far-flung civic centers and the relative youth of its artistic institutions, was there a strong sense of an independent class of cultural producers of the kind that had led to the European *bohème*. Culture in the United States was instead understood in terms that owed more to an eighteenth-century British understanding of that term: as an acquired set of ideas and behaviors that conferred upper-class status distinction. The question applicable to Mann's case was thus not simply, Would Americans believe his representative legitimacy as an icon of German culture? but also, Why should they care?

When he first set foot on US soil, in 1934, Mann was already famous there, thanks to a relentless marketing campaign that promoted him as the "greatest living man of letters" and sought to convince American readers that his books contained profound ideas that would be useful to them on their own paths of social advancement. Had this been the last of it, Mann's career would no doubt have entered a phase of precipitous decline over the course of the 1930s, as had happened to previous German literary giants who had been similarly promoted, for instance his archrival Gerhart Hauptmann. But by the time that he stepped off the *Queen Mary* in 1938, millions of Americans were desperately seeking answers to such questions as, What were the origins of Nazism? Were the Germans inherently evil? Could peace ever be made with Hitler? Thomas Mann provided them with answers in speeches, essays, and interviews. During the period from 1938 to 1945, Mann's importance as an interpreter of the current situation in Europe easily outpaced his role as the author of demanding and culturally prestigious fiction. Over the course of these years, Alfred A. Knopf issued five new volumes of speeches and essays to balance five works of fiction. The novels were heftier works, but the essays and speeches sold better. The lecture transcript *The Coming Victory of Democracy*, for instance, sold more copies even than *Joseph in Egypt*, the most widely acclaimed literary work that Mann published during his American exile.[27]

Modernism and the Media

Thomas Mann's success in the United States was thus fundamentally the result of two serendipitous acts of cultural translation: a thoroughly Germanic notion of culture unexpectedly gained relevance with an American audience, and a model of the world republic of letters developed in Europe following the First World War became useful to a world rapidly hurtling toward a second global catastrophe. Ultimately, however, such large conceptual abstractions are of limited use in explaining what actually happened, and they undercut a full consideration of the many different agents who played a part in the creation of Thomas Mann's rather singular status in the United States.

In recent years, literary histories of the early twentieth century have increasingly become cognizant of those decades as collectively forming what the critic David Trotter calls "the first media age."[28] On its most basic terms, this simply means recognizing that during this period, cinema, telephone, radio, and later also television joined print culture as important channels for the distribution of information, while print itself was transformed by such technical advances as newspaper photography. Thomas Mann took a keen interest in the medial advances of his age, from his astute meditations on recording technology and X-ray photography in *The Magic Mountain* to his several unsuccessful attempts to pitch films to Hollywood.

Much more importantly, the notion of a "first media age" reminds us that literary works and literary authorship were themselves increasingly mediated during the early twentieth century. Readers interested in obtaining the latest book by Thomas Mann, for example, no longer simply went to the local bookstore or lending library. Instead, they first might have studied the extensive advertising supplements produced by Alfred A. Knopf, which featured blurbs, summaries, and sometimes excerpted passages. Their interest piqued, they could have turned to the reviews, purchase recommendations, and literary advice columns that flooded the journals and newspapers of the period. Their minds made up, they then might have gone to the local bookstore—or they have might have chosen to place an order via the Book-of-the-Month Club instead. If they decided on the latter route, their reading matter would have been dispatched to them via the US Postal Service with a speed and efficiency made possible only by recent advances in labor organization and rationalization. Similarly, readers interested in learning more about Thomas Mann's political opinions could simply wait until he made a stop in a nearby town as part of a tour organized by a professional lecturing bureau. To get there, they would hop into their cars, while Mann would arrive by high-speed luxury train.

Mediation of this sort always goes hand in hand with a certain loss of autonomy: no author can control the newspaper headlines, and the question of who gets to interact with a prestigious literary figure will always partly be decided not only by ledger books but also by train schedules, highway maps, and other factors. What makes the case of Thomas Mann so

intriguing, then, is that even as he developed into a self-conscious manipula-
tor of his own public image, he also doubled down on the ostensible purity
of his art. In his 1947 work *Minima Moralia*, the exiled philosopher Theodor
W. Adorno sniffed, "Every intellectual in emigration is, without exception, mutilated, and does well to acknowledge it to himself, if he wishes
to avoid being cruelly apprised of it behind the tightly closed doors of his
self-esteem. He lives in an environment that must remain incomprehensible to him. . . . Between the reproduction of his own existence under the
monopoly of mass culture, and impartial, responsible work, yawns an irreconcilable breach."[29] Adorno's statement, though it has often been echoed in
the decades that followed, is remarkably myopic. During the very years in
which he wrote *Minima Moralia*, Adorno also served as a musical consultant
to Thomas Mann on his novel *Doctor Faustus*, unquestionably an "impartial,
responsible" work. Yet Mann was quite comfortable with the "reproduction
of his own existence under the monopoly of mass culture," and even took
an active hand in it.

The account that follows, then, will chart how a social role for the author
was invented and successfully popularized in an age of total war—an age in
which modern literature's traditional insistence on social autonomy itself
represented a political act. The first chapter explores Mann's changing self-
understanding as a writer during the decades prior to the Nazi seizure of
power. After that, the story moves to America. Each subsequent chapter
focuses on a different social formation in the United States, along with some
of the representative institutions and actors that it produced: the middlebrow commercial networks of the 1920s, the Popular Front of the mid-1930s,
the military-industrial complex of the Second World War, and the secretive
cabals of the early Cold War period, to name just the most important examples. In each case, the guiding question will be how these social formations
participated in creating and mediating a specific image of Thomas Mann. My
emphasis throughout these chapters is on "Thomas Mann" the author figure, not Thomas Mann the flesh-and-blood person, a fact that I have sought
to highlight by naming each of my chapters after one of the epithets and
marketing slogans that were used to promote him.

The novels and stories that Mann wrote throughout the 1930s and 1940s
provide one of the best windows into his own changing understanding of the
social role of the writer. The main chapters of the book are thus separated
by "literary interludes" that each focus on one of the main works Mann
produced during his American period. For reasons of space, I have left out
the comparatively minor novella *The Transposed Heads* (1941) as well as the
novel *The Holy Sinner* (1951), published toward the very end of his stay in the

country. Readers who are unfamiliar with these largely forgotten late works will hopefully find in these interludes an inspiration to rediscover them. Those, however, who simply wish to learn about Mann's changing fortunes in the United States can skip them without danger of losing the thread of the narrative.

CHAPTER 1

The Teacher of Germany

An author like Thomas Mann has made deeper strata of the German spirit and soul accessible to the world than any number of books that merely present experience or memory in formulaic fashion. . . . In the continuities that connect Thomas Mann to Nietzsche and Wagner, European intellectual circles get a clear sense for the continuity of German spiritual development.

—Max Rychner, "The Nobel Prize in Literature 1929"

Whenever I meet Thomas Mann, 3,000 years of tradition look down upon me.

—Bertolt Brecht, letter to Karl Korsch, July / August 1941

That Thomas Mann should at one point be celebrated in the United States as the leading voice of the "other Germany," and as an intimate enemy of his native country's official government, would have come as a surprise to many who read his works during the time of the First World War. In his exhaustive summation of his political views of the time, the paradoxically titled *Reflections of a Nonpolitical Man* (1918), Mann argues that a true artist is obligated to refrain from any intervention in public affairs. He further describes this attitude as distinctively German and casts scorn on writers who try their hand at journalistic commentary, a stance he associates with French and English public life.

Twenty years later, these earlier remarks would occasionally still come to haunt him. In December of 1938, for example, the *New York Herald Tribune* published a letter to the editor that condemned America's embrace of Mann as a spokesperson of the other Germany, and demanded, "Read his 'Friedrick und die Grosse Koalition' [sic]—there's a copy in the New York Public Library—and observe the sea-change that has in recent years transmogrified his political theorizing."[1] The author of this letter, a certain Thomas A. Baggs, was poorly informed about Mann's oeuvre in translation, for "Frederick and the Grand Coalition" was, in fact, the only one of the author's patriotic wartime writings that *had* been translated. But the larger point stands. For example, Mann had written that Germany would inevitably win the war, because "history will not crown ignorance and error with victory" (*GKFA*, 15.1:45). Had ordinary Americans in the late 1930s been aware of such chauvinistic remarks, they would most likely have abandoned him.[2] Mann himself was keenly aware of this, and made sure that *Reflections of a Nonpolitical Man* was never translated into English during his lifetime.

Viewed from a different perspective, however, *Reflections* actually foreshadows rather than negates Mann's later role in America. For its very existence is premised on the assumption that an author and his country are conjoined by a representational link, and that both the words and the actions of an individual reflect the larger character of the national community. This assumption—or rather this active desire to become representative—guided Thomas Mann's career from the very beginning and remained intact throughout his various reinventions and transmogrifications.

During the years of the Weimar Republic, Mann's representative aspirations became the subject of much commentary and even more ridicule. As early as 1919, the conservative journalist Hanns Elster bestowed upon Mann the epithet "precaeptor Germaniae" (teacher of Germany), an honorific title that had first been applied to the Renaissance humanist Philipp Melanchthon and indicated an author who through his writings guided the nation to self-understanding.[3] Conservative opinion cooled off considerably after Thomas Mann publicly embraced the Weimar constitution in 1922. A satirical drawing by the right-wing caricaturist Arthur Johnson relentlessly mocks him as panegyrist of the republic (figure 1.1). Liberal and left-wing opinion was often similarly scathing. The Austrian essayist Jean Améry, for example, wrote an amusing piece in which he spoofs the obeisance that Thomas Mann so often seemed to expect (and usually received) from the Weimar public by summarizing the breathless narration that a German radio reporter provided from the 1929 Nobel Prize awards ceremony: "Thomas Mann just arose from his seat, and now his figure, so accustomed to wearing a tailcoat [seine frackgewohnte Gestalt], is approaching the podium with bounding steps."[4]

In reality, Thomas Mann wasn't nearly as rigid and pretentious as his fiercest critics liked to suggest. His copious and often agonized reflections concerning his representative status reveal that he was instead intensely attuned to the social flux around him. And his later career in America demonstrates that he ultimately owed his fame to his ability not to resist, but rather to

FIGURE 1.1. Arthur Johnson, "Thomas Mann, Panegyrist of the German Republic," *Kladderadatsch*, July 22, 1923, n.p.

respond to, unprecedented historical conditions. Whatever else it might have been, Nazism was a powerful manifestation of modernity. In successfully positing himself as its antipode, Mann was not expressing blind obeisance to tradition but rather engaging in a dialectical dance that transformed the social role of the author into something that it had never been before.

Role Models and Literary Antecedents

The most obvious symptoms of Mann's search for representational forms that would be suitable for his own era can be found, paradoxically, in his near-constant reflections upon the literary past. Mann's numerous speeches and essays about his poetic forebears do not simply form an attempt to appropriate these figures as sources of authority. The outrage with which conservative circles greeted his 1933 lecture "The Suffering and Greatness of Richard Wagner" (in which Mann accuses Wagner of bourgeois pretentiousness and questions whether the idea of the "total work of art" is really as artistically profound as the composer's disciples would argue) already demonstrates this.[5] Mann's critical reflections should instead be seen as attempts to better understand the present by analyzing both its similarities and its differences to the recent past.

One of the most important antecedents whom Mann used as a reference point in this process of historical self-triangulation was Johann Wolfgang von Goethe. Mann's literary engagement with the older writer was multifaceted and encompassed such internally diverse projects as the story "A Weary Hour" (1905), the essays "Goethe and Tolstoi" (1923), "Goethe as a Representative of the Bourgeois Age" (1932), "Goethe's Career as a Writer" (1933), "Goethe's *Faust*" (1938), and "Goethe and Democracy" (1949), as well as the historical novel *Lotte in Weimar* (1939). Indeed, it is notable that with the exception of a single essay on Gotthold Ephraim Lessing ("Lessing," 1929) and a few crucial remarks about Martin Luther, Mann never turned his gaze on any earlier figure in German literary history.

Goethe was not the first writer ever to be acclaimed as the archetypal spokesperson of the German cultural tradition. The example of Philipp Melanchthon has already been mentioned, and during the 1780s German readers celebrated the novelist Christoph Martin Wieland as their "classical national author."[6] Goethe, however, was the first person to outline a theory of artistic representativeness that took into consideration the extent to which authorial reputations are both created and continually undermined by social change. In his classic pronouncement on the subject, "Literary Sansculottism" (more commonly translated as "Response to a Literary Rabble-Rouser," 1795), he argued that Germany would never be able to produce a truly "national" author because the country was "politically splintered despite representing a geographical unity" and lacked a "real cultural center where writers can gather and find a common guideline to aid their development."[7] Goethe also fretted about the increasing influence of a "mass public without taste."[8] In other words, he displayed a keen analytical understanding of the dawning age of nation-states, as well as of the constraints that govern artistic production in bourgeois societies, in which writers can no longer depend on the aristocratic patronage of the feudal court system. In the two essays that Mann wrote to commemorate the centenary of Goethe's death, "Goethe as a Representative of the Bourgeois Age" and "Goethe's Career as a Writer," he took great care to emphasize this modernizing aspect of the great author's legacy.

A second foundational rumination on representative authorship within the German tradition, Friedrich Schiller's "On Naïve and Sentimental Poetry," was also published in 1795. Like Goethe, Schiller was a lifelong intellectual touchstone for Thomas Mann, who paid heartfelt tributes to his forebear in the story "A Weary Hour," the abandoned essay manuscript "Intellect and Art" (1909–12), and the "Essay on Schiller" (1955), among others.[9] As was the case with "Literary Sansculottism," "On Naïve and Sentimental Poetry" had been written in response to the trauma of the French Revolution. According to Schiller, the revolution reveals the fundamentally fragmented nature of modern societies. In such societies, artists will have to commit to one of two choices. They can either strive for an ideal depiction of their surroundings, treating the world as if it could somehow be made whole again, or they can adopt a reflective and critical attitude, acknowledging that they will invariably produce fragments. To artists choosing the former path, Schiller gives the name "poets" (Dichter); to those choosing the latter he refers as "writers" (Schriftsteller).[10]

Over the course of the nineteenth century, Germans began to self-identify as citizens of a "country of poets and thinkers" (Land der Dichter und Denker).[11] The concept of the critical and reflective "writer" was instead associated with neighboring France and to a lesser extent also with Great Britain and the United States. In the early years of the twentieth century, as tensions between Germany and the western European nations intensified, it was joined by the more derogatory term "man of letters" (Literat), which referred to a professional scribbler or hack, somebody capable of adopting any viewpoint whatsoever as long as there was money to be made from it.[12]

The irony, of course, is that German society in the late nineteenth century was more fractious than it had been at any point in the country's past. The second industrial revolution, set in motion by the dawn of the electrical and petrochemical ages, belatedly threw what had been a largely agrarian nation into a condition of modernity. And modern societies inevitably splinter into a number of discrepant groups—workers, capitalists, beleaguered farmers and artisans, bureaucrats, intellectuals—whose outlooks contradict one another as a consequence of the differing roles that they play in the social collective. Writers certainly do not escape this process. At the same time that popular sentiment in Germany thus enshrined the poet as a kind of oracular figure, the sole guarantor of a national identity that in real life seemed lost amid the squabbles of partisan interest groups, the people doing the actual writing were busy carving out a social niche for themselves that was as insular as any other.

In light of this gap between image and reality, it will be evident why Thomas Mann raised considerable hackles when, to mark the centenary of Goethe's death, he pronounced him a prototypical "representative of the bourgeois age" and—even worse—spoke of his "career as a writer" (Laufbahn als Schriftsteller) rather than of his "calling as a poet." Mann even explicitly stated that "it is a fruitless and futile mania of the critics to insist on a distinction between the poet and the writer—an impossible distinction, for the boundary between the two does not lie in the product of either, but rather in the personality of the artist himself" (ED, 44, translation modified; GW, 10:181–82). This was not an innocent pronouncement but rather a highly self-aware effort to enlist Goethe's prestige as a quintessentially "German" artist for a reformed understanding of what might actually constitute such a representative function.

Mann's inspiration for this process of redefinition was Friedrich Nietzsche, from whom he borrowed the term "insight" (Erkenntnis, a word that is sometimes also translated as "knowledge" or "understanding") as the principal goal for which the modern writer should strive. In his first major aesthetic manifesto, the 1906 essay "Bilse and I," for example, Mann wrote, "There is an intellectual school in Europe—Friedrich Nietzsche created it—which has accustomed us to combine the concept of the poet with that of the one who strives for insight. Within this school, the border between art and criticism has become much less definite than it used to be" (GKFA, 14.1:105–6). Four years later, in the unpublished essay "On the Social Position of the Writer in Germany," he again asserted that the modern man of letters is "an artist of insight, separated from art in the naive and trusting sense by self-consciousness, intellect, moralism, and a critical disposition" (GKFA, 14.1:225). Intellectual activity and a moral sense here combine with self-consciousness to reinforce the image of an artist as someone who is painfully aware of living in a fragmented world, in which all viewpoints are inevitably subject to further disputation and critique.

This insistence on critical reflection and an awareness of things as they actually are was largely rooted in Mann's lifelong respect for his forefathers, who rose to their prominent social position through bourgeois pragmatism and commercial calculation. Already in 1895, for example, he wrote a letter to his friend Otto Grautoff in which he placed the "writer with a strong *intellectual talent*" above the mere poet, but the businessman above both (*GKFA*, 21:58; emphasis in original). By contrast, Mann had very little patience for the conventional German understanding of the "poet" as a purveyor of idealized alternatives to reality, or of what in one of his notebooks he calls creations that "arise from Orphic depths with slurred speech" (GuK, 158). "No modern creative artist," so he insisted, "can regard the critical faculty as something that is opposed to his inner nature" (*GKFA*, 14.1:86). Everything that he ever wrote about Goethe, Schiller, and indeed Wagner can consequently be read as an attempt to disentangle these figures from their traditional role in German intellectual life and recuperate them as forerunners of his own conception of the modern writer. This would prove to be a lifelong task, and the frustration is evident in Mann's 1925 response to the conservative German professor Conrad Wandrey, who had sent him a manuscript once again extolling the virtues of the Germanic poet type: "What is certain is that this a difficult and almost always awkwardly executed opposition. You do know that Goethe, in contrast to Shakespeare, considered himself to be a writer, don't you?" (*GKFA*, 23.1:136).

Artistic Habitus and the Contrast with Stefan George

Figuring out how to position himself in relationship to an existing discourse concerning representative authorship was only the first step in Thomas Mann's struggle for self-definition. He also needed to show that he could fully inhabit the new subject position that he had articulated. This was a task at which he succeeded marvelously, and indeed, nowadays he is much less remembered for his written commentaries on the social position of the modern writer than he is for his remarkably theatrical attempts to live as one.

This attempt to embody what it might mean to be a modern writer, and to subordinate his public appearance to a specific set of rules to which the sociologist Pierre Bourdieu would refer as a "habitus," can be contrasted with the quite different strategy of the previous generation of cultural producers, the literary *bohème*. The *bohème* had come into being in the 1850s, when artists first tried to articulate a distinctive identity, a code of behavior that would separate the professional from the mere amateur.[13] Mann still experienced bohemian culture, with its eccentric mannerisms, strategically

dissolute lifestyles, and outlandish manners of dress, in his adopted home of
Munich-Schwabing during the 1890s, and it left an imprint on his earliest stories. By that time, however, bohemianism had already largely given way to
something else altogether, namely the ideology of *l'art-pour-l'art*. While the
bohème had endeavored to carve out a social space for the artist in the modern
world, the disciples of *l'art-pour-l'art* went one step further and turned their
backs on that world. They advocated for the purity of art and for the independence (both financially and sociologically) of cultural production from
society at large.

The foremost representative of this tendency in Germany was the poet
Stefan George, who gathered around him a circle of admirers who believed
his art to be an expression of the true, the "secret" Germany. In the words
of George's disciple Friedrich Wolters, this secret Germany hovered "in the
free space of its own self-created atmosphere" above "the domains of ethnic and economic borders, unconfined by topography or customs unions."[14]
Much like Mann, George was supremely conscious of the fact that his ability
to embody a specific vision of modern authorship crucially depended not
only on the quality of his writing but also on choices of personal comport-
ment, such as dress, work habits, and interpersonal attitudes. Blessed with an
aquiline nose vaguely reminiscent of Dante Alighieri, George thus affected
priestlike vestments and would wander around Munich swathed in an aura
of noble asceticism.[15]

Mann detested Stefan George and parodied his influence in several of
his works, most notably in the short story "At the Prophet's" (1904) and in
the final chapter of *The Magic Mountain*. The literary critic Daniel DiMassa
blames this animosity largely on the fact that both authors were gay and yet
held very different views about same-sex attraction.[16] It is just as true, however, that Mann had no patience for George's attempts to lead art away from
society, to close it in upon itself until it could only be appreciated by the properly initiated. If literature was to be guided by the artist's critical faculties,
then it needed to open out upon the world. By cultivating a consciously bourgeois lifestyle that in many ways was outwardly indistinguishable from that
led by successful lawyers, merchants, or politicians, Mann was thus setting
out in the exact opposite direction from that chosen by George and his circle.

Much more was at stake than just the question of how one dressed and
presented oneself in public, however. The final decades of the nineteenth
century were also a period in which the publishing landscape became cleft by
an ever-widening chasm between popular outlets hoping primarily to make
money and those catering to a self-defining clientele. Journals and to a lesser
extent publishing houses had, of course, always catered to diverse audiences,

and differences in aesthetic preferences are one of the ways in which social hierarchies become instrumentalized.[17] But rapid urbanization, widespread employment, and a noticeable rise in literacy all combined to rapidly accelerate this development. As new mass-market dailies catered to the urban masses—many of them also printing fiction and cultural reviews—a number of more intellectual journals came into being hoping to defend the needs of modern art.[18] Similarly, once the larger publishing houses began issuing cheap reprints of the German classics, making it difficult for younger artists to compete in an already-saturated market, smaller firms came to their rescue.

George, unsurprisingly, elected to position himself against the demands of the market, self-publishing most of his works in his journal *Blätter für die Kunst*, as well as in the publishing house that went with it.[19] Mann chose a different route. His early stories appeared in or were contracted by smaller publications, such as the naturalist magazine *Die Gesellschaft*, the art nouveau journal *Pan*, and the satirical weekly *Simplicissimus*, which also offered him an editorial position.[20] But by 1897, he had established a permanent base in the pages of the *Neue deutsche Rundschau* (later simply *Neue Rundschau*)—the house journal of the S. Fischer publishing firm, which aimed to introduce demanding modern fiction to the center of German social life. Three years later, Mann was offered the chance of a lifetime when Fischer agreed to publish his debut novel *Buddenbrooks*, though at the insistence that he cut his manuscript by half. Audaciously, Mann refused, arguing that the integrity of his work depended upon it—and he prevailed. The initial printing of *Buddenbrooks* was a commercial flop, though the novel found an audience when Fischer lowered the price and released it as a single volume rather than in a more cumbersome two-volume edition. Soon it went through print run after print run, and by the late 1920s, it had become one of the bestselling German novels of all time.

For Mann, this combination of initial failure followed by spectacular success was perhaps the best of all possible outcomes. On the one hand, his refusal to compromise on his work even in the face of market opposition established him as someone who could creditably defend the autonomy of modern art. The subsequent success of his stories, on the other hand, vindicated him as someone who could speak to, and ultimately also for, an entire society. In the early years of the twentieth century, Mann could therefore shift gears and begin to produce with a wider audience in mind, knowing that his reputation as a writer of quality was assured. He was nevertheless careful how he went about this, and in 1908, when he placed one of his stories ("A Railway Accident") in a mass-market daily for the first time, he still felt compelled to inform friends and family that "it was really nothing at all. A thing of one afternoon, done only on account of the surprisingly decent fee they pay. Christmas is expensive" (*GKFA*, 21:404). Soon, however, he grew bolder. He convinced Fischer to license a mass-market paperback of his novella *Tristan*, and by the early 1920s, he was routinely driving hard negotiations with his publisher in order to persuade a reluctant Fischer to try to reach for more popular markets. The celebrated outcome of these endeavors was the so-called people's edition of *Buddenbrooks*, which sold almost one million copies between 1929 and 1935.[21]

Finding the right kind of presentation for his stories was only part of the battle. Two further qualities were required to complete Mann's self-realization as the kind of modern writer that he envisioned. First, he needed to acquire visibility as a public figure, and as someone who could command respect not only through his writing but also through the force of his personality. This he achieved primarily by embarking on a series of highly successful reading tours, but also through less conventional strategies, such as his innovative use of author photographs to suggest a modern professional identity.[22] The second quality that was required to truly live up to the Nietzschean ideal of the modern intellectual was self-reflexivity, or an awareness of the fact that his works were themselves a part of German society and thus available to critique from vantage points other than his own. Mann's early endeavors in this regard have a certain roguish quality to them. In 1901, for example, we find him giving his friend and admirer Otto Grautoff detailed instructions on what the latter should say in a book review of Mann's recently published *Buddenbrooks* (*GKFA*, 21:179). Throughout his life, Mann studied reviews of his works very carefully, and frequently responded to them either privately or in print.[23] He also went out of his way to befriend professors from around the world who took an interest in his stories, and he was an early member of the Bonn Society for Literary History, the first-ever German academic society devoted exclusively to contemporary literature.[24] In 1909 he also became one of the founding members of the Association for the Protection of German Writers (Schutzverband deutscher Schriftsteller), a lobbying organization for literary professionals. Through the association, an interest group created *by* cultural producers *for* cultural producers, Mann could creditably fight for the independence of modern art from mere economic demands while simultaneously ensuring that it was firmly anchored in larger German society.

By the second decade of the twentieth century, then, Thomas Mann had not only philosophically articulated, but also publicly modeled, an entirely modern conception of what a writer should be, one that stood profoundly at odds with conservative understandings of the "poet." This modern conception of the writer's role meshed only uneasily with Mann's simultaneous ambition to be perceived as the mouthpiece of his nation. In his 1901 instructions to Otto Grautoff, he had already urged his younger friend first and foremost to stress "the *German* character of the novel" (*GKFA*, 21:179). And several years later, he confided in his notebooks that he possessed an "inclination to see myself as a national factor, to regard myself as essentially national" (*Nb.*, 2:120). But if modern writing was defined not only by the embrace of the critical faculty but also by self-awareness, and thus by a cognizance of the writer's perspectival limitations, then how could a truly modern artist ever claim to speak for an entire nation? Throughout the early 1900s Thomas Mann wrestled with this question, and his literary projects of that period bear the imprint of his struggle. He tried—with mixed success— to adapt classic forms of German literature to the twentieth century: the novella (with *Tonio Kröger*, 1903), the historical drama (with *Fiorenza*, 1906), and even the novel of development, or bildungsroman (with *The Magic Mountain*, which he began in 1913). Ultimately he concluded, however, that such forms could only be used as a matter of parody (*GKFA*, 15.1:175–76). And he also began—and then quickly abandoned—a number of monumental projects, such as the essay "Intellect and Art" or a historical novel about Frederick the Great, in which he would presumably have sought to shed critical light on the vagaries of the German national experience.

Mann's struggles did lead him to one noticeable success, the 1912 novella *Death in Venice*. The protagonist of this story, Gustav von Aschenbach, has completed all the projects that Mann himself had abandoned over the previous years; we are also told that he enjoys the "homage" (*SD*, 381; *GKFA*, 2.1:506) of his nation. Official school textbooks carry excerpts from his stories, and a well-meaning aristocrat has even bestowed upon him an honorific title of nobility. But Aschenbach's greatness is also predicated on his conscious renunciation of the intellectual ideals for which Mann himself was striving, of "criticism" and of "insight." As a young man, we learn, he "had done homage to intellect, had overworked the soil of knowledge [Erkenntnis] and ground up her seed-corn" (*SD*, 385; *GKFA*, 2.1:512). But as he matured, he had "turned his back on the realm of knowledge and passed it by with averted face, lest it lame his will or power of action" (*SD*, 386; *GKFA*, 2.1:513). It is precisely this renunciation of knowledge, and particularly of critical self-knowledge, that will lead to Aschenbach's eventual downfall in Venice when his encounter with Tadzio forces him to confront truths about himself that he is ill-equipped to handle.

Political Engagement and the Contrast with Émile Zola and Maximilian Harden

Mann's struggles to reconcile his self-conception as a modern writer with his ambition to be perceived as a "national factor" can be usefully contrasted with those of the older colleague to whom he would later be compared during his American exile: the French author Émile Zola. When he published his famous open letter "J'accuse" in the Paris daily *L'aurore*, Émile Zola, then fifty-eight years old, already stood at the peak of his influence and was arguably the most famous novelist in all of France. With essays such as "The Experimental Novel" (1880), he had also elevated the naturalist movement into the public consciousness, and was thus recognized as a principal voice of modernism in literature. The social context from which he had sprung was very different from that of Thomas Mann, however. As the historian Christophe Charle has shown, the strong influence that Auguste Comte's philosophical positivism exerted upon French educated society in the 1890s caused an entire generation of French intellectuals to adopt scientism as its guiding credo, especially since this worldview served as a useful rallying cry in a battle with the aging grandees who held prestigious posts in the academies and *grandes écoles*.[25] Zola's naturalism was the literary outgrowth of this scientistic movement. Naturalism claimed to carry into the artistic sphere the same impassioned analytical gaze, the same ambition to speak truth for truth's sake that also characterized recent advances in the hard as well as social sciences. And it furthermore believed that that a scientific disposition was the only way to adequately render human social life, because human actions could—at least on a general level—be attributed to extrapersonal forces capable of objective study.

With his intervention in the Dreyfus case, Zola applied his ambition to cultivate a neutral analytical stance to the realm of social affairs.[26] When the *Nation*, in 1937, published Mann's letter to the dean of the philosophical faculty at Bonn as "I Accuse the Hitler Regime," it clearly meant to draw a parallel to this earlier intervention. In reality, however, the two acts were quite differently motivated. Thomas Mann knew Zola's novels, was influenced by naturalist thought in the early stages of his career, and later in life even declared that Zola had been one of the "gods" "of his youth (*GW*, 13:134). And yet he never commented on "J'accuse" or on the Dreyfus affair more generally when it happened. This silence is all the more remarkable because the affair was widely discussed in Germany.[27]

Mann's silence can be explained by the fact that he neither regarded his own intellectual stance as detached and scientistic, nor was he as yet willing to admit that modernity might sometimes place the cultural producer into militant opposition to other social institutions, such as the military, parliament, or the courts. By birth, Mann belonged to the typically German social class of the *Bildungsbürgertum*: a subsegment of the bourgeoisie that defined its status not just through its accumulated wealth but primarily through education and specifically through cultural erudition. As Gangolf Hübinger has argued, the *Bildungsbürger* believed himself to be equally at home in the scientific, cultural, and political spheres of society.[28] It was only during the latter years of the nineteenth century, when scientists, writers, and politicians all began to develop their own professional ethos, that this self-understanding slowly began to fall apart. And Mann had no interest in the scientistic worldview that began to take hold in the research laboratories of the empire. His preferred terms for intellectual activity, *Geist* and its adjectival correlate *geistig*, are instead of humanistic origin and could also be translated as "spiritual."[29] Lacking such a scientistic basis, Mann also did not follow Zola in the assumption that the foremost social role of the artist should be to proclaim "truth." Instead, he believed that writers should use their intellectual powers to analyze the opposing viewpoints that were an inevitable consequence of any modern society, and then produce artistic statements that would expose these viewpoints to public scrutiny while withholding judgment of their own.

Two further factors undoubtedly contributed to Thomas Mann's apparent reluctance to comment on the Dreyfus trial. The first was his fraternal rivalry with his older brother, Heinrich, who was himself a highly regarded novelist. Heinrich's admiration for modern French literature, and for the works of Zola in particular, was well known, and Mann thus made a strategic choice to seek other means of defining his artistic identity.[30] The second was Mann's reluctance to embrace journalistic activities. Émile Zola had launched his manifesto not in a small literary magazine with close connections to the naturalist movement but rather in the socialist daily *L'aurore*, which was then edited by Georges Clemenceau, the future president of the republic. Clemenceau, furthermore, immediately recognized the significance of what he was about to publish. He posted broadsheets all over Paris and increased his print run more than tenfold, from the usual twenty to thirty thousand to roughly three hundred thousand copies. "J'accuse," then, was a genuine intervention in the public sphere of its country, targeted not solely at the more educated liberal and socialist clientele that ordinarily read *L'aurore*, but at a mass public (figure 1.2). It appealed to its readers as citizens of the French Republic, not as individuals holding specific political beliefs or cultural pedigrees.

Deuxième Année. — Numéro 87

Cinq Centimes

JEUDI 13 JANVIER 1898

Directeur
ERNEST VAUGHAN
ABONNEMENTS

Directeur
ERNEST VAUGHAN
LES ANNONCES SONT REÇUES :
242 — Rue Montmartre — 142

L'AURORE

Littéraire, Artistique, Sociale

J'Accuse…!

LETTRE AU PRÉSIDENT DE LA RÉPUBLIQUE
Par ÉMILE ZOLA

LETTRE

A M. FÉLIX FAURE

Président de la République

Monsieur le Président,

FIGURE 1.2. Émile Zola's "J'accuse" on the front page of *L'aurore*, January 13, 1898. Public domain/Wikimedia Commons.

By contrast, Mann's relationship both with the popular press and with the concept of a "German public" was much more complicated. Of course he was anxious to become a well-known and widely read author, but this goal was initially secondary to being perceived as a writer of quality. Broadsheets and popular newspapers were unlikely to be helpful in this strategy; Mann's ambivalence about publishing his "Railway Accident" in the Viennese *Neue Freie Presse* contrasts tellingly with his unbridled joy about seeing his novella *Tristan* reprinted by the mass-market publisher Reclam. Reclam had made its reputation by offering affordable editions of the classics. As such, it was a focal point for the self-perception of the *Bildungsbürgertum*, the social stratum that Mann identified as his primary audience, and whose internal cohesion was actively threatened by the thought that everyone, even workers, was now reading newspapers.

Mann's hesitation to embrace the medium of the popular newspaper was undoubtedly aggravated by a public scandal that occurred in 1906 and formed a rough German equivalent to the Dreyfus case: the Harden-Eulenburg affair. In November of that year, the journalist Maximilian Harden, whose every move Mann followed with a mixture of envy, awe, and disgust, published an article in which he accused Kaiser Wilhelm II of having endangered national security through an alleged relationship with a member of his general staff, Prince Philipp zu Eulenburg.[31] The accusations and resulting trials held the German public spellbound for several years. Whereas Zola emerged from the Dreyfus affair a hero, however, having exposed the illiberal and deeply anti-Semitic mindset of the French military, Harden could not score a similar success. Sued for defamation, he lost both in a court of law and in the court of public opinion. The consensus, essentially, was that he was a ruthless journalist who had tried to engineer a public scandal in order to increase the circulation of his paper. The affair, furthermore, had disastrous consequences for Germany's gay subculture, which had previously thrived amid a cultural milieu that was actually more welcoming than that of most other European nations in the early twentieth century.[32]

As a closeted gay man, Thomas Mann followed the Eulenburg affair closely. He commented publicly on it only once, in a 1907 response to an opinion survey in the daily newspaper *Der Morgen*, in which he praised Harden's "political seriousness, his sense of responsibility, and his will towards the positive" (*GKFA*, 14.1:179).[33] Privately, however, he clearly entertained doubts. In his working notes to "Intellect and Art," for example, he described Harden as a "man of letters who has been perverted into becoming a politician" and who "compromised Germany . . . through the whole Eulenburg affair" (GuK, 217). These phrases outline very clearly Mann's evident revulsion at the thought of cultural production as a form of political activism, a verdict that easily could have been applied to Zola in the Dreyfus affair.

For perhaps the first time in his writings, Mann in this passage also used the term "man of letters" (Literat) to refer to a particular author type from which he was trying distance himself. Although Mann in his published writings prior to the First World War employed the words *Literat* and *Schriftsteller* fairly interchangeably (see, e.g., the essay "The Artist and the Man of Letters" of 1913), he was privately attempting to draw finer distinctions between the writer who critically analyzes for the benefit of others and the man of letters who abuses his analytical powers for a partisan purpose.[34] Soon enough, he would also employ this distinction publicly, with explosive results.

Representation and the Contrast with Heinrich Mann and Gerhart Hauptmann

Germany's invasion of Belgium in August 1914 greatly intensified the pressure on Thomas Mann to finally find an adequate form for his representative aspirations. Surely now, more than ever, the nation needed a spokesperson who could represent its cultural values to the world? Mann's initial response to the call was revealing. Shortly after the invasion, he published an essay titled "Thoughts in Times of War," in which he strongly supported the actions of the German government. And in early 1915 he followed up with his essay "Frederick and the Grand Coalition," in which he reshaped some of the materials that he had accumulated for his abandoned historical novel into an essay examining the causes of the Seven Years' War.

The outbreak of the war coincided with a new and even more intense confrontation with Heinrich that finally forced Thomas Mann to publicly position himself vis-à-vis Zola. In the spring of 1915, Heinrich published an essay in which he praised the French writer as a militant intellectual. The essay begins with the sarcastic observation that "writers who affect a self-assured and 'representative' [weltgerecht] demeanor during their twenties will generally see their talents wither by mid-career."[35] It didn't take a lot of skill to identify this as a barb aimed at his younger brother, who was about to turn forty and had not published a major novel since *Buddenbrooks* fourteen years earlier (*Royal Highness*, in 1909, had met with only tepid critical and commercial success). Thomas Mann took this insult quite personally. Mere personal insult alone cannot explain, however, why he decided to set aside all work on his novel *The Magic Mountain* and devote the next three years to his *Reflections of a Nonpolitical Man*. To arrive at some account for this, one also has to keep in mind that Heinrich's essay was intended as a partisan intervention in debates about modern authorship, a conscious taking of sides for Zola and against Thomas. It contains the fateful line "a war can be necessary and moral as long as it is the outcome of a long struggle for truth."[36] The meaning of these words is obvious, given Zola's well-known insistence that the obligation of the modern writer was to struggle for truth not only in fiction but also in social affairs. They constitute a clear endorsement of the writer as a political agent, right down to the point of agitating for war. And of course they also provide tacit support for the French side in the First World War, a fact that only hastened Thomas's resolve to align himself with the German position instead.

Reflections of a Nonpolitical Man is, therefore, first and foremost an attempt to outline a conception of the modern writer that might be placed in conscious opposition to that offered by Zola and Heinrich. On a personal level, the book is also a sustained attack on the hated brother. Going in a more general direction, it is furthermore a polemical attempt to contrast German and French national characters. But the personal and the general are really two sides of the same coin: attacks undertaken not as much for their own sake as in an attempt to bolster Mann's own representative strivings.

Reflections is the only place in Mann's entire oeuvre in which he offers an (albeit brief) analysis of Zola's intervention in the Dreyfus affair, confessing that he did not want "Dreyfus to be condemned and then acquitted for political reasons—for the acquittal of an innocent person for political reasons is no less repulsive than his conviction on the same basis" (R, 189; GKFA, 13.1:285). The logic underlying this conclusion is hair-raising, but the assumption that judicial decisions should be based on deliberations about justice, not political expediency, is clearly sound. Zola would, of course, have agreed with this rather elementary point. But the two men part ways over the question whether it should be the task of the writer to pursue political causes in an attempt to restore justice in situations where it was abrogated. Mann clearly thought not.

What then was to be the task of the representative writer? One answer that Mann gives in *Reflections* is that it is to steer away from the corrosive influence of partisan politics, and instead to try to remain impartial by making the best case for *both* sides on any given issue. This strategy Mann calls "aestheticism," though he is careful to differentiate himself from the *l'art-pour-l'art* understanding of that term by insisting that he does not mean "dying in beauty or always having figures of speech such as 'wine leaves in the hair' on one's tongue" (R, 161; GKFA, 13.1:244). As quintessential examples of aesthetes, Mann instead lists a diverse set of writers (Schiller, Gustave Flaubert, Arthur Schopenhauer, Lev Tolstoy, August Strindberg, and

Nietzsche, among others) who each aimed for such a complex depiction of reality. In his 1803 play *The Bride of Messina*, for example, Schiller has the same character praise both peace and war within a few lines of one another. Had Schiller advocated only for the former, we might have acclaimed him as "enlightened and praiseworthy." Had he spoken only for the latter, we would have perceived him as an "enemy of humanity to be combatted." In either case, however, he would have acted as a "politician"—that is, as a partisan of particular interests. "To immerse himself deeply into the essence of peace and war with the same dilettantish empathy," however, "was aestheticism" (*R*, 161; *GKFA*, 13.1:245).

"Aestheticism" is thus the answer with which Thomas Mann responds to the banner of "truth" that Zola carried into the public sphere. Zola believed that the modern writer deserves to represent society to itself because the writer has learned to cast an indiscriminating eye on the world, to set aside social pieties and clearly describe what is actually the case. From this he furthermore inferred a mandate for political activism as the writer attempts to change the world for the better. Mann makes a different argument. The specific virtue of artists is that they are pledged to an aesthetic view of the world, and thus aim to represent all facets of it. This does not mean that they cannot have strict opinions. Schiller, for instance, lived in a most violent age and definitely had some personal thoughts about the preferability of peace to war. Writers, however, should not issue prescriptions but should act as a kind of catalyst: by making us rehearse all sides of an issue, they force us to come to our own conclusions.

Mann's biographers have often pointed out—usually in a critical tone—that he never fully renounced *Reflections of a Nonpolitical Man*, not even after his political journey had driven him to embrace the western "civilized world" that he so bitterly attacked in 1918. Instead, Mann generally insisted that *Reflections*, far from representing a momentary lapse in critical judgment, was actually a crucial stepping stone in his development as a writer.[37] Indeed, Mann's greatest literary achievement of the 1920s, *The Magic Mountain*, is perhaps better read as a continuation of some of the main arguments of *Reflections* than as a recantation of them. Back in 1916, shortly after he had set aside the manuscript for his novel, Mann had argued that the most characteristically "German" of all literary forms, the bildungsroman, could nowadays only be appropriated as parody. But in writing *Reflections*, he found that this was not necessarily true. The character of the Italian humanist Ludovico Settembrini, who appears as a vaguely Satanic tempter figure in the early sections of *The Magic Mountain*, was now reshaped into a spitting image of "civilization's man of letters." Just as importantly, he was given an intellectual antagonist in the form of Leo Naphta, who manages to combine characteristics of an ultramontane Catholic, a Communist, and a fascist demagogue all in one complex personality. Standing between these figures is the protagonist Hans Castorp, who lends a sympathetic ear to both, but pledges allegiance to neither, and instead draws his own conclusions. *The Magic Mountain* offers a powerful example of what *Reflections* calls an "aesthetic" point of view, for it is not just Hans Castorp who profits from the exposure to Naphta and Settembrini. By accompanying Castorp on his intellectual path, the reader is exposed to the multiple conflicting ideologies of the interwar period as well. And like Castorp, the reader will learn how to critically evaluate them all, without being forced (or even invited) to take sides.

Castorp's "aesthetic" openness can usefully be contrasted with the general demeanor of another character in the novel, namely that of Mynheer Peeperkorn. Peeperkorn is in many regards the exact opposite of the novel's young protagonist. Whereas Castorp lacks a strong personality and tends to be at his best when he gets to react to other characters (he never formulates any ideas of his own but proves to be a master dialectician, brutally skilled at turning a point against the person who originally made it), Peeperkorn exudes authoritarian charisma and repeatedly shows himself capable of shutting down an interlocutor with a simple gesture. In one telling scene, for instance, the quarreling Naphta and Settembrini instantly fall silent when Peeperkorn points toward an eagle that is soaring above them in the mountain air. In a novel that is obsessed with talking, Peeperkorn also stands out because he is practically aphasic. He seems incapable of completing even simple sentences and instead persuades through the nonverbal force of his personality.

The comparison with Peeperkorn is useful not only because it brings Castorp's own qualities into sharper focus but also because the Dutch planter is a thinly veiled parody of Mann's foremost rival in the race to become Germany's most distinguished writer of the interwar period, Gerhart Hauptmann. As winner of the Nobel Prize in Literature in 1912, Hauptmann was perhaps the most famous German author of the 1920s, not just in Germany itself but internationally. He also happened to share a publisher with Thomas Mann, which made the rivalry between the two men all the more intimate. Hauptmann had leapt onto the literary scene in the late 1880s as the principal German exponent of the naturalist movement. By the 1920s, however, he had settled into bourgeois respectability as the author of neoclassical dramas and verse epics. When the empire collapsed, there were rumors that Hauptmann would be offered the presidency, and throughout the 1920s he was revered as an incarnation of the German national spirit. In 1922, on the occasion of

Hauptmann's sixtieth birthday, the *actual* German president, Friedrich Ebert, even felt compelled to declare that "By honoring Gerhart Hauptmann, the German nation honors itself."[38]

Thomas Mann publicly adulated and privately resented his older contemporary, as *The Magic Mountain* documents. Mynheer Peeperkorn's appearance and speech patterns are unmistakably modeled on Hauptmann, a fact that was widely remarked upon in the Weimar press and led to some tense moments between the two authors. Hauptmann understandably felt betrayed by his younger colleague, since two years earlier, on the occasion of Hauptmann's sixtieth birthday, Mann had still paid obeisance to him as a "king of the Republic" (GR, 109; *GKFA*, 15.1:515). What Mann primarily resented about Hauptmann was that the older man seemed to have built up a representative façade that was backed up by very little substance. Hauptmann fancied himself to be the last great German poet in the tradition of Goethe, and he certainly cultivated a public persona to go along with these claims.[39] But in truth, much of his best work was long behind him. It had furthermore been written at a time when Hauptmann still took a self-consciously antagonistic stance to the German state, as the author of scandalous naturalist plays and as a supporter of the socialist party who even inspired the personal ire of the kaiser. Hauptmann had little to say about public life in the Weimar Republic, and when he did speak—so Mann clearly thought, judging by his depiction in *The Magic Mountain*—he spoke in platitudes.[40]

Despite all this, Hauptmann largely succeeded at positioning himself as the foremost spokesperson for the new Germany. *The Magic Mountain* was, among many other things, a gauntlet thrown down in protest against these representative aspirations. The novel is an incomparably more modern work than anything that Hauptmann ever wrote. It rejects the self-enclosed neoclassical style associated with the late Hauptmann and instead aims for a radical openness of both form and content.[41] It is precisely this openness that makes it uniquely suited to speak for an internally conflicted society like the Weimar Republic. Political reactionaries were dismayed by the novel, but among a younger generation, Mann now firmly established himself as the foremost literary spokesperson for his country.

In the Interwar Republic of Letters

By the mid-1920s, then, Thomas Mann stood at the pinnacle of his fame and influence in Germany. And increasingly, this fame spread across the country's borders as well. This was not at all a foregone conclusion, for the European interwar republic of letters was still to an astoundingly large extent governed by national prejudices. When Mann and his wife visited Oxford in May 1924, for instance, many of the local dons refused to meet him because (as his translator Helen Tracy Lowe-Porter put it) they did not think he displayed the "sense of guilt" that was felt to be "the proper attitude of all worthy Germans."[42] The following year, the *Times Literary Supplement* devoted only half a column to the newly published *Magic Mountain*.[43] Mann's works never sold particularly well on the British Isles, and it was largely Alfred A. Knopf's influence that convinced the British firm of Martin Secker (later Secker & Warburg) to publish them at all.[44] In France matters stood even worse. A French translation of *Death in Venice* did not come out until 1925. Following its success, Mann was able to persuade the publishing house Kra to take on translations of all of his novels (*GKFA*, 23.1:224), only to have its editor-in-chief, Léon Pierre-Quint, try to back out of the deal once the German volumes arrived on his desk and he realized how long they were (*GKFA*, 23.1:280). *La montagne magique* finally appeared in 1931, *Les Buddenbrooks* in 1932.

Despite these obstacles, Thomas Mann quickly gained preeminence as a representative of the German cultural tradition not only within the confines of his own country but also abroad. A series of widely publicized lectures around Europe was perhaps the most important motor of this development. Unlike Mann's earlier speaking commitments, which had mostly comprised readings from his fictional works and were confined to cities that either lay within the German Reich or could boast of large German-speaking minorities, these new lectures were devoted to broader intellectual themes and were frequently written specifically for the occasion. In keeping with Mann's continued reluctance toward overt political action, he almost always spoke on literary topics. But the attentive audience member never had to burrow very deep in order to discover some kind of applicability to contemporary social problems.

Perhaps the best illustration of this is the 1922 lecture "On the German Republic," a large part of which is given over to a comparison between two seemingly antithetical writers: the royalist German poet Novalis and the bard of the American republic, Walt Whitman. True to the aesthetic method already propagated in *Reflections*, Mann pays equal attention to both figures, only to then show that they have much more in common than we might initially assume. The conclusion that Mann draws from these similarities is that the German people ought to give a republican form of government a fighting chance, rather than rejecting it as alien to their traditions. "Goethe and Tolstoi," "Lessing," "Freud's Position in Modern Intellectual History" (1929), and "The Suffering and Greatness of Richard Wagner" represent similar attempts to show Germans how a careful study of their own cultural history might lead them toward reconciliation with the western world. And the Germans were clearly listening, for they flocked to such lectures in droves, as Mann proudly noted in his correspondence with his publisher.[45]

Increasingly, Mann also delivered his talks abroad. Unlike his later lecture tours in the United States, his visits to cities such as Amsterdam, Paris, London, Stockholm, or Warsaw generally were noncommercial in nature and came about at the invitation of some kind of hosting organization, such as the local PEN Club. At a time when the reading public in France and Great Britain still viewed German authors with a great deal of suspicion, Mann thus forged personal connections with colleagues in the former enemy countries, for example, with André Gide in France or with John Galsworthy, H. G. Wells, and George Bernard Shaw in England (Galsworthy was the first president of International PEN, and played a crucial role in bringing Mann to London). In return, Mann also tried to introduce foreign-language authors to the Weimar Republic. He thus wrote an important foreword to S. Fischer's 1926 edition of Joseph Conrad's *The Secret Agent* and for a time served as the coeditor of the book series Novels of the World (Romane der Welt) for the Knaur publishing house.[46]

The list of authors with whom Mann associated during the 1920s reveals an important fact about his representative strivings and allows us to shed new light on the nature of literary relations in the interwar republic of letters. Gide, Galsworthy, Wells, and even Conrad—these were all authors who were born between 1855 and 1875 and who therefore belonged to the very first wave of what we now call modernist literature. They rose to prominence and into middle age in the decades before the First World War, and thus before the cataclysmic events that formally and politically radicalized the subsequent generation. These were authors who had struggled to first establish and then defend the autonomy of modern art and who by the 1920s occupied positions as the de facto "elder statesmen" of the European republic of letters. Thomas Mann belonged to the very tail end of this generation. He was young enough to recognize slightly younger contemporaries who would exceed him in stylistic daring, such as Alfred Döblin (born in 1878), James Joyce (1882), or Franz Kafka (1883), as competitors, but still old enough to adopt an attitude toward his craft that owed more to the previous generation. This strange transitional position has led many later critics to underestimate the innovative nature of Mann's works, especially since Mann's authorial habitus has come to be so strongly enshrined in the collective literary memory.[47] But it needs to be stressed that Mann's alignment with such people as Gide or Galsworthy was not just a reactionary gesture in the context of the early 1920s. It represented a lesson learned from the horrors of the war in its own right and was thus a legitimate a response to modernity.

The metaphor of "elder statesmen" seems entirely appropriate to describe the particular redefinition of representative authorship in which Thomas Mann participated during these years. For these prestigious middle-aged writers forged not only personal but also institutional connections across national barriers in an attempt to prevent another world war. The various national PEN Clubs—Mann joined the German one in February 1925 (*Br. LF*, 514)—are a prime example of this. Similar in function to the *Schutzverband* that Mann had helped found before the war, they nevertheless differed from this purely national project by virtue of the fact that they were interconnected both through their practical activities and through their charter status as autonomous subsidiaries of International PEN. The Nobel Prize Committee provides another example. Though the first Nobel Prize in Literature had been handed out in 1901, and although technically only members of the Swedish Academy were eligible to participate in the awards deliberations, the Nobel Prize during the 1920s changed from a fairly parochial institution that heavily favored Nordic writers into a major force in European (though not yet "world") literature. Writers from all over the continent tried to influence prize decisions either directly (past laureates were able to submit recommendations, as Thomas Mann did on several occasions after his 1929 win) or indirectly (though vigorous lobbying activities). Privately endowed, the Nobel furthermore stood above the meddlesome influence of national governments.

At the same time, the interwar republic of letters was never completely "independent of political boundaries," as has sometimes been claimed.[48] The metaphor of the "republic" here proves entirely apt, for after all, republican systems of government are characterized by the fact that their principal actors function as representatives of larger social collectives. Thomas Mann's hosts in Holland, France, England, Poland, or Sweden always invited him with the explicit understanding that he would speak to them as the representative of German letters and culture. And Mann gladly obliged. In 1926, for example, he gave a well-received lecture, "The Intellectual Situation in Contemporary Germany," in Paris on the invitation of the Carnegie Foundation for International Peace. At the same time, he always stressed the fundamental unity of cultural producers across the continent. In an address to the PEN Club in Warsaw (figure 1.3) he remarked, "We [European writers] are bound, determined, and preordained by birth and tradition. We live our lives within verbal and spiritual webs that we ourselves extend as we maintain and develop the culture of our people" (*GW*, 11:403). Mann nicely summarized

FIGURE 1.3. Thomas Mann visiting the Polish PEN Club in Warsaw, March 1927. Thomas-Mann-Archiv, ETH Zurich. Photographer: Atelier Karol Pęcherski.

his position at another point of the Warsaw lecture, when he pointed at a French colleague and declared, "whatever this man is and means for his country, I am and mean for my country as well. I am to Germany what he is to France. And thus national character becomes a more or less formal concern, a mere external difference that is due to chance. The essential, personal and human elements that unite us are revealed underneath" (GW, 11:403).[49]

Thomas Mann's 1929 Nobel Prize can similarly be seen as a symptom of the reassertion of national characteristics within an international context. Mann owed his prize primarily to the advocacy of the powerful Swedish literary critic Fredrik Böök, a Germanophile who admired Mann primarily because he believed him eminently capable of popularizing the German cultural heritage for an international community.[50] The 1929 award was specifically given to *Buddenbrooks* (by then almost three decades old) rather than to the more stylistically advanced *Magic Mountain* because Böök believed the older novel stood a better chance of representing German life and German thought on a global stage.

This paradoxical combination, whereby a writer is at once intimately bound to the traditions of his or her country and, precisely by so being bound, part of a larger community of cultural producers that all share in the same condition, stood at the heart of Mann's hopes for European peace. As he put it in some remarks to the French PEN Club in Paris,

> The social union of poets and writers, their amicable correspondence from country to country, is of the greatest importance in our day. . . . There can be no hostility that runs deep enough to permit war between nations whose intellectual advocates are friends. Economic and political conflicts have never been enough to set people at war with one another. Intellectual tension, alienation and strife have always been necessary as well, and these we must prevent and correct. The PEN Club may not have a very predisposing name, but the idea that undergirds it may grow into an important factor for peace and for the reconciliation between nations. (*GKFA*, 15.1:1094–95)

These are unquestionably idealistic and perhaps even otherworldly sentences. Yet they are also unmistakably a product of their times. Their goal is to lead Germany back into the community of European nations, rather than to underline its exceptional status as a "nation of culture," a *Kulturnation*. It is important to remember in this context both the weakness of the political parties in the Weimar Republic and the inefficiency of the League of Nations on an intergovernmental level. As Thomas Mann noted in a letter to Ernst Robert Curtius shortly before his departure to address the Carnegie Foundation, "The main efforts to achieve an amicable understanding [between France and Germany] will probably have to be made by us [intellectuals]" (*Reg.*, 25/215). In the absence of effective political action, the thought that writers might lead the way toward European reconciliation may not have seemed quite as unrealistic as it does today.

Idealism aside, we can discern in Mann's various interwar addresses a visionary program statement for an international republic of letters. According to this vision, organizations such as the PEN Clubs function as anchors that ground an international intellectual community within the realm of geographical boundaries and linguistic differences. As chartered entities that come into being within specific national spaces, the clubs both serve these spaces and represent them to the rest of the world. The writers who congregate within them have a similarly representative function. At the same time, however, the centers operate as portals that lead from the national world into a realm of intellectual activity and camaraderie, which knows neither linguistic nor political divisions. Looking back on the past decade in an autobiographical essay that he published in 1930, Mann would interpret his activities in the PEN Clubs and similar institutions as an entirely logical outgrowth of the reigning political circumstances, writing that "the official elevation of literary intellect into an organ of national life . . . was a logical consequence of social developments in Germany and only confirmed existing circumstances" (GW, 11:136).

Both the PEN Clubs and the Swedish Royal Academy, which awards the Nobel Prize, are nongovernmental organizations. This does not mean, however, that Mann believed international understanding could only come about in complete independence from political interference. Rather, it is a case of governmental systems sheltering and supporting spaces for free creative and intellectual expression within their midst. To the extent that this assessment insists on the fundamental segregation of culture from politics, it represents a continuation of the position already advanced in *Reflections of a Nonpolitical Man*. At the same time, Mann took seriously the implication that cultural producers needed to do their part to remind the governing classes of the need for an independent creative sphere. As a founding member of the Section for Poetic Art of the Prussian Academy of the Arts, Mann worked tirelessly toward just this purpose.[51]

Mann's personal vision of a semiautonomous republic of letters, anchored within national cultures and protected by national governments, yet at the same time international in scope, helps explain why his break with the Nazi regime in 1936 was brought about by such a seemingly trivial occasion as the revocation of his Bonn doctorate. It would be easy to attribute Mann's consternation over his lost title entirely to his personal vanity, as some people already did during his own lifetime.[52] Mann's outrage and disappointment make perfect sense within the context of his worldview, however. Over the course of the nineteenth century, Germany's once-parochial universities had established themselves as the very best in the world precisely because of their guiding ideal that they would be state supported yet at the same time entirely autonomous from political demands.[53] This commitment toward intellectual autonomy, backed by the financial and administrative heft of the German states (and later the Second German Empire), made their humanistic faculties important institutional pillars of the field of cultural production, as well as of the European republic of letters. An honorary doctorate of letters was thus one of the highest forms of accreditation that a modern writer could possibly achieve. Tellingly, even Gustav von Aschenbach, who seems to have overcome all the obstacles in front of which his creator stumbled, is able to win a certificate of nobility, but not an honorary doctorate.[54]

To be stripped of this degree thus meant far more than a personal insult to Thomas Mann. It also illustrated to him the true nature of totalitarian dictatorship, which consists precisely of the dissolution of boundaries between the separate fields that comprise a modern society, and their submission to the dictates of charismatic politics. And since Mann's self-perception as Germany's representative in the European republic of letters was built on the notion of a field of cultural production whose autonomy was guaranteed by the power of the state, the attack on the independence of the university meant an attack also on his professional identity. When he arrived in New York in February 1938, his representative status thus was not nearly as self-evident as his confident address to the American nation might indicate. Thomas Mann needed to construct a new kind of representative status, one that would be appropriate to his condition as an émigré and one in which US cultural institutions would play a significant and hitherto underappreciated role.

CHAPTER 2

The Greatest Living Man of Letters

At the time when Buddenbrooks *first became a matter of comparative, instead of merely national literature, it was natural enough to define the scope of its author in terms of Mr. Galsworthy, Mr. H. G. Wells, Samuel Butler, Romain Rolland. Today, with* The Magic Mountain *coming into its logical position in a whole world's excited awareness, these comparisons begin to strike qualified judges as unconsciously trivializing. The names which [would be appropriate instead] are Dante, Goethe, Balzac, Shakespeare.*

—Promotional brochure published by Alfred A. Knopf, 1930

Ever since the days when such formidable mediocrities as Galsworthy, Dreiser, Tagore, Romain Rolland or Thomas Mann were being accepted as geniuses, I have been perplexed and amused by fabricated notions about so-called "great books." That, for instance, Mann's asinine Death in Venice, *Pasternak's melodramatic, vilely written* Dr. Zhivago, *or Faulkner's corn-cobby chronicles can be considered "masterpieces," or at least what journalists term "great books," is to me the same sort of absurd delusion as when a hypnotized person makes love to a chair.*

—Vladimir Nabokov, in a televised interview, 1965

For the majority of the years that Thomas Mann spent cultivating his reputation as a representative writer first in Germany, and then on the European scene, he remained a nonentity in the United States. The first American edition of a Mann story (*Tonio Kröger*, in a translation by Bayard Quincy Morgan) wasn't published until 1915; the first of his novels (*Royal Highness*, translated by A. Cecil Curtis) followed in 1916. Both were commercial failures. H. L. Mencken was thus almost certainly correct when he asserted, in an editorial for his journal the *Smart Set*, that there were "but half a dozen [people] who could name offhand the principal works of Thomas Mann" in the United States in 1920.[1] This disinterest, furthermore, was mutual. Mann's diaries, letters, and essays of the period show little curiosity about the United

States. As late as 1929, he dismissed Americans as a "childish race" in print (*GW*, 10:703). He would not set foot in the New World until 1934.[2]

In light of this rocky start, it is all the more surprising to discover that by around 1930, Mann's books and the author himself were routinely showered with hyperbolic praises in the American press. This development began in 1922, when the little magazine the *Dial* introduced Mann to the US public as "generally and rightly looked upon by his countrymen as their most distinguished living man of letters," and reached a first high point in 1930, when Alfred A. Knopf, hoping to capitalize on Mann's recent Nobel Prize, published a brochure (quoted in the first epigraph to this chapter) that not only compared the author to Dante and William Shakespeare but also declared him to be "a very great man indeed."[3] By then, the locution "the greatest living man of letters" had already become a fixture of marketing materials; in 1934 the respected journalist Dorothy Thompson gave it the veneer of a neutral judgment when she titled one of her reviews "The Most Eminent Living Man of Letters."[4] *Time* magazine's cover profile of the author, the first such story dedicated to a non-Anglophone writer, was published the same year and simply called "Great Mann."[5] Other journalists and critics coined even more outlandish epithets: "man of genius and gentleman," "the greatest interpreter of the human spirit," "the dean of novelists."[6]

Given that Mann himself did not visit the United States until well after this discourse had become entrenched in the American press, it clearly did not owe anything to his personal charisma or even to his own active interventions. The flattering descriptions were, instead, the creation of actors in the American cultural field, especially Alfred A. Knopf. Indeed, publishers in the 1920s began to discover the considerable value of promoting not only books but also authors. A 1922 article in the *New York Tribune* averred that following the First World War, "the simple [promotional] paragraphs of an elder age assumed a new and more interesting form, dealing not only with the books, but with their authors, concerning whom all sorts of personal information was set afloat and widely read and quoted."[7] Ordinary readers eagerly participated in this process, and embraced the authors who were promoted to them as inspirational figures. The books that these readers purchased served a recreational as well as an educational and practical function. They were tools for finding one's way in a changing world and thus often acquired meanings that their original creators could neither anticipate nor fully control.

Thomas Mann's rise to literary prominence in the United States thus took place within the larger context of a newly emerging and distinctively American cultural formation, the "middlebrow." The mere evocation of this term may on first sight appear both slanderous to Mann's reputation and deeply insulting to his present-day readers. For after all, is the middlebrow not by definition antithetical to "serious" modern literature, and more specifically to that other developing cultural category of the 1920s with which Mann is more commonly and more favorably associated, to "modernism"?

Vladimir Nabokov certainly thought so. In the second epigraph that introduces this chapter, he gestures toward the middlebrow by his repeated derogatory use of the phrase "great books," a lexical conjunction that entered the American vocabulary around 1920 and reached its peak usage around 1940. As Nabokov himself recognizes, the notion of the "great book," which is closely related to that of the "great man of letters," can only partially be reduced to seemingly synonymous terms such as the "masterpiece." It is instead, as the cultural historian Joan Shelley Rubin has shown, a signature phrase of the middlebrow idiom.[8] Nabokov then follows up on his condemnation by providing some book recommendations of his own, all of them gospel texts of the modernist movement: *"My* greatest masterpieces of twentieth century prose are, in this order, Joyce's *Ulysses*, Kafka's *Transformation*, Bely's *St. Petersburg*, and the first half of Proust's fairy tale, *In Search of Lost Time.*"[9]

However, in a bit of irony that seems to have escaped the Russian master, this pronouncement itself makes use of one of the most characteristic forms of the middlebrow, the ranked list. With pedantic earnestness, Nabokov lays down the law: not just what texts should count as great literature, but also their internal hierarchy. This telling detail suggests that modernism and the middlebrow perhaps aren't as antithetical to one another as Nabokov himself believed. And indeed, the novel that Nabokov ranks above all others, *Ulysses*, was published in the United States in the Modern Library imprint at Random House, another institution that Rubin identifies as essential to the development of middlebrow taste. There, it stood side by side with a 1932 reprint of *The Magic Mountain* by that "formidable mediocrity" Thomas Mann.[10]

Modernism and the middlebrow have, in other words, never truly stood in opposition to one another. "Ordinary" readers have always shown an appetite for experimental literary texts (from Joyce's *Ulysses* [1922] to David Foster Wallace's *Infinite Jest* [1996]), and the high priests of modernism frequently acquired their place in the canon through a process of commodification virtually indistinguishable from that also applied to more conventional celebrities.[11] Some authors of stylistically ambitious fiction, like Ernest Hemingway, have reveled in this crossover dimension. Others, like Jonathan Franzen, have been appalled by it. Thomas Mann, who was certainly a more formally demanding author than either Hemingway or Franzen, belongs in the former camp. Although he never compromised in his fiction, he also delighted in his popular success, and saw no inconsistency between his reputation as a literary heavyweight and the fact that his face adorned the front pages of magazines in American dentists' offices.

The process by which Mann was canonized as the "greatest living man of letters" in the New World certainly had many similarities to his staging as a representative writer in the Old. But there were enormous differences as well, and these would turn out to be consequential for literary history, including literary history back in Germany.

The Struggle for American Culture

As the last chapter already made clear, the German word *Kultur* and the English word "culture" are at best highly problematic synonyms. Nineteenth-century German society was characterized by a dearth of democratic civic traditions, for which the burgher class compensated with an exaggerated pride in its own cultural achievements. In America the situation was very different. The United States in the late nineteenth century was a country rich in republican customs, but as yet without many hegemonic cultural traditions that could have played a dominant role in reinforcing national identity. American identity was then (and indeed continues to be to this day) far more likely to be defined by social values like the ones codified in the Bill of Rights or the Gettysburg Address than by poems, folk songs, or popular plays. This fact does not imply, of course, that Americans did not *have* any culture of their own, as chauvinist discourse in Germany liked to aver at the time. But it does mean that culture was talked about differently and that it played a different role in society at large.

The few intellectuals, almost all Anglo-Saxon by heritage, who *did* worry about the nature of "American culture" during this period mostly modeled their thought on English thinkers. In contrast to the German-speaking world, English critics viewed culture primarily as an expression of class identity rather than of nationality. To be "cultured" meant to be able to display wit, beauty, and refinement and to thereby testify to the intellectual and spiritual suppleness that were thought to be prerequisites for elevated social positions. In America the Unitarian theologians who clustered around Harvard University in the early nineteenth century wedded these so-called "genteel virtues" to an expressly religious program that viewed a cultured sensibility as an important step toward the attainment of salvation.[12] This fusion of aesthetic refinement with moral responsibility also gave rise to a specifically American conception of the representative writer. Such writers were tasked with the secular equivalent of the social function traditionally performed by the clergy. That is, they were "duty bound to remain immersed in democratic society—guiding, criticizing, and elevating it."[13] In sharp contrast to the German tradition, in which poets were expected to refrain from social commentary and writers who strayed too far into contemporary affairs risked being denigrated as mere *Literaten*, American intellectuals thus from a fairly early period onward drew an intimate connection between elite literary activity and civic engagement. This emphasis would later also become one of the distinguishing characteristics of middlebrow culture.

Initially, however, the social transformations of the twentieth century seemed a threat to the equation between culture and democracy. The rapid modernization and urbanization of the United States created a fear of what in the parlance of the time was known as the "standardization" of minds. American civilization, so conservative thinkers fretted, was extremely good at channeling social energies toward economic improvement, but it lacked the institutions necessary to instill a sense of culture in the masses. At the same time, the late nineteenth and early twentieth centuries were a period of unprecedented immigration to the United States from non-English-speaking countries. Many of these immigrants were illiterate, a fact that only increased conservative fears about the ability of Anglo-American culture to guide and elevate the populace. These fears were matched by equally strong worries that immigrants might cling to the traditions of their respective countries of origin rather than embrace the cultural identity of their new home. In a famous address given on Columbus Day 1915, the former president Theodore Roosevelt thus averred that "there is no such thing as a hyphenated American who is a good American. The only man who is a good American is the man who is an American and nothing else."[14]

One need only remember that this address was given less than half a year after the sinking of the *Lusitania* to realize that one of its main targets was the German American community, which in the early twentieth century offered by far the strongest challenge to the dominance of Anglo-Saxon traditions in America.[15] Indeed, there was something of a battle going on at this time between the American and the German approaches to culture and to representative art. This battle can best be illustrated with a reference to two different publishing projects undertaken in the United States during the years immediately before the First World War, which both attempted to introduce a popular readership to "classic" (i.e., representative) works of literature. These two projects mark the opposite poles of the cultural force field in which Thomas Mann's reception would unfold during the interwar period.

On one side of this force field stood the fifty-one-volume anthology *The Harvard Classics*, which Charles William Eliot, the president of Harvard University, compiled and published in 1909. Popularly known as the "Five Foot Shelf," *The Harvard Classics* represented a practical response to a thesis that Eliot had advanced on several earlier occasions in speeches and letters, namely that in an age in which only 3 percent of adult Americans possessed a college degree, all basic elements of a liberal education might nevertheless be obtained by spending just fifteen minutes a day reading from a collection of books that could fit on small bookshelf. The motivation behind the endeavor was thus civic and educational in nature: in a twentieth-century spin on the genteel tradition, Eliot hoped to instill in his harried readers the virtues of republican democracy by providing them with a universally accessible version of a liberal education.

During the 1920s, Eliot's "Five Foot Shelf" would inspire the rise of the so-called Great Books courses at American colleges and universities— first at Columbia, where John Erskine began teaching a version of such a class in 1920, and later also at the University of Chicago. The defining feature of these courses was that they approached time-honored books as though they were contemporary works. Discarding philological erudition and hermeneutic acrobatics, the teachers in Great Books courses instead challenged their students to reflect on the ways in which Plato, Shakespeare, or Ralph Waldo Emerson might speak to the problems of contemporary society. Thomas Mann, too, eventually found a home in these courses, where his reputation lives on long after he fell out of favor with mainstream American society.

There was another important feature about Eliot's project that would have ramifications for Mann's reception during the interwar period. Like the Great Books courses that followed in its wake, it treated scientific treatises, autobiographical reflections, essays, and even holy scriptures as exactly equivalent to literature. After all, what counted most in a text was not in what context or by whom it was written, but rather what it had to say to the reader. As a result of this preconditioning, American readers tended to treat Mann's literary and nonfictional works on equal footing, instead of regarding the author (as his own countrymen did, and largely continue to do to this day) as primarily a novelist whose essays were of secondary importance.

Eliot's attempt to adapt the genteel tradition to the needs of the modern American nation can be contrasted with the anthology *The German Classics of the Nineteenth and Twentieth Centuries*, which the Harvard German professor Kuno Francke launched in 1913. If Eliot's *Harvard Classics* was a populist attempt to provide a liberal education to a fragmented public, the Francke edition represented an unmistakable attempt to agitate for German *Kultur* in an age in which American public opinion was rapidly turning against it.[16] It was published in twenty sumptuous volumes, each with an imperial eagle embossed in gold leaf on the cover (figure 2.1). The cheapest version, bound in buckram, sold for ninety dollars and was thus priced well out of reach of the average consumer. The most expensive version, the "Emperor edition" in pigskin, retailed for $675, or roughly the price of a Ford Model T.

In sharp contrast to Eliot's *Harvard Classics*, the Francke edition stuck to a very conservative definition of *Kultur*, anthologizing only traditional literary genres, such as plays, poems, and short stories. Its aim was not to lead

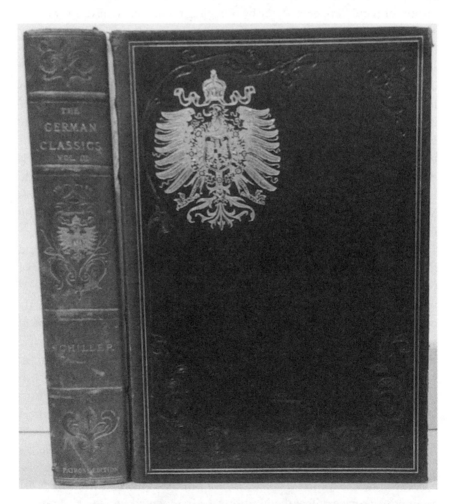

FIGURE 2.1.   A volume of the Kuno Francke edition of *The German Classics*, showing the imperial gold eagle and fine leather binding, 1914. Carpe Diem Fine Books, Monterey, CA.

its readership toward civic engagement but rather to promote the endur-
ing value of German cultural traditions in an age in which many Americans associated Germany primarily with Prussian militarism and the kaiser's
bellicose rhetoric. Despite—or perhaps precisely because of—these intentions, however, the whole project was soon overshadowed by the disastrous
spirit of hypernationalism that seized so many German intellectuals in the
fall of 1914. Julius Petersen, for example, a Basel professor who wrote the
introductory essay to the volume dedicated to contemporary short stories,
warned his readers that "the wild alarm *Germania est delenda* is trumpeted as
a so-called duty of human civilization" and reassured them that the authors
whose works he had anthologized had "heard the call to arms" summoning
them to a defense of the fatherland.[17]

The Francke edition serves as a vivid illustration of how different the German and American approaches to culture really were in the early twentieth
century. But its significance is increased even further by the fact that Peters-
en's volume was the place in which the first Mann story to be rendered into
English, Bayard Quincy Morgan's translation of *Tonio Kröger*, was published.
Petersen's claims, of course, accurately describe Thomas Mann's own world
view in 1915, a time when the author would proudly characterize his *Reflections of a Nonpolitical Man* as a form of "intellectual military service" in the
struggle of German *Kultur* against French and British "civilization" (R, 1,
translation modified; GKFA, 13.1:11). Ironically, then, the most important
thing about the Francke edition for Mann's later reception in America may
be that it utterly failed. The grand dinner that Francke organized to celebrate
the launch of his anthology in the spring of 1913 also proved to be the swan-
song of the project. Subscriptions dropped off almost immediately after the
German army invaded Belgium, and by 1915 the German Publishing Society,
which Francke had founded to finance the project, had gone bankrupt.

Two important facts resulted from this development. First, it meant that
Mann's chauvinistic wartime opinions remained largely unknown in America. A few American journals published reviews of *Reflections of a Nonpolitical
Man*, and Mann's name would later also appear in early histories of the war,
such as Charles Francis Horne's *The Great Events of the Great War* of 1920, in
which he is called a mouthpiece of "the Boches" who declared "that Kultur
is above morality."[18] But most ordinary Americans never learned about his
early political utterances. The second and even more important consequence
of Francke's failure was that Mann's name never became associated with the
older conception of representative art that *The German Classics* so thoroughly
embodied. This was important, because over the course of the First World
War, the American reception of German culture changed dramatically.

There was a tremendous and frequently violent backlash against all things German, and even artists who had no connection to the kaiser's policies were frequently subject to book burnings and acts of iconoclasm.[19] Immigrants changed their names en masse and abandoned their prior practice of voluntarily segregating themselves in German-speaking communities. The notion that German culture might thrive on American soil without any kind of cross-pollination with other traditions was irrevocably dead.

Van Wyck Brooks, Randolph Bourne, H. L. Mencken, and the Rise of Middlebrow Culture

The First World War had a devastating effect on the attempt to transplant a German notion of *Kultur* to American soil, but it proved equally cataclysmic to the genteel tradition. A new generation of intellectuals moved to the forefront of cultural life in the United States during the second decade of the twentieth century. Arguably the three most important figures in this transition were Van Wyck Brooks, Randolph Bourne, and H. L. Mencken. Between them, these three men would help provide a theoretical foundation for what we now commonly call the "middlebrow." Each in his own way would also contribute to Mann's rising fame in the United States during the 1920s.

For present purposes, the most important of the three was Van Wyck Brooks, who rose to prominence in the United States through the publication of his book *America's Coming-of-Age* in 1915, as well as through his editorship of the *Seven Arts*, a short-lived but highly influential little magazine that appeared from 1916 to 1917. In *America's Coming-of-Age*, Brooks argued, greatly influenced by William Morris's critique of the division between culture and practical life in capitalist societies, that contemporary American culture had become riven into, "on the one hand, a quite unclouded, quite unhypocritical assumption of transcendent theory ('high ideas'), " and on the other "a simultaneous acceptance of catchpenny realities."[20] To these two opposite poles—culture lost in theoretical abstraction vs. culture as a cliché reproduction of existing circumstances—Brooks gave the names "highbrow" and "lowbrow," proudly noting that they represented a genuinely American contribution to cultural theory: "I have proposed these terms to a Russian, an Englishman, and a German, asking each in turn whether in his country there was anything to correspond with the conceptions implied in them. In each case they have been returned to me as quite American, authentically our very own, and, I should add, highly suggestive."[21]

The point of the opposition between highbrow and lowbrow as Brooks originally proposed it was not to differentiate between aesthetically complex and therefore "good" art, on the one hand, and simplistic popular trash on the other. For Brooks, highbrow and lowbrow were, instead, equally undesirable elements. "The 'Highbrow' is the superior person whose virtue is admitted but felt to be an inept unpalatable virtue; while the 'Lowbrow' is a good fellow one readily takes to, but with a certain scorn for him and all his works," he wrote.[22] What was missing, according to Brooks, was the "genial middle ground" on which reflection and practice, sophistication and common sense might meet.[23] Curiously, it took almost two decades until someone (the literary critic Margaret Widdemer in the pages of the *Saturday Review of Literature*) introduced the term "middlebrow" to designate this meeting place.[24]

Thomas Mann was not among the European interlocutors whom Brooks consulted to gauge the originality of his conceptual coinage. But when an American journalist in the late 1930s accused Mann of expressing "middle-class" rather than "high-brow" ideas in his writings, he eagerly aligned himself with the middlebrow, albeit with a telling interpretive twist. In his 1943 Library of Congress lecture "The War and the Future," he recalled the encounter in the following terms: "Such a person holds a false and reactionary concept of the banal. . . . What the high-brow journalist was characterizing as 'middle-class ideas' is actually nothing else than the liberal tradition. It is the complex of ideas of freedom and progress, of humanitarianism, of civilization; in short, the claim of reason to dominate the dynamics of nature, of instinct, of blood, of the unconscious—the primitive spontaneity of life" (*LC*, 24; *GW*, 12:918). Indeed, if we understand the term "middlebrow" in the original adulatory sense given to it by Brooks, rather than as a synonym for artistic pretension, then Thomas Mann can without hesitation be called a "middlebrow" author. He was, after all, as proud of the intellectual ambition of all his works as he was of his "common touch," and of the fact that ordinary readers felt drawn to his works. Novels such as *The Magic Mountain* or *Doctor Faustus* were, furthermore, written with the unmistakable ambition to affect a transformation in German social life through aesthetic means.

The congruence between Brooks's vision and Mann's writing is nicely illustrated by a long novella that the little magazine the *Freeman* serialized in 1922–23, at a time when Brooks oversaw its cultural pages: the self-proclaimed "idyll" "Bashan and I" in a translation by Herman George Scheffauer. "Bashan and I" (which was retitled "A Man and His Dog" when Alfred A. Knopf published it in a new translation by H. T. Lowe-Porter) is a decidedly odd story, a lengthy paean to the loving relationship between a man and his short-haired pointer, written in the first person and based on autobiographical material. Beneath the tranquil surface of the story lurk unplumbed depths, however. In one of the most memorable and disturbing scenes, the narrator and his dog, out on a ramble through the wooded parks surrounding Munich, stumble upon the residues of a suburban development that was abandoned fifteen years earlier. The project is described in terms that recall Goethe's *Faust* but lead up to a bathetic anticlimax: "The building society conceived things on a rather large scale. They enclosed the river between dykes, they built quays and planted gardens, and, not content with that, they had embarked on clearing the woods, dumped piles of gravel, cut roads through the wilderness. . . . But no one walks there save Bashan and myself, he on the good stout leather of his four paws, I in hobnailed boots on account of the gravel" (*SD*, 465–66; *GW*, 8:565–66).[25] The historian David Blackbourn has pointed out that large-scale land reclamation efforts, particularly in marshy environments like the one described here, formed an integral part of German claims to cultural superiority over the course of the nineteenth and early twentieth centuries.[26] As if to drive home this point, the deserted streets in the unfinished development are named after German authors of "quality" literature from the last three centuries: Christian Fürchtegott Gellert, Martin Opitz, Paul Fleming, Gottfried August Bürger, Adalbert Stifter.

What, then, the story seems to ask, is the relationship between these signs of victorious German culture and the general desecration that seems to have befallen them? How might we connect the narrator's feigned reverence with his hobnailed boots and his no-doubt less respectful canine companion? And what sort of "idyll" is this exactly? Is it an innocent exercise in the suburban bucolic or would it behoove the reader to remember the phrase inscribed in so many pictorial idylls: *et in Arcadia ego*? The story thus highlights the tensions between traditional high culture and the pragmatic demands of the modern age without, however, coming down on either side. Cultural monuments, so "A Man and his Dog" seems to inform us, are perhaps best approached in casual attire, yet at the same time, they also provide reflective meaning and contemplative substance to what otherwise would be a mere forest walk. It is a decidedly middlebrow attitude, and one that, though expressed in an entirely German formal and conceptual vocabulary, might have struck Brooks as congruent with his American cultural criticism.

Brooks's editorship at the *Seven Arts* was closely intertwined with the work of that journal's most influential contributor, Randolph Bourne. In his most famous essay, "Transnational America" (1916), Bourne takes issue with the then-popular metaphor of the United States as a "melting pot"—a crucible that strips immigrants of their heritage and molds them into uniform Americans. Claiming that the most vital and energetic regions of America can be found in the Midwest, where German and Scandinavian settlers had stuck to their cultural traditions, Bourne argues that here, the "foreign cultures have not been melted down or run together, made into some homogeneous Americanism, but have remained distinct but cooperating to the greater glory and benefit, not only of themselves but of all the native "Americanism" around them.[27] The result, so he concludes, is a kind of "federated ideal," a notion of America as "transplanted Europe, but a Europe that has not been disintegrated and scattered in the transplanting as in some Dispersion. Its colonies live here inextricably mingled, yet not homogeneous. They merge, but do not fuse."[28]

Randolph Bourne was, in short, America's first theorist of what we now call "multiculturalism," even if still of a blatantly Eurocentric sort. But his vision of American society as inherently "transnational" (a term that Bourne appears to have invented) also sounds surprisingly similar to the vision of a European republic of letters that Mann would advance a decade later in his lecture to the Warsaw PEN Club, or in essays such as "On National and International Art." Both writers propose that the antidote to what Bourne calls the "weary old nationalism" afflicting twentieth-century Europe might consist not in the overcoming of national sentiments altogether, but rather in a new federation of cultures, all proud in their historical achievements and yet willing to emphasize their commonalities over their differences.[29]

Bourne died in the global influenza pandemic that followed the Armistice, but not before his ideas had spread to other people who would seek to implement them in the world of practical affairs. The publisher Scofield Thayer was one such man. In 1919 he took over the little magazine the *Dial*, purged it of its previous sympathies with Soviet bolshevism, and let it be known that he henceforth intended it to function as a "*Seven Arts* without politics."[30] The Thayer *Dial* is nowadays generally remembered as a lighthouse of the modernist movement, made eternally famous by the fact that it published T. S. Eliot's *The Waste Land* and bestowed upon him the lucrative Dial Award for 1922. But a closer look reveals that the qualities that made the *Dial* distinctively modernist are surprisingly hard to differentiate from those characterizing the emerging category of the middlebrow. The journal's editorial line was defined by a kind of cultural synopticism, that is, a belief that the world's cultures shared deep communalities and could therefore communicate with one another across vast distances of time and space while remaining true to their individual natures. The opening page of *The Waste Land*, with its multilingual dedication and epigraph as well as its references to Arthurian legends and to Richard Wagner, was a prime example of this quality. Thayer's decision in 1921 to start publishing Thomas Mann stories such as *Tristan* or *Death in Venice*, which like Eliot's poem fused material drawn from modern life with mythical elements, can be seen in the same vein.

It is but a short step from the "modernist" synopticism of *The Waste Land* to the "middlebrow" pragmatism of the Great Books movement, which similarly insisted that *The Satyricon*, the Grail legend, and Wagner operas all stand at equal distance to the modern reader. Thayer, in fact, had little patience for the thesis that historical cataclysm might force ruptures in the production and reception of literary texts. When he published his very first Mann story, for example ("Loulou" in a 1921 translation by Kenneth Burke), he prefaced it with an essay by the British diplomat Alec W. G. Randall, which advances the somewhat astonishing thesis that "the flood of literature produced in Germany after the Armistice . . . does not indicate in the least a change of imagination, a transformation of intellect on the part of German writers."[31]

When viewed as a form of pedagogy, this antihistoricist commingling of world cultures in the pages of the *Dial* serves as a powerful, if unorthodox, realization of Bourne's vision for a transnational America. That Thayer indeed had pedagogical intentions along those lines is documented by his decision to hire a number of cultural correspondents in various European countries, whose contributions went a long way toward making the *Dial* the kind of federation of cultures that Bourne had envisioned. The illustrious list of names included Maxim Gorki for Russia, Hugo von Hofmannsthal for Austria, and José Ortega y Gasset for Spain. The German correspondent chosen by Thayer was Thomas Mann, who was thus from the very beginning represented in the pages of the *Dial* not just as an author of stories like the pathbreaking *Death in Venice* but also as a journalist and essayist.

Between 1922 and 1928, Mann published a total of eight "German Letters" in the *Dial*. In the scholarly literature, these have been dismissed as "odd jobs," and indeed a letter that Mann wrote to his German publisher shows that he accepted the commission primarily because the American journal paid him in dollars at a time when his income was threatened by galloping inflation (*GKFA*, 22:445).[32] Despite all this, however, both the topic and the tone of his letters document a marked (though clearly unplanned) congruence with the larger aims of the *Dial*. The very first letter, for example, consists of a sharp attack on Oswald Spengler, the proponent of a segregationist "morphological" model of cultural differences, and invokes Goethe's conception of world literature to argue that "the cultural life of Europe was never more plainly 'in the sign of trade' than before the great war," that "translation flourishes," and that as a result of it "France, Italy, Spain, America" are now "taking [German spiritual products] into their languages "(GL, 646).

The third bright star in the firmament of American cultural criticism of the 1910s and 1920s was H. L. Mencken, the editor (with George Jean Nathan) of the literary magazine the *Smart Set* from 1914 to 1924, and the sole editor of the *American Mercury* from 1924 to 1933. If Brooks's theorization of the middlebrow and Bourne's arguments for transnationalism went a long way toward conceptually defining a particularly American notion of culture (cosmopolitan and intellectually sophisticated, yet without ever losing sight of the common man), then Mencken did more than anybody else to disseminate this new vision among the larger populace. Bourne and Brooks enjoyed stellar reputations in intellectual circles, but journals such as the *Seven Arts*, the *Dial*, and the *Freeman* barely registered more than ten thousand subscribers. The *Smart Set*, by contrast, counted more than sixteen times that number, while the more intellectually rigorous *American Mercury* still reached circulation figures of over eighty thousand. Their editor-in-chief became a veritable celebrity. The journalist Walter Lippmann called Mencken "the most powerful influence on a whole generation of Americans."[33] Thomas Mann's son Klaus fell under Mencken's spell as well when he first came to America, referring to him as a "legend" in his autobiography *The Turning Point*.[34]

Mencken was the son of German immigrants, took an active interest in all things German, and was particularly well-versed in the philosophy of Friedrich Nietzsche. It is thus not surprising that he became acquainted with Thomas Mann at a fairly early date, reading him in German long before any of his stories ever appeared in the United States. Curiously, though, especially in light of his highly prolific output, Mencken never once reviewed any of Mann's stories for the American press, nor did he publish them in either the *Smart Set* or the *American Mercury*. His active contribution to Mann's fame in the United States was instead confined to a single, albeit decisive, intervention: it was he who in 1921 persuaded Alfred A. Knopf to acquire the American rights to Mann's works, despite the fact that Knopf's earlier attempt to publish *Royal Highness* had been a commercial failure.[35]

Like Randolph Bourne, Mencken in his essays of the 1910s and early 1920s relentlessly agitated against the Anglo-Saxonist vision of the United States as a "melting pot," fashioning himself in the process as a champion for German American culture.[36] Beyond this crusade, however, Mencken's real significance for Thomas Mann lay in the fact that he managed to make US literary culture a part of the larger fashionable social life. The *Smart Set* began its existence in the early twentieth century as a belletristic extension of the society pages, publishing the amateur literary efforts of the New York idle rich. The names of its contributors mattered as much to the readership as the actual contents of any given issue. When Mencken and Nathan took over, the journal became much more respectable, but it still profited immensely from the implication that it provided a peek at the life of "the smart set" in the dual sense of that term. Mencken's outsized personality and the fortunes of his journal were, in fact, inseparably coupled. Mencken and his contributors helped naturalize the idea that literature, theater, and the arts were a necessary part of an up-to-date lifestyle. Two much longer-lasting magazines took up this basic message and helped make it a part of an unmistakably American identity: *Vanity Fair* (founded in 1914) and the *New Yorker* (founded in 1925). Like Mencken's earlier publication, these journals combined society items and sophisticated criticism into a new form of cultural expression.

Thomas Mann profited from this development because his strongly articulated authorial habitus—his elegantly tailored suits, his impeccable manners, his charisma at the microphone, and even his large and highly interesting family—made him a natural target of interest for an American readership accustomed to consume cultural news alongside the society columns. To be sure, Mann's personality and habits were entirely different from those of most US celebrities, and he frequently felt ill at ease during public social occasions in his adopted country. His diaries contain very little information about the various parties at which he was fêted and frequently register only his exhaustion, even when he found himself in the company of bona fide movie stars (see, e.g., *Tb.*, April 3, 1938; *Tb.*, March 18, 1940). But precisely this difference made him an irresistibly attractive subject for the larger American public. Mann was not a down-on-his-luck refugee in a threadbare suit like so many other German intellectuals who streamed to the United States in those days. He came crowned in an aura of European sophistication and mystery, almost like a latter-day Count of Monte Cristo. No wonder, then, that US magazines devoted extensive coverage to his works and that both *Life* (in 1939) and the *New Yorker* (in 1941) ran rather gossipy biographical essays about his stay in America.[37] Mann reciprocated the attention by making the *New Yorker* his regular reading material, though like so many others since then, he seems to have opened it mainly for the cartoons (*Tb.*, April 30, 1941).

Alfred A. Knopf and the Making of a Modern Classic

Between them, Brooks, Bourne, and Mencken thus staked out a new and typically American cultural formation. This formation aimed to be intellectually attuned to modern existence while remaining accessible to the larger populace. It tried to be cosmopolitan in nature, assimilating influences from around the world (or at least the western hemisphere) as long as they seemed useful to the exigencies of modern American life. And finally, it aspired to be glamorous. Thomas Mann embodied all these qualities, and in so doing became the prototype for an authorial type that remains important to the international publishing industry even in the twenty-first century.

Of course Thomas Mann initially spoke very little English, and throughout the 1920s remained stubbornly uninterested in American affairs. He required the help of others in order to become a success on the US literary market. In popular thought, we often reduce the complex processes by which books or authors are inserted into languages and cultures that are not their own to the singular dimension of "translation." But translation involves far more than just the juxtaposition of words from one language to another. Translation is an alchemical process that alters the base elements that it touches. Etymologically, the word derives from the Latin for "to ferry across," and just as Gustav von Aschenbach discovers that he is not quite himself anymore after a mysterious ferryman carries him across the Venetian lagoon, so the American Thomas Mann ended up a very different author from the German one.

The first thing that Mann needed was a publisher, someone capable of making his oeuvre available to a general readership and of promoting it with all the financial might of a major press. He found such a publisher in Alfred A. Knopf, a man who from the very beginning embraced the new cultural precepts established by Brooks, Bourne, and Mencken. Born in 1892, Knopf founded his eponymous publishing house at a very young age in 1915. He aspired to make the very best in European literature accessible to an American readership, in editions marketed specifically to a middlebrow audience. He took great pride in the facts that the very first order for his books in 1915 came from Marshall Field's department store in Chicago and that Midwestern bookstores consistently ranked among his best clients.[38] One of the earliest books that Knopf acquired for his new press was a 1916 English translation of Mann's *Royal Highness* by A. Cecil Curtis, which Knopf bought sight unseen from the British firm of Sidgwick and Jackson.[39] It proved to be a spectacular failure, no doubt because a few months after the sinking of the *Lusitania* nobody in the United States wanted to read a love story between an American heiress and a fictional prince whose external appearance resembled that of Kaiser Wilhelm II. After Mencken convinced him that Mann was nevertheless an author worth pursuing, Knopf and his wife Blanche immediately traveled to Europe, where in 1921 they met with Samuel Fischer and secured from him the exclusive American rights to Mann's oeuvre under the stipulation that Knopf publish *Buddenbrooks* and at least one subsequent book every year thereafter.[40]

These imposing demands would have a profound effect on the ways in which Knopf marketed Thomas Mann in the United States. It was simply not possible to satisfy the pace stipulated by Fischer with literary translations alone, especially since Mann specialized in such long novels. For a while Knopf was able to fulfill his contractual obligations by offering reprints and by buying up existing translations of Thomas Mann works. By the late 1920s, however, he was forced to add collections of nonfictional works. These were initially selected to shed further light on the intellectual context from which the fictional masterpieces had sprung. A reviewer of the 1933 volume *Past Masters and Other Papers*, for example, described the essays contained therein as "foothills surrounding the *magnum opus* [i.e., *The Magic Mountain*]. They make it easier of access, and they contain the same rich vein of gold, lying even closer to the surface."[41] Soon, however, they acquired a life of their own, and Mann became equally known as an essayist and as a novelist. In Germany, such a development would likely have done harm to his reputation as a first-rate writer. In America, however, with its more capacious definition of what constituted "culture," it only increased his fame. By the early 1930s, Mann's now well-established name in America was positively inseparable from that of Alfred A. Knopf, and Knopf reacted forcefully whenever Mann did anything that might have endangered that exclusive relationship, offering improved contractual arrangements where necessary, but also threatening legal action against competing firms.[42]

Knopf's greatest strength lay in marketing, and he developed a meticulously curated promotional strategy for his firm. The critic Catherine Turner has summarized this strategy with the words, "Knopf sold the works that he published as the functional equivalent of civilization rather than just as good books. Even works like Mann's, which questioned accepted definitions of civilization, were sold for their abstract quality to signify civilized life."[43] The promotional slogans that Knopf employed for *The Magic Mountain* (a work that certainly "questions accepted definitions of culture") illustrate what this meant in practice. In a 1927 ad in *Publisher's Weekly*, Knopf advertised the recently released tome as a *"Divine Comedy* for our disastrous age," and in a pamphlet that he released to capitalize on Mann's 1929 Nobel Prize, the work is described as "a complete *Pilgrim's Progress* for the physical and psychic life of modern man."[44]

Two qualities are worth highlighting about these sentences. First, they place Mann's works within an international web of cultural classics, a strategy reminiscent both of the pedagogic philosophy underlying the Great Books movement and of Thayer's editorial line for the *Dial*.[45] Second, they highlight the use value of these difficult works for the practical life of modern man, thereby realizing the central tenet of Brooks's "genial middle ground" between highbrow and lowbrow culture. Similar strategies can be found throughout the many different ads that Knopf placed for *The Magic Mountain* during the period 1927–30.

Knopf did not content himself with vague phrases such as "the physical and psychic life of modern man," however. He was quite specific about the practical lessons that ordinary American readers might be able to draw from Mann's works. In marketing *The Magic Mountain*, for instance, Knopf adapted the novel's famous climactic sentence—*"for the sake of goodness and love, man shall let death have no sovereignty over his thoughts"* (MM, 496–97; GKFA, 5.1:748, emphasis in original)—as a promotional slogan. He glossed this phrase for potential customers with the explanation that Mann's novel presented an instructive picture of "the world that achieved its logical self-expression in 1914" and that it juxtaposed this image with a "vision of goodness and love."[46] From an early point onward, Mann's talents at novelistic depiction where thus intertwined in the minds of ordinary readers with the distinctively middlebrow claim to explain the contemporary world as it was and as it ought to be. This link would only become stronger when his essays were published.

Knopf's efforts to promote Mann as an artist capable of synthesizing an entire era of European thought in a way that would be accessible to ordinary Americans meant that the publisher consistently downplayed two important features about his author. The first was Mann's rarefied style. Knopf never made any efforts to promote Mann as being somehow among the most "advanced" or "original" writers of his time. His focus was instead exclusively on promoting Mann as a modern classic—a writer whose work may have been ambitious and demanding, but ultimately also timeless and accessible to anyone willing to invest the prerequisite effort. The second was the author's political engagement. During the 1920s, when Mann's political work was confined mostly to speeches, and during the early 1930s, when he fell silent about the Nazis, this aspect was easy enough to manage. But once the publication of *An Exchange of Letters* had established Mann as a major voice of the antifascist exile community, Knopf's job became much harder. In vain did he implore his charge, "Tommy, you are a Dichter and you must dicht!" (*Reg.*, 54/26).

Knopf instead tried to popularize Thomas Mann as a personality rather than just as a name on the title page of long and difficult novels. In this, of course, he was reacting to the governing spirit of the 1920s—the decade in which artistic labor became socially fashionable in America. Particularly illustrative in this regard are the events surrounding Mann's first visit to the United States in 1934, on the occasion of his fifty-ninth birthday and of the US release of the novel *Joseph and His Brothers* (later retitled *The Tales of Jacob*). To mark the occasion, Knopf hosted a glamorous gala reception to which he invited local politicians, industrial titans, and celebrity guests.[47] He also convinced mayor Fiorello H. La Guardia to provide his German guest with a police motorcycle escort and rented a boat so that journalists would be able to intercept the arriving author on his ocean liner before he ever set foot on American soil (*D*, 211; *Tb.*, May 29, 1934). The fruit of all these efforts was extensive media coverage, the most important piece of which was the "Great Mann" story in *Time* magazine.

Behind the scenes, however, Knopf had to struggle mightily to make this promotional success happen. After all, the Nazis had been in power for little more than a year, and while Mann's outspoken words about Hitler in the latter days of the Weimar Republic were not widely reported in the United States, prominent Americans were nevertheless wary of getting entangled in European affairs that they as yet little understood. Knopf consequently assured the politicians and titans of industry whom he invited that "the purpose of [Mann's] visit is purely literary, and no political significance whatever is to be attached to it."[48] Clearly not everyone found this argument convincing. Arthur Hays Sulzberger, for example, the publisher of the *New York Times*, wrote back to explain that he was having a "pretty difficult job here at *The Times* in keeping free of all political aspects of the present situation in Germany," and that he would therefore have to decline the invitation.[49]

By the time that Mann settled in the United States for good, this situation had changed, of course. Indeed, when reporters swarmed the author in 1938 to record his opinions about the Anschluss, they were utilizing Mann's fame to advance a narrative that was diametrically opposed to the one his publisher had originally tried to pitch. There is a dialectical logic to this process: first, Mann was stripped of the status as a merely German writer and instead promoted as the author of modern classics. He was furthermore billed as an intensely charismatic figure whose mind corresponded with those of the literary giants who walked before him and who could teach his readers to look beyond the plight that afflicted them in modern industrial societies. After Hitler came to power and it became clear that the biggest threat to American social beliefs emanated not from any abstract cultural malaise but rather from the concrete actions of specific individuals across the Atlantic Ocean, this preceding process of literary beatification gave Mann an advantage that so many of his less fortunate countrymen lacked. Because he so manifestly stood above the partisan fray, Mann was able to speak out against Hitler and be perceived as a voice of reason rather than be dismissed as an agitator for a specific political agenda, as were so many of his fellow German émigrés.

Helen Tracy Lowe-Porter and the "English Garb" of Thomas Mann

In his attempts to popularize Thomas Mann for a US audience, Knopf possessed an invaluable ally in the translator Helen Tracy Lowe-Porter (whose first and middle names were invariably reduced to initials on the title pages of the books that she translated, since female translators were still commonly regarded as intellectually suspect). Mann knew this as well, as he demonstrated in an unpublished 1939 letter to Knopf:

> If there's anything that can reconcile me to the unnatural fact that my books—which are all very German works indeed—today are almost nonexistent in their original languages and live their uprooted and necessarily imprecise life practically only in translation—~~masterful translations in some cases, it is true~~—then that thing would be (apart from the knowledge of the lawless and forced nature of present circumstances and the sure conscience of their ephemeral character) the vicarious interest of the educated American public in my work: a splendidly good-natured receptiveness that has only been deepened by highly intelligent reviews, and which proved itself movingly adequate to Mrs. Lowe-Porter's admirable translations of *Buddenbrooks*, *The Magic Mountain*, and the Joseph novels.[50]

As these lines show, Mann was very much aware that his present impact as a writer was almost exclusively due to the wide distribution and warm reception of his works in English translation, and he knew that he owed this reception in no small part to Helen Tracy Lowe-Porter. At the same time, however, his decision to strike out the clause in which he praises her translations as "masterful," leaving only the more toned-down description of them as "admirable," indicates he was also aware of her many faults as an interpreter of German prose.

During the early 1920s, several translators (most prominently among them Kenneth Burke and Herman George Scheffauer) worked concurrently to produce new translations of Thomas Mann stories. This situation changed when Martin Secker and Alfred A. Knopf hired Lowe-Porter to translate *Buddenbrooks* and eventually installed her as Mann's sole authorized translator for the Anglophone market—against the express wishes of the author, who at the time expressed reservations about her linguistic abilities and was also displeased to see *The Magic Mountain* translated by a woman (*GKFA*, 23.1:154).[51] Mann would have preferred Scheffauer, a native speaker of German with whom he would later briefly collaborate on a German book series, but Knopf blocked this suggestion with the forceful assertion: "Mr. Scheffauer's reputation is nothing like as important or noticeable, outside perhaps of Germany today, as you would seem to think."[52] Why Knopf ultimately preferred Lowe-Porter over Scheffauer has never been decisively established, though contrary to what is frequently written he appears to have acted not out of any personal predilection, but simply on the advice of his British business partner.[53] At any rate, in the following years Lowe-Porter quickly established herself as the English-language voice for Thomas Mann (so established, in fact, that when Kenneth Burke published an essay on Thomas Mann in his 1931 collection *Counter-Statement*, he chose to quote from her translation of *Death in Venice* rather than from his own).[54] As Knopf moved aggressively to consolidate his holdings, Lowe-Porter would eventually also retranslate most of the stories that had been rendered by other translators in the early 1920s.[55]

The quality of Lowe-Porter's Mann translations has attracted an enormous amount of critical commentary.[56] The initial evidence is fairly damning. Lowe-Porter may well not have said, as her obituary in the *New York Times* quoted her as saying, that "the Germans are too anxious to impress their German style on English. I want to get rid of German because English is what I want to be."[57] But she did confess that "I sometimes do not really understand T. Mann until I have dressed his thought and put English garb on it" and prefaced her very first translation, of *Buddenbrooks*, with the admission that she had intended to "transfer the spirit first and the letter so far as might be."[58] Perhaps most damningly, she also once boasted "of never sending a translation to the publisher unless I felt as though I had written the book myself."[59]

Unreflective criticism of these utterances ignores, however, that mainstream translation theory in the early decades of the twentieth century still favored readability in the target language over fidelity to the source language—an attitude that we find both in the Anglo-French theorist Hilaire Belloc, whom Lowe-Porter apparently read, and in the German theorist Ulrich von Wilamowitz-Moellendorf, whose influence cast a long shadow over the philological training of Lowe-Porter's husband, Elias Avery Lowe, in Germany during the early 1900s.[60] It also turns a blind eye to the fact that Lowe-Porter borrowed her metaphor of "dressing Mann's thought and putting English garb on it" (on another occasion, she also speaks of "chang[ing] the garment of his art into one which might clothe her for the marketplace") from the author himself.[61] In his 1939 lecture "The Making of *The Magic Mountain*," Mann explains that "oddly enough, it is not a difficulty for me, but rather the reverse that I have to discuss *The Magic Mountain* in English. I am reminded of the hero of my novel, the young engineer Hans Castorp. At the end of the first volume, he makes an extraordinary declaration of love to Madame Chauchat, the Kirghiz-eyed heroine, veiling its strangeness in the garment of a foreign tongue" (MoM, 41; GW, 11:602–3).

Mann is referring, of course, to the famous section of *The Magic Mountain* that is composed entirely in French, in which Hans Castorp not only finds the courage to declare his love for Madame Chauchat, but also discovers a number of things about himself simply because he is forced to dress his self-reflection in the "garment of a foreign tongue." This was not the only time Mann employed this metaphor. Almost twenty years earlier, on March 16, 1920, Mann received his author's copy of A. Cecil Curtis's translation of *Royal Highness* in the mail. Thumbing through the pages of this volume, Mann confessed that: "Truly, *the garment of this foreign tongue* fits as though it had been custom-made. . . . No, perhaps I'm not so truly 'national' after all" (GKFA, 2:232; emphasis mine). Although it is true that Mann on many later occasions complained about the inevitable flattening and the occasional distortion that his thoughts suffered in English, we thus also find a long-standing acknowledgment that the opposite might equally be the case and that translation into another language, far from disguising his intentions, might in some ways help to reveal his true nature.

What conclusions can be drawn, then, if we approach Lowe-Porter's Mann translations not simply as the products of professional malpractice, but rather as the outcome of a conscious (and ultimately highly successful) effort to clothe his art for the American marketplace? The first observation is that Lowe-Porter's English greatly reduces both the syntactic and the symbolic complexity of Mann's compositions. When Lowe-Porter requires five leisurely sentences to render what Mann accomplishes in three in the opening paragraph of *Death in Venice*, for example, she obscures an important expression of the disciplined "classical" style that characterizes the novella (SD, 378). And when she translates the crucial word *Edelrost* in the opening paragraph of *The Magic Mountain* not as "patina," but rather as "mould" (MM, v), she misreads a key metaphor intended to alert the reader to the fact that Hans Castorp's seven years in Davos should be read not as a process of decay but rather as one of transubstantiation and ennoblement. Even the translation scholar David Horton, who has conducted what is not only the most rigorous but perhaps also the most sympathetic study of Lowe-Porter's renditions to date, has to concede that "the rich intricacy and integration of the original is frequently reduced in Lowe-Porter's version, toning down precisely the multiple qualifications and ambivalences which are considered so central to Mann's style."[62]

Qualification and ambivalence (in other words, irony) are indeed unmistakably the biggest victims of Lowe-Porter's translations. One of the most characteristic elements of Mann's prose is his subtle way of combining description and commentary in a single sentence, by letting a narrator utter a sentence that at first sight appears straightforwardly descriptive but that actually, through the use of linguistic pastiche or of grammatical markers such as modal particles and inexplicit modifiers, expresses an inner distance to the subject matter at hand.[63] No wonder, then, that Erich Heller, the author of an important early study of Mann's ironic narration has lamented that "in English, alas, the ironically draped velvet and silk [of the original creations] often look like solemnly donned corduroy and tweed."[64]

T. J. Reed, another pioneering British critic of Mann's oeuvre, has given us a less colorful but more nuanced version of the same assessment. What Lowe-Porter's translations bring to the fore by a kind of distillatory process, so he claims, are those elements of Mann's art that he assimilated from the larger German cultural tradition and then dissolved in his ethereal prose style: "cultural matter is what remains when the volatile element of irony has been driven off by translation."[65] Even this assessment is still overly simplistic. First of all, Mann's irony can never be separated from his relationship to German culture. In *Death in Venice*, for example, irony was a fundamental component in what Oliver Jahraus has called Mann's strategy of "hybrid representation"—his way of completely assimilating a representative style only in order to show that he had already transcended it.[66] In *The Magic Mountain*, on the other hand, it was the signal of Mann's turn toward democracy: the device by which he was able to repeat many of the same claims that he had articulated six years earlier in *Reflections of a Nonpolitical Man* and yet do so as if his formerly sacrosanct opinions were now surrounded by scare quotes.

Just as importantly, however, Lowe-Porter transformed Mann's text not only through a strategy of stylistic reduction ("driving off") but also through one of addition. Anybody who compares extended passages of her prose to the German original, for instance, is quickly struck by the large number of foreign terms, especially from the French but also from the Italian and the Latin, that she introduces. In *Death in Venice*, for instance, the simple German term *Fahrlässigkeit* (*GKFA*, 2.1:509), meaning "carelessness," is rendered as *"laissez-aller"* (*SD*, 383), while the phrase "es schien folglich, daß er nicht allzu sehr ruhen dürfe" (*GKFA*, 2.1:524; evidently he ought not rest too much) is translated as "evidently it would not do to give himself up to sweet *far niente*"

(SD, 393). In *The Magic Mountain*, Joachim Ziemssen's "ritterliche Haltung" (*GKFA*, 5.1:116; chivalrous posture) becomes a *"preux chevalier"* (*MM*, 75), while the term *Gereiztheit* (*GKFA*, 5.1:1034), so crucial for the last chapter of the novel, is rendered not simply as "petulance," but rather with grand flourish as *"hysterica passio"* (*MM*, 681). Lowe-Porter's love of foreign terms is so pronounced that it even induces her to commit one of her most famous howlers, when she translates the word *Baiser* (*GKFA*, 5.1:230) not according to its German meaning as "meringue" but rather according to its French meaning as "kiss" (*MM*, 150), and thereby accuses poor Frau Stöhr, who is merely guilty of having transgressed the dietary strictures of the Berghof sanatorium, of having committed adultery.

The reason for all these unnecessary additions is clearly that Lowe-Porter hopes to emphasize Mann's immersion not solely in the German cultural tradition but rather in European humanist culture at large. The middlebrow nature of this strategy is revealed by her simultaneous sprinkling of what we might best identify as the debased detritus of an American liberal arts education around the pages of her translations. Thus, Mann's invocation of Mme. de Staël's phrase "alles verstehen heißt alles verzeihen" (*GKFA*, 2.1:513; to understand all is to forgive all) is retranslated back to the original *"tout comprendre c'est tout pardonner"* (*SD*, 386), while elsewhere a simple "Eintritt dieses Ereignisses" (*GKFA*, 5.1:490; coming to pass of this event) turns into a "crossing of the rubicon" (*MM*, 323) and a musical phrase delivered "mit Ausdruck" (*GKFA*, 5.1:506; with great expression) is rendered with pedantic preciseness as having been played *"con espressione"* (*MM*, 333). Lowe-Porter also greatly overemphasizes Mann's play with archaic phrasings. In the opening paragraph of *Death in Venice*, for example, she renders the phrase "an einem Frühlingsnachmittag des Jahres 19., das unserem Kontinent monatelang eine so gefahrdrohende Miene zeigte" (*GKFA*, 2.1:501) as "in that year of grace 19—, when Europe sat upon the anxious seat" (*SD*, 378)—a curious formulation taken straight out of the sermons of the nineteenth-century American revivalist preacher Charles Grandison Finney.

The combined effect of all these changes is that they turn *Death in Venice* and *The Magic Mountain* from mere masterpieces into "Great Books" of a kind that ordinary readers in interwar America could easily recognize. Since Mann's journey to his mature political vision was obscured in the Lowe-Porter translations, in which the narrator keeps speakers such as Naphta and Settembrini at a continuous safe distance rather than tempting the reader to adopt their points of view, Mann came across as a foam-born master exegete of the contemporary European soul. Alfred A. Knopf, as we have already seen, was keen to reinforce precisely this image of Thomas Mann as an author who, through his ability to synthesize the intellectual big picture, was able to keep aloof from the social and political strife of his era.

The *Saturday Review*, the Book-of-the-Month Club, and the Shaping of Public Opinion

Knopf's marketing strategy, which established Thomas Mann as the celebrity author of literary classics, and Lowe-Porter's tendency to privilege affirmative content over stylistic ambiguity in her translations both were the direct product of a distinctively American cultural climate that came into being during the 1920s. But their efforts were accepted and elaborated when Mann's works were distributed to the larger American public. His reinvention for the US market was thus not exclusively, or even primarily, the work of any one figure within the publishing industry. It instead arose as a natural response to a particular cultural moment. Nothing makes this clearer than a look at the two most important instruments for the mass dissemination of literary culture in America during the 1920s and 1930s, the *Saturday Review of Literature* and the Book-of-the-Month Club.

The *Saturday Review of Literature* was founded in 1924 by the Yale professor Henry Seidel Canby, one of the most important arbiters of middlebrow taste in America during the interwar period and an admirer of Thomas Mann (he served as the master of ceremonies for the 1934 gala reception honoring the author). The broad expansion of literary culture in US society during the 1920s created an unprecedented thirst for accessible literary reviews, especially since few Americans in the early twentieth century had access to a well-stocked bookstore staffed by a knowledgeable sales force.[67] The genteel magazines of the late nineteenth century, such as *Harper's*, *Scribner's*, or the *Atlantic Monthly*, could not cater to this demand. Daily newspapers, such as the *New York Times* or the *New York Herald Tribune*, eagerly stepped in to fill the gap. The *Saturday Review*, as well, began its life as a supplement to a daily paper (the *New York Evening Post*) before Canby, sensing the opportunity of the moment, established it as an independent publication whose circulation would eventually number in the hundreds of thousands.

The *Saturday Review* was from the very beginning aimed squarely at a middlebrow readership, a fact that distinguished it from *Publisher's Weekly* (targeted mostly at trade professionals). This did not mean that it was parochial in scope or unsophisticated in intention. From our contemporary vantage point, the 1920s are often described as an "isolationist" decade. While this moniker may very well apply to official US policy, a closer look at the *Saturday Review* reveals that it only imperfectly describes the attitudes and interests of ordinary Americans, who were, after all, keenly aware of such developments as international radio broadcasting or the first attempts at transatlantic aviation. From the very beginning, Canby's newspaper reviewed important new American books and titles published abroad, even if they weren't yet available in translation. Collective reviews of the latest fiction to have been published in Germany became a regular feature in the *Saturday Review*. They were typically written by knowledgeable native correspondents and appeared as often as semimonthly. Another regular column, the "Reader's Guide" by May Lamberton Becker (author of several popular advice books and nicknamed the "reference librarian of the nation"), frequently featured queries by readers desiring to know, for example, "what novels of fairly recent appearance in French, Russian and German have been translated into English."[68] The *Saturday Review* also published quite sophisticated essays on the current state of literary translation and on the economics of what we nowadays call "world literature." A 1925 article by Ernest Boyd, for example, compares the translation practices of English and American firms, pointing out that most translations into English to have appeared after the Great War had been commissioned (though not necessarily executed) by Americans—a situation which, of course, precisely describes what also happened in Mann's case.[69]

Thomas Mann's name made frequent appearances in the *Saturday Review*, so much so that the paper highlighted its early coverage of the famous author as one of its proudest achievements when it commemorated its tenth anniversary in a series of articles. Mann was first presented to a general readership in May 1925, at a time when his fame was otherwise still confined to the little magazines. Ironically, the person to introduce him was Frank Thieß, who twenty years later would come to lob bitter accusations at his colleague for having moved to America.[70] Two weeks later, the *Saturday Review* printed an appraisal of the German edition of *The Magic Mountain* by A. W. G. Randall, which was followed in short order by an article on the Dial Press's *Death in Venice and Other Stories*. In August of that same year, readers were also given a first interview with the author. The steady coverage only intensified after the 1927 publication of the American edition of *The Magic Mountain*, and by 1929 Mann's reputation was so secure that US publishers featured him in blurbs for quite undemanding publications, such as the photo book *Animals Looking at You*. In later years, Thomas Mann's image would also repeatedly appear on the cover of the *Saturday Review*.

This coverage of Thomas Mann produced a very specific image of the author for an American audience. He was promoted as an icon of cultural distinction, as somebody who could be used to signal taste and familiarity with European culture at a time when Americans were still unsure about their own grandeur as a nation. Evidence for this is provided not only by the reviews themselves but also by the many other occasions on which his name appears in the paper. The ranked mini-list also employed by Nabokov was a common vehicle in this regard. Readers were supplied with ammunition for their next after-church or cocktail-hour conversation by being told that Mann ranked as a "close second" to John Galsworthy as "the greatest living master of the large-scale family novel," or that "Bashan and I" could be considered as one of the three greatest contemporary fictions about men and their dogs.[71] May Lamberton Becker in particular was a serial offender in this regard, dropping Mann's name into her answers to numerous readers' queries. But Mann's works were also highlighted in other ways. In December 1927, for example, two editors of the *Saturday Review* featured *The Magic Mountain* in their annual list of Christmas recommendations, alongside middlebrow reads such as *Trader Horn*, *The Rise of American Civilization*, or *Adventures in Reading*.[72]

As a result, the *Saturday Review* increased Thomas Mann's readership and, more importantly, created a much larger audience that knew him by reputation and was capable of repeating certain clichés about his works. And these clichés stood in a symbiotic relationship both to the publishing strategies pursued by Alfred A. Knopf and to the translation choices made by Helen Tracy Lowe-Porter. In the 1925 interview with Mann, for example, the interviewer Aldo Sorani informed American readers—long before they would have been able to make up their own minds about the German author's novels—that "the novel of today turns away from narrative." Instead, in *The Magic Mountain*, "a thesis heads each chapter, made up of at least two dissertations. Nothing happens beyond the contrast of views."[73] Later reviews told readers that in Mann's novels "individuals are presented only as the exponents of groups," that "instead of plot, he chooses a pattern," and that instead of "creating" new worlds, he "interpreted" the existing one.[74] Some of these assessments were no doubt meant to be negative, but in their sum, they created a definite image of Thomas Mann as a very specific kind of writer: a novelist of ideas, whom one read for his philosophical disquisitions, not out of admiration for his literary method, his plots, or his character portraits.

By the time that Mann first arrived in the United States, however, the *Saturday Review of Literature* was no longer the most important instrument for disseminating his fame among the American public. As a book review, the paper could inform people about literature, but it could not induce them to buy it—and during the hardships brought on by the Great Depression, ordinary readers certainly thought twice about every penny that they spent on leisure activities. Another publishing revolution of the mid-1920s, how-ever, the Book-of-the-Month Club, could directly distribute novels into read-ers' homes, whether they had consciously chosen those titles or not.[75] The importance of mail-order book publishing in the United States during the 1930s is hard to overestimate. At the start of the Great Depression, there was one bookstore in the United States for every thirty thousand people, and fully a third of the population lived in small towns without direct access to bookstores whatsoever.[76] Harry Scherman, a successful ad man with exper-tise in mail-order circulars, founded the Book-of-the-Month Club in 1926 with the express goal of reaching this untapped market, and he succeeded admirably. A year after it launched, the club already had sixty thousand mem-bers; in 1947, its peak year, that figure stood at almost nine hundred thou-sand. Throughout the 1940s, the Book-of-the-Month Club was one of the largest customers of the US Postal Service, comparable in mail volume to such companies as Sears or Montgomery Ward. There were many copycat book clubs as well, and *Time* magazine estimated in 1946 that there were as many as three million subscribers in total.[77]

The Book-of-the-Month Club naturally targeted a middlebrow audience, and most of its regular judges were also frequent contributors to the *Satur-day Review*. This included Henry Seidel Canby himself. Despite this overlap between the two institutions, however, it took more than a decade for one of Mann's works to be chosen. An anxious 1934 letter to Alfred A. Knopf by the journalist Dorothy Canfield Fisher, who was fretting about whether to recommend *Joseph and His Brothers* to the club, shows what the difficulty may have been: "I wonder—just on the general subject of translations, whether it isn't legitimate to make some of these slight changes in the style of the original which would bring it more within the spirit of the language into which it is set? For example, where the German sentences are notably lon-ger and more involved than any now constructed by people writing in Eng-lish, would it be a crime to break them up into shorter ones?"[78] Canfield Fisher's fears appear to have been well founded. Mann's sales figures for the Book-of-the-Month Club (roughly eighty thousand copies of *Stories of Three Decades*, his first selection, and just over two hundred thousand copies of *Doctor Faustus*, his second-to-last) were impressive for an author of serious, stylistically difficult fiction but still noticeably lower than the club average, which stood at roughly ninety-five thousand copies per title in the mid-1930s, and at roughly three hundred thousand copies per title in the mid-1940s.[79]

In light of such adverse sales considerations, then, the fact that the club disseminated no fewer than five Thomas Mann titles during the period from 1936 to 1951 seems all the more significant.[80] There are two probable reasons for this. The first is that the club judges, for all their consciousness of the limitations of their audience, genuinely believed that it was their task to introduce ordinary Americans to the higher ideas of their time. In this regard they were faithful followers of Van Wyck Brooks. The strategies that the club pursued to achieve this aim closely mirrored those pioneered by Knopf a decade earlier. It deemphasized the Germanic nature of Mann's thought and instead positioned him in a long line of western literary classics. Canby's appraisal of *Joseph the Provider*, for example, draws explicit comparisons to Milton's *Paradise Lost*.[81] It also deemphasized stylistic novelty and emphasized intellectual depth. Clifton Fadiman's review of *Doctor Faustus*, which is arguably Mann's most radical novel from a stylistic viewpoint, begins with the words, "Like all of Dr. Mann's novels, this is reading meant for intellectuals. The reader must go slowly, because the novel brims over with aesthetic, religious, and philosophic asides."[82] And finally, it ran lots of feature stories on Thomas Mann as a person, which invariably focused on his iron discipline, his ability to write on trains, and his beautifully furnished home office in Pacific Palisades—qualities that would have served to connect the intellectual sphere in which Mann moved with the world understood and admired by the club's white-collar audience (figure 2.2).

The second reason for the continual promotion of Thomas Mann was that the club, much like the *Saturday Review*, clearly viewed it as part of its core mission to satisfy American interest in European culture. As early as 1929, just as he wrapped up his duties as a foreign correspondent for the *Dial*,

In his study at Santa Monica . . . but he could concentrate in a boiler room

FIGURE 2.2. A photo of Thomas Mann, documenting the Book-of-the-Month Club's efforts to make the author relatable to an American white-collar audience. *Book-of-the-Month Club News*, October 1948.

Mann became a member of the club's "European advisory committee." And over the subsequent two and a half decades, the club again and again chose books in translation to disseminate to its audience—including no fewer than twenty-nine titles by German-language authors, though no other writer came close to matching Thomas Mann's popularity.[83] The majority of the chosen titles were historical works of fiction and fictionalized biographies, such as Franz Werfel's *The Forty Days of Musa Dagh*, about the Armenian genocide, or Stefan Zweig's *Mary, Queen of Scots*. This pattern casts light on another way in which standard narratives about Mann's place within literary modernism give way to competing accounts about his relationship to middlebrow culture with only a slight change in perspective. Both *Joseph and his Brothers* and *Doctor Faustus* have frequently been celebrated as paradigmatically modernist engagements with myth and as ambitious modernist epics. Most of the American readers of these novels, however, would instead have approached them as easily recognizable examples of time-honored popular forms: the historical novel and the artist's novel.

Each of the four novels distributed by the club sold well over one hundred thousand copies, while *Joseph in Egypt* and *Doctor Faustus* surpassed the two hundred thousand mark. The peak of Mann's fame and financial fortune in the United States thus came in the early 1940s. By then, however, the marketing strategies first designed by Knopf almost two decades earlier had long been overtaken by the calamitous rush of world history. The carefully curated image of Thomas Mann as the embodiment of European sophistication, as the spiritual heir to the classics of the western canon, and as the author of philosophical novels capable of standing up to the chaos of modern existence may still have sold books in Topeka, but it held no more appeal in New York. In the mid-1930s "engagement" had become the new watchword in US intellectual circles, and Brooks's vision of a "congenial middle ground," where high culture might fructify the barren soil of ordinary reality, now seemed almost laughable.

Even the *Saturday Review* did not entirely escape this development. In May of 1937, it ran an editorial about the youth of the day, who apparently believed that "the Thomas Mann cult is a vast reservoir of sentimentality, and [that] in these desperate days it is our duty to root out the sentimental."[84] This was such a notable departure from the paper's previous editorial line that Canby himself took to the pen to issue a rebuttal. Mann could still be helpful, so he claimed two weeks later, because he dealt in large ideas and could therefore answer the only question that really mattered, which was, "Is Western Civilization really crumbling then?"[85] Canby expressly did not allude to what would seem to be the most obviously interesting thing about Thomas Mann in 1937: the fact that he was an exile from Hitler's Germany, who might have been uniquely qualified to offer an informed personal perspective on the rise of European fascism and the threat that it posed to intellectual life. Instead, he praised him only as a purveyor of abstract thoughts, a novelist of ideas. The bombshell publication of Mann's letter to the dean in the pages of the *Nation*, and later on of *Reader's Digest*, would change all this and alter Mann's reception in the United States almost overnight.

Interlude I: *Joseph in Egypt* (1938)

On February 28, 1938, almost exactly a week after Thomas Mann's triumphant arrival in New York, Alfred A. Knopf published *Joseph in Egypt*, the third in the monumental series of biblical novels on which the author had begun working twelve years earlier. The book was greeted with rapturous enthusiasm and marked the high point of Mann's critical acclaim from a purely literary point of view: while even greater laurels were as yet in store for him, they would all be given more for his services to democracy than for those to modern fiction.

Unsurprisingly, middlebrow reception networks led the celebratory charge. Henry Seidel Canby called *Joseph in Egypt* an "epoch-making story" in the *Saturday Review of Literature*, while Book-of-the-Month Club critic Clifton Fadiman spoke of a "masterpiece" "at once contemporary and classic."[1] But other critics struck a more thoughtful tone, asking whether a book like *Joseph in Egypt* was really what the world needed at this point in time. In the pages of the *New Republic*, for example, Malcolm Cowley wrote, "The philosophy that Mann develops in the Joseph story is a noble structure, full of wisdom, but it is also full of dark rooms and calculated mysteries. This is an age when mysteries are to be distrusted. When reasonableness and good sense are being threatened on all sides by all sorts of myths—as they are today—and by glorifications of force, instinct, blood, race, the soil, it is dangerous to praise legends at the expense of history."[2] To Mann, such questions would have seemed familiar, for Marxist intellectuals back in Germany had been hitting him with even more forceful versions of the same argument ever since the publication of *The Tales of Jacob* back in 1933.

The comparative restraint of Mann's American interlocutors owed a lot to the fact that the country as a whole was as yet but slowly awakening to the new political realities of the fascist era. This slow awakening, however, was conducive to a level of intellectual nuance rarely on display in Mann's Old World critics. The journal *Partisan Review*, for example, which would soon develop into the foremost intellectual medium in the United States, staged one of its first attention-grabbing debates on contemporary culture in 1938 and 1939, when it ran a half-dozen essays deliberating whether Mann's new novel was in any way useful to left-wing social action. The debate pitted William Troy, on the one hand, against a core team of *Partisan Review* editors (among them William Phillips, Dwight Macdonald, and Howard Rosenberg), on the other.

At the heart of this debate stood Mann's decision to write a "mythic" novel, a decision that all participants rightly understood as representative of a central trend within modernist literature. To identify the *Joseph* novels as "mythic" in intention did not simply mean that they drew inspiration from stories passed down through the millennia. Nor did Mann earn the appellation through his exhaustive studies of the latest scholarship in anthropology, Egyptology, Judaic studies, and similar fields, although this attention to detail was certainly one point that separated his oeuvre from lesser contemporary works. No, to write a "mythic" novel meant to produce a literary work whose individual parts were put together according to the compositional logic of ancient mythology rather than those of modern narrative. And this implied, among other things, a conscious disregard for scientific causality. For Mann's defenders, such a mythic approach represented a genuinely original tool with which the artist might join the scientist and the political theorist in the critique of the fascist mind. Mann, so Troy asserted, had "come to myth . . . only after the most conscious and deliberate threshing-out of all the problems involved in giving adequate expression to our cultural predicament."[3] Unsurprisingly, this was a view that Mann himself shared. In several letters and essays of the period he reiterated that he had discovered the importance of mythical thinking for the present day through his study of psychoanalysis. As he put it in the 1936 lecture "Freud and the Future," "myth is the foundation of life; it is the timeless schema, the pious formula into which life flows when it reproduces its traits out of the unconscious" (*ED*, 422; *GW*, 9:493). And indeed, Mann's description of the episode in which Joseph's jealous brothers throw him into a well has struck many a reader as a trenchant analysis of the fascist mob mentality.

Mann's detractors were not so sure of this. For one thing, they doubted the author's abilities as a social commentator. Mann was constantly taking "the most extreme and reckless political positions" while "protesting his inadequate understanding of the subject, thus claiming the indulgence granted the amateur," Dwight Macdonald charged in a blistering editorial.[4] For another, the emphasis on myth necessarily implied a corresponding disregard for the scientific study of society and history, that is, for Marxism as an outgrowth of the enlightenment. "The European man of Thomas Mann . . . lacks science, the most characteristic product of the human mind. The extension of scientific method into history has helped to strip it of legends and prejudices, introducing order, direction, and law," wrote William Phillips, and "we cannot accept Mann as our historic contemporary because he is not concerned with contemporary history."[5]

The *Partisan Review* debate was part and parcel of a larger discussion about the uses of myth for left-wing politics that profoundly altered US society over the course of the late 1930s, and which will receive more comprehensive treatment in the following chapter. What makes it of special interest for the present purposes, however, is the fact that the *Joseph* novels derive their specific compositional form not from "myth" in the abstract, but from the Jewish stories about the patriarchs that were eventually compiled in the book of Genesis. As most cultural histories of the 1930s point out, the years following the Great Depression were the time when Jewish intellectuals first won for themselves a place at the heart of intellectual life in America, and *Partisan Review* was one of their main vehicles of expression. Virtually all the critics who debated the merits of *Joseph in Egypt* in the new journal had left traditional Jewish families for the allure of a more cosmopolitan life guided by the lodestars of Karl Marx, Vladimir Ilyich Lenin, and Leon Trotsky. At the same time, Mann, who as late as April 1933 had privately complained about the "hostile-antagonistic, base, and un-German" nature of the Jewish people (*Tb.*, April 10, 1933), was now coming around to a decidedly philo-Semitic position. In his 1937 essay "On the Problem of Anti-Semitism," he even argued that "the Jews in a German context represent the intellectual element physically, by virtue of their blood and race" (*GW*, 13:483). Problematic as these sentences may be (the critic Todd Kontje has rightly pointed out that "Mann rejects anti-Semitism, but he does not reject the idea that Jews are different from Germans, nor does he reject the concept of race"), they publicly positioned the writer in opposition to the Nazi party and contributed to his eventual loss of citizenship.[6] Over the course of the coming years, interlocutors in the United States would repeatedly link Mann's exile to the diaspora of the Jews, a process that culminated when the author dedicated the cornerstone of the Palestine Pavilion, funded by the New York Zionist Meyer Weisgal, at the 1939 New York World's Fair.

It is indeed true that the *Joseph* novels derive the originality of their compositional form not just from a preoccupation with myth in the abstract but rather from a careful study of Jewish myth, which thereby is put into tacit opposition to the Nazi worldview. One of the characteristic elements of all mythical thinking is the erasure of the boundaries between the individual and the typical, the present and the past. "Primitive" peoples imagine themselves to be coeval, and to a certain extent identical, with the spirits of their ancestors, a pattern of thought that Sigmund Freud applied with great success also to an analysis of modern psychic life in studies such as *Totem and Taboo* (1913). The first of the *Joseph* novels, *The Tales of Jacob*, exhibits precisely this same pattern when it tells the stories of Joseph's patriarchal forefathers nonsequentially, thereby blending their distinct identities into one larger archetypal construct. But as Dieter Borchmeyer explains, the second novel, *Young Joseph*, gives a distinctively Jewish twist to this larger idea when it turns this fascination with the simultaneity of the nonsimultaneous into a quest for—and eventual discovery of—a transcendent (rather than immanent) God.[7] In the chapter "How Abraham Discovered God," we read about Abraham contemplating the origin of things:

> It began with Abram thinking that to mother earth alone was due service and worship, for that she brought forth fruits and preserved life. But he observed that she needed rain from heaven. So he gazed up into the skies, saw the sun in all its glory, possessed with the powers of blessing and cursing; and was on the point of deciding for it. But then it set, and he was convinced that it could not be the highest. So he looked at the moon and the stars—at these with particular expectation and hope. (*J*, 283; *GKFA*, 7.1:401)

In this scene, the fruits, the earth, the heavens, the sun and the stars are all simultaneously present and yet also described as an ever-widening circle of entities in which each successive object either begets or at least encompasses the ones that came before it. The specifically "Jewish" nature of this thought process reveals itself only when Abraham leaps from this contemplation of the immanent to a deliberation of the transcendent—to that which does *not* seem to be simultaneously present with everything else, and yet conditions all of it: "His soul was greatly troubled and he thought: 'High as they are, had they not above themselves a guide and lord, how could the one set, the other rise? It would be unfitting for me, a man, to serve them and not rather Him who commands over them.' And Abraham's thought lay so painfully close to the truth that it touched the Lord God to His innermost and He said to Himself: 'I will anoint thee with the oil of gladness more than all thy fellows'" (*J*, 284; *GKFA*, 7.1:401–2).

This capacity to not only think mythically but also combine mythical thought with analytical method is what ultimately distinguishes Mann's protagonist Joseph and enables his meteoric rise to governor of Egypt once he is called to interpret the dream of Pharaoh. But there is a contemporary political relevance to all this as well, for Abraham's struggle to reach the transcendent cause behind visible reality lays the foundation for the Jewish people as social community, through the original covenant with God. In this regard, *Young Joseph*, written in 1931–32 and published in the German original in 1934, is much more radical than the essay "On the Problem of Anti-Semitism" of 1937. If the latter still speaks of the "race," "blood," and "physiognomy" of the Jews, thereby replicating the rhetoric of the Nazis, the novel recognizes that lineage and blood are just the biological chain that connects the present generation to Abraham's covenant, which in turn is the true precondition of Jewish identity. It thereby undercuts the very foundation of racialized anti-Semitism, rendering its ostensible "problem" null and void.

In his 1943 Library of Congress lecture on the *Joseph* novels, Mann proudly drew attention to the Judaic content of his literary creation, claiming that "the selection of the old testamental subject was certainly not mere accident; most certainly there were hidden, defiantly polemical connections between it and certain tendencies of our time which I always found repulsive from the bottom of my soul; the growing vulgar anti-semitism which is an essential part of the Fascist mob-myth" (*LC*, 11; *GW*, 11:663). The *Joseph* tetralogy did not become as popular as it did in the United States because it was viewed as a Jewish cycle, however. It instead derived its enormous appeal from the fact that, starting with the second novel, it leaves the realm of the patriarchs behind and henceforth focuses on the fortunes of young Joseph, whose story offers everything that one might expect from a gripping yarn: love won and scorned, betrayal and treachery, rise to great wealth followed by unexpected catastrophes. And with the start of the third novel, once Joseph enters into Egypt, the strictly Judaic conception of a transcendent creator is also matched with a more universal equivalent, that of the Egyptian sun-god Atum-Rê, whose symbol is the isosceles triangle, an emblem of mathematical symmetry and perfection.

Among the many things that distinguish Atum-Rê from the God of the Jews (or at least ostensibly distinguish between them, for Mann leaves open the possibility that they are one and the same) is that anybody can convert to the cult of Atum-Rê, as Pharaoh himself will do. The introduction of Atum-Rê to the story thus allows Mann to construct the model of a social community founded not on race and blood (not even in the incidental sense exemplified by the Jewish people), but rather on the conception of subservience to a universal transcendent idea. In this, of course, his Joseph story merely echoes standard narratives about Christianity as a more universal successor to Judaism that have been offered over and over again since at least the *Lectures on the Philosophy of Religion* by Georg Wilhelm Friedrich Hegel. Indeed, Borchmeyer suggests, Atum-Rê's triangle can be read as a not-so-subtle allusion to the Holy Trinity.

That Mann's thought and fiction underwent a kind of "religious turn" over the course of the 1930s is by now well-established in the secondary literature and will also become evident from his activities chronicled in subsequent chapters.[8] Just as interesting, however, is the fact that the *Joseph* novels, in drawing an arc from Judaism to Christianity, participate in a larger American trend during this period to theorize a "Judeo-Christian tradition" that could be placed in opposition to what sources at the time often referred to as "godless fascism." In his "Fireside Chat" of September 3, 1939 (two days after Nazi Germany invaded Poland), for example, Franklin Delano Roosevelt defined the difference between the average American and the average Nazi with the words, "Most of us in the United States believe in spiritual values. Most of us, regardless of what church we belong to, believe in the spirit of the New Testament."[9] And in 1942, the interfaith National Conference of Christians and Jews released a statement declaring, "We the undersigned individuals of the Protestant, Catholic, and Jewish faiths, viewing the present results of Godlessness in the world . . . realize the necessity for stressing those spiritual truths which we hold in common."[10]

A letter that Agnes E. Meyer wrote to Thomas Mann in the late summer of 1937, after she had finished reading *Joseph in Egypt*, illustrates how easily the novel fit into this typically American thought pattern:

> I am back in the turmoil after a month of complete isolation. We have a cattle ranch in Wyoming and while my family went to see our live stock exhibited, I rode further into the mountains and established a camp in a veritable paradise. There I lay beside the bank of a mountain stream in which I was supposed to be fly-fishing, and in the shade of those enormous fir trees which would be out of proportion in any country but our own I read your account of Joseph's experience in Egypt. . . . Many a time I tossed the book aside because my imagination was compelled to follow the current of your thoughts in much the

same way as the water in the mountain stream before me pursued its way between meandering banks. To have read this extraordinary book in the silence and majesty of such a natural setting is an experience that I shall never forget. (*Br. AM*, 91)

In Meyer's overactive mind, the rocky landscape of the *Joseph* novels became one with the mountainous terrain of Wyoming. In this way, Mann's efforts to wrest the powers of mythology away from the grip of fascism were supplemented with a celebration of the western United States—the same landscape in which that most American of prophets, Joseph Smith, had already located the true home of the lost tribes of Israel. And Meyer was far from the only reader to respond in this fashion. In the pages of *Harper's*, for example, the historian John Hyde Preston ruminated on the "earth-form that is so unmistakable in a Thomas Mann," and which he searched for in vain in the works of American-born authors such as Theodore Dreiser or Sinclair Lewis.[11] Willa Cather, too, was smitten by the book to such an extent that she read it three times in quick succession. Her close friend Fanny Butcher would later claim that Cather found in the *Joseph* novels a "book that carried her into a new world . . . the oldest world of all."[12]

Of course, when he began his work in 1926, Mann could hardly have anticipated that his decision to devote a novel cycle to Jewish themes would eventually come to be read as an antifascist gesture. The world had changed a lot in the intervening twelve years. But this simple fact also points toward a final interesting point to be raised about the American reception history of *Joseph in Egypt*. The praises of the middlebrow critics who promoted the novel are consistently undercut by a certain conceptual confusion about the point in history to which Mann's latest creation might belong. For Clifton Fadiman, *Joseph in Egypt* is "at once contemporary and classic," "written both today and always."[13] For Canby, it is at once "significant for a new age" and strangely out of time, capable of being summarized only by means of an "interim report."[14] As will by now be clear, this conceptual confusion is at one level a symptom of an intellectual crisis that confronted middlebrow culture in the face of a newly political era. It was no longer possible to hide behind vague rhetoric of "timeless mastery," as so much American criticism of Mann had done during the 1920s and early 1930s. On another level, however, the confusion also responds to the form of Mann's project itself, which was that of the novel cycle.

There had certainly been many novel cycles before; the turn of the century in particular produced many infamous mammoth-projects, such as Émile Zola's twenty-volume *The Rougon-Macquarts* (1871–93), or Romain

Rolland's ten-volume *Jean Christophe* (1904–12). But rarely before had the publication history of one of these projects encompassed so much social upheaval as was the case with Mann's *Joseph* novels, and never before had an author so actively responded to this upheaval in the compositional form of a cycle. It seems extremely unlikely that Mann would have characterized Joseph's brothers as an atavistic mob if the Brownshirts hadn't conquered the streets of Munich while he was at work on the second novel in the early 1930s. And it seems similarly unlikely that Mann would have given the cult of Atum-Rê quite as much prominence in *Joseph in Egypt* if he had not actively searched for a humanistic counterpoint to the Nazi ideology once he had been forced into exile. Certainly, it is inconceivable that *Joseph the Provider* would ever have taken the form of an allegory on the New Deal if its author had not emigrated to the United States.

These responses to contemporary political events tie not only the content but also the form of the novel to concrete historical moments. At the same time, however, the continuous plot and especially the motivic structure of the cycle create a larger formal unity, a means by which the allegorical elements that characterize parts of the novels (the brothers as Brownshirts, Joseph as Roosevelt) are integrated into a larger mythical structure.

This dual temporal structure parallels that of the world republic of letters, which also exists contemporaneous to political reality and yet simultaneously transcends it. All authors swim in the social currents of their era. But once they reach a certain classic status, they are also lifted out of the rivers of history, to a place where their works exist side by side with those of their poetic forebears. Charles William Eliot's "Five Foot Shelf" of *Harvard Classics* had been one visual expression of this simultaneity, premised on the notion that the close spatial proximity of so many high-powered texts might yield something greater than the sum of its parts: a socially transformative liberal education. Eliot's experiment had provided the foundation for middlebrow culture. With *Joseph in Egypt*, Mann was updating this middlebrow ideology for an era of antifascist struggle. His steady work on a cycle of novels even in the face of personal chaos and social upheaval, combined with the fact that each successive novel seemed to draw strength and intellectual depth from the ones that had preceded it, sent a powerful message of opposition to Nazi Germany. Hitler might have been able to force Mann into exile, threaten his friends and family, and deprive him of his material possessions. But he could not sever the nourishing bonds to cultural tradition from which Thomas Mann derived sustenance.

CHAPTER 3

The First Citizen of the International Republic of Letters

> *We are glad that you are here, Thomas Mann, no nation can exile you. Yours is a larger citizenship, in no mean country. Wherever men love reason, hate obscurantism, shun darkness, turn toward light, know gratitude, praise virtue, despise meanness, kindle to sheer beauty; wherever minds are sensitive, hearts generous and spirits free—there is your home. In welcoming you, a country but honors itself.*
>
> —Dorothy Thompson, "To Thomas Mann," April 1937

> *It is not just a matter of you being honored however; rather, the country that is honoring you is well aware that it is honoring itself when it honors the intellectual principle that you represent to the world.*
>
> —Gottfried Bermann Fischer, letter to Thomas Mann, July 1935

Thomas Mann was an early enemy of national socialism. In 1921, at a time when the Nazi Party still had fewer than four thousand members, he already dismissed it as "Swastika nonsense" (*GKFA*, 15.1:436). Over the coming years, he became one of the most prominent defenders of the democratic constitution of the Weimar Republic, and an increasingly vocal critic of Adolf Hitler and his followers. Joseph Goebbels was a jealous admirer of *Buddenbrooks* and may well have hoped to convert the author of the *Reflections of a Nonpolitical Man* to the Nazi cause. But if Mann's declaration "On the German Republic" of 1922 did not already put an end to such ambitions, his 1925 appeal "Save Democracy!," in which he urged his fellow Germans to reject the presidential aspirations of the Nazi's preferred candidate, Paul von Hindenburg, certainly did.[1]

The high point of the tensions between Mann and the Nazis came in October 1930, when the author delivered a lecture called "German Address: An Appeal to Reason" in Berlin's Beethoven Hall, the same venue in which he had pledged his allegiance to the republic eight years earlier. The lecture had been drafted in direct response to the Reichstag elections of the previous month, in which the Nazi Party had won the second-largest share of the vote; Mann attempted to analyze the causes of the national-socialist success and urged the middle classes to join forces with the social democrats. The Nazis sent about thirty storm troopers in rented tuxedos to disrupt the occasion. Led by the playwright Arnolt Bronnen, the SA men booed lustily and forced Mann to leave the hall via a back door immediately after the conclusion of his lecture (figure 3.1). Ever since that day, Mann's name occupied a top place on the Nazi list of "undesirable elements" to be arrested immediately after a seizure of power.

The contrast between Mann and Arnolt Bronnen could not have been more overt: on the one hand, a proud and independent artist using his acquired cultural capital to stand up for his beliefs by putting himself in direct opposition to powerful political forces. On the other, a servile scribbler who contorted his own aesthetic convictions in order to flatter the Nazis and who, after 1933, became the programming director of a state-run television station. Given this contrast, it comes as all the more of a disappointment to learn that Thomas Mann, after he made the decision not to return from a lecturing tour that had taken him outside Germany when Hitler came to power,

FIGURE 3.1. Audience members react to Nazi hecklers at Thomas Mann's "German Address," 1930. Ullstein Bild Dtl./Getty Images.

did not utter a single public word against the Nazis for three full years. It is of little consolation to note that his diaries and letters were as strident as ever or that, like many other incredulous Germans at the time, Mann believed that Hitler would be impeached or otherwise removed from office once his deluded supporters figured out that his promises had all been lies. Nor is it entirely satisfactory to remember that Mann rightly feared he might be stripped of his citizenship if he drew too much attention to himself. In the end, it is all too obvious that economic considerations played a part as well and that Mann, despite the fact that he could undoubtedly have lived off of his international royalties, feared the loss not only of his German audience but also of the considerable revenue stream that it brought with it.[2]

It took a prolonged campaign from Mann's two oldest children, Erika and Klaus, to convince Mann to finally speak out. The fact that his Jewish publisher, Gottfried Bermann Fischer, was forced to leave Germany at great personal and financial loss left a deep impression on him as well. In February 1936 the *Neue Zürcher Zeitung* published an open letter in which the author justified his decision not to return to his native country. It concluded with some powerful lines by Mann's favorite poet, August von Platen:

> To flee one's fatherland is far more sage
> Than still to bear among a childish race
> The yoke of the unthinking rabble's rage.
> (*GW*, 11:793)[3]

The German government was surprisingly slow to respond to this provocation. A full ten months went by before the Nazis stripped Mann of his citizenship and banned his books, which had previously been publicly burned but still tolerated for sale. By then Mann had already become an honorary Czechoslovak citizen, while Gottfried Bermann Fischer had successfully emigrated to Vienna, taking most of the material assets of his publishing house with him. Still, this final confrontation set wheels in motion that inexorably led to Mann's decision, during his 1938 North American lecture tour, to take out his "first papers" and apply for US citizenship.[4] Too great was his fear that tiny Switzerland might eventually be overrun by the German army, and there were also rumors of Nazi raiding parties secretly crossing the Swiss border to abduct undesirable émigrés.

Among Mann's more politically engaged followers in the United States, his public turn against the Nazis was just as eagerly anticipated as it was within the European refugee community. Mann's antifascist story "Mario and the Magician" had received an overwhelmingly positive American reception when Knopf published it in 1931.[5] In September 1933 the *New York Times* published an interview by the reporter David Ewen, who had introduced himself to Mann as a music journalist and had managed to tease some unguarded statements out of his reluctant subject. "I cannot return to Germany until justice and freedom have preceded me there," the famous author said, and "Hitler appeals not to the intelligence of a people; he appeals to their emotions."[6] Mann was forced to issue an immediate retraction. A year later, the *New Republic* printed an open letter by Harry Slochower—a Brooklyn College professor who was then one of the most distinguished academic interpreters of Mann's work in America—urging him to break his silence. A whole slew of literary celebrities, including Sherwood Anderson, Kenneth Burke, Malcolm Cowley, Clifton Fadiman, James T. Farrell, Langston Hughes, and John Dos Passos, lent their signatures as well.[7] When Mann finally spoke out, the most vocal supporter announcing his new stance to the American public was the journalist Dorothy Thompson, whom *Time* magazine in 1939 declared to be one of the two most influential women in America (the other was Eleanor Roosevelt).[8] Thompson, a long-time Berlin correspondent for several American newspapers, was especially famous for a no-holds-barred 1932 interview with Adolf Hitler, and for the fact that the Nazi government had thrown her out of the country in 1934. At a banquet in Mann's honor, she delivered a short address that she subsequently published as an editorial for the *New York Herald Tribune*, which in turn was nationally syndicated.

Thompson's description of Mann, quoted in the first epigraph to this chapter, might initially seem to be merely a restatement of the slogan "the most eminent living man of letters" that the journalist had employed three years earlier, also in the pages of the *Herald Tribune*. But if the general effect of the earlier epithet (and similar remarks in the middlebrow press) had been to disembody Thomas Mann and lift him up into the realm of an abstract spiritual greatness, the later description is much more grounded in political reality. Thompson argues that the "larger citizenship" earned by Mann's globally recognized artistic achievements more than compensates for his loss of German civic rights. She does not treat the metaphorical and the literal understanding of "citizenship" as disparate concepts, in other words, but rather implies that the one exists on the same plane as the other. At the same time, Thompson's praise is not as disinterested as we might at first assume it to be. For the notion of a larger cultural citizenship glides effortlessly into an encomium to the American republic, the nation that has offered Mann the promise of a new political citizenship to replace the one that he lost.

A similar shift can be observed in the honorary degree citations that Thomas Mann received from American universities during these years. In

1935, Harvard University had praised him as an "interpreter of life to many in the western world" and as a "contemporary guardian of the great tradition of German culture."[9] In subsequent years, the praise became more expressly political. Hobart College, in 1939, called him "the first Citizen in the International Republic of Letters [and] standard bearer of the growing army of artists who believe . . . that democracy must be militant." It also went on to point out that "you represent, par excellence, the ideals of the liberal colleges in this, your adopted fatherland."[10] The University of California at Berkeley, in 1941, called him a "native of Germany, but belonging to all mankind; by the malignancy of a freedom-destroying regime, and by our good fortune, citizen of the United States."[11] In both cases, Mann's avowed membership in an international republic of letters was thus first translated into the political realm and then patriotically appropriated.

Over the course of the late 1930s, in other words, Mann's reputation as a "great man of letters" was adapted for a new and more belligerent age that found its culmination with the outbreak of the Second World War. By turning Mann into an anti-Nazi icon, Americans were simultaneously taking a stand themselves. One of the most important factors driving this process was Mann's physical presence in the country, which opened up entirely new avenues of reception.

Harvard 1935

Publishers, promoters, and journalists acting according to their own commercial agendas were largely responsible for crafting Mann's public image in the United States during the 1920s and early 1930s. Things got much messier during the second half of the 1930s. For one thing, Mann himself became an increasingly visible presence on the American scene and influenced his reception through his own words and actions. This influence was not always welcome; both Alfred A. Knopf and Agnes E. Meyer (the powerful wife of the *Washington Post* publisher Eugene Meyer, who adored Mann and appointed herself as his patron and protector) implored the author to be more guarded about his political views. Another reason why Mann's reception became more complex in the late 1930s was that his image had now been cultivated for more than a decade and could no longer be so easily manipulated. American audiences had built up a complex set of expectations, and as new works by the German author were published (Knopf had by now pretty much exhausted Mann's extensive back catalog and was forced to translate whatever the author handed him to fulfill his contractual obligations), they sometimes collided with existing assumptions.

Perhaps no other episode illustrates this complex web of entanglements as clearly as the story of Mann's 1935 degree from Harvard University, the one that he would exploit for such great effect when he broke with the Nazis. This story begins on March 15, 1935, when the author received a letter from Dr. James B. Conant, the president of Harvard, informing him that the university's governing board had voted to confer upon him an honorary doctorate of letters at Harvard's 299th commencement exercises. Mann was torn. On the one hand, he recognized that such an award would send an unmistakable signal to the Third Reich, noting in his diaries that "the matter is dear to me, because of Germany" (Tb., March 15, 1935). On the other hand, he feared interrupting work on his novel *Joseph in Egypt* and perhaps also sensed that accepting the degree might stir up a hornet's nest in Berlin. In the end, he sent a dilatory telegram and only leaped into action after a friend who had held a visiting professorship at Columbia impressed upon him the significance of a Harvard degree (D, 236; Tb., March 16, 1935).[12] On June 10, 1935, Mann embarked for New York, and ten days later received the Harvard doctoral hood amid the "tremendous acclamation" (D, 242; Tb., June 21, 1935) of the roughly six thousand invited guests at the commencement ceremony. Indeed, the *Boston Post* specifically reports that Mann, along with fellow honoree Albert Einstein, received the loudest applause of any of the honorary degree recipients.[13]

It is worth asking what exactly the Harvard students and parents were celebrating when they gave Mann such a tremendous welcome. Innocent as this query may seem, two very different, and seemingly contradictory, narratives may be advanced to answer it. Together, they illustrate the complex role the German author had come to play within American popular consciousness by the middle of the 1930s.

The first narrative takes us to the circumstances immediately surrounding the 1935 commencement ceremony. When he wrote to Thomas Mann that March, James B. Conant was in the second year of what would eventually turn out to be one of the most transformative presidencies in the history of Harvard University. A research chemist by training, Conant's main priority throughout the 1930s was to accelerate Harvard's transformation from an elite liberal arts college with a smattering of adjoining graduate programs into a full-blown research university. To this end, he abolished athletic scholarships and instituted policies governing faculty promotions that anticipated the modern tenure-track system. He also staunchly defended the idea that academics should be held accountable first and foremost to the scholarly ethos of their profession, and not to the dictates of creed or country. This belief put him on a collision course with the Massachusetts legislature, which in early 1935, amid widespread fear of radical anarchism following the Great

Depression, enacted a teacher's loyalty oath, requiring all instructors in the commonwealth to swear allegiance to both the state and the federal constitutions. By contrast, Conant (who publicly testified against the oath) believed that teachers should be evaluated solely on their competence to guide students toward leadership in their respective fields. "Leadership," he further explained in an interview with the *New York Times Magazine* published less than two weeks before the commencement exercises, needed to be fostered not only in technical disciplines, but also in "cultural" ones: "writers, poets, philosophers, artists, professors, lawyers, doctors." Conant concluded that "in all these walks of life, the distinguished men profoundly influence the thought and action of the whole country."[14]

Mann, whose Nobel Prize was less than six years old and whose *Tales of Jacob* was still cluttering up nightstands across the country, was clearly invited because he was regarded as a "cultural leader" who might set an excellent example for future Harvard students. Kenneth Murdock, dean of the Faculty of Arts and Sciences and a close ally of Conant's, even approached the Harvard German Department with a proposal to hire Mann as a visiting Kuno Francke Professor, though the department declined, pointing out (probably rightly) that Mann would have been unlikely to fulfill the teaching duties that traditionally came along with that title.[15] Conant's influence is even more readily discernable in the case of Albert Einstein. Only a year earlier, the committee responsible for selecting honorary degree recipients in the physical sciences had still rejected Einstein's nomination on the ludicrous grounds that he "had done nothing of original value since 1915" (covert anti-Semitism was a far more likely explanation).[16] Following an inquiry by Conant, the physicist's name was added to the lists for the 1936 tercentenary, and eventually moved up to 1935.

Thomas Mann and Albert Einstein may well have been the most celebrated degree recipients at the 1935 commencement exercises. But they were not the most talked-about by a long shot. Also receiving honorary doctorates that day were three close allies of Franklin Delano Roosevelt: the agricultural secretary (and later vice president) Henry A. Wallace, the senior diplomat Norman Davis, and the liberal publisher William A. White (figure 3.2). To Conant—and to his closest associates in this matter, such as George R. Agassiz, chairman of the Committee on Honorary Degrees of the Board of Overseers, and Jerome D. Greene, secretary of the Harvard Corporation—these men undoubtedly represented further examples of lives lived in the service of democratic citizenship and cultural leadership; the degree citation for Henry A. Wallace, for example, barely mentions politics and instead turns him into a moral beacon when it lauds his "courage to

FIGURE 3.2.   The 1935 honorary degree recipients of Harvard University. Seated from left to right: Norman Davis, William A. White, Albert Einstein, James B. Conant, Henry A. Wallace, and Thomas Mann. Boston Public Library, Leslie Jones Collection.

attempt an uncharted journey in our modern wilderness." To the genteel conservatives who dominated Harvard social life, however, these men (and especially Wallace, a chief architect of the New Deal) were the embodied anathema of all they held dear. The Republican congressman Hamilton Fish, Harvard '10, gave a long speech on Class Day (the day preceding the commencement exercises, reserved for alumni activities) in which he lambasted Conant and Wallace, and praised Calvin Coolidge.[17] Other alumni made their displeasure known by letter or telegram. "Why in hell give Wallace a degree? . . . A degree to him is surely the bologna," cabled one of them. "A departure of the University from its traditional standards of Americanism," fulminated another.[18] The flood of letters was so unrelenting, and so obviously at odds with the self-understanding of the Conant administration, that it caused Jerome D. Greene to muse, "It has been astonishing to me to find that there are Harvard Graduates who consider that the function of a university, whether in appointing professors or in conferring academic honors, is thereby to certify their espousal of the particular doctrines and beliefs of the persons thus honored."[19]

The "tremendous" applause that greeted both Mann and Einstein at the 1935 commencement may, in other words, have seemed so enthusiastic only because it contrasted with the far more restrained reception reserved for Wallace, Davis, and White, who took to the podium immediately prior to and immediately after the distinguished German guests. Some of the students, parents, and alumni of Harvard University who were in the audience that day may not have known much about Mann at all. Many others surely knew who we was but still embraced his particular brand of "cultural leadership" as an unthreatening counterexample to the ostensible radicalism of the New Deal figureheads.

There is a second narrative that can be put forward to answer the question why Mann received such an enthusiastic reception, however. This second explanation starts a year earlier, at the university's even more tumultuous graduation exercises in 1934. This was Conant's first commencement as university president, and he had had little influence over its advance planning. He would presumably have relished an opportunity to somehow disinvite its most controversial participant, even though there was no possibility of doing so, since said participant was an alumnus, not an honorary degree recipient. Ernst "Putzi" Hanfstaengl, Harvard '09, was a German American who had wormed his way to the inner seats of power of the Third Reich by playing piano for Adolf Hitler. By 1934 he was the head of the German Foreign Press Bureau, a role that put him in charge of all propaganda efforts in the United States.[20] He was ostensibly in town to celebrate his twenty-fifth graduation anniversary but also made it publicly known that he intended to donate a substantial sum of money to support Harvard's study-abroad programs in Germany.[21]

Hanfstaengl was a charismatic man who had made many influential friends during his time at the university, and Harvard in general was then characterized by an atmosphere of casual anti-Semitism. It thus doesn't surprise that many members of the campus community looked forward to his visit and that the *Harvard Crimson* even demanded he be given an honorary degree.[22] But these were hardly sentiments shared by the larger Boston public. The commencement weekend consequently descended into turmoil. On Class Day, Hanfstaengl, protected by two members of the Boston Police Anti-Radical Squad, marched across campus, giving a wave that, as the *Boston Post* noted, "was an exact replica of the Nazi salute and tickled the crowd" (figure 3.3). Meanwhile, members of the class of 1924 dressed up as Bavarian mountaineers and celebrated the recent repeal of prohibition by rolling out a beer truck and practicing their goose step amid raucous shouts of "Heil Hitler!" The commencement ceremony itself (from which Hanfstaengl, who was originally supposed to attend as an honorary marshal, wisely stayed absent) was interrupted by the repeated "down with Hitler" cries of two

FIGURE 3.3. Ernst "Putzi" Hanfstaengl salutes the crowd at the 1934 Harvard commencement. Boston Public Library, Leslie Jones Collection.

female members of the Communist Party USA, who had chained themselves to a balustrade and were only removed with great difficulty by the Cambridge police.[23]

Conant cannot have cherished his memories of this disaster, nor did he presumably soon forget the press conference at which Hanfstaengl was asked point-blank by a local rabbi whether he advocated the "extermination" of the Jews, or the editorial in the *New York Times* which concluded that "Dr. Hanfstaengl may or may not be a very charming person, but a university is no place for a man who devoted the best part of his lifetime to destroy intellectual freedom, humiliate the finest minds, and burn the books they produced."[24] Indeed, Conant already went into damage-control mode that very same weekend. At a speech to the Harvard alumni association, he pointedly observed that "whatever be the outcome of the uncertain future which the whole world faces, the universities must stand firm by their principle which insures the right of free inquiry and free debate."[25] And the theme of his baccalaureate sermon, delivered while the campus was abuzz with the news that Harvard had turned down the Hanfstaengl bequest, was "For what shall it profit a man if he shall gain the whole world but lose his own soul."[26] In light of all these facts, most accounts of the Hanfstaengl controversy come to the same conclusion: the invitations to Albert Einstein and Thomas Mann (arguably the two most prominent émigrés from Nazi Germany at the time) were likely issued in an attempt restore the university's reputation in time for its 1936 tercentennial. This was also the opinion of the *Boston Post* and of at least one alumnus who wrote in to President Conant.[27]

This second way of accounting for Thomas Mann's favorable reception at the Harvard commencement exercises illustrates that Americans were willing to embrace him as an anti-Nazi icon even before he formally broke his silence on the matter. After all, Mann—whatever he may have said or not said—was one of the most illustrious émigrés from Hitler's Germany, and American audiences formed their own interpretive strategies in order to make sense of his literary fame in the changing political landscape of the 1930s. Furthermore, these interpretive strategies had an undeniably self-serving component. In celebrating Mann, the Harvard community was able to simultaneously celebrate its alleged return to the humanistic values that had been so badly tarnished the previous year.

On first sight, these two interpretations seem to be at odds with one another. After all, the first, which juxtaposes Mann with Henry A. Wallace and other New Dealers, locates the source of the writer's appeal in his apolitical reputation. The second, which juxtaposes him with Ernst Hanfstaengl, locates this appeal instead in the growing public perception of Mann as an anti-Nazi figurehead. As the widely diverging alumni responses to the award make clear, however, there is actually no reason to choose one interpretation over the other. Both were true at the same time: conservative attendees may well have viewed Mann primarily as an antagonist to Wallace; more liberal ones, as an antagonist to Hitler. In either case, however, the spectators were driven by motives that Mann himself could not possibly comprehend and that were deeply American in nature.

The Popular Front

The students, parents, and alumni of Harvard University weren't the only people to project complex and internally contradictory feelings upon Thomas Mann following his public declaration for the anti-Nazi cause, of course. The 1930s were a period in which the accepted relationship between culture and politics underwent a profound shift in American intellectual life, and Mann became both an object for, and an active participant in, the debates that ensued. Americans did not simply wait to have their German interlocutor explain the Nazi mind to them. They had theories, ambitions, and agendas of their own.

The reputation as the "greatest living man of letters" that Thomas Mann had acquired over the 1920s and early 1930s was, at heart, profoundly apolitical. Antifascists scouring the American literary scene for some kind of alternative aesthetic, however, would have found slim pickings. During the years of the Great Depression, the Communist Party USA threw its organizational, financial, and theoretical heft behind the so-called proletarian school of literature most ably represented by authors such as Mike Gold and Jack Conroy. The writers of the proletarian school found a receptive outlet in the party's cultural paper, the *New Masses*, and a social support system in the party-sponsored John Reed Clubs. With very few exceptions, however, their literature failed to rise to any great heights; instead, they offered doctrinaire Marxist analyses of US society in prose that generally "mimicked the flatness of Hemingway without his implied depth of feeling."[28] In both subject matter and style, they were worlds removed from Mann's rather patrician aloofness and from his coolly ironic technique.

This divergence is made especially clear in a letter that Agnes E. Meyer wrote to Thomas Mann in April 1937, exactly a week after she first made his acquaintance when she interviewed him for the *Washington Post*: "The mere mention by you of Goethe's name gave me a flash of insight and enables me to do a longer analysis of your significance as *Kulturmensch* as opposed to the political leader, the universal as opposed to the local point of view. Your development as an artist clarifies this whole question amazingly and gives the answer to our proletarian school of writers who must remain ineffective just because they are political and therefore local and limited" (*Br. AM*, 77). It's not hard to see from the cloying style of these lines why Mann would in subsequent years frequently refer to his American patron with the exasperated epithet *die Meyer*. But the argument is not without internal logic and furthermore is highly illustrative of the American cultural landscape during the mid-1930s. Mann is described as a *Kulturmensch* and directly contrasted with the "political leader," an opposition that would have made sense both from within the German tradition, where *Kultur* and *Politik* were natural opposites, and from the American middlebrow perspective, which aimed at intellectual improvement rather than the implementation of specific political programs. Meyer furthermore juxtaposes Mann's "universal" vision to the "local and limited" focus of the proletarian novelists, a statement that implicitly pits the Berghof sanatorium, with its cosmopolitan inhabitants and wide-ranging philosophical allusions, against the naturalistic description of Depression-era tenements and coal towns in novels such as Gold's *Jews without Money* (1930), or Conroy's *The Disinherited* (1933).

Meyer was a Republican, and her reference to the proletarian school was not entirely innocent. Aware of Mann's recent political turn, she was clearly worried that the writer whom she so admired might pivot toward Marxism. In another letter from this period she implores him, "If the clouds should gather more darkly in Europe and the Marxists raise a clamor for your enlistment against the negative and destructive power of fascism, I beg you not to forget that the rational forces of democracy need your individual leadership to preserve the orderly progression of freedom and justice over here" (*Br. AM*, 75).

Meyer's fears were not unfounded. While representatives from the Communist Party USA weren't exactly knocking on Mann's hotel doors to recruit him for their cause, the cultural landscape in America had shifted in such a way as to bring the previously separate poles of proletarian and middlebrow literature much closer together. In August 1935, the Communist International, fearing that its previous denigration of non-Communist leftwing parties as "social fascists" might leave the Soviet Union isolated in case of an attack by Nazi Germany, adopted a new policy that soon came to be known as the "Popular Front." It called for an international collaboration of leftwing thinkers, a strategic alliance with social-democratic and liberal forces, and a de-emphasis of the proletarian nature of the coming revolution. On a tactical level, the cultural historian Serge Guilbaut notes, "the Popular Front would have to attract prestigious figures, well-known bourgeois artists and writers, in order to confront the enemy with a strong and credible image, the image of a united and dynamic front." Of further importance was "the Popular Front's rehabilitation of the notion of culture that had been defended by the bourgeoisie against earlier communist attacks. By defending the national cultural heritage, the revolutionary party was able to forge an alliance with the middle classes, which might otherwise have been susceptible to a similar culturally based appeal from the fascists."[29]

In America, as in most of western Europe, a number of new organizations came into being to advocate for these strategic and tactical goals of the Popular Front. Foremost among these was the American Writers' Congress (held in 1935), which gave birth to the League of American Writers (in existence 1935–43), as well as the American Artists' Congress (1935–42). Thomas Mann made an obvious target of interest for these groups. He was both a quintessentially bourgeois artist and a well-known defender of the notion of "national culture."

The distance that the Popular Front needed to bridge in order to reach out to the German author was not nearly as large as it might seem at first glance. Although most contemporary commentators categorize Mann as a liberal, or sometimes even as a conservative, he had also been flirting with socialist ideas ever since the days of the 1918 Spartacus uprising, when Communist activists staged an unsuccessful revolution in Germany (see, e.g., *D*, 22–23; *Tb.*, November 12 and November 29, 1918).[30] Already in 1930 he had, furthermore, anticipated the central insight of the Popular Front when he argued that "the political place of the German bourgeoisie is now next to social democracy" (*GW*, 11:889). His work with organizations such as the Association for the Protection of German Writers or the international PEN Clubs during the days of the Weimar Republic had also acquainted him with the kind of programmatic committee work that characterized the ever-expanding archipelago of Popular Front organizations. Now that the die had been cast against Hitler, Thomas Mann threw himself into the new struggle. In cooperation with his more overtly political brother Heinrich, Thomas wrote speeches, planned meetings, and collected money. His manifesto, "A Declaration in Support of the Struggle for Freedom" appeared in the Popular Front magazine *Das Wort*, published in Moscow, on July 21, 1937. Three months later he sent greetings to the Communist-backed European Conference for Justice and Freedom in Germany (*Tb.*, October 27, 1937). Most importantly, however, he participated in the efforts to create a German People's Front in Paris, sending a letter of praise to the organizing committee in March 1937 (*Tb.*, March 21, 1937) and then, after this committee's work came to naught, personally organizing an inaugural meeting, for which he also raised money, in September 1938.[31]

These networking efforts soon touched the American Popular Front as well. If Mann's first two trips to the United States had largely been celebratory occasions—in 1934, to promote the release of *The Tales of Jacob*, and in 1935 to receive his honorary doctorate—his third trip in April 1937 assumed a different face entirely. Nominally, he came to deliver a series of lectures in celebration of the Graduate Faculty of Political and Social Science, otherwise known as the University in Exile, which had been founded as a refuge for displaced Jewish academics at the New School for Social Research. But while in New York, he also addressed a gathering of the North American Committee to Aid Spanish Democracy, gave a lecture attacking anti-Semitism at Carnegie Hall, promoted the American Guild for German Cultural Freedom, and spoke out in favor of a proactive stance against fascism at the former home of the New York Shriners, the Mecca Temple. The North American Committee to Aid Spanish Democracy was a Popular Front organization plain and simple, and his appearance there encouraged the organizers of the 1937 American Artists' Congress to issue an invitation to Mann as well. He was unable to attend but sent a telegram that received extensive coverage in the American press. The next year, following his decision to permanently relocate to the United States, Mann also participated in the widely publicized "Save Czechoslovakia!" rally that coincided with the Munich Conference. There, he spoke in front of an audience of twenty thousand, the largest gathering he ever addressed in the United States.

Mann's decision to promote Prince Hubertus zu Löwenstein's American Guild for German Cultural Freedom (an organization that nobody would suspect of proximity to the Communist Party) just two days after he spoke to the North American Aid Committee demonstrates that his engagements were not driven by any specific political agenda. Mann did not actively seek out the Popular Front, he simply seized every opportunity that presented itself in order to speak on topics close to his heart. In later years, his ignorance (or carelessness) as to the exact nature of the organizations with which he corresponded would repeatedly get him into trouble. From the perspective of the American Popular Front, however, these appearances provided valuable PR opportunities. And in turn, the wide publicity that they received went a long way toward revising America's image of the famous author. Previously he had been a remote entity, who resided far away on his "magic mountain" and communicated with the US public mostly through dense and voluminous tomes. Now, however, he became a living person, who frequented raucous New York political assemblies and received coverage in the news section of the papers, rather than just in the cultural pages.

The most important effect that the advent of the Popular Front had on Thomas Mann's reception in the United States was literary rather than personal, however. By shifting the cultural landscape in America, the Popular Front opened up avenues of reception that had been closed off during earlier periods. Put in the simplest terms, Mann could now be read in a different way, even if his literary works did not self-evidently illustrate his newly adopted political outlook.

Popular Front Strategies

Several factors contributed to this process. The first and arguably the most important was that the Popular Front strategy of downplaying doctrinaire Marxist aesthetics and references to the class struggle short-circuited any lingering conceptual opposition between "culture" and "politics." The defense of cultural traditions, even in their most abstract and universal sense, could henceforth be recognized as an inherently political act. As the liberal intellectual Lewis Mumford put it in his opening address at the First American Artists' Congress: "The time has come for the people who love life and culture to . . . be ready to protect and guard, and if necessary, fight for the human heritage which we, as artists, embody." Embodiments of "human heritage" were a genre that Mann specialized in, and here it was given political acuity. As Mumford further proclaimed, "[Dictators] rightly believe that if the forces represented by the artist are allowed to exercise their will, they will disrupt the Fascist regime. The irrepressible impulse of Art may upset the whole Fascist program."[32]

A year after Mumford spoke these words, the Spanish Republic came into being, proudly standing up against Hitler and Benito Mussolini while giving a home to left-wing artists and intellectuals. By the time that the American Artists' Congress met for the second time, in December 1937, however, Francisco Franco's forces were already on the march, and Pablo Picasso, who was to have been the keynote speaker, could only send a telegram in which he offered rather weak assurances that "the Democratic Government of the Spanish Republic has taken all the necessary measures to protect the artistic treasures of Spain." The impact of this message was completely overshadowed by the competing telegram that the congress organizers had solicited from Thomas Mann, and which was read out by his daughter Erika, who happened to be in attendance. "Of all speakers of the evening," *Time* magazine informed its readers in a full-page special, "Erika Mann had the simplest and to many listeners the most significant words to justify the American Artist's Congress." The message that she delivered read in part as follows: "One frequently hears it said that the artist should stick to his own craft, and that he merely cheapens himself when he descends into the political arena to participate in the struggles of the day. I consider this a weak objection, because of my conviction, or rather my clear realization, of the fact that the different spheres of humanity—whether artistic, cultural, or political—are really inseparable."[33]

To anybody who had been paying any attention to Mann's career over the last three decades, these words must have appeared odd indeed. This was a man, after all, who had once published an eight-hundred-page book called *Reflections of a Nonpolitical Man*, in which he argued for the exact opposite of what he was now claiming. But because *Reflections* had never been published in America, it became possible for Mann to redefine the very foundations of his artistic and intellectual outlook in a manner that he could not have achieved in Europe, with its far tighter networks of cultural exchange and reception.[34] Over the course of the coming years, Mann again and again repeated his message of art as an inherently political activity, virtually always in front of sympathetic audiences. The dissenting voices were few, the most important among them that of James T. Farrell, a prominent leftist critic of the Popular Front strategy, who in a letter to the editor of the *New York Herald Tribune* accused Mann of affecting a "language of incantation and exhortation" when he focused on art rather than on a scientific analysis of social life.[35]

American audiences were primed to receive what Mann had to tell them in large part because the Popular Front had similarly equated culture and politics as it attempted to unite bourgeoisie and proletariat against fascism. Needless to say, few of the middle-class Americans who came to hear Thomas Mann lecture maintained any conscious links with left-wing activist circles, though as the cultural historian Michael Denning notes, "a 1942 *Fortune* poll found that 25% of Americans favored socialism and another 35% had an open mind about it."[36] Furthermore, the reach of the Popular Front in the late 1930s extended well into the middlebrow canon. In the Pulitzer Prize–winning play *There Shall Be No Night* (1940) by Robert E. Sherwood, for example, which is set to the backdrop of the 1939–40 Winter War between the Soviet Union and Finland, one of the characters gives an impassioned speech comparing the Finnish national epic, the *Kalevala*, to the Declaration of Independence. The parallels to Mann, whose proclamations against Nazism were steeped in allusions to Goethe, Wagner, and Nietzsche, are obvious.[37]

By the late 1930s, then, the American public was used to seeing "culture" discussed in a political context. A second crucial factor leading to new avenues of reception for Thomas Mann lay in the international orientation of the Popular Front and of cultural movements throughout the 1930s more generally. Over the course of this decade, the interest in foreign peoples surged as a series of military conflicts shook the globe: the Italian invasion of Abyssinia in 1935, the Spanish Civil War of 1936–39, the Second Sino-Japanese War of 1937, and finally the Winter War.[38] Furthermore, as Michael Denning notes, the culture of the Popular Front not only amplified but also "transformed the ways people imagined the globe. It did this in its daily work of helping refugees, organizing tours, and holding benefit performances and dances for Spanish and Russian war relief. But it also did this through the international stories [that it] dramatized."[39] In other words, American interest in the world moved from the merely belletristic to the political, from unmodified exceptionalism toward an embrace (however hesitant and partial) of international solidarity.

As a prominent émigré writer, Thomas Mann could readily satisfy these interests. Even on the rare occasions on which he did not speak about

Germany explicitly, his mere presence told an international story of its own. But Mann went much further than that. A common theme of many of his addresses between 1937 and 1939 was the transnational character of German art. Already in December 1936, in a letter to the editor of the *New York Times*, Mann had declared, "To the extent to which German culture transcends beyond the borders of the Reich ethnologically and linguistically, its conception is higher than that of the State. That is Germanic freedom. No president of an official chamber of culture can subdue it" (SP, 18; *GW*, 13:638). And when he spoke to the American Guild, he similarly invoked a continuing German spirit "deprived of any support in the state" (*GW*, 11:943).

This transnational posture would have been impossible to convincingly maintain without the groundwork that had been laid by middlebrow reception networks during the 1920s. The American conception of Thomas Mann had, in truth, always been transnational in the sense that he was promoted as the exponent of abstract and portable cultural values. What changed now was that this transnationalism acquired a political edge. Suddenly Thomas Mann the German author who carried culture with him into exile was placed in opposition to all university deans and "presidents of official chambers of cultures." When Mann, upon arriving in America in February 1938, declared, "where I am is Germany," he was thus merely giving a pithy shape to a sentiment that both he and the American press had expressed many times before. Perhaps this is another reason why only one newspaper bothered to quote him verbatim.

A final factor enabling new avenues of reception for Thomas Mann, besides the political reorientation of culture and the new openness toward international affairs, came with the American left's embrace of popular mythology as a weapon against fascism. No other moment crystallizes this development as well as the day in April 1935 on which Kenneth Burke took to the podium at the First American Writers' Congress to deliver a lecture titled "Revolutionary Symbolism in America." Burke had come a long way since serving as one of Thomas Mann's earliest translators into English in the years following the First World War. Over the course of the 1920s, he had turned into the de facto face of the Greenwich Village *bohème* and a key spokesman for international modernism. As late as 1931, he celebrated Mann as an apolitical, thoroughly modernist artist, lumping him together with André Gide to ask, "Are not these men trying to make us at home in indecision, are they not trying to humanize the state of doubt? . . . Perhaps there is an evasion, a shirking of responsibility, in becoming certain too quickly, especially when our certainties involve reversions to an ideology which has the deceptive allurement of tradition."[40] But over the course of the next few years, which also marked his transition from the *Dial* to the more mainstream *Nation*, he moved further to the left and reconsidered his former positions. In a 1934 review of Mann's *Past Masters and Other Papers* in the *New Republic*, he no longer spoke of a "home in indecision" but instead lamented the German author's tendency to fall "into what [Harry Slochower] has called the 'bottomless pit of indiscriminate sympathizing.' "[41] Given the overwhelming presence of injustice, bigotry and oppression in the world, Burke now argued, the artist was morally obligated to pick a side.

Also in the early 1930s, Burke began to develop the outlines of what would later come to be known as his "philosophy of symbolic action": a theory of how the symbolic nature of human language conditions our responses to the world. It was in this capacity as a theoretician of symbolic action that Burke took to the stage in 1935 and urged that the terms "the masses" or "the workers" henceforth be replaced with "the people" in all left-wing publications: "In suggesting that 'the people,' rather than 'the worker' rate highest in our hierarchy of symbols, I suppose I am suggesting fundamentally that one cannot extend the doctrine of revolutionary thought among the lower middle class without using middle-class values."[42]

From the very beginning, both Burke himself and his proposals were greeted with frank skepticism by the hard left. Joseph Freeman, the editor of the Communist literary journal the *New Masses* is supposed to have shouted either "We have a snob among us!" or "We have a traitor among us!" (accounts vary).[43] The lingering confusion between these two alternatives illustrates what strange bedfellows modernists (i.e., the snobs), the middle class (i.e., the traitors), and the Communist left made at this singular moment in US cultural history. At any rate, Burke's suggestions quickly became Popular Front dogma, especially when they were vindicated by very similar instructions from Moscow after the Seventh Congress of the Communist International. Throughout the late 1930s, American artists with leftist sympathies began to churn out works celebrating not the class struggle of the international proletariat but rather the heroic spirit of ordinary American people, including such mythological figures as the American cowboy and frontiersman. The murals of the Works Progress Administration are one famous expression of this tendency; Aaron Copland's compositions, such as *Billy the Kid* (1938), *Fanfare for the Common Man* (1942), and *Appalachian Spring* (1944), another.[44] This new celebration of ordinary people found its summit in the veneration of Abraham Lincoln. The American volunteers who fought in the Spanish Civil War called themselves the Abraham Lincoln Brigade, and over the course of the late 1930s, numerous works dedicated to the American president were published, centrally among them Daniel Gregory Mason's *Lincoln Symphony* (1936), Robert E. Sherwood's Pulitzer Prize–winning play *Abe Lincoln in*

Illinois (1938), and Carl Sandburg's four-volume biography (final volume 1939). In the celebration of the common man, coupled with the adjoining cult of Lincoln, the American Popular Front found a powerful rejoinder to the Nazi racial mythology, complete with its deification of the führer.

Thomas Mann's literary output during the 1930s could easily be assimilated to this general climate. From 1926 to 1943, he was at work on his monumental *Joseph* tetralogy, a retelling for a modern audience of stories drawn from the book of Genesis. The four volumes were published in America in 1934, 1935, 1938, and 1943, to increasing acclaim. Their publication sparked an important debate about Mann's mythic method and its relevance for popular politics. And Mann himself, much like the Popular Front artists around him, conceived of what he was doing as a conscious rebuttal of fascism. In a 1941 letter to Karl Kerényi, the Hungarian philologist who served as his mythological advisor, he wrote, "It is essential that myth be taken away from intellectual fascism and transmuted for humane ends. I have for a long time done nothing else" (*MH*, 103; *Br. KK*, 100).

Measure and Value

Amid all these changes to the conditions governing his American reception, Mann himself was busy rethinking what it might mean to be a representative writer who was cut off from the official cultural life of his nation. In this endeavor he was far from alone, since all the political émigrés of the time to some extent found themselves in the position of representing their countries, whether they had consciously wanted to in the past or not. There were two general trajectories that emerged. The first was defined most succinctly by the Dutch writer Menno ter Braak, who proclaimed in the pages of the émigré journal *Das neue Tage-Buch*, "Well written books that have been composed in good taste but could also have been written by any other author . . . are 'meaningless.' It's something else that matters, namely the contemporary relevance."[45] Authors who followed this advice consequently turned toward "engaged literature," believing that under conditions of fascism, politics superseded aesthetics. The other trajectory was the one taken by Prince Hubertus zu Löwenstein, who founded his German Academy on the belief that aesthetics rather than politics were what counted most at this point, and that "true" German literature could easily be separated from the corrupted institutions of the Nazi state.

For all his initial sympathies with the Löwenstein project, Mann ultimately chose a different route. In early August 1937, a few months after his return to Switzerland from his third trip to the United States, he launched the inaugural issue of a new periodical called *Mass und Wert* (*Measure and Value*, sometimes also translated as *Standards and Values*). Although *Measure and Value* was never commercially successful and folded with the outbreak of the Second World War, Thomas Mann's name on the masthead nevertheless gave the journal outsized importance within the émigré community.[46] The foreword for the inaugural issue also provided Mann with a welcome opportunity to sum up his evolving stance as a representative writer.

As a German-language publication, *Measure and Value* never saw wide distribution in America. But since the journal was published by the Swiss firm of Emil Oprecht rather than by Gottfried Bermann Fischer, Alfred E. Knopf could not assert his exclusive contractual bond with Fischer. Agnes E. Meyer, who had remained in continuous contact with Mann throughout the summer of 1937 and had repeatedly signaled her eagerness to publish some of his writings in the *Washington Post*, pounced at this opportunity. She secured the rights to translate Mann's foreword herself. It appeared on Sunday, August 15, in both the *Post* and the *New York Times*—an early example of a Mann text that was published nearly simultaneously in German and English translation.[47]

In his foreword, Mann seeks to chart out a course for art that would avoid the twin extremes of politics and aestheticism that characterized so much of the German emigration. After briefly sketching the two opposing positions, he launches into a paean to art's "revolutionary traditionalism" (*OD*, 90–91; *GW*, 12:800). Art is "traditional," according to this account, because it aims to "preserve something which has heretofore comprised the dignity of mankind: the idea of a supra-personal, supra-party, supra-national measure and value." At the same time, however, it is also revolutionary "in that it would not take [its goal] untried out of any past whatever but would undertake to test it in utter sincerity by present conditions" (*OD*, 92–93; *GW*, 12:802). Far from being a mere reaction to local circumstances, in other words, art aims for truths that would encompass all humanity. At the same time, these truths need to be able to stand up to the violence imposed by fascist societies.

If Mann had left it at these rather banal pronouncements, then the many reviewers who criticized his essay as being vague and impractical would certainly have been justified. But the foreword to *Measure and Value* eventually articulates an original point. For Mann brings the discussion around to a consideration of Nazi totalitarianism, which he contrasts with an alternate model of totality in social life:

> Totality: there is only one, the totality of humanity, of the human. In it the politico-social field is a segment and part. . . . From the delusion

that one can be a man of culture and unpolitical much harm to Germany has ensued. But must the German always go from one extreme to the other? Must he always, when he corrects his blunders, make them worse. . . ? Must he now insist on "totalizing" politics and the State—which is far worse than his previous neglect of them, the first being a sin of omission against humanity as a whole, while the second, the forcing of everything human into the political sphere, is a crime and can only result in the committing of more and more crimes? (*OD*, 95–96; *GW*, 12:805)

The most interesting thing about this passage is the apparent renunciation of *Reflections of a Nonpolitical Man* contained in the line "from the delusion that one can be a man of culture and unpolitical much harm to Germany has ensued." Instead, the foreword to *Measure and Value* argues that "culture" is not so much an antithesis to "politics," but rather a larger set that encompasses it.[48] Against the Nazi state, in which culture is entirely subjected to the dictates of politics, Mann thus pits an alternate conception of a "human totality" in which politics is but one "segment and part" of a larger cultural vision. In so doing, he also assigns a prominent leadership role to the artist, rather than to the political demagogue.

What would it mean to submit politics to culture in the way that Mann here proposes? The passage just quoted recalls Mann's definition of "aestheticism" in *Reflections*, where the term refers to an attitude that tries to avoid partisan prejudices and aims to consider all sides of any given issue. To consider politics as a subsegment of "human totality," then, would mean to implement practical actions not according to the dictates of a programmatic vision, but rather out of a desire to achieve the harmonic synthesis of competing viewpoints.[49] Put slightly differently, it implies the submission of practical action to a larger noumenal vision—to an idea of culture that isn't bounded by empirical particulars, such as language and history, but rather applicable to "humanity as a whole."

The foreword to *Measure and Value* remains disappointingly vague as to what such a universal idea of culture might actually look like. Strong clues can be found in the essay's rhetorical structure, however, for the foreword abounds in religious allusions and explicit invocations of Christian ideas. "Whenever we are concerned with values and their defence, with the preservation of a universally applicable human standard," Mann thus proclaims, "we must stand, firmly and in freedom, upon the human culture of Occidental Christianity" (*OD*, 97; *GW*, 12:806). And about the Nazis he says, "Their inhuman activities must bring them into conflict with every sort of freedom, that is clear; but in particular the freedom of the Christian must be a thorn in their sides, and so now we see them in the act of 'conquering Christendom'" (*OD*, 96; *GW*, 12:805).

Mann's decision to give such a Christian cast to his *Measure and Value* foreword may well have been motivated by the success of an address he had given just a few months earlier, during his April 1937 visit to New York City. This lecture was delivered to the University in Exile at the New School and took as its theme the phrase "To the Living Spirit," which had adorned one of the main buildings at the University of Heidelberg until 1936, when the Nazis replaced it with the inscription "To the German Spirit." Much of the New School lecture was cobbled together from talking points that Mann also used elsewhere during this period. But religious undercurrents seeped into his text as well. Thus Mann calls upon the modern writer to take a "spiritual stand" (geistiger Standpunkt) against Nazi barbarism (LS, 265; *GW*, 13:337). This was a common locution in his writings that can be traced all the way back to the earliest days of his representative strivings. Here, however, it is developed in an unprecedented fashion. Within the span of a few pages, it is linked to the "world spirit" and then the "will of God—which the spirit of man must serve" (LS, 268; *GW*, 13:340). Mann also compares his own past reluctance to take a "spiritual stand" against Nazism to the hesitation of Moses to become a vessel for the Lord. The entire passage culminates in a quotation from Goethe: "The spirit of man will never soar above the sublimity of the moral discipline of Christianity as it shines radiantly in the Gospels" (LS, 269, translation modified; *GW*, 13:341).

Mann's decision to take such an uncharacteristic swerve into Christian theology was more than a little awkward, given that he was addressing an audience comprised largely of émigré Jews. But the lecture clearly was a success, as witnessed by the fact that the New School adopted the phrase "To the Living Spirit" as its motto soon after. And this success, in turn, may well have convinced Mann that going forward, the easiest way to position himself as a cultural antagonist to Nazism was through a religiously inflected language.

This strategy put Mann at odds with other dominant currents of the émigré press. At one point of his foreword to *Measure and Value*, for example, Mann turns the discussion directly toward socialism: "Socialists, yes we are that. Not necessarily because we swear by the Marxist philosophy. It is not quite in our line to envisage the spiritual as the 'ideological superstructure' or to see the creative fundamental fact of life in the light of economic class-conceptions" (*OD*, 98, translation modified; *GW*, 12:807). Adherents of the international Popular Front were genuinely mystified by this passage and by the vaguely spiritualized understanding of "socialism" that it proposed. Fritz

Erpenbeck, the editor-in-chief of the Moscow-based Popular Front journal *Das Wort*, dismissed Mann with the words, "Those who believe they can create *Measure and Value* from the myth of a "spirituality" that hovers self-righteously above society are unfree, for they are slaves of social reality."[50] The philosopher Ernst Bloch, writing in the pages of the Prague-based *Neue Weltbühne*, was more conciliatory, stating that "the most valuable goods of humanity are saved by [Mann's] reflections and put into opposition to fascism."[51] He too, however, ultimately expressed doubts whether a spiritualized antifascism could ever lead to anything but political quietude.

In the American context, on the other hand, these vaguely religious allusions readily fed into the general tendency to think of the United States as a Judeo-Christian nation at war with "godless fascism." Mann's remarks also provided welcome opportunities to dissociate their author from the streams of Marxist refugees then pouring across US borders to the chagrin of many conservative Americans. Meyer's *Washington Post* thus printed Mann's remarks about socialism under the unauthorized subheading "Science, Art, Culture Not of Class Origin." The *New York Times* chose the subheading "Transcending Marxian Limits" for the same paragraphs.[52] Even as Mann's proximity to the US Popular Front won him new audiences, then, his traditional middle-class readership created its own image of what the author stood for.

Princeton 1938–1940

By the time of his 1938 arrival in the United States, Mann clearly no longer was the same "greatest living man of letters" who had been heralded during the time of the Great Depression. The earlier epithet had been rooted in a rather vague and thoroughly apolitical understanding of international culture as a means for social improvement. During the mid-1930s, however, ordinary Americans began to display a greater interest in politics, and their understanding of international affairs became more sophisticated. Mann developed new and more ambitious representative aspirations as well. His notion of humanist culture as a "totalizing force" that could be placed in opposition to totalitarian politics displayed strongly Christian undertones and resonated with concurrent attempts by the American Popular Front to harness "myth" as an intellectual tool against fascism.

No other term was as central for Mann's reinvention as a representative writer, however, as "tradition." Tradition was the concept that transformed the eternal recurrence of the same promised by myth into a solid weapon against the Nazis. If the totalitarian state controlled all the cultural institutions through which new German-language literature was produced, validated, and disseminated, then Mann could at least take recourse in the cultural authority bestowed by the past. Alfred A. Knopf, as a publisher of contemporary literature, could be of only limited help in this endeavor. Universities, as the places where the literary inheritance of bygone ages was shaped into a coherent form, were much more valuable interlocutors. It thus proved to be extremely fortuitous that Mann, thanks to the intervention of his inveterate patron Agnes E. Meyer, received an offer to join the faculty of Princeton University as a lecturer in the humanities during the 1938–39 academic year, an appointment which was renewed for the spring semester of 1940. The Mann family would remain in Princeton for three years, until they relocated to Los Angeles, where they would spend the final eleven years of their American exile.

The Special Program in the Humanities that Mann joined at Princeton wasn't just any other college major. It was a trailblazing initiative, one of the first programs set up in the United States to facilitate interdisciplinary communication among scholars working in what had only recently come to be known as "the humanities."[53] Its creation in 1936 was a direct response to the formation of similar interdisciplinary initiatives in the social and hard sciences.[54] From the very beginning, the Special Program was also intended to include visiting lectureships by leading intellectuals from outside academia.[55] The first visiting lecturer to be hired in this capacity was the Pulitzer Prize–winning poet Archibald MacLeish, who left the university upon his appointment as the new librarian of Congress. His departure created a vacancy for Mann, whose reputation as a novelist and essayist, cultural commentator, and anti-Nazi polemicist made him an ideal fit for such an interdisciplinary endeavor.

While Mann's actual activities at Princeton were fairly circumscribed (he gave roughly a dozen public lectures and preceptorials during his two years at the university and had only very limited contact with any of the undergraduate students), his engagement there was far from random. Princeton's primary motive in hiring Thomas Mann was neither to support his creative writing nor even to provide a sinecure for one of the foremost representatives of the "great tradition of German culture" that Harvard had praised three years earlier. The university was interested in Mann as a syncretizing figure; he was valuable as a public symbol for the organic diversity of the humanities and also as a reminder of their relevance beyond the walls of the ivory tower. These ambitions are most readily discernable, perhaps, in the citation for the honorary doctorate that the university bestowed upon the author at the end of his first year as a lecturer. Here, he is praised as "a disciple" not merely "of Goethe and Schopenhauer" but also of "the great humanists of all time," as "a student of music who has drawn from this art significant lessons for literature," and as somebody who is "equally at home in ancient Egypt and contemporary Europe."[56] He is portrayed, in other words, as somebody able to summon at a moment's notice centuries' worth of interdisciplinary humanistic knowledge to serve both his art and his political interventions.

In line with these conditions and expectations, the majority of Mann's lectures and preceptorials at Princeton were facilitated by faculty members who weren't themselves experts in Germanic literature, such as the university's dean (and professor of French literature), Christian Gauss; the comparatist Harvey W. Hewett-Thayer; and the English professor Robert K. Root. Among Princeton's teachers of German, only a young professor by the name of Hans Jäger seems to have taken an interest in the famous visitor, and invited him to address his upper-division students. History does not record what the undergraduates thought of Mann's lecture "Über mich selbst" ("On Myself"), which was delivered over the course of two days in the author's characteristically uncompromising German.[57]

This lack of interest within Princeton's Germanic division can be partly explained by its weak standing within the university as a whole; during the 1930s, German at Princeton could not boast of a single full professor, and the Germanic division did not separate from the Department of Modern Languages and Literatures to form an entity in its own right until after the Second World War.[58] But more importantly, it is symptomatic of the larger state of the discipline in the United States during the late 1930s, when most leading German scholars and departments strenuously tried to remain aloof from contemporary affairs, either out of misguided cultural elitism, or—as unfortunately happened all too often—out of covert Nazi sympathies.[59] Princeton was no exception in this regard, despite the fact that virtually all the instructors there were American-born. In Ruth B. Bottigheimer's diplomatic phrasing, once war was declared, "the university as a whole threw itself into the military effort. . . . In the Germanic division, however, courses revolved not around military German, but instead around Goethe."[60]

As a polarizing figure who refused to keep literature and politics separate from one another, Mann aroused the suspicion of many a German professor, not just at Princeton but across America. Tellingly, virtually all the earliest academic exponents of Thomas Mann in the United States—such as Ludwig Lewisohn, Harry Slochower, Anna Jacobson, Howard Nemerov, and Lienhard Bergel—were Jewish, and thus outsiders in their profession. Hermann Weigand, the only notable gentile among this group, has vividly recalled the casual anti-Semitism that reigned in American German departments during the 1930s.[61] Similarly, the extant correspondence between Knopf and Fischer documents the opposition from conservative academics that the American publisher anticipated when Jacobson tried to publish an annotated college teaching edition of "Disorder and Early Sorrow" in 1927 (*Br. AJ*, 25).

Ordinarily, this opposition among a fairly small and institutionally circumscribed set of early readers might remain tangential to the larger story of Thomas Mann's reception in the United States. Much like Princeton, however, used its hire of the famous German author to underscore a fundamental change in the way in which it conceptualized its humanities programs, so Mann used his Princeton years to carefully evaluate what American academics might have to contribute to his ongoing transformation as a representative writer.

The crucial moment in this regard came in early May of 1939, when Mann received an invitation from Christian Gauss to speak to an upper-division course about *The Magic Mountain* during the final week of classes. Separated from the notes that had gone into the novel's composition by fifteen years of a rather tumultuous life, Mann revisited one of the few reliable works of criticism that he had at his disposal, namely Weigand's 1933 study *Thomas Mann's Novel "Der Zauberberg"* (*Tb.*, May 3, 1939). Weigand, who taught at Yale and had been on friendly terms with the Manns since the mid-1920s, had sent the author a copy of his monograph immediately after it was published, and Mann, then still getting used to his new role as an exile, had greeted it with evident gratitude, praising it as "phenomenal in its penetration and comprehension" (*Br. HW*, 119).

Mann's diaries do not record what sections in particular he reread as he prepared his 1939 lecture, but it stands to reason that he would have started with the chapter that he had praised six years earlier as the "heart and soul" (*Br. HW*, 119) of the entire study, the one titled "What is German?" There, Mann would have found an eloquent argument for Hans Castorp as the "embodiment of spiritual Germany" that was based centrally on the analytical category of language.[62] Working closely with *Reflections of a Nonpolitical Man* (a fact that made Weigand one of the first critics to recognize *Reflections* and *The Magic Mountain* as intimately linked rather than as antithetical poles in their author's political development), Weigand argues that Mann's ironic attitude in the novel represents first and foremost an attempt to implement what *Reflections* (and by implicit extension also the foreword to *Measure and Value*) had called an "aesthetic" attitude toward politics. Weigand's analysis therefore runs counter to many competing accounts of irony in modernist literature (both in Mann's own time and in ours) that read the trope primarily as a way of evading politics.[63] Instead, Weigand sees *The Magic Mountain* as an attempt to persuade German readers to embrace "logical clarity and psychological analysis" in language as a necessary precondition for pursuing national interests. He thereby also provides a concrete example of what it might mean to subsume politics to the larger "totality" of culture.

A second important source for Mann as he prepared for his lecture was an unsolicited manuscript titled "The Quester Hero: Myth as Universal Symbol in the Works of Thomas Mann" that he had received sometime earlier from a correspondent at Harvard named Howard Nemerov. In later years, Nemerov would acquire considerable fame in his own right as a poet and literary critic, serving two nonconsecutive terms as the poet laureate of the United States. In 1939, however, he was a mere junior at Harvard College. Had Mann realized this, he possibly would never have read Nemerov's manuscript, since he took a rather dim view of American undergraduates ("curious fellows" he called them, once he had delivered his lecture for Gauss's seminar [*Tb.*, May 10, 1939]).[64] The text was so sweeping and magisterial, however, that Mann assumed he was dealing with a talented junior professor.[65] Nemerov's main purpose in "The Quester Hero" is to detach *The Magic Mountain* from the merely national generic traditions (such as the bildungsroman) with which previous critics had associated it, and instead resituate it in the grander category of "quester narratives." As prime examples of such narratives, Nemerov cites the various medieval Grail legends but also invokes the Upanishads, the Egyptian Book of the Dead, the Polynesian legends of Maui, and various others.[66] Here, then, was an audacious and sweeping account arguing for Thomas Mann's place in world literature in the very grandest sense, an argument that bestowed upon him a kind of authority that the Nazis would never be able to touch.

Mann's reading of these critical sources allowed him to revisit a sensitive matter that had preoccupied him for at least the last five years. In 1934, following his return from his first journey to America, he had published a short essay in the cultural pages of the *Neue Zürcher Zeitung* called "Voyage with Don Quixote." It is a curious piece that combines an impressionistic account of Mann's transatlantic journey with literary notes about *Don Quixote*, especially the second part of that novel. Only on prolonged reflection does the deeper relation of these two themes emerge. For *Don Quixote* is, among many other things, also the tale of an author—Miguel de Cervantes—who lost control over his own literary creation when, in the absence of copyright regimes in the early modern period, an imposter issued an unauthorized sequel to his runaway bestseller. In his essay, Mann refers to this development as "terribly depressing for an author" (*ED*, 436; *GW*, 9:436), and he obviously related it to his own fate now that he was cut off from Germany, without any direct control over his reception there. True, he needed not fear that some Nazi storm trooper would write an unauthorized sequel to *The Magic Mountain*. But what if the state-controlled press and public education departments conspired to cast his works in a revisionist light? Allusions to the uncertainties surrounding the exile experience correspondingly abound in the essay. The steamer, for example, carries a group of Jews who are emigrating to America, and who are visited in their steerage accommodations by a young German onto whom Mann appears to have projected some of his own features.[67] There is also a lengthy analysis of Cervantes's story of the Moor Ricote, who is banished from Spain for his religion but returns in disguise because he cannot bear the pangs of exile.[68]

Five years later, Mann's warm reception at American universities and the intelligent, sympathetic reception he received from American critics convinced him that the Nazis would never be able to rewrite his place in cultural history. For beyond the German tradition of which he had for so long felt himself to be a part, there lay a larger, global cultural community: an "international republic of letters," as Hobart College had called it. Princeton's Special Program in the Humanities, in which scholars of all the European literatures taught side by side with historians and political scientists, provided a concrete institutional manifestation of this larger community. In the transcript of the lecture that he addressed to Christian Gauss's students, which was later published as "The Making of *The Magic Mountain*," Mann goes so far as to state, "I have been much helped by foreign criticism and I consider it a mistake to think that the author himself is the best judge of his work. He may be that while he is still at work on it and living in it. But once done, it tends to be something he has got rid of, something foreign to him; others as time goes on, will know more and better about it than he" (MoM, 45; GW, 11:614). For an author who was then regularly attacked in the German press in the most defamatory ways imaginable, this was quite an astounding thing to say. But Mann had come to recognize that there were defenders and able interpreters of the German tradition outside the Reich, and indeed, that there were other traditions of which it was worth being a part. This realization would be one of his central sources of consolation over the coming years, as he took up his cultural battle with Nazism in earnest.

Interlude II: *Lotte in Weimar* (1939)

Literary tradition, and specifically the question of how the public perception of an author is shaped by circulation and criticism, is one of the main topics of the first fictional work that Mann completed during his American exile: the novel *Lotte in Weimar*. This book was first published in America in 1940 as *The Beloved Returns*, though the British edition was called by the original title, and subsequent reprints have adopted this name as well. *Lotte in Weimar* is not strictly speaking a product of Mann's American period; he hatched the idea in 1933 (*Tb.*, November 19, 1933) and began working on it in earnest during the summer of 1936 (*Tb.*, August 25, 1936). Roughly half the novel, including the entirety of the crucial seventh chapter, was written in the United States, however, and Mann explicitly connected his literary work to his duties at Princeton when he wove a hidden allusion to the project into one of his preceptorials there (*GW*, 9:655).

Lotte in Weimar was inspired by the most unprepossessing of sources: a brief entry in Goethe's diaries for the year 1816 that reads, "Lunch with the Ridels and with Madame Kestner." The literary interest of this passage lies in the fact that "Madame Kestner" was none other than Charlotte Kestner née Buff, the real-life person who inspired the character of Lotte in *The Sorrows of Young Werther*, written after Goethe unhappily fell in love with her during the summer of 1772. The two models for one of the most famous romances in literary history were, in other words, reunited more than forty years after the fact, at a time when both were widowed and in their sixties. The basic tone of Mann's novel is dictated by the conflict between the rich dramatic potential of this event and its insultingly cursory treatment in Goethe's diaries.

Mann depicts Charlotte as a somewhat simple yet fundamentally likable woman whose entire life has been shaped by her involuntary fame as the heroine of an exceedingly popular and scandalous work of literature. She has come to Weimar to seek some kind of recompense, to finally merge with the more glorious literary character to whom people have been comparing her all her life, and perhaps even to rekindle her love affair with Goethe. Goethe, by contrast, is depicted as a remote and impersonal artist at the peak both of his literary powers and of his social and political influence at the Weimar court.

Given that Mann was an exiled artist who was painfully aware that his continuing acclaim and financial health would increasingly depend on the support of an English-speaking audience, *Lotte in Weimar* was a decidedly odd project to pursue. Mann had already published three volumes of his *Joseph* tetralogy to enormous success. Why did he not simply get on with it and write the fourth volume? Even his staunchest supporters in the United States had to concede that ordinary Americans would probably be overwhelmed by a novel that presupposed intimate familiarity with the details of Goethe's life and works. Agnes E. Meyer, at the conclusion of a long and glowing review for the *New York Times Book Review*, voiced fears that "some of the allusions to Goethe's works may be overlooked," while Clifton Fadiman, another long-time admirer, spoke of the novel as a *"jeu d'ésprit"* in the pages of the *New Yorker*.[1] Indeed, the critical reception was muted, and the Book-of-the-Month Club, which just two years prior had chosen *Joseph in Egypt* as one of its monthly selections, accorded the novel only the much more modest honor of a "recommendation." Nowadays *Lotte in Weimar* is virtually never read in the English-speaking world.[2]

The tiny crowd that actively promoted the book clearly recognized that if *Lotte in Weimar* was to have any success at all, it needed to be linked to Mann's political turn. Thus, Meyer called it "a book with a message for our times" and summarized her hero's recent attempts to bring "his German heritage of individualism and subjective idealism into the social field."[3] Alfred A. Knopf, displaying a considerable amount of chutzpah, proclaimed it "the first serious novel of European life since *The Magic Mountain*."[4] Many readers of *Lotte in Weimar* have since come to the conclusion that if the novel can be called a political statement at all, then that statement is to be found in Mann's depiction of Goethe as a counter-pole to the blusterous Romantic nationalism of his day. "They [the Romantic nationalists] think they are Germany, but I am" (*BR*, 331; *GKFA*, 9.1:327), Goethe declares at one point, even if only in an inner monologue. Taking into consideration Mann's well-documented tendency to identify with the earlier poet, one can further conclude that the novel's portrait of Goethe was intended as a sketch of how a contemporary artist might position himself vis-à-vis political power at an even darker point in German history. Tellingly, Goethe's reflection on his representative status is followed just a few lines later by a sentence lifted verbatim out of Mann's *Exchange of Letters*: "I am better suited to represent German traditions than to become a martyr for them" (*GKFA*, 9.1:327).[5] Such a reading can be complemented by two further facts that have so far received scant attention in the critical literature on *Lotte in Weimar*. First, Charlotte too can be seen as a vehicle for Thomas Mann's self-projection, and second, the highly original form of the work provides a commentary on the role that criticism and literary tradition play in establishing the author as a counter-pole to totalitarian power.

It is Charlotte, rather than Goethe, who stands at the center of the novel. Eight of nine chapters are devoted to her; only "The Seventh Chapter" (which is distinguished from the others by the fact that it is the only one to have a definite article in the title) is focused entirely on the poet. The six chapters that precede the Goethe interlude are devoted to successive encounters between Charlotte and members of Weimar court society during the hours following her arrival. The eighth chapter concerns a luncheon at Goethe's house, while the ninth tells the story of a final encounter (which may be entirely imaginary) between the two protagonists.

The common theme of the early encounters is that they comically juxtapose two different conceptions of art. Charlotte clings to a conception of aesthetics that was practiced by the young Goethe during his *Sturm und Drang* period, when he sought to create art by elevating intense personal experiences onto a higher and longer-lasting plane. She thinks of herself as a kind of objective correlative of Goethe's Lotte and has come to Weimar to finally assume that halo of glory that has so long been denied to her during her rather pedestrian life as Charlotte Buff. To this end, she has even brought with her a forty-year-old dress that she wore during her youthful flirtation with Goethe, which the poet immortalized in his novel. Outwardly of course, especially in conversations with her daughter Lottchen, Charlotte would never admit to all this. Her basic attitude is humorously summarized in an early conversation with Mager, the fictional head waiter of the Weimar inn in which she has just taken up rooms: "But my dear Herr Mager, you go too far, you greatly exaggerate, when you simply identify me, or even the young thing I once was, with the heroine of that much lauded book. . . . The character in the novel is quite different and distinct from my former self, to say nothing at all of my present one. For instance, anyone can see that my eyes are blue, whereas Werther's Lotte is well known to have black ones" (*BR*, 14; *GKFA*, 9.1:21).

Charlotte's principal obstacle is that she has aged several decades since her days as a real-life model for Lotte, and so appears utterly ridiculous when she dons her old dress to attend the luncheon at Goethe's house. This is not her only problem, however. Charlotte also fails to appreciate that she herself, and not just the fictional Lotte, also became an object of the public imagination the moment that she was touched by world history during Goethe's courtship. Other people now project hopes and fears onto her that have little to do with her actual life and everything to do with that of the poet. These two main problems are symbolically connected with one another through the fact that Charlotte in her old age is prone to fits of "trembling and nodding of the head" (*BR*, 5; *GKFA*, 9.1:12): she is quite literally unable to move into sharp focus in her own right.

Over the course of the opening six chapters, Charlotte first encounters two fictional characters, the waiter Mager and a young Irish dilettante named Miss Rose Cuzzle, who tours the courts of Europe to collect autographs and make sketches of famous people. Mager is the archetype of a naive reader who cannot distinguish between reality and fiction; he gratefully participates in Charlotte's fantasy of herself as Lotte. Things already turn darker with Rose Cuzzle, however, who is interested in the older woman exclusively because of her past association with Goethe and thus approaches her as a trophy to be bagged for her collection. After that, Charlotte meets a number of historical figures from Goethe's inner circle. In the critical literature these historical figures have often been compared to planets that orbit the star of the great writer, suffering increasing distortions in their own rotations the closer they get to him.[6] They also exert a gravitational pull of their own on Charlotte.

The first of these historical figures is Goethe's personal secretary, Friedrich Wilhelm Riemer, a would-be poet who blames his personal failures on Goethe's overwhelming presence and hopes to find a fellow victim in Charlotte. The second is Adele Schopenhauer, the daughter of Goethe's friend Madame Johanna Schopenhauer. She presides over a salon of self-declared "muses" and is clearly drawn to the older woman as both a model and a foil. The third interlocutor is Adele's friend Ottilie Pogwisch, who is betrothed to marry Goethe's son August but has recently found herself the target of amorous advances by the father as well. Ottilie does not appear in person but rather as the heroine of a lengthy story told by Adele. This story explores how Ottilie fell in love with a French soldier during the Napoleonic Wars, and in so doing also uses Charlotte's own *Sturm und Drang* love affair to define the amorous fantasies of a different period, the Romantic movement. The final interlocutor is August himself, who is consumed by fear and loathing of his father and hopes to find in Charlotte a sympathetic ear.

Charlotte's problems, which stem from her insistence on an objective correlation between her own person and the discursive construct of "Lotte," can usefully be contrasted with an entirely different approach to art practiced by the aging Goethe. In contrast to his *Sturm und Drang* self of the 1760s, the Goethe of 1816 embraces what might be called an "aesthetics of impersonality." Rather than creating art from autobiographical experiences, he subordinates individual existence to a larger realm of typological correspondences. During the summer of Charlotte's visit, he is busily at work on his *West-Eastern Divan*, a composition that requires him to capture the poetic spirit of a Persian writer who has been dead for more than four hundred years. In the seventh chapter of the novel, he explicitly reflects on this impersonal method as an improvement upon his earlier attempts at autobiographical transfiguration: "marvelous, how it always is the same. . . . *Divan* and *Werther* are . . . closely related—same thing on different levels, ascent to a climax, repetition and refinement of life" (*BR*, 319; *GKFA*, 9.1:317).

Goethe's typological immersion—his willingness to subordinate the unique story of his own life to a larger story assembled from literary and historical sources—is so strong that even Charlotte can feel it. During the luncheon with Goethe, she suddenly has a vision in which the poet appears before her as one of his cultural forerunners:

> She felt by no means pleased that the friend of her youth, after the brief private colloquy, had shifted his attention to the whole circle. . . . And yet she could not help sympathizing with their characteristic pleasure; their characteristic, one might almost say mythically conditioned pleasure in this patriarchal monologue by the presiding father of the house. An old verbal association and vague memory came into her mind and obstinately persisted. "Luther's Table-Talk," thought she, and defended the impression against all the dissimilarity of the actual features. (*BR*, 409; *GKFA*, 9.1:403)

All these aesthetic games were of immediate significance for Mann's self-reinvention as a representative writer during the years prior to the Second World War. Mann knew that one of the objections that might reasonably be raised against his attempts to speak as the voice of German culture was that he had not lived in the country since 1933. How could he with any authority comment on developments that he had not himself experienced? The underlying premise of this accusation—that artistic and intellectual expression must necessarily be rooted in autobiographical experience—is one with which Mann had had to grapple ever since the earliest days of his career. When *Buddenbrooks* was published, Mann had to confront angry accusations by his relatives and by the townspeople of Lübeck that he had exploited their lives for literary purposes. Local shopkeepers even began selling "keys" to the novel. Six years later, journalists in Munich went digging through the city's trash when it became known that offprints of "Blood of the Walsungs" (1906) had been accidentally remaindered to be used as packing paper instead of being pulped after Mann's father-in-law intervened to stop publication of the salacious story.[7] Mann's first summation of his own aesthetic philosophy, the essay "Bilse and I," was written the very same year and took explicit aim at the charge that he produced nothing but romans-a-clèf. Mann instead defined art as a process of "transmutation," in which the artist takes possession of experiential materials and makes them entirely his own. "These works are not about you," he informed his readers, "only about me, always just me!" (*GKFA*, 15.1:110).

Despite these protestations, the fact remains that virtually all the works Mann produced prior to 1933 were rooted to some extent in autobiographical experience.[8] *Buddenbrooks* (1901) and *Tonio Kröger* (1903) draw heavily on childhood reminiscences of Lübeck. "Blood of the Walsungs" (1906) as well as "Disorder and Early Sorrow" (1926) give private insights into Mann's family life. *Death in Venice* (1911), *The Magic Mountain* (1924), and "Mario and the Magician" (1930) were inspired by observations made on trips around Europe. When Mann tried to depart from an autobiographical approach, the results were usually critical and commercial failures, as with the novel *Royal Highness* (1905) and the play *Fiorenza* (1906).

Obviously, none of these works remains at a purely autobiographical level. All are elevated into the timeless and impersonal realm of art in some fashion, frequently through the juxtaposition of mythical or pseudomythical elements: Wagner's Ring Cycle in "Blood of the Walsungs," the cult of Dionysus in *Death in Venice*, the legend of Venus Mountain in *The Magic Mountain*. But it was only with the first *Joseph* novels that Mann decisively turned toward a different style: the style of impersonality that he also ascribes to the mature Goethe. All of Mann's late works still utilize autobiographical materials, but in a much more subdued fashion than was previously the case. Instead they step before us primarily as fanciful elaborations of source materials taken from world literature: the *Joseph* novels and the novella *The Tables of the Law* (1943) are based on the Old Testament, *The Transposed Heads* (1940) on the Indian story collection *Kathāsaritsāgara, Doctor Faustus* (1947) on the sixteenth-century Faust chapbook, and the late novel *The Holy Sinner* (1951) on the medieval verse epic *Gregorius*.

This shift had two main effects. First, it emphasized that authoritative stories could be told without roots in autobiographical experience—including political stories about contemporary life, for reviewers were quick to pick up on *Joseph the Provider* as a commentary on the New Deal and *Doctor Faustus* as an allegory on recent German history. Second, it established cultural tradition as an alternate source of authority for such stories. Crucially, Mann's conception of tradition in this context was much more expansive than was customary at the time. The works of his late period intermingle German and world literature, giving new breath to foreign materials in his native language and introducing half-forgotten German materials to a global audience through the mechanism of translation.

Mann's basic problem in the United States, however, was personal in addition to literary in nature. His art of impersonality allowed him to tell stories without basing his authority in lived experience. But many Americans were more drawn to him by his personality than by his writings. How might he maintain his reputation as an "ambassador," a "representative German"? *Lotte in Weimar* provides an answer to this question as well. The seventh chapter of the novel is notoriously written in stream-of-consciousness style and takes us into the mind of Goethe. Many critics of the novel have interpreted Mann's decision to employ this particular formal device (the only time he did so in his entire oeuvre) as a kind of rear-guard action: a response to James Joyce especially, whom Mann was jealously watching as a rival to the claim of being Europe's foremost novelist.[9]

There is an important difference between the Joycean stream of consciousness and the one employed in *Lotte in Weimar*, however. Joyce, like other modernist masters such as Virginia Woolf or Alfred Döblin, builds his stream of consciousness from the detritus of the everyday world, from sense impressions that constantly bombard the protagonists of his novels. As a result, these streams are fragmented and disorganized. Thomas Mann's stream of consciousness, by contrast, has an inward orientation. It takes in external particulars only occasionally and devotes its main attention to Goethe's creative process. It is also much more grammatical and traditionally organized than most passages we find in a novel like *Ulysses*.

The reason for this is that the seventh chapter, in addition to presenting a stream of consciousness, is also a magnificent example of literary montage. Goethe's thoughts are neither random nor, indeed, created by Thomas Mann. Instead they are copied from a bewildering array of primary and secondary sources. The primary sources include Goethe's own literary works, his letters and diaries, and his recorded conversations with contemporaries, as well as a number of pieces by Mann and by authors with no apparent connection to the great poet. The secondary sources comprise biographies and critical works written about Goethe during the century after his death. The full extent of this montage remained obscured to even the most perceptive of Mann's contemporary readers. It took the patient philological labor of an army of later exegetes to uncover.[10]

"Goethe," in other words, does not exist in this novel as an autonomous subject. His most personal thoughts are reconstituted from utterances that have entered into world literature, and just as importantly, from words that other people have said about him. His representative authority, his claim that "they think they are Germany, but I am" is rooted entirely in a century of criticism and literary circulation. Goethe is an exemplary German not because he was born in Frankfurt or lived his life within German territory, but rather because critics and literary successors recognized him as such and propagated this claim throughout global culture. By engaging with American literary criticism, and by taking a place in American university life, Thomas Mann was setting in motion a similar process, a process that would ensure his continued relevance even in an age in which the Nazis controlled all newspapers and publishing houses, all high schools and universities, all institutes and academies back in Germany.

CHAPTER 4

Hitler's Most Intimate Enemy

Mann's style has become direct, terrible, powerful. His enemies will be amazed by the tragic violence of the voice of a man they always derided as the master of ceremonies of German prose. They will be amazed all the more by the fact that Mann speaks as a patriot, thus seizing the claim staked out by the present rulers of Germany.

—Günther Anders, "Germany in Exile," 1937

Thomas Mann is giving a voice to his deep-seated hatred against the Führer, whom he targets with expressions like "ten times a failure," "extremely lazy," "a man who has spent long periods in institutions," "a disappointed bohemian artist," "a fifth-rate visionary," "a cowardly sadist," and "a plotter of revenge fantasies." His two latest publications, Europe Beware! *and "This Peace" also belong to this genre of vile propaganda.*

—Report by the Sicherheitsdienst, the secret intelligence services of the SS, 1939

In March of 1942, Thomas Mann testified before the House Select Committee Investigating National Defense Migration, better known by the name of its chairman as the Tolan Committee. Created shortly after the attack on Pearl Harbor, the Tolan Committee was charged with determining the fate of the so-called enemy aliens in the United States; it now lives in infamy for having rubberstamped the mass internment of Japanese American citizens. Mann had taken early notice of these measures, and on December 27, 1941, had nervously written to his friend and patron Agnes E. Meyer: "I wanted to ask you about my position as an 'enemy alien.' Am I really one? I don't mean 'in reality,' of course. For in reality, I am *pretty friendly*. But technically? I was stripped of my citizenship by Hitler, and am thus not a German subject. I carry a Czech passport" (*Br. AM*, 349; italicized words are in English in original). Self-interest was thus an at least partially motivating cause when he spoke to the congressional representatives on behalf of the German exile community. Eager to prove his loyalty to his adoptive country, Mann, who had begun formal immigration proceedings shortly after his arrival in 1938 and became a proud US citizen in 1944, stated for the record that he was "only awaiting a call from the government" to give a more public form to his hitherto "more or less personal" contributions to "defense work."[1]

The call from the government never came. Thanks to his powerful allies among the East Coast social set, Mann and his wife had twice already (once in 1935, shortly after he received the honorary degree from Harvard, and once in January 1941) visited the White House, where they had dined with the Roosevelts.[2] But although these encounters instilled in Mann an almost idolatrous devotion to the US president, they seem to have left much less of an impression on his host. It is not known whether Roosevelt ever more than thumbed through the copies of Mann's books that the German author gifted to him on these occasions. Certainly they didn't inspire him to place a call to his literary guest when the United States entered the war in December 1941.

Nor did other government departments make a concerted effort to recruit the famous writer. An employee of the Office of Strategic Services (OSS, the wartime forerunner to the CIA) did take Mann out for dinner in December 1943, but although the details of the encounter are a little hazy, it appears not to have been a recruitment event. The OSS mainly reached out because it wanted to dissuade Mann from any further involvement with an émigré Marxist action committee whose goals ran contrary to the office's strategic interests.[3] Mann left this meeting with the false impression that the US government had already made up its mind to occupy Germany "for a minimum of 50 years" and to enforce a "quarantine" policy according to which "for 30 years no Allied child should be permitted to get in touch with a German child." When he shared this news with other émigrés, it sparked the rumor that Mann fully approved of such punitive measures. The resulting outrage cast a long shadow over his postwar reception in Germany.[4]

Mann did record a series of propaganda broadcasts—the majority at the behest of the BBC, a few also for the Voice of America—that collectively form the closest thing he ever did to "defense work" for any Allied country. Throughout all these, however, he maintained complete editorial independence; there is no reason to believe any government official ever tried to influence what he was saying. This comparatively aloof position contrasts directly with the stance taken by Mann's children. Both Erika and Klaus put their literary talents at the service of the US Army: Erika as a battlefield correspondent who accompanied the troops from the D-Day landing to the banks of the Rhine, and Klaus as a reporter for the *Stars & Stripes* covering the Italian campaign. Their younger brother Golo, who had studied under the famous philosopher Karl Jaspers and would later in life become a well-regarded historian, found a way to be active as well, working as an intelligence analyst for the OSS.

Mann's example is nevertheless more fascinating than that of his children precisely because he never directly aligned himself with the US government. The 1930s were a decade in which governments of various stripes throughout the world discovered the value of employing artists to drum up support within a populist base. Great as the individual differences may be, this statement holds as true for Nazi Germany as it does for fascist Italy, Communist Russia, or indeed New Deal America with its Works Progress Administration.[5] Mann was a patriotic resident of the United States who throughout the war years carefully refrained from criticizing his adoptive country. His testimony to the Tolan Committee, for example, does not include a single word about the Japanese American internment.[6] But his voice and his aims were always unmistakably his own, and he agitated for the United States because he equated the American cause with that of liberal democracy, not because of any government commission.

In so doing he created a novel role for the artist: fully engaged with the political events of the day through a variety of twentieth-century media and yet fiercely protective of an independent stance. Mann's relocation to California can serve as a symbolic marker of this transition. In September of 1940, the author purchased a plot of land in the Los Angeles suburb of Pacific Palisades. The house that he commissioned from the German American architect Julius Ralph Davidson was completed in January of 1942, and the author and his family would live at 1550 San Remo Drive for the next decade, until their permanent return to Europe in 1952.[7]

Like other German émigrés before and after him, Mann was attracted to California in large part because of the Mediterranean climate ("here one can find Egypt and Palestine all in one place, which should be pretty good for my *Joseph*," he excitedly reported to his sometime assistant Ida Herz [*Reg.*, 40/452]). But it cannot have escaped him that in making the move he was also putting a vast distance between himself and the networks that had previously supported him in the United States. His publisher lived in New York City, his translator in Princeton. Agnes E. Meyer spent most of her time in Washington, DC. The university communities that had sustained him up to this point all belonged to the East Coast as well. Los Angeles had its own distinctive social circles, of course, but although Mann was endlessly fascinated by the American movie industry, he was comically ill-adapted to the partying lifestyle of the Hollywood Hills. Other than a few half-hearted attempts to develop treatments for the screen, he made no effort to join it. Nevertheless, it would be equally unfair to lump him in with other residents of "Weimar on the Pacific," as the German exile community in Pacific Palisades has often been called.[8] This label implies isolation and a fixation on the past. Mann, by contrast, showed himself willing (even if sometimes reluctantly) to fundamentally reinvent his life in response to globally transformative events. In this regard, he wasn't unlike many of the other people who streamed to Los Angeles in these years, attracted by the booming military economy that increased the population of the metropolitan area to a size larger than that of thirty-seven states.[9] It was from his base at the heart of what has sometimes been called the "fortress California" that Mann pursued his dual goal of strengthening the American war effort while simultaneously maintaining his reputation as an intellectually uncompromising author of quality fiction. It was during his residency in Pacific Palisades as well that he reached the apogee of his trajectory as an anti-Nazi celebrity in the eyes of the American public.

Brother Hitler

It is safe to say that when Mann published his open letter attacking the Nazis in the *Neue Zürcher Zeitung* in 1936, he did not yet have a firm grasp on what his new oppositional stance would mean for his public role as a writer. His understanding of this role developed only gradually over the following years, always in dialogue with an American audience that pursued its own interests. An important turning point came in the spring of 1938, however, just a few weeks into the transatlantic lecture tour that followed Mann's triumphant arrival in New York and his declaration that "where I am, there is Germany."

On March 20, 1938, the author and his family arrived in Salt Lake City, where he was scheduled to give a lecture at the University of Utah the following evening. Salt Lake City did not suit Mann, who struggled with the high altitude and later declared the visit, which included an audience with the octogenarian president of the Mormon Church, to have been "strange" (*Tb.*, March 22, 1938). Nevertheless, it was as part of this stop that Mann made a pronouncement that would come to mark an important turning point in his developing self-understanding as a writer. During a routine interview with the local newspaper, the *Deseret News*, he declared himself to be "Hitler's most intimate enemy," an epithet that the paper reproduced as an oversized photo caption on its front page (figure 4.1).[10]

Needless to say, there is little reason to believe that Hitler actually wasted much thought on his self-declared principal antagonist in America; he referred to Mann publicly on only one known occasion.[11] Mann's statement is of interest not because it is literally true but because it noticeably differs

FIGURE 4.1. Front-page photo of Thomas Mann in the *Deseret News*, March 21, 1938. Deseret News Publishing Company.

from self-descriptions he had offered until this point. In *An Exchange of Letters*, for example, he had still characterized himself as a reluctant martyr, someone dragged into the antifascist struggle against his own will and inclination. Now his rhetoric was bellicose and self-affirmative. In his open letter in the *Neue Zürcher Zeitung*, he had haughtily dismissed the Nazi supporters as an "unthinking rabble." Now he was suddenly alluding to an intimate acquaintance with their führer.

Had Mann's remark been the last of it, it could be dismissed as merely a slip of the tongue during one of an interminable series of press junkets. Two days earlier, however, during another lecture stop in Tulsa, Mann had mentally resolved to accept a commission for an essay about his exile experiences extended by *Cosmopolitan* magazine (*Tb.*, March 19, 1938). This essay would eventually come to be recognized as his most important programmatic statement from the early war years, and it develops themes that are only hinted at in his brief comment to the *Deseret News*.

The *Cosmopolitan* commission was Mann's first assignment for an American magazine, and the first major project begun following his arrival in the United States. It also marked a conscious pivot away from his European readers toward an American audience.[12] *Cosmopolitan* was a very different outlet from any of the magazines in which he had published in Europe, and Mann at first struggled with his assignment. After working on the project for about a month, he decided that both the tone and the length of what he had written rendered his essay "too weighty" for the proposed venue, and he consequently withdrew from the commission (*Tb.*, May 11, 1938).[13] Later that summer he stripped his manuscript of the original autobiographical reflections and condensed it to a short character sketch of Adolf Hitler, which he called "The Brother" and intended to include in his forthcoming essay collection *Europe Beware!* When Gottfried Bermann Fischer pointed out to him, however, that a direct attack on Hitler would make it difficult to distribute the volume in neutral countries such as Sweden and Switzerland, Mann began to reconsider an American publication. Fortunately for him, the Chicago-based *Esquire* had meanwhile also expressed an interest in a commission (*Br. GBF*, 189), and eventually published the essay as "This Man Is My Brother" on March 3, 1939. The American publication preceded a German one in the Paris-based journal *Das neue Tage-Buch* by three weeks, and thus became the first thing Mann ever wrote to be published in English before it was in his native language. What's more, the English version is to a certain degree the more authentic one, since Leopold Schwarzschild, the editor of *Das neue Tage-Buch,* retitled the essay "Brother Hitler," thereby violating Mann's artistic intention to write about Hitler without ever mentioning his name. (The title "Brother Hitler" has since stuck, and I will follow convention by using it throughout the rest of this book.)

"Brother Hitler" perfectly illustrates the successful fusion of modernist technique with middlebrow marketing that characterizes Mann's American period. Much like his novels, the essay is stylistically uncompromising, marked by introspection, intertextual allusions (especially to the works of Friedrich Nietzsche), and formidable syntactic complexity. At its hearts stands a veritably Proustian sentence of 337 words, which Helen Tracy Lowe-Porter tried to tame by splitting it into no fewer than fourteen separate sentences for her English translation. In the author's preface to the 1942 collection *Order of the Day*, Mann opined that of all his essays from this period, "Brother Hitler" was "closest to the artistic sphere" (*OD*, xv; *GW*, 13:178).[14] Nevertheless, *Esquire* was an unmistakably middlebrow venue and surrounded the essay with advertisements for fashionable men's clothing.[15] In the same way that distribution networks such as the Book-of-the-Month Club placed his novels into the hands of readers who otherwise might never have discovered them, so *Esquire* carried Mann's image of proud cultural autonomy into American living rooms through commercial channels.

Mann's basic thesis about Hitler is already expressed by the *Esquire* title: "This Man Is My Brother." It would be easy to conclude that the German author must have been benighted when he wrote these words. After all, why would he publish an essay arguing for a spiritual kinship with Hitler at the precise moment that he was building a reputation as an anti-Nazi intellectual? Attempts to discredit Hitler by drawing attention to his past as a middling artist were an established genre by the late 1930s.[16] Mann's essay, however, was different. He actually seemed to mean it when he referred to the führer as his brother!

"Brother Hitler" develops the theme of a spiritual kinship between writer and dictator in two separate ways. On the one hand, Mann postulates that Nazism is rooted in certain cultural tendencies of the fin-de-siècle and acknowledges that his own stories derive from this very same source. Referring to Hitler as a "disappointed bohemian artist" (*OD*, 154; *GW*, 12:846) who is "possessed with a fundamental arrogance which thinks itself too good for any sensible and honourable activity" (*OD*, 156; *GW*, 12:850), he draws a direct link between the führer and such dilettantish characters as Detlef Spinell, which populate Mann's early fictions and give life to their creator's aesthetic self-doubts. Mann even acknowledges that so accomplished a story as *Death in Venice* can, with historical hindsight, be accused of containing fascist tendencies. It was conceived, so "Brother Hitler" argues, as a "challenge to the psychologism of the age" and contains "much talk of simplification and resolution of mind." As such, it brims "with ideas which twenty years later were to be the property of the man in the street" (*OD*, 158–59; *GW*, 12:850).

The second way in which Mann connects the artist to the dictator is by pointing out that Hitler, even if he has ceased to paint, remains an artist at heart. His tools of political persuasion are incantatory (and therefore aesthetic) rather than rational and discursive. The fascist rallies are essentially second-rate (*verhunzt*) Wagnerian spectacles.[17] This insight is not particularly original and can also be found, for example, in Walter Benjamin's much-quoted and nearly contemporaneous essay "The Work of Art in the Age of Its Mechanical Reproducibility" (1936), which speaks about fascism as the "aestheticization of politics." Mann fundamentally differs from Benjamin in the conclusion that he draws from his analysis, however. Whereas Benjamin advocates for a Marxist aesthetic that would subordinate art to the demands of politics, Mann instead concludes that the main task of the artist should be to wrench his tools away from the dictator, to claim ownership over them and use them to advocate for higher principles: "Art, certainly, is not all sweetness and light. But neither is it all a brew of darkness, not all a freak of the tellurian underworld, not simply 'life.' More clearly and happily than ever will the artist of the future realize his mission as a white enchanter, as a winged, hermetic, moon-sib mediator between spirit and life" (*OD*, 161; *GW*, 12:852).[18]

The reference to the artist of the future as a "winged, hermetic, moon-sib mediator" was, of course, a sly allusion to Mann himself, who had always identified with the Greek god Hermes, and who was about to begin work on the concluding volume to his great *Joseph* tetralogy, the protagonist of which shows himself to be repeatedly intoxicated by the moon. With "Brother Hitler," Mann had therefore created a manifesto for an intellectual project that would keep him busy over the next decade. Art, harnessed for ill ends, had given rise to Nazism, and as an artist Mann was better positioned than nearly anybody else to diagnose this problem. At the same time, the democracies of the future would clearly require the support of artists, whose task it would be to stay alert to any misappropriation of their trade. Art could never be subordinated to political concerns, not even those of a liberal democratic state. Instead, its goal would have to be to advocate for the abstract spiritual values (such as love of freedom and equality) that fertilize the ground upon which democracy flourishes. This is a topic to which Mann would return again and again over the next four years, as he toured the country delivering lectures with titles such as "The Coming Victory of Democracy" or "The War and the Future."

Harold R. Peat Presents the World's Greatest Living Man of Letters

Thomas Mann had always been a talented and enthusiastic public speaker. He gave his first public reading at the age of twenty-five (*Br.*, 1:24), and soon after was a regular on the European lecture circuit. Contemporary listeners describe him as naturally soft-spoken, but when microphones were invented, he took to them with gusto and relished staging his readings almost as if they were theatrical performances; Mann's diaries from the 1930s contain many postmortems of an evening's lecture.[19] We can gain a sense of what he must have been like as a public speaker from a rather unlikely source, namely a short television recording that was made in 1929 and recently rediscovered in the German Federal Archives.[20] Television in 1929 was still a completely experimental medium, and there were no receivers in private households. It is thus all the more impressive that Mann, despite the fact that he presumably had never seen a televised image before, unfailingly looks into the camera as he delivers his remarks; he is poised and speaks in clearly audible, rhythmically structured sentences.

Mann received his first invitation to lecture in the United States in February of 1928. It was extended to him by the Leigh-Emmerich Lecture Bureau, which proposed that he tour twenty-five cities over the course of three months, on terms that were apparently financially quite favorable (*GKFA*, 22:337).[21] Nothing came of this project, and so Mann's earliest appearances in America in 1934 were not in front of a paying public; rather, they catered to invited guests in New York and at Yale University. His English was then still quite poor, and this undoubtedly distracted from the quality of his performances. Extant recordings of his lectures from the 1940s confirm that he gradually improved and eventually acquired a measured and dignified, though still by no means fluent, style of delivery. For the inevitable question-and-answer period that followed his American lectures (a convention that he detested), he required the help of a translator.

Mann's resounding success as a speaker to refugee aid organizations in 1937 clearly demonstrated his appeal to an America that was rapidly waking up to global affairs. It is thus not surprising that shortly after his return to Switzerland he was contacted by the New York literary agent Harold R. Peat, who wanted him to tour the United States and lecture about democracy (*Tb.*, August 1 and 6, 1937). Peat was himself a veteran orator who had spun his experiences in the First World War into a series of engagements during the 1920s. By the late 1930s, he ran one of the biggest lecturing bureaus in the country, counting H. G. Wells and Winston Churchill among his other clients.[22] The deal that Peat proposed to Mann—initially for a transcontinental tour covering twelve cities—was far too remunerative to turn down, though the author was at first skeptical whether he would be able to rise to the occasion. "Democratic idealism? Do I really believe in it? Am I not just assuming a role?" his diaries note (*Tb.*, November 27, 1937). By January 1938, however, Mann had clearly vanquished his doubts and privately boasted that the lecturing tour on which he was about to embark would be "exactly the right thing for the United States, and a support for Roosevelt's policies" (*Br. RS*, 129). Eventually he delivered his lecture text "The Coming Victory of Democracy" on fifteen occasions in fourteen cities during the spring and summer of 1938, receiving a total of fifteen thousand dollars for his efforts.

The large sum confirms Mann's desirability as a lecturer: Hans Rudolf Vaget points out that in 1938 fifteen thousand dollars was roughly equivalent to the annual salary of a college professor. The amount also falls in the same ballpark as the twenty thousand dollars that Mann would receive in royalties for his book sales over the following year.[23] Indeed, according to an article in *Time* magazine, a fee of one thousand dollars per appearance put the German author in the same league as such American celebrities as Sinclair Lewis or Dorothy Thompson; among literary figures, only H. G. Wells and Aldous Huxley received substantially more that year.[24] On average, somewhere between two thousand and six thousand people attended each lecture, and pirated transcripts of Mann's remarks soon began to circulate. Alfred A. Knopf guarded vigilantly against such efforts, and at the end of the lecture tour published "The Coming Victory of Democracy" as a short book.[25] It sold more than twenty-five thousand copies in 1938–39 alone, benefiting from an endorsement by Eleanor Roosevelt, and reached an even wider audience when it was excerpted in *Reader's Digest*.[26] Given this success, it is not surprising that Mann was hired for four more tours in 1939, 1940, 1941, and 1943 (figure 4.2). All in all, he gave ninety lectures in this fashion, addressing paying audiences at universities and local lecturing societies alike; Vaget has calculated that he spoke in public 134 times if one adds in his various appearances as a guest of academic honor societies, as a banquet speaker, and similar.

Mann's success did not take place in a vacuum. Public lecturing had long been recognized as a distinctively American activity. In 1857 *Putnam's Magazine* described the Lyceum theaters, a nationwide web of organizations that sponsored public programs and entertainments, as "the one institution in which we take our nose out of our English prototypes . . . and go alone."[27] And a few decades later, the so-called Chautauqua movement brought edifying lectures mixed with religious instruction to rural America by means of

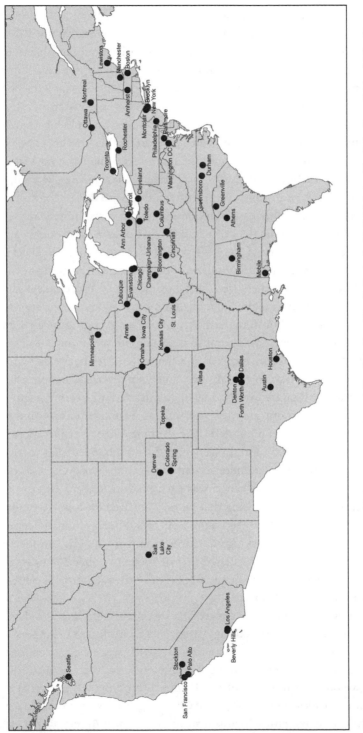

FIGURE 4.2. The cities visited by Thomas Mann on his lecture tours, 1938–43. Mat Sisk, Navari Family Center for Digital Scholarship, Notre Dame Hesbugh Libraries.

giant collapsible tent structures. The appeal of the Chautauqua circuits was so strong that their routes transformed American geography. In fact, the very land where Mann built his American house had originally been cleared by the Southern California Conference of the Methodist Episcopal Church, which erected a flourishing Chautauqua operation in what was soon to be known as Pacific Palisades during the early 1920s.[28]

The importance of this tradition was not lost on Thomas Mann's oldest daughter, Erika, who was herself a highly accomplished and widely success-ful lecturer and who frequently accompanied her father as a translator. In an article that she wrote for *Liberty Magazine*, she explains that "lecturing is a strictly American existence. Nowhere else in the world is it a full-fledged profession. In no other country I know of can you spend your life—and earn your living—merely traveling about and making speeches."[29] By the mid-1940s, when Erika wrote these lines, the thirst of small-town America for edification in lecture format was already a popular target for gentle mockery by coastal elites. Her article too traffics in anecdotes like the one about how she once had to ride part of the way to her destination in a milk van, and it is accompanied by satirical drawings. But it also ends on a more profoundly reflective note: "In his turn, the lecturer learns many things from his audi-ences. The most reassuring piece of knowledge he may gain from them is this: They are earnest, grown-up people endowed with reasoning minds and feeling hearts. . . . At this most crucial moment in the history of their coun-try, they are far more concerned, far more deeply aroused and disquieted, than some of their leaders may choose to realize."[30]

Indeed, the literature on popular lecturing in the United States has long highlighted that such lectures are best approached neither as a source of diversion for bored rural communities nor as a top-down system for the transmission of knowledge. Instead, they should be understood as perfor-mative occasions in which a variety of new identities came into being. The first of these were new professional identities that were created, in the words of Donald M. Scott, not through the "occupancy of a particular office," but rather through "an underlying commitment to use the possession of knowl-edge."[31] Doctors, for example, gained popular recognition as a group distinct from quacks in part through the public display of their professional knowl-edge in edifying lectures. Thomas Mann was no exception in this regard, and the start of his lecturing activities in 1938 initiated a new stage in his public reception as a major writer in the United States.

During the 1920s and early 1930s, Alfred A. Knopf monetized his exclu-sive rights to Thomas Mann primarily by issuing translations of books that the author had published many years earlier; Mann's reputation was, in other words, closely tied to the public intimation of him as a "classic." By the mid-1930s, Knopf had exhausted this back catalog and had moved on to promoting Mann as a contemporary writer who was in touch with the political issues of the day. With the author's permanent resettlement in the United States and the start of his lecturing activities, finally, Mann's personal presence—his availability for lectures, interviews, banquets, and other social occasions—seriously began to compete with his writings as a source of fame in the US market. For better or worse, the author now began to eclipse his literary work.

The promotional brochure that Harold R. Peat used to advertise Mann's 1938 lecture stops provides a glimpse of this transformation (figure 4.3). While Peat still employs the old slogan of Mann as the "Greatest Living Man of Letters," the photo that accompanies it is radically different from the ones used in previous American advertisements. During the late 1920s and early 1930s Mann was frequently photographed with averted eyes and furrowed brow, often with pen in hand. The joint effect of these conventions was to give him a remote, intellectual appearance—the visage of a man whose genius was best approached through his writing. The Thomas Mann portrayed by Peat, by contrast, has his face confidently turned toward the viewer and sports a slightly ironic frown; he is sitting at ease in an armchair and dangling a cigarette. He looks, for all intents and purposes, as if he is ready to engage in a battle of wits—in fact, his posture could easily be transposed to one of the political talk shows of the early television era twenty years later, such as William F. Buckley's *Firing Line*.

Coverage in the local press did its part to shift audience interest from Thomas Mann's books to Thomas Mann as a personality. It was not unusual for papers such as the *Cleveland Plain Dealer* or the *Dallas Morning News* to run up to half a dozen stories during the weeks building up to a Thomas Mann visit. Most of these were simple summaries of Mann's past work and his current reputation, but there were articles clearly meant to whip up excitement and human interest as well. The *Plain Dealer*, for instance, ran a human-interest piece about a young lady ("22 and pert as they make them") who had cycled 140 miles each way to hear Mann speak in Cleveland.[32] And the reports that followed upon a Mann appearance rarely failed to comment on the social dimensions of the visit—in some cases devoting noticeably more space to who had attended than to what was being said.[33] As a result of such coverage, Mann's public image in America was profoundly transformed during the five years of his lecturing activity. Even more important than that, however, were the changes it brought about in his audience.

HAROLD R. PEAT *has the honor to present*

THOMAS MANN

"The Greatest Living Man of Letters"

·NOBEL PRIZE WINNER·

in his First American Lecture Tour

SPEAKING ON

"The Coming Victory of Democracy"

CONSTITUTION HALL   THURS.   8:30 P.M.

Auspices: The Washington Forum   **MAR. 10**

Tickets at Mrs. Dorsey's Bureau, 1300 G.St. (Droop's) NA 7151.
83c, $1.10, $1.65

FIGURE 4.3. Promotional brochure advertising Thomas Mann's lecture tour for "The Coming Victory of Democracy," 1938. Redpath Chautauqua Collection, University of Iowa Libraries, Iowa City, Iowa.

The Itinerant Lecturer of Democracy

It is difficult to determine precisely what ordinary Americans thought of Thomas Mann, since newspapers generally did not think to interview any spectators. The *New York Times* journalist Charles Poore, however, noted that by July of 1938, crowds were cheering Mann when his face was shown in a cinema newsreel.[34] A photo story that was published in *Life* magazine in 1939 also documents the eagerness with which ordinary Americans crowded to the author's lectures (figure 4.4). The residents of Tulsa, Oklahoma, who examined Mann's books on that occasion were clearly there in part because it was a glamorous social occasion. Decked out in their Sunday best, cigarettes in hand, they were having the time of their lives. But they were also discovering, and presumably debating, a political message. Among the books for sale

FIGURE 4.4. Audience members at Thomas Mann's 1939 lecture in Tulsa, Oklahoma, peruse the book exhibit. The LIFE Picture Collection/Getty Images.

depicted in the photo, alongside numerous copies of *The Magic Mountain*, are *Essays of Three Decades* and the anti-Nazi *Exchange of Letters*, which the two older ladies at back right are perusing with some earnestness.

In his study of the early US lecture circuit cited earlier, Donald M. Scott notes that lecturing tours instilled in their audiences a "sense of belonging to a national public."[35] Indeed, by the 1930s lecture tours had a long history of providing ordinary listeners with reflective occasions on which they could ponder what it meant to be an American. As one scholar of the early twentieth-century lecture circuit notes, "all the relevant concerns of the time—citizenship, race, community, gender, politics, government, quality of life, foreign affairs" were examined by traveling orators.[36] And this included occasions on which "speakers and audiences could contemplate the ambivalent relationship of the republic to the world beyond its borders."[37] Consider only the example of Charles Zueblin, an urban sociologist who was one of the most prominent lecturers in America during the time of the First World War. Zueblin gave lectures with titles that could easily have been dreamt up by Mann: "Education for Freedom," "Evolution and Revolution," "Democratic Culture." Their central thesis, namely that "democracy is not a form of government, but a faith and a life" sounds suspiciously similar also to the lesson conveyed by "The Coming Victory of Democracy."[38]

Mann was thus not offering anything that was, strictly speaking, new to the American lecture circuit. Lectures on democracy as a way of life, on the need to anchor republican values in a wider cultural sphere, and on the need to intervene in world affairs had energized American audiences during the last world war as well. What was new is that these lectures now came from a German, albeit one who consistently stressed his intention to take up US citizenship. This basic fact again points to a shift in Thomas Mann's public image in America. During the 1920s readers had been attracted to his books because they seemed signifiers of a fairly abstract vision of European cultural greatness. The audiences that now thronged to his lectures were motivated by concrete events in German and central European history, events that made headlines in the United States as well and challenged ordinary Americans to take a stance: the book burnings on Berlin's opera square, the Munich Agreement, the Nazi invasion of Poland.

By speaking out on these issues, Mann waded into hotly contested terrain and held forth on questions that cut to the very heart of what it might mean to be an American. For the American public in the late 1930s hardly stood in uniform opposition against fascism and Nazi militarism. At numerous rallies and training camps, the German American Bund promoted a favorable view of the Third Reich. Reactionary preachers, wandering lecturers, and radio personalities, most infamous among them the Roman Catholic priest Father Charles Coughlin, spread anti-Semitic messages not at all dissimilar to the ones expounded by the propaganda ministry of Joseph Goebbels. The influential America First Committee, which could boast of a membership of roughly eight hundred thousand right before Pearl Harbor and possessed a powerful spokesperson in Charles Lindbergh, did its best to "keep America out of the war" by pursuing a policy of appeasement.

The activities of most of these groups and individuals were heavily focused on the upper Midwest, not only because this region was home to the population centers of Milwaukee, Chicago, Detroit, and Cleveland but also because it was here that an exceptionally large proportion of German Americans was to be found. For much the same reasons, Thomas Mann was a frequent guest lecturer in this area between 1938 and 1943. (He had a personal motivation as well, since his favorite daughter, Elisabeth, lived in Chicago with her husband, Giuseppe Antonio Borgese.) It is thus likely that at least some of the visitors who heard Mann speak in locations such as the Cleveland Music Hall (May 1938), the Masonic Temple of Detroit (March 1939), or the auditorium of Ohio Wesleyan University (February 1940) would have also heard speakers with views quite antithetical to his in close spatial and temporal proximity. During the question-and-answer sessions that followed his lectures, Mann was sometimes asked to comment on the other side.[39] He also incorporated a passage attacking isolationism into his 1941 lecture script "How to Win the Peace," which was later published in *Order of the Day* as "The War and the Future."[40]

One particularly dramatic example of such a spatial and temporal juxtaposition is presented by the "Save Czechoslovakia!" rally that was staged in Madison Square Garden on September 25, 1938, concurrent with the Munich Conference. Drawing an audience of over twenty thousand, this was the largest gathering that Mann ever addressed. He did so with evident success. The *New York Times* reported that "the greatest demonstration of the meeting came at the end of Mr. Mann's short and eloquent address, when he declared: 'Hitler must fall.' 'This and nothing else will preserve the peace.' For several minutes the Garden was a bedlam of sound as the crowd cheered and clapped for the somber, obviously nervous, tall German who forsook his fatherland when Hitler came to power."[41] It was a sweet but all-too-fleeting victory for Mann, who recorded his excitement in his diaries: "A most impressive event. . . . They will fight!" (*Tb.*, September 25, 1938). Only five days later, however, Chamberlain signed away the Sudetenland. And less than five months after the "Save Czechoslovakia!" rally, the German American Bund staged a pro-Nazi gathering of comparable size in the very same hall, with

Bundesführer Fritz Julius Kuhn inveighing against "Frank D. Rosenfeld" and his "Jew Deal" (figure 4.5).[42] When he reported on the isolationist rallies in one of his radio addresses to occupied Europe, Mann thus struck a very different tone concerning audience sizes:"20,000 applauding spectators is not so much considering the dimensions of this country," he now claimed somewhat hypocritically (GW, 11:1005).

Existing studies of this rhetorical battle for the soul of America have always tended to devote outsized attention to the side that stood sympathetic to fascism. Even in their own day, the speeches by bund sympathizers and the radio addresses by Father Coughlin were recognized as rhetorically sophisticated attacks on liberal democracy.[43] Thomas Mann's speeches have never even remotely drawn the same level of scrutiny. To some extent this is understandable. Compared to the topical columns written by his friend, the journalist Dorothy Thompson, Mann's speeches and wartime essays were frequently perceived as unfocused and overly intellectual. The *Minnesota Daily* of February 17, 1940, for example, reported that "Mann's concepts were lofty and, to some, confused."[44]

Analytical rigor was hardly the point of Thomas Mann's lectures, however. The ordinary people who came to hear the author speak by the thousands were not primarily drawn by the promise of intellectual nuance. They were attracted by the promise of celebrity and by Mann's biography as an antifascist émigré, which lent his pronouncements a kind of authenticity that was clearly an attraction in its own right. A reporter for the *Philadelphia Evening Bulletin*, for example, admitted that on Mann's "mental integrity and his courageous defense of his own beliefs there can be no reflection."[45]

Mann understood and actively fostered such projections. If there is one thing that the Weimar experience had taught him, it is that democracy is an attitude as well as an intellectual stance and that its defense requires passion in addition to education. This is the great theme of "The Coming Victory of Democracy," in which Mann recognizes that "America needs no instruction in the things that concern democracy" but also argues that "even physical things die off, disappear, are lost, if they are not cared for" (OD, 115; GW, 11:911). The congruence of Mann's theme and his listeners' emotional attitudes is vividly demonstrated in a report on Mann's address to a private gathering at the house of the Hollywood producer Jack Warner, written by the gossip columnist Gladys Lloyd Robinson. Mann was introduced by his old friend and fellow émigré Bruno Frank, who gave a boosterish address culminating in the words, "The real Germany, that Germany which will live, does not bear the features of a fanatic; that Germany is reflected in the features of the man who is with us this evening."[46] Robinson's account picks

Figure 4.5. A color guard of the German American Bund stands at attention in front of a portrait of George Washington in Madison Square Garden, February 1939. Bettmann/Getty Images.

up on this spirit, praising Mann's "burning and dynamic personality" and his "renewed warmth," while also reporting in great detail on the author's belief that "democracy has indeed grown stale" and that it risks losing out to a fascism that appeals only "through the sheer sensation of novelty and excitement."[47]

On at least this one occasion, Mann's "burning personality" seems to have indeed enkindled a lasting flame, for the lecture marked the beginning of Warner's support for the Hollywood Anti-Nazi League. His sponsorship would prove to be greatly beneficial not only from a financial but also from a public relations point of view, since it elevated the league above the reproach of merely being a Communist front.[48] Charismatic conversions to the antifascist cause were an important and intended outcome of Mann's lecturing activities, and the author may well have had the American tradition of itinerant preachers in mind when he self-deprecatingly described himself as an "itinerant lecturer [Wanderredner] of democracy" (GW, 10:397).

Antifascist Conservatism

In addition to their largely emotive, rather than intellectual, appeal, there is another reason why Mann's wartime lectures are now largely forgotten. They belong to a strain of émigré fascism theory that exerted a profound influence in America during the late 1930s but has so decidedly fallen out of favor that it is now barely recognizable as a coherent tradition. When we think about the intersection of fascism theory and intellectual emigration during the 1930s and 1940s, we are instantly drawn to names such as Franz Neumann, Theodor W. Adorno, Max Horkheimer, or Siegfried Kracauer—figures, in other words, who approached their topic from a Marxist perspective. Mann's collaboration with Adorno on Doctor Faustus is well-known, but only recently have scholars begun to examine his close links to a number of quite different intellectual influences from the conservative end of the political spectrum. These influences include his son-in-law, the Italian historian and literary critic Giuseppe Antonio Borgese (author of Goliath: The March of Fascism, 1937); the German cultural philosopher Erich Kahler (Der deutsche Charakter in der Geschichte Europas [German Character in the History of Europe], 1937), who was Mann's close friend and neighbor during the Princeton years; the penitent ex-Nazi Hermann Rauschning (The Revolution of Nihilism, 1939), who corresponded with Mann and contributed a foreword to the anthology The Ten Commandments, in which Mann first published his novella The Tables of the Law; and the German American political theorist Peter Viereck (Metapolitics: From the Romantics to Hitler, 1941), who received an early career boost when Mann blurbed his book, and who went on to become one of the most prominent conservative intellectuals in the United States during the 1950s.[49]

Borgese, Kahler, Rauschning, and Viereck were quite diverse thinkers, and no single common thread unites all of their works. Nevertheless, there are a few broad themes that can each be connected to several of these writers and that characterize Mann's speeches and essays during the late 1930s and early 1940s as well. The first of these is a tendency to approach the rise of National Socialism as primarily a problem for cultural history, rather than for political or economic theory. Viereck, for example, opens *Metapolitics* with an extensive quotation from William Butler Yeats's poem "The Second Coming," and his first chapter with another from Goethe's *Faust*. Rauschning proclaims confidently that "it would be simplifying much too much if we were to identify [the sources of Nazism] with the world economic depression, or with the loss of the world war, or with the unchanging character of Prussian imperialism. These things played their part, but the roots of the development in Germany lie deeper. They lie in moral and intellectual processes, some of them of long duration."[50] As this final sentence suggests, the writers under discussion here also liked to think in terms of the *longue durée*. Viereck locates the origins of Nazi ideology among the German Romantics, while Kahler (who never opted for conciseness where a monumental approach might serve just as well) reaches back to the fall of the Roman Empire and the age of the great migrations. Borgese begins his equally far-reaching exploration of Italian fascism with a chapter on Dante.

Mann had similarly declared fascism to be an essentially cultural problem, and he doubled down on this proposition during wartime. In "The War and the Future," for example, he argues that "what we call National-Socialism is the poisonous perversion of ideas which have a long history in German intellectual life" and claims that economic explanations are "largely pretexts and rationalizations" for "Germany's acts of violence" (*OD*, 253–54). He also consistently linked his country's reluctance to embrace liberal democracy with the legacy of German Romanticism, occasionally reaching further back in time to the age of the Reformation.

A second characteristic feature of conservative fascism theory during the 1930s is that it postulates German identity as divided into two oppositional parts, one cosmopolitan and good, the other provincial and bad. In this, it differs from the conservative discourse of the 1910s (the so-called Ideas of 1914), which located the primary motor of cultural conflict in a struggle between a unified German *Kultur* and a similarly monolithic western European civilization. Viereck makes the terms of this argument especially clear: "Just as Mason and Dixon's line today still runs through the hearts of many

Americans, so through the centre of German hearts runs the great Roman wall. Speaking metaphorically, on one side of the wall are the classical, rational, legalist, and Christian traditions (often mutually conflicting) of the Romanized German; on the other side (often mutually conflicting) are the paganism of the old Saxons, the barbaric tribal cults of war and blood, and the anti-rationalism and anti-legalism of the romantics."[51] Kahler similarly argues that in Nazism, "everything that is European is exterminated as 'foreign' with a vindictive fervor—but what remains of 'Germanness' once all these foreign elements have been expelled is nothing more than a muddle-headed immaturity."[52] Rauschning claims that conservative German nationalism veered into National Socialism once it abandoned "the intellectual and historical unity of Western civilization," and Borgese interprets Italian fascism as a "Great Involution" responding to the revolutionary legacy of the European Enlightenment.[53]

Although Mann's *Reflections of a Nonpolitical Man* ranks among the most important products of the "Ideas of 1914," he had, in point of fact, always argued that German *Kultur* was at least partially European in nature. Germanic cultural greatness, for Mann, was of an essentially musical sort and thus easily capable of spreading across national borders.[54] In his speeches and writings of the late 1930s and early 1940s, he further developed this point. In the essay "This War" of 1939, for example, he claims that "it is . . . clearly observable to every friend of Germany . . . that she can only be great and happy within a Europe purged of the poison of international politics. . . . More than all other peoples would the German people take full advantage of such conditions: they would be rid of the curse of power-politics, more disastrous to Germany than to any other country" (*OD*, 225).

A final characteristic shared by all the thinkers under examination here is the tendency to inflate their cultural narratives to a point where they veer into the metaphysical, even the theological. The titles generally say it all: fascism is not just a matter of politics, but of "metapolitics"; Hitler's seizure of power, not just a social revolution, but rather "the revolution of nihilism." Mussolini's fascism is not just a social movement, but rather a "Goliath." Viereck's book even includes an extensive discussion of Alfred Rosenberg as the prophet of a new Nazi religion that takes Hitler as its messiah.

Mann was similarly drawn to grandiose narratives of a theological bent, partly out of personal predisposition and partly out of strategic considerations for his American audience. Thus he declares in "The Coming Victory of Democracy" that "democracy and fascism live, so to speak, on different planets, or, to put it more accurately, they live in different epochs. The fascist interpretation of the world and of history is one of absolute force, wholly free of morality and reason and having no relation to them." (*OD*, 143; *GW*, 11:935). And in "The War and the Future," he speaks of the world as "the universal setting for a single battle—a battle of faith and conviction, a religious struggle where the cause is everywhere the same" (*OD*, 243).

As much as he may have borrowed from Borgese, Kahler, Rauschning, and Viereck, however, Mann's ultimate purpose was entirely his own. This purpose was the demand that a privileged place in the antifascist struggle be given to artists. In "The War and the Future," Mann claims that "the 'political' is now no longer what it used to be: a problem for experts, a game played according to certain accepted rules. . . . Now it is a matter of ultimate values, of the basis of our civilization, of the very idea of humanity" (*OD*, 240). These "ultimate values" include, for Mann, not only liberty and equality but also culture. As a result, the artist is "simply forced to stand his ground in the conflict of convictions; because life has taught him—taught all of us—that the problem of humanity is one, and its different spheres and expressions inseparable from another" (*OD*, 239). Here, we again encounter the conviction, already expressed in the foreword to *Measure and Value*, that art is of social value primarily because it can provide "knowledge of the unity of the world, the totality of all things human" and thus serve as a counter-point to "the total State" dreamed up by the Nazis (*OD*, 242).

Mann was, in other words, forging an arsenal of concepts and propositions for use by artists in the ongoing struggle with fascism. But the weapons he proposed would hardly have proven effective if they had not also reminded his audience of very similar ones that were then being given experimental shape in a wholly different idiom by American-born public intellectuals.

Crisis, Responsibility, and the "City of Man"

The main characteristics of the conservative antifascist school of émigré writers, especially the tendency toward portentous metaphysical speculation on a grand scale, also apply to a number of American thinkers of the period. The intellectual historian Mark Greif has called the decade stretching from the Great Depression to the end of the Second World War the starting point of the "age of the crisis of man," to draw attention to the tremendous number of contributions in fundamental anthropology that were published during this period. Everywhere in America, "man" was perceived to be in crisis and in search of a new definition. Greif himself has noted the close relationship between this preoccupation and the intellectual migration from Weimar, and indeed both Rauschning and Kahler would provide important contributions to the phenomenon.[55] But there were plenty of home-grown contributors to the "crisis of man" discourse as well, including several who wrote or published important essays on Thomas Mann during this period: Reinhold Niebuhr (*The Nature and Destiny of Man*, 1943), Lewis Mumford (*The Condition of Man*, 1944), and Dwight Macdonald ("The Root is Man," 1946).

Mann certainly was well aware of the "crisis of man" genre. In May of 1943, for example, he encouraged Kahler, who was putting the finishing touches on *Man the Measure*, by saying, "Contemporary experience has, after all, awakened a certain receptivity to such synoptic and daring books. Niebuhr's *The Nature and Destiny of Man* is . . . a sign of the times" (*EF*, 68; *Br. EK*, 2:54). One year later, he took a more negative view of the same phenomenon when he complained to Agnes E. Meyer that most American critics insisted on reading *Joseph the Provider* as yet one more example in a line of "overstuffed monstrosities" à la Mumford's *The Condition of Man* (*Br. AM*, 575).

The real importance of the "crisis of man" genre, however, lay in the way in which it overlapped and to some extent preconditioned another movement that would profoundly influence the reception of Thomas Mann during these years. This movement is often referred to as "responsible liberalism," a name derived from one of its earliest manifestos, "The Irresponsibles," by the poet Archibald MacLeish.[56] Other figures generally subsumed under the label include the urban sociologist and philosopher of technology Lewis Mumford, the theologian Reinhold Niebuhr, and the novelist and literary critic Waldo Frank. All these people exchanged letters with Thomas Mann and met him in person on at least one occasion. More importantly, however, they also reviewed his books, generally cementing his burgeoning reputation as a politically informed writer whose works contrasted with the general tendency toward "disillusion and dissolution" prevalent among so many other members of the modernist generation.[57] Finally, all the responsible liberals except Frank cooperated with Mann on projects of cultural warfare.

The responsible liberals had several things in common that naturally drove them to seek out affiliations with Thomas Mann. First and most importantly, they were strong defenders of democracy who believed that American liberalism had become overly complacent in the face of fascism. They advocated for a strongly interventionist trajectory in international politics, although their arguments were rooted not in pragmatism or realpolitik but rather in liberal idealism (indeed, the American pragmatists collected around the anti-interventionist philosopher John Dewey were among their principal enemies). Second, democracy for them was primarily an expression of a social code comprising justice, liberty, and equality, rather than an operative procedure. Established liberalism in the United States, so they claimed, had too long neglected this fact in favor of an exclusive focus on material wellbeing. Third, they shared a self-consciously "tragic" view of life, which caused them to dissent from progressive narratives that saw social life as continuously improving and leading toward the happy reconciliation of individuals and their community. Fourth and finally, they were willing, more perhaps than any other intellectual cohort in the United States since the days of the Civil War, to follow words up with actions. MacLeish served his government as librarian of Congress from 1939 to 1944. Niebuhr acted as a consultant to the State Department on a number of occasions throughout the 1940s. Mumford and Frank held no government posts but nevertheless caused a tempest in the intellectual world when they clamorously resigned as contributing editors from the *New Republic* over the magazine's perceived timidity in foreign affairs.[58]

Responsible liberalism had roots in the early 1930s, but a flashpoint in its development came with the German invasion of France in the spring of 1940. This is when MacLeish published "The Irresponsibles" in the pages of the *Nation*, pointedly stating that "history will have one question to ask of our generation. . . . Why did the scholars and the writers of our generation, witnesses as they were to the destruction of writing and scholarship in great areas of Europe and the imprisonment and murder of men whose crime was scholarship and writing. . . —why did the writers of our generation in America fail to oppose these forces while they could?"[59] Mumford and Frank contributed essays asking much the same question and titled respectively "The Corruption of Liberalism" and "Our Guilt in Fascism" to the *New Republic*.

The spring of 1940 is also when Mumford and Niebuhr found themselves sitting at a conference table with Thomas Mann to discuss the role that intellectuals might play in the battle with Nazism. The occasion for this meeting was the "City of Man" conference of May 24–26, 1940, which was coincidentally also the weekend of the Dunkirk evacuation. Jointly convened by Borgese, Mumford, Niebuhr, and Mann (along with Robert M. Hutchins, the president of the University of Chicago, and William Allan Neilson, the recently retired president of Smith College), this gathering of intellectuals brought together an eclectic group of conservative antifascists, American responsible liberals, and émigré intellectuals. Other attendees who put their names to what would eventually become *The City of Man: A Declaration on World Democracy* included Van Wyck Brooks, Dorothy Canfield Fisher, and the émigrés Hermann Broch, Oscar Jászi, and Hans Kohn.

The conference consisted of a series of six workshops that jointly aimed at a discussion of the problems afflicting contemporary democracy and at the

search for a future world order. Mann presided over the third of these meetings, dedicated to "definitions and redefinitions of democracy." Lewis Mumford, in his autobiography, notes that the author "was silent most of the time:
but his deep feeling in the reading of his paper on democracy impressed
everyone: at one point he could hardly keep back his tears."[60] Mann himself
remembered the occasion thus: "I presided over the morning meeting in the
Blackwell-Room and gave my all to my address, which left a deep impression.
The conference itself is diffuse and unfocused" (Tb., May 25, 1940).

The "City of Man" conference allows for an interesting glimpse into the
history of twentieth-century political ideals. First, it serves as clear testimony
of the ways in which European conservative antifascist thinking fused with
American liberalism to produce an abstract diagnosis of contemporary ills
and a prescriptive remedy. The City of Man veers between conservative and
liberal poles, and cannot be entirely reduced to either of them.[61] The conservative predisposition is perhaps most apparent in passages lamenting the
"decline of Western civilization" and invoking "discipline and loyalty" as "the
collective purpose of democracy."[62] By contrast, the touch of the responsible
liberals can be felt in passages such as the one describing democracy as a
"faith militant and triumphant" that is now "disintegrating into a routine of
'liberties and comforts,'" or in the assurance that "the signers of this document neither bid for power nor shrink from responsibility."[63]

Second, however, this heterodox union of European and American ways
of thought also created a remarkable vision for a possible postwar future, a
vision that enjoyed brief prominence during the early 1940s but was then
extinguished by the onset of the Cold War. This vision was that of a world
government. "Peace," the declaration confidently asserts, "cannot rest upon
coalitions and ententes, or upon half-hearted security pacts; it cannot be
achieved through structures like the League of Nations, which presumed to
dispense justice without exercising power, or through one-sided lame lead-
erships like that of England's and France's rulers." It can be founded "only
on the unity of man under one law and one government." This universalist
vision is advanced through recognizable allusions to the European intellectual heritage (the reference to Saint Augustine's City of God is explicit, while
Immanuel Kant's philosophical sketch on "perpetual peace" has clearly heavily colored the phrasing), but the overall plan for the future is just as much
American. "The New Testament of Americanism must identify itself with
World Humanism," the declaration asserts. "'Separation' must be replaced
with 'unity,' Independence must be integrated into Interdependence."[64]

The City of Man shares with Mann's speeches and essays of the early 1940s
the conviction that democracy itself is in peril in a totalitarian age and that

the foundations of western political thought will have to be reconceived through a simultaneous engagement with western intellectual and cultural history. It is not surprising that several of the declaration's cosigners would, during the years immediately following the war, become actively involved in the World Federalist Movement, a kind of rival organization to the United Nations. More surprising is that Mann, too, made a swerve toward world democracy immediately following the "City of Man" conference. In his lecture "The Theme of the *Joseph* Novels," which he delivered at the Library of Congress on November 17, 1942, we find an interpretation of *Joseph the Provider* that sees the protagonist's ascent to the governorship of Egypt as the culmination of a cosmopolitan trajectory: "in Joseph the ego flows back from arrogant absoluteness into the collective, common; and, the contrast between artistic and civic tendencies, between isolation and community, between individual and collective is fabulously neutralized,—as according to our hopes and our will, it must be dissolved in the democracy of the future, the cooperation of free and divergent nations under the equalizing scepter of justice" (*LC*, 14–15; *GW*, 11:666).

In the Fortress of Freedom

The "City of Man" is not the only example of a project of cultural warfare that united responsible liberals and émigré intellectuals during the years of the Second World War. Mann's affiliation with the Library of Congress provides another illuminating case for how his desire to take a public stance against the Nazis both nourished and was nourished by homegrown American movements. The seeds for this affiliation were sown in October of 1941, when Thomas Mann signaled to Agnes E. Meyer that he was under some financial strain and would welcome relief from a magnanimous benefactor (*L*, 376–77; *Br. AM*, 325–26). Given Mann's highly remunerative career as a public lecturer, the basis for his claim is somewhat doubtful. It is more likely that he was simply tired of his itinerant existence and longed for a source of income that would allow him to devote more attention to his art while continuing his customary patrician lifestyle. Meyer responded by reaching out to an old friend, Archibald MacLeish.

MacLeish's appointment as the nation's ninth librarian of Congress had taken place under somewhat unusual circumstances just weeks before the outbreak of the Second World War. He had been hand-picked by Franklin Delano Roosevelt, but his selection was opposed both by conservatives in Congress, who objected to his liberalism and ostensible Communist sympathies (the term "fellow traveler" was coined during the MacLeish confirmation hearings), and by the American Library Association, which understandably wanted to see a trained librarian, not a poet, appointed to the post.[65] Ironically, MacLeish's five-year tenure in Washington would be distinguished by his professionalism, his reflections on the nature and purpose of modern librarianship, and by his public defense of American democracy. Mann's appointment as a consultant in Germanic literature related to all three of these concerns.

When MacLeish assumed his post, the Library of Congress was in a rather sorry state. MacLeish's predecessor, Herbert Putnam, had occupied the job for four decades and retired an eighty-year-old man. Over the course of his long tenure, Putnam had expanded the library's holdings from one to six million volumes and established the Library of Congress Classification System on a national scale. But he also remained stuck in the managerial customs of the Gilded Age, ruling over his domain as though it were a personal fiefdom and ignoring developments in modern librarianship.[66] When MacLeish took over, the library was understaffed, and the librarians were underpaid. The cataloging backlog amounted to over 1.5 million volumes.[67] Part of the new librarian's energy was consequently spent on mundane administrative tasks: increasing the budget, reorganizing departments, fighting with the Civil Service Administration for higher wages, and hiring dozens of new catalogers. But MacLeish also advanced and then implemented an audacious vision for the Library of Congress. During 1940 and 1941 especially, MacLeish's name was everywhere in the American public sphere. He spoke and wrote about libraries as bastions of democracy, a topic that moved his lectures into the vicinity of Mann's. Whereas Mann remained mired in philosophical abstractions, however, MacLeish gave his thoughts a more pragmatic and institutionally grounded direction. President Roosevelt during this time started using his famous description of the United States as an "arsenal of democracy." For MacLeish, the Library of Congress was a part of this arsenal; it was to be what one contemporary account described as a "fortress of freedom."[68]

MacLeish's vision essentially had two parts. First, he wanted to breathe new life into the library's founding purpose as a servant of the government, without thereby limiting its service to the general public. When the Library of Congress was founded in 1800, it was generally perceived as a public version of the eighteenth-century gentleman-scholar's personal library. Over the course of the nineteenth century, it grew into a great research institution, similar to many college libraries. MacLeish believed that the Library of Congress should differentiate itself from these other libraries by placing emphasis on those materials necessary for the operation of a government bureaucracy: statistical materials and maps as well as government documents and bibliographic materials from all countries in the world.[69] After Pearl Harbor, he phrased this vision in an increasingly militant light, writing that "today, the Library of Congress is, physiologically speaking, the nerve center of our national life. It is alive with activity essential to the nation's defense, to vital legislation, to the expanded needs and extraordinary demands of a nation at war. Every resource at its command is strained for national service."[70]

Second and even more importantly, however, MacLeish wanted the Library of Congress to serve as an educational institution for the values and ideals of democracy. During a fiery speech that he gave at the Carnegie Institute in Pittsburgh just weeks after assuming his new office (and less than two months after the outbreak of the Second World War), he declared that "we will either educate the people of this Republic to know, and therefore to value and therefore to preserve their own democratic culture, or we will watch the people of this Republic trade their democratic culture for the non-culture, the obscurantism, the superstition, the brutality, the tyranny which is overrunning eastern and central and southern Europe."[71] And in an equally combative appearance before the American Library Association the following year, he charged that the fundamental fault of professional librarianship as it then existed had been its failure "to arrive at a common agreement as to the social end which librarianship exists to serve."[72] MacLeish's ideal of the librarian as a curator and educator working on behalf of ordinary Americans in times of war has obvious roots in the middlebrow culture of the 1930s that did so much to promote Thomas Mann's rise into a literary superstar. Tellingly, Dorothy Canfield Fisher, who had worked with Alfred A. Knopf and Helen Tracy Lowe-Porter to promote the German author through the Book-of-the-Month Club, wrote to MacLeish after reading his Carnegie address to express her full-throated approval and tell him about her father, who she claimed had held very similar ideals during his tenure as the head librarian of the Ohio State University.[73]

The two poles of MacLeish's vision—government service and democratic education—came together in his plans for a new category of fellowships through which intellectuals and artists from outside the library might be hired to help professionalize its collection, lend their expertise to the government, and reach out to the general public. The Library of Congress had, in fact, already sheltered a number of honorary "consultants" since the early 1920s. A 1945 recollection by Luther H. Evans, Archibald MacLeish's successor as librarian of Congress, gives a good impression of why they were deemed unsuitable by the ambitious poet-librarian: "A group of greybeards who spent their morning hours in eager anticipation of the learned discourse around the "round table" beginning at half past twelve, and their afternoons in childlike slumber at home, they had been the darlings of their septuagenarian master [Putnam]. But to Mr. MacLeish these superannuated gentry were objects first of consternation and then of actual concern. The "round table" died suddenly and left no heirs."[74] Although most of these consultants were academics, at least one was a practicing writer: Joseph Auslander, whose term as consultant in poetry had begun in 1937. MacLeish despised Auslander, whom he had once privately described as "a word fellow" with "the labial not to say digital dexterity of a masturbating monkey."[75] Unsurprisingly, he set about immediately to have him removed, and eventually succeeded in having the consultant position replaced with a rotating lecture series called The Poet in a Democracy. The sponsor of this lecture series was Agnes E. Meyer, who would soon also come knocking with an inquiry on behalf of Thomas Mann.

The rest of the consultant system turned out to be harder to replace. Instead of the lifetime appointments of the earlier advisers, MacLeish envisioned a set of rotating year-long fellowships for young and ambitious academics. From the very beginning, he set his sights on the stream of refugee intellectuals (especially social scientists) that was then arriving from Europe as a possible target group. Along with his assistant R. D. Jameson, administrator of consultant services, MacLeish spent a great amount of energy throughout 1940 corresponding with the Emergency Committee in Aid of Displaced Foreign Scholars, the International Red Cross, and the American Council of Learned Societies.[76] MacLeish's efforts on behalf of refugees were greatly hampered by the paucity of available funds and the difficulties of hiring noncitizens into government employment. The Carnegie Corporation eventually provided him with funds to employ a number of young American academics on leave from their respective institutions, a program that would continue until 1944. Unlike the earlier consultants, these fellows were selected largely to help develop bibliographic materials in areas that had a clear military applicability: recent European military history, population studies, naval history, war bibliography, and so on.[77] There were also a number of part-time associate fellows, initially drawn from inside the library, but then increasingly from other parts of America's burgeoning war apparatus.

When Agnes E. Meyer wrote to MacLeish in October of 1941 and proposed that she finance a "Consultantship in German Literature" at the Library of Congress, her proposal therefore could not have fallen on more fecund ground. MacLeish had already extolled Mann as the quintessential "responsible" artist in his widely read piece "The Irresponsibles." He had already worked with Meyer to establish a Poet in a Democracy lecture series, very similar in intent to what Meyer was now proposing. And he had begun a new scheme for the employment of outside intellectuals at the library, clearly highlighting émigrés as a desirable recruiting group. Although Mann's initial title from 1941 to 1942 was that of "consultant" (probably because Meyer had been involved with library affairs for the past two decades and remembered the older nomenclature), this title changed to the more modern one of "fellow" in late 1942.

Mann's duties to the Library of Congress were light. He was to take up residency for two weeks out of every year and give a public lecture during this period. In addition he was to be available for "advice and information" in conjunction with the library's holdings in German literature.[78] In reality Mann never abided by the residency requirements and was rarely if ever consulted in bibliographical matters. He also gave only five lectures over the course of his nine-year tenure: "The Theme of the *Joseph* Novels" in 1942, "The War and the Future" in 1943, "Germany and the Germans" in 1945, "Nietzsche's Philosophy in the Light of Contemporary Events" in 1947, and "Goethe and Democracy" in 1949. Mann's unsigned staff identification card, still on file in the Library of Congress, provides silent testimony of his seeming disengagement (figure 4.6).

The author's light duties provoked malicious gossip in the press and forced MacLeish to issue a sharp rebuttal in which he pointed out, among other things, that Mann's position was paid for out of private funds, not taxpayer

FIGURE 4.6.   Thomas Mann's staff card, identifying him as an employee of the Library of Congress, 1943. Consultants and Fellows File, box 25, folder Thomas Mann, Manuscript Division, Library of Congress.

dollars.[79] In reality, however, both parties derived significant benefits from the arrangement. Mann gained a steady source of income as well as a highly visible platform in the nation's capital. The lecture scripts that he prepared for the Library of Congress are, without exception, more carefully argued and intellectually nuanced texts than the ones that he took on the road for his job as an itinerant lecturer. His speeches were even more important, however, as illustrative examples of MacLeish's vision for responsible liberalism and for the educative role of modern libraries. They were exhibit A for the Library of Congress's transformation from the treasure house of culture that it had become under Putnam into a "fortress of freedom." MacLeish's awareness of this fact is clearly documented by the introductions he gave for Mann's talks in 1942, 1943, and 1945. On the occasion of Mann's 1943 lecture, for example, MacLeish informed his audience that

> we owe it to the Nazis that we have recovered a sense of what it is to have put together a great collection of books, and to have surrounded these books with scholars, with men of learning. It is the great glory of this country, among other glories, that it possesses here a great library, which is not only the greatest collection of materials that men have ever put together, but a collection of materials around which are gathered scholars and writers. *It is my very great pride to introduce to you tonight not Thomas Mann, one of the great novelists of our time, but Thomas Mann, Consultant in Germanic Literature at the Library of Congress.* (Br. AM, 989–90; emphasis mine)

As symbolic occasions, the Mann lectures were indeed memorable. They took place in front of overflow crowds in the library's richly appointed Elizabeth Sprague Coolidge Auditorium and attracted important government dignitaries. The initial lecture and subsequent party at Meyer's house were attended by the vice president, Henry A. Wallace; the attorney general, Francis Biddle; and the secretary of the treasury, Henry Morgenthau, as well as several Supreme Court justices and Edward Wood, Viscount Halifax, the British ambassador. Less than a year after the United States had entered the Second World War, Mann was thus being courted as a representative public intellectual speaking on behalf of Germany to members of the American government.

Mann's affiliation with the Library of Congress provided him with an important opportunity to affirm his function as a representative German. Even more importantly, however, it also provided a forum in which he could present both his fictional and his nonfictional work of the early 1940s as a form of cultural warfare. Thus in the 1942 lecture "The Theme of the

Joseph Novels," he was able to present his about-to-be-concluded tetralogy, which he had begun almost two decades earlier, as a project ideally suited to contemporary times, arguing that "there were hidden, defiantly polemic connections between it and certain tendencies of our time which I always found repulsive from the bottom of my soul," such as anti-Semitism (*LC*, 11; *GW*, 11:663). In his 1945 lecture "Germany and the Germans" he provided a summary of the lessons to be drawn from Nazism now that the end of the Third Reich was at hand. Perhaps the most intimate connection between the "fortress of freedom" and Mann's cultural war work came about in 1943, however, when decided to write his agitatory novella *The Tables of the Law* on Library of Congress stationery.

Interlude III: *The Tables of the Law* (1943)

The novella *The Tables of the Law* has always occupied a singular status among the works of Thomas Mann. It is his only mature work of fiction to have been written on commission, his only story to appear in English before it did in German. And it starkly divided both contemporary reviewers and later critics, some of whom dismissed it as a second-rate coda to the gargantuan *Joseph* cycle that Mann had completed just a few months earlier, while others declared it to be a key summation of Mann's political and sociological thought.[1]

The importance of this strange little text for Mann's attempts to promote himself as a representative of all things German is illustrated by an episode that took place less than a year after its publication. In July of 1944, Henri Peyre, the Sterling Professor of Modern French Literature at Yale University, published an open attack on Thomas Mann in the letters section of the *Atlantic Monthly*. Peyre accused Mann of agitating for a soft peace with Germany and dredged up previously untranslated quotations from the time of the First World War that cast their author in an extremely unflattering light. Mann struck back three months later, with a short essay to which the *Atlantic* gave the title "In My Defense." Throughout much of this piece, he is indeed noticeably on the defensive, poking at bibliographic errors in Peyre's account and listing the names of his anti-Nazi treatises. But he rouses himself toward more programmatic heights on the final page of the essay, where he describes himself as "a man who is exerting the vital powers of his declining years to play a rightful part in the current struggles of humanity, and to combine his duties as a world citizen with the task of furthering and completing a life's work that may have some value for some people" (IMD, 102; GW, 13:210).

Edward A. Weeks, the editor of the *Atlantic*, sent advance proofs of Mann's reply to Archibald MacLeish, who felt compelled to put in a word on behalf of his fellow in German literature: "I can imagine how difficult it is for a man living here as an exile to face the blasts of ill-will. . . . Only you can judge . . . how far the *Atlantic's* pages ought to lend themselves to Mann's enemies."[2] Whether Mann ever learned of this intervention is uncertain, but no sooner had "In My Defense" appeared in print than he wrote to McLeish to inquire "whether I may present to the Library the original handwriting of [*The Tables of the Law*]. My special reason for this offer is the fact that the whole story is written on the particularly pleasant stationery of the Library—a misuse for which I can best atone by this dedication" (*L*, 456; *Br.*, 2:398).

Perhaps Mann was being ironic, but the fact remains that had he merely been looking for a suitable repository for his manuscript, Yale's Beinecke Rare Book and Manuscript Library, which already possessed a substantial part of his personal papers, would have made far more sense. Instead, he chose to leave it to MacLeish's "fortress of freedom," a fact that underscores the expressly political nature of this work.

Certainly nobody would deny that *The Tables of the Law* was begun as a literary form of cultural warfare against Hitler. Sometime over the summer of 1942, a certain Arnim L. Robinson, an Austrian literary agent and would-be film producer, approached Mann with the idea for an anthology movie for which ten different authors would write scripts illustrating the biblical Commandments and their perversion by the Nazis. By the time that Mann assented to the project, in November 1942, it had already been downsized to a collection of novellas, for which Mann was supposed to provide a foreword. Other notable contributors recruited for the project included Rebecca West, Franz Werfel, Bruno Frank, and Sigrid Undset. For unknown reasons, however, Mann never got started on the foreword and chose to write a novella instead, which Robinson used to illustrate the first Commandment: *Thou Shalt Have No Other Gods besides Me.* (The work acquired its current title when it was published as a stand-alone volume the following year.) Hermann Rauschning wrote the foreword in Mann's stead, providing some choice quotes by Hitler concerning the Decalogue. "The day will come when I shall hold up against these commandments the tables of a new law," the führer was supposed to have said.[3]

The Ten Commandments: Ten Short Novels of Hitler's War against the Moral Code was published in late 1943, to decidedly middling reviews. The anonymous reviewer for the *New Yorker* expressed the central point of concern rather well by stating that the collection proved not only the Nazi transgression against the Decalogue but established "just as conclusively that moral indignation doesn't necessarily make good fiction." Thomas Mann wasn't spared from these verbal lashes, with the reviewer declaring his story to be "none too subtle."[4] This summary assessment glosses over the fact that Mann's story differs from the others in an important way, however. Whereas the other nine writers stuck closely to their commission, writing tales that are set in Nazi-occupied Europe and didactically examine the German betrayal of the Ten Commandments, Mann's contribution instead retells the story of Moses related in the book of Exodus, from Moses's birth to his second descent from Mount Sinai. The story makes no reference to Nazism for much of its duration. Only in the final paragraph does Mann work in a reference to Hitler (and to Rauschning's foreword), when he has Moses proclaim about the Decalogue: "But woe to the man who shall arise and speak: They are no longer valid! [For] the Lord says, I shall raise my foot and shall trample him into the mire, to the bottom of the earth shall I cast the blasphemer, one hundred and twenty fathoms deep" (*TC*, 70; *GW*, 8:853).

Given the chance to display his reputation as "Hitler's Most Intimate Enemy" in an explicit project of literary warfare, then, Mann chose to do something else, offering only an oblique critique of Nazism. Hans Rudolf Vaget has interpreted this decision as a consequence of the many years devoted to the *Joseph* novels. Having spent almost two decades researching and writing about the world of the Old Testament, so his account goes, Mann couldn't resist the temptation to try his hand at one more biblical story. As a result, a "creative impulse which had originally been contemporary and politically motivated was overtaken and eclipsed by the older, well-established interest in reinventing the theme of the artist"—the artist here being Moses himself, who shaped the contours of his people.[5]

This particular line of reasoning only makes sense if Mann's "well-established interest in reinventing the theme of the artist" can indeed be interpreted as standing in opposition to his "contemporary and politically motivated" creative impulses. In truth, however, the two ambitions are one and the same, as the essay "Brother Hitler" already made clear. For Mann, the reinvention of the artist's role *was* a political act, for the artist and the dictator are "brothers." The crimes of the latter thus force the former to reexamine his role in society.

The intertwined experiences of artist and dictator are symbolized in the story by the figure of Moses. As Mann himself admitted in his autobiographical reflections on the 1940s, *The Story of a Novel*, he gave his biblical protagonist the external appearance of Michelangelo, "in order to depict him as an artist toiling laboriously over refractory human raw material" (*SN*, 16; *GKFA*, 19.1:419). This reference to an artist who works with "human raw material" already suggests the link to the fascist dictator, but in order to further strengthen the allusion, Mann projected aspects of Hitler's characteristic personality—his tendency to violent outbursts, his peculiar speech pattern, and his habit of energetically shaking his fists whenever he spoke—onto his protagonist. Mann's description of other leading Israelites completes the picture: his Joshua appears as the devoted leader of a paramilitary troupe of "Avenging Angels," his Aaron as a silver-tongued propaganda minister, his Miriam as an unflagging organizer of the Hebrew people.

Thomas Mann's Moses is thus at once Michelangelo and Hitler, artist and dictator. Having asserted the fundamental congruence of these two archetypes, Mann now faced the challenge to explain how the artist might rise above his dictatorial sibling, and how the weapons of fascist demagogy might be turned into tools for democracy. His open letter to Henri Peyre provides a partial indication of how he went about doing this. There, it will be recalled, Mann goes out of his way to describe himself not just as an engaged intellectual but as somebody who is striving, through his art, to fulfill his duties as a "world citizen."

It is worth remembering in this context that the exodus story has a long and distinguished literary prehistory, with which Mann was intimately familiar.[6] It is a story par excellence of identity formation, an archetypal myth to which persecuted peoples turn when they try to describe their own struggles to maintain a sense of self in the face of systematic oppression. This is the way it was used in Mann's own time by Jewish novelists such as Sholem Asch, and it is the way, even more importantly, in which it had been used by African American preachers, artists, and intellectuals since at least the early nineteenth century.[7] Just four years prior to *The Tables of the Law*, for example, Zora Neale Hurston had published a novel called *Moses, Man of the Mountain*. In it, Hurston's predominantly African American readers would have found an image of Moses that was based less in scripture than in Hurston's anthropological fieldwork in Haiti, where she had studied local adaptations of the Jewish myth. "There are other concepts of Moses [than the Judeo-Christian one] abroad in the world," Hurston declares in her author's preface, and "all across Africa, America, the West Indies, there are tales of the power of Moses and great worship of him and his powers. But it does not flow from the Ten Commandments. It is his rod of power, the terror he showed before all Israel, and to Pharaoh, and THAT MIGHTY HAND."[8]

There is no reason to believe that Mann had ever heard of Hurston, much less read her novel. But her approach to her source material, which extricates the exodus story from its original Judaic context, appropriates it to describe the experiences of a different ethnic group, and emphasizes Moses's role as a leader of his people, taps into a time-honored literary tradition. For obvious reasons, Mann could not follow in the footsteps of this tradition. He was writing on behalf of Germany, and to equate the German experience with that of the Israelites would have begged the question of Pharaoh's place in the allegory. For Hurston, the matter was simple. She could depict Pharaoh as a protofascist leader, obsessed with the creation of a "New Egypt" and with eugenic policies vis-à-vis the Israelites. ("The birthing beds of Hebrews were matters of state. The Hebrew womb had fallen under the heel of Pharaoh.")[9] Doing so not only allowed her to evoke villainy with a few broad brushstrokes, but also to link American slavery to contemporary German Nazism. Had Mann tried the same thing, he would have fallen victim to the "two Germanys" argument of Prince Hubertus zu Löwenstein and some émigré groups, which tried to draw firm boundaries between a "good" and a "bad" Germany.

Mann's decision to project aspects of Hitler onto the protagonist of his Moses story can thus be read as a way around this difficulty, a way of showing that the "good" and the "bad" Germany were inescapably mixed with one another. To further emphasize this point, Mann hit upon another narrative trick, which consisted of making his protagonist the biracial child of an Egyptian princess and a Hebrew slave. This departure from the biblical source material, which was inspired by his reading of Sigmund Freud's study *Moses and Monotheism*, earned him a certain amount of enmity in the US religious press, though it has since been hailed as one of his more original accomplishments in *The Tables of the Law*.[10] (In reality, as Barbara Johnson and others have discussed, treatments of Moses as biracial or even outright Egyptian were fairly commonplace in the 1920s and 1930s; Hurston, for example, uses the same trope for her own ends when she strongly suggests that Moses may have been the son of an Ethiopian prince.)[11]

Perhaps Mann's most consequential decision in composing *The Tables of the Law*, however, was to focus on precisely that aspect of the story which Hurston, in her attempt to portray Moses as an archetype for the African American experience, chose to downplay: his role as a lawgiver. As the title of Mann's novella indicates, he treats the Decalogue as Moses's crowning achievement; by contrast, episodes such as the crossing of the Red Sea or the battle between the armies of Joshua and of Pharaoh are only stations on the way to Mount Sinai. *The Tables of the Law* also ends with Moses's second descent from the mountain.

Viewed at the simplest level, this decision to focus on the Decalogue establishes Moses as a universal, rather than group-specific, hero: the founder of a global Judeo-Christian tradition rather than of the tribe of Israel. But it does more than that as well; it allows Mann to conceptually flesh out the link between the political leader and the artist. To call the Ten Commandments an artistic achievement may on first sight appear as a stretch, but Mann makes the metaphor literal. Whereas the Bible provides contradictory accounts of whether Moses copies down the Decalogue himself or whether Yahweh does the writing for him, Mann's Moses is the sole creator of the tables of the law.[12] More than that, Mann depicts him as actually inventing the script in which the Decalogue is written. He is therefore not merely a scribe to the divine but an actual artist—that is, somebody who creates a new form for the content that he is about to put down. When Moses embarks upon this task, he first thinks about the hieroglyphic and syllabic scripts he encountered during this travels in Egypt and Midian, mourning chiefly that there exists no similar script in "the language of his father's blood" (*TC*, 58; *GW*, 8:864). But gradually he hits upon a much more innovative idea, an alphabetical script tied not to concepts or syllables but rather to phonemes: "Thus one could form any word one liked, any word which existed, not only in the language of his father's kin, but in all languages" (*TC*, 59; *GW*, 8:865).

The script, much like the content that it represents, thus strives for universal relevance. The allegorical implications of this are clear. Under conditions of fascist dictatorship, so Mann argues in *The Tables of the Law*, it cannot possibly be the role of the engaged artist to merely preserve the cultural heritage of a threatened group, or even to further group solidarity by adding to this heritage. This is, in fact, exactly what Aaron attempts to do when he casts the figure of the golden calf, responding to the demand of the Israelites to be "a people like other peoples" that is permitted "to carouse before gods which are like the gods of other peoples" (*TC*, 65; *GW*, 8:871). (The ensuing quarrel between Aaron and Moses, in which Moses seems more concerned with denigrating Aaron's sculptural abilities than correcting him on theological grounds, only adds to the impression that we are, in fact, witnessing a debate about the proper role of art.) The role of art should instead be to connect a cultural tradition to the wider flow of the world. Mann's Yahweh is precisely not "like the gods of other peoples" in that his law claims universal relevance and is expressed in a form accessible to all. In the open letter to Henri Peyre, Mann spoke in this context of the duties of the artist as world citizen, and his description of the law-giving act atop Mount Sinai is a programmatic statement also for world literature: a vision of artistic creation carried out with the foreknowledge and open embrace of translation and global cultural mobility.

The composition of *The Tables of the Law* overlapped with the Battle of Stalingrad and the Casablanca Conference, at which the Allied Powers settled on the unconditional surrender of Nazi Germany as the only acceptable outcome of the Second World War. Far from being a mere epilogue to the epic sweep of the *Joseph* novels, the story thus acts as a kind of literary gateway through which the contours of a new world are already dimly discernible. A letter that Mann wrote to the philosopher Robert S. Hartman in April 1943 documents that Mann perceived a clear connection between his literary work and the political shape of things to come. He wrote, "The tendency towards some kind of world-organization is undeniably there, and nothing of the sort is possible without a certain degree of secularized Christianity, without a new Bill of Rights, a universally binding basic law of human rights and human dignity" (*Br.*, 2:305).[13] The hard work of bringing about such a new world was being performed on the battlefields of Europe. The nature of that battle would play its part in the ongoing transformation of Thomas Mann's place within world literature.

CHAPTER 5

A Blooming Flower

And somehow, as I rode through the night now increasingly loud with gun-fire, I kept thinking about the flowers I had seen on the balcony railings of those empty and shell-torn houses. And I thought that perhaps those flowers might well symbolize the whole struggle in Spain—those flowers blooming so bravely there in the face of fascist fire; those flowers like the brave and beautiful books of Thomas Mann and others that Hitler burned in his bonfire in Berlin.

—Langston Hughes, "Madrid's Flowers Hoist Blooms to Meet Raining Fascist Bombs," 1937

The "problem of the book" is no longer a German question, but a European one, just as the question of the survival of German culture long ago became the question of the survival of European culture.

—Gottfried Bermann Fischer, in an interview with the Jewish-German newspaper *Der Aufbau*, 1940

On May 10, 1942, CBS first aired what was to become one of the most frequently retransmitted radio plays of the war years. Written by Pulitzer Prize–winning poet Stephen Vincent Benét, narrated by Academy Award–nominated actor Ralph Bellamy, and introduced by America's highest-paid radio journalist, Raymond Gram Swing, *They Burned the Books* was an unabashed propaganda broadcast, its release timed to coincide with the ninth anniversary of the book burnings in Berlin's Opera Square. The literary qualities of the script were dubious. Benét was far from a subtle writer even under the best of circumstances, and no one would claim that this play ranked among his better works. But it captured the spirit of the times. Not only was it frequently rebroadcast in America, but it was also translated into German for transmission into the Reich. The following year, on the tenth anniversary of the book burnings, Bellamy participated in a live performance of the play in front of an audience of thousands at the New York Public Library, while former Republican presidential candidate Wendell Willkie invoked it in a commemorative address.[1]

They Burned the Books consists of two parts. In the first, Benét invokes the ghost of the Jewish poet Heinrich Heine to testify to the Nazis' rewriting of German literary history. In the second, he uses the example of an American classroom studying the Gettysburg Address to illustrate what might happen if the Third Reich ever conquered the United States. The first part concludes with the following exchange between Heine and his Nazi opponent:

NAZI: We'll shut your mouth!
We'll find you in the graveyard where you lie,
Dig up your rotten bones and scatter them,
Scatter them till there's nobody in all the world
Who's heard of Heinrich Heine!
HEINE: (MOCKING) Dig deep! Dig well!
Scatter my bones, break up my burial stone,
Erase my name with all your thoroughness,
Your lumbering, fat-headed, thoroughness,
Smelling of beer and bombs!
And yet, while there's a book, there will be Heine!

Upon which Bellamy intones,

Yes.
There will be Heine. There will be all those
Whose words lift up man's heart.
But only if we choose.
This battle is not just a battle of lands,
A war of conquest, a balance-of-power war.
It is a battle for the mind of man,
Not only for his body.[2]

Needless to say, Benét also provides his listeners with a list of authors whom the Nazis burned, and Thomas Mann figures among them. This would have surprised nobody, for Mann's status as a persecuted author had been extensively reported in the American press. Langston Hughes, in one of his dispatches from the Spanish Civil War for the *Baltimore Afro-American*, memorably invokes the image of Mann's books going up in flames, their pages curling up like petals and thereby forming "beautiful flowers," as a symbol of antifascist resistance. And Walt Disney, in his 1943 propaganda short "Education for Death," depicts Nazi thugs setting fire to a stack of books that prominently includes a Thomas Mann volume. This symbolic prominence was somewhat at odds with historical reality, for while over-zealous Nazis did indeed toss his volumes onto the flames at book burnings throughout the Reich, his works were not part of the carefully staged performance on Opera Square explicitly referenced by Hughes, and indeed they weren't even officially banned until three years later.

These repeated references to book burnings throughout the 1930s and early 1940s highlight the extent to which media featured as weapons in Thomas Mann's struggle against Nazism. This was already true about the American home front, of course. As the photos from Mann's lecture tours prove, Alfred A. Knopf made sure that every stop along the way was provided with an ample supply of books, which eager listeners could purchase and take home with them, in order to further ruminate on what they had heard (figure 5.1). And Mann's rise to literary stardom in the United States would have been impossible without the intervention of newspapers and tabloids, book clubs and radio broadcasts.

This dynamic took on a completely different dimension on the European continent, however. Ever since 1933, Thomas Mann had been unable to personally connect to his core readership in the Reich, and once the Second World War broke out, even a visit to the exile communities in London, Stockholm, or Switzerland was out of the question. In the language of *They Burned the Books*, the Nazis had been able to "scatter his bones." But true to Benét's prophecy, the author lived on in his books—and not just in these, but also in a number of other media, from radio broadcasts to hand-printed propaganda pamphlets.

The US government was keenly aware of the power of books and other media. In a foreshadowing of what Dwight D. Eisenhower, as president, would later christen the "military-industrial complex," Washington and the publishing industry came together to devise effective means of weaponizing literature, of turning books into tools in a cultural battle with Nazism. Benét's radio play was sponsored by the Writers' War Board, an organization put together by the author Rex Stout at the behest of the US Department of the Treasury, which mobilized over two thousand professional writers during its first year alone to produce stories, poems, radio scripts, and novels in support of the war effort.[3] It frequently worked in close collaboration with the Council on Books in Wartime, a similar brain trust put together by America's publishers, perhaps best remembered nowadays for its slogan "Books are Weapons in the War of Ideas." Librarians jumped on the bandwagon as well, and for part of the war, every editorial in the *Library Journal* began with a quote by the commissioner of education, John W. Studebaker: "When people are burning books in other parts of the world, we ought to

FIGURE 5.1. Thomas Mann signing books with his daughter and translator Erika during a 1939 lecture stop in Tulsa, Oklahoma. The LIFE Picture Collection/Getty Images.

be distributing them with greater vigor; our books are among our best allies in the fight to make democracy work."[4]

Thomas Mann, too, benefited from such government-industry collaborations, for example, when NBC and CBS gave him access to their studios to record propaganda broadcasts that were then carried into Nazi-occupied Europe by both the BBC and the Voice of America. His main intermediary on the continent, however, was his old German publisher Gottfried Bermann Fischer, who fought a battle of his own to keep Mann's books available in those countries that had not yet been conquered by the Nazis. Both forms of transmission—the transmission of Mann's voice via radio waves and the transmission of his books via increasingly convoluted distribution networks—were beset by all sorts of difficulties during wartime. But both were essential in keeping the author's influence alive in a time when he was unable to personally connect to his readership.

The Voice of Germany

Thomas Mann was a nearly omnipresent figure in the European republic of letters during the interwar years. His frequent reading tours took him to most of the European capitals, and he impressed his audiences with his stentorian voice and superbly composed appearance. Mann's fame, more than that of almost any other writer, was an *embodied* one. The early years of his exile in Switzerland did not change this fact. Unlike many other émigrés, who retreated inward into the husks of their private lives, Mann continued to travel and to engage with his audiences.

When he departed for America, however, Mann left behind a void in Europe. The author's physical absence from the continent lasted for almost a decade, from 1938 until 1947, when he returned to Switzerland in order to participate in the annual gathering of International PEN, where he delivered the address "Nietzsche's Philosophy in the Light of Contemporary Events." For roughly half this period, however, Mann was nevertheless present on the continent, albeit in disembodied form. Between November 1940 and December 1945, he produced a total of fifty-eight propaganda broadcasts, which the German Service of the BBC carried into the heart of the Reich under the program title *Listen, Germany! (Deutsche Hörer!)*. Occasionally, Mann also recorded English-language addresses for the Voice of America, which were then broadcast to places as far apart as Bombay and Lisbon, Cairo and Stockholm.[5] Interested listeners in Germany and other parts of Europe would therefore have been able to hear his voice, at least assuming they had both the courage and technical wherewithal to tune their radios to the forbidden

"enemy frequencies." Collectively, these addresses form an important document of Thomas Mann's self-presentation as an author and show how he
adapted some of the same rhetorical strategies that had proven effective in
the United States for a European audience. They also provide perhaps the
clearest example of Mann's transformed presence in Europe once the war
made a personal return to the continent impossible.

The story of Mann's involvement in propaganda broadcasting begins in
September 1940, when Erika, his oldest daughter, arrived in London with
the intention of reporting on the Battle of Britain for an American audience.[6] Thanks to a sham marriage with W. H. Auden, who had agreed to the
arrangement when the Nazis stripped her of her German citizenship in 1935,
Erika held a British passport. She also happened to be a personal acquaintance
of Duff Cooper, Churchill's minister of information, and used this connection to persuade the BBC to allow her to record several radio addresses that
were broadcast over the German Service between September 6 and October 14. Over the course of her negotiations, she mentioned that she and her
father had discussed plans for a joint radio project: Thomas Mann would
compose short comments on "any vital subject of the moment," disguised
as personal missives to his daughter, and then cable them to London, where
Erika would read them over the air. Erika's letter to the BBC suggests that
the plan was hatched under the heady influence of Mann's addresses to large
Popular Front gatherings in America during the previous three years, since
she proposes that such radio transmissions might be "successful with a large
number of middle-class and formerly 'social-democratic' Germans."[7]

The BBC was skeptical of such a father-daughter cooperation, perhaps
because it regarded the volatile Erika as a difficult partner. Instead, it suggested that the older Mann cable his statements directly to the BBC, where
they would be read by one of the male broadcasters employed by the German Service. On October 19, the author therefore had a personal interview
with the BBC's New York representative (*Tb.*, October 19, 1940), and a week
later he submitted a five-hundred-word telegram, which was broadcast on
November 6. Three further telegrams followed in late November, December, and January 1941.

The BBC's decision to effectively give Thomas Mann his own program
violated the station's policy not to identify any of its émigré broadcasters by
name. This policy had been instituted because the German Service was eager
to emphasize its putative objectivity. It wanted to be recognized as a source
of information to which German listeners might turn to get the "truth,"
rather than the propaganda lies of their own radio services. Alerting those
listeners to the fact that many of the contributors to the programs were, in

fact, refugees, would have risked tarnishing the service as an "émigré station."[8]

Thomas Mann was clearly regarded as a contributor who was so eminently respectable that he would stand above the fray. His inaugural broadcasts begins with the confident words:

German Listeners:

A German writer speaks to you whose work and person have been outlawed by your rulers, and whose books, even if they deal with the most German matters, with Goethe, for example, can only speak to foreign, free nations, in their language, while for you they must remain silent and unknown. . . . In war-time there is no way left for the written word to pierce the wall which the tyrants have erected around you. Therefore I am glad to take the opportunity which the English radio service has offered me to report to you from time to time about all that I see here in America, the great and free country in which I have found a homestead. (*LG*, 3–4; *GW*, 11:986–87)

Mann unapologetically characterizes himself as a "German" writer whose works "deal with the most German matters." He thereby stakes out his representative claims. He also draws attention to the fact that his books, though censored and physically imperiled in the Reich, nevertheless "speak" to foreign countries in translation. This phrasing neatly anticipates the rhetorical tropes also deployed in Benét's play or in the publications of the American Library Association, and furthermore links the circulation of literature to the war effort. This connection is made especially clear when Mann describes the propaganda broadcasts of the German Service as compensatory measures for the interrupted movement of his books.

The BBC evidently agreed with Mann that his voice was a vital component of his overall message, for starting with the fifth broadcast in March 1941, the author was allowed to record his own texts. Doing so constituted a significant technical challenge. To transmit a message from the East Coast of the United States all the way to Germany via shortwave radio would have already been difficult enough, given the active interference by Nazi jamming stations. To make matters worse, the Mann family relocated to California that same spring. A complicated work-around was thus devised. About once every month, Mann drove to the NBC Studios in Hollywood, where his text was recorded onto a phonograph record. This record was then flown to New York, where it was played in front of a microphone and transmitted to London via transatlantic telephone lines (*LG*, vi; *GW*, 11:984). At BBC headquarters, the transmission was pressed onto yet another record for editing purposes and then broadcast into Germany.[9] The overall loss in signal quality resulting from this process was so great that the BBC on several occasions discussed (but ultimately discarded) plans to instead have the master discs taken across the Atlantic aboard Royal Air Force bombers.

Complex transnational and transmedial processes were thus required to deliver Mann's voice to his European listeners. An authorial persona that had originally been built upon immediacy and embodied charisma was dissolved into something far more ethereal by the vicissitudes of wartime. It is perhaps only fitting that the phonograph should play such an important part in this transformation and that Mann would never address his audiences directly, but only through the time-lapse medium of recording technology. For after all, it was Mann himself who in the concluding chapter of *The Magic Mountain* had provided such a powerful testimony to the record player's capacity to "haunt" our existence. In that novel, a spellbound Hans Castorp listens over and over again to the final act of Giuseppe Verdi's opera *Aida*, in which Aida and her lover Radames, the once-powerful general who has now been cast out of the national community by the high priest Ramfis, are vocally transfigured even as they pine away in a tomb. It wasn't an entirely inappropriate metaphor for the fate of what was once Germany's most prominent author.

Mann, as we have already seen, was an experienced and confident radio speaker, a fact that is borne out by the surviving recordings of his addresses in the German Radio Archives. The first broadcast that he made in his own voice once again begins with a reflective remark regarding its own composition.

German Listeners:

What I had to tell you from afar, until now was brought to you by other voices. This time you hear my own voice.

It is the voice of a friend, a German voice; the voice of a Germany which showed, and will again show, a different face to the world from the horrible Medusa mask which Hitlerism has pressed upon it. It is a *warning* voice—to warn you is the only service which a German like myself is able to render you today; and I do this serious and heartfelt duty although I know that no warning can be issued to you which is not long familiar to you, which has not long been alive in your own fundamentally uncheatable knowledge and conscience. (*LG*, 21; *GW*, 11:997)

In this passage Mann presents Nazism as a "horrible Medusa mask" that has been pressed upon *all* of Germany, and refers to his own voice not as a call coming from abroad but rather as emanating from the true entity that lies beneath. On the one hand, this strategy enables him to build a bridge to his audience and to suggest that his listeners, too, have for a long time and deep down in their "uncheatable conscience" known that the Nazis were evil. On the other, it disabuses those same listeners of the notion that they can somehow extricate themselves from the vengeance of the Allied bombardments. The Medusa mask weighs upon all Germans, whether they like it or not.

Mann's argument anticipates the one he would make four years later in his lecture "Germany and the Germans," and is all the more significant for the medium in which it was raised. In the early 1940s, neither the British government nor the programming directors of the BBC as yet had any clear sense of where they stood on the question of German war guilt. In fact, Lindley M. Fraser, an influential contributor to the German Service, which he would eventually come to direct, spent the latter part of 1942 delivering lectures with titles such as "The Part Played by Broadcasting in Modern Warfare." Fraser believed that in order to be an effective propaganda instrument, the radio would have to tirelessly reiterate a distinction between the Nazis and ordinary Germans, in order to dissuade the latter from fighting to the bitter end.[10] In the United States, Reinhold Niebuhr, whose reflections on the guilt question exerted enormous influence in government circles, expressed a similar viewpoint in a scathing review of *Listen, Germany!*[11] The fact that Mann's own message so widely diverged from what increasingly became received wisdom in Allied government circles shows that while his interventions were mediated by the international propaganda networks of the Second World War, they cannot simply be reduced to them. They instead formed a part of a longer process of authorial self-stylization.

The One and Only German Preacher

Mann sustained his broadcasts throughout the duration of the war, ceasing only after the unconditional surrender in May 1945. His broadcasts soon lost what little anchoring in topical commentary they may have originally possessed, however. His initial assignment as a foreign correspondent did not particularly suit him. He was interested in more fundamental questions. Even more than the speeches that he delivered on the American lecture circuit, Mann's radio addresses are marked by a hortatory attitude and the use of overtly biblical language, which has been exhaustively cataloged by the German critic Bernd Hamacher. Among other things, Mann employs phrases such as "but I say unto you" (ich aber sage euch) and "have no fear" (fürchtet euch nicht) that are taken from the Sermon on the Mount (Mt 5.28) and the Christmas story according to Luke (Lk 2.10), respectively.[12] He casts Hitler into the role of the Antichrist, calling him "the most godless of all creatures, who has no other relationship to God the Lord than to be a scourge of God" (*LG*, 67–68; *GW*, 11:1024), and reminds his German listeners that the führer "makes you believe that he is the man of the millennia, come to place himself in Christ's stead and to supplant the Saviour's doctrine of human brotherhood under God" (*LG*, 14; *GW*, 11:993). He even goes so far as to compare himself to a prophet when he says that "my conviction grows daily that the time will come, and is already approaching, when you will be grateful . . . that I warned you, when there was still time, to beware of the vile powers in whose yoke you are helplessly harnessed today" (*LG*, 58–59; *GW*, 11:1019).

As was already the case with his American lecture scripts, Mann's appropriation of biblical language must primarily be seen as an ingenious rhetorical ploy. He knew that these phrases would trigger affective responses in his audience; not for nothing did he primarily pilfer from passages that even Germans who were less-than-enthusiastic churchgoers would have recognized. At times, his American strategy could even be adapted wholesale for the German context. In April 1943, for example, Mann read the final paragraph of his recently completed novella *The Tables of the Law* over the ether. The Moses story as a whole, drawing as it did on the mythic inheritance of the Old Testament rather than on the prophetic diction of the New, and originally crafted for an American audience that was just then discovering its "Judeo-Christian" inheritance as a counterpoint to fascism, would hardly have made a suitable subject for the BBC broadcasts. But the final paragraph, with its strongly implied criticism of Hitler and its messianic tone, was perfect for the new context.

Most importantly, however, Mann also tied his new rhetorical strategy to his long-standing ambitions to be recognized as the true spokesperson of the German cultural tradition. In doing so, he positioned himself in explicit opposition to Adolf Hitler. In the preface to the first printed edition of his radio addresses, for example, he boasts that "my allocutions have been referred to, in an unmistakable fashion, by my Führer himself" (*LG*, vii; *GW*, 11:985). The term "allocution" originally referred to any exhortatory or moralizing discourse, but in contemporary German is generally reserved for the official pronouncements of diplomatic representatives, especially those of an apostolic nuncio.

This complex self-presentation would have been impossible if other speakers had read Thomas Mann's missives on his behalf. The efficacy of Mann's radio addresses depended upon the ways in which the author simultaneously styled himself as present and absent. Present, because his voice persisted even in the face of the "wall" that Nazi tyranny had erected around Germany. But also absent, because it spoke from a place beyond immediate reach. And in contrast to the rhetorical strategies employed by most other speakers on the BBC German Service, this distant place wasn't equated with Britain, the United States, or any other concrete location beyond the borders of the Reich. Mann had no use for the standard propaganda strategy of telling the enemy how well things were going in the Allied countries: how much better off the workers were, how inexorably military production was ramping up, and so on. He spoke to Germans from a truly immaterial and unlocatable place.

The American media scholar Melissa Dinsman has described Mann's radio addresses as "haunted," a description that holds true to a perhaps even greater degree than Dinsman herself recognizes.[13] Dinsman adduces two "ghostly" facets of Mann's performances: First, his exhortatory discourse was quite literally disembodied by the medium of the radio, especially at a time when Nazi jamming stations frequently corrupted the BBC signal. Second, Mann draped himself in the garb of cultural tradition and addressed his listeners as the haunting voice of a happier past. To these we can add two further dimensions: first, Mann's own understanding of what he was doing as a thoroughly modern activity, a production of German *Geist* brought about in what his opening address called the "free" world outside the "walls that tyrants have erected"; and second, his affectation of a hortatory, at times even messianic, attitude.

The dust-jacket illustration of the first US edition of *Listen, Germany!* nicely encapsulates these various facets. Its three floating heads highlight the disembodied nature of his radio work and cast Mann in the role of someone who speaks from the repressed depths of the German cultural heritage (figure 5.2).[14] At the same time, Dinsman suggests, the arrangement of the heads into a geographical constellation—the United States, Britain, and Germany—points to the ways in which Mann has transplanted German "spirit" into the extraterritorial realm of the world republic of letters. Finally, and perhaps most overtly, the collage also gestures toward the Holy Trinity.

The BBC actively encouraged Mann's swerve away from a primarily factual toward a primarily hortatory and prophetic style. On July 11, 1941, Erika, who had just paid a business call to BBC headquarters in London, cabled her father to say,

BBC DELIGHTED WITH YOUR SPEECHES BUT I AGREE SUGGEST YOU SHOULD REMAIN AS GODLIKE AND GENERALLY

FIGURE 5.2. Dust-jacket illustration of the first US edition of *Listen, Germany!*, 1943. Alfred A. Knopf/Random House.

VALID AS POSSIBLE OMITTING COMMENT ON DAILY EVENTS
BUT RATHER TALK ABOUT GERMAN SOUL GOOD AND EVIL
ETC STOP . . . BEING ONE AND ONLY GERMAN PREACHER
ABOVE CLOUDS YOU MIGHT STICK TO ETERNAL CONCEPTS
NEVER DESCENDING TO LOWER SPHERES STOP[15]

There is of course a fair bit of self-irony in these lines. The BBC, however, seems to have missed it—Cyril Conner, the station's overseas liaison manager, commented instead that the telegram was "somewhat strange in language." He expressed hope that "no doubt [Mann] and his daughter understand each other's language best."[16]

Such earnestness and eagerness to embrace Mann's prophetic message was perhaps to be expected. The so-called broadcast talks—the program rubric under which the BBC slotted Mann's radio addresses—had been invented by the corporation's first director general, John Reith, and had quickly developed into a core component of the station's broadcast identity. Reith was a devout Scottish Presbyterian, and his leadership of the BBC was strongly inflected by his religious values. There were no broadcasts on Sundays before 12:30 p.m., for example. More importantly for the purpose at hand, however, Reith also believed in the radio as a vehicle of public instruction and moral elevation. This was the primary purpose he assigned to the broadcast talks, which quickly became an important instrument for the buttressing of religious values, national identity, and imperial ideology. Much as Mann's attempts to reinvent himself in the United States found an ideal vehicle in the Methodist Chautauqua lecturing tradition, so his radio rhetoric found an accommodating vessel in the established format of the BBC radio talks, conditioned as they were by Presbyterian values. It is certainly not surprising, then, to find one of his supervising producers at the station praising his broadcasts by stating that "their value tends, if anything, to increase with time because of the prophecies contained in them."[17]

Three things might thus be noted about Thomas Mann's radio addresses. First, they derive their considerable power from their willingness to rethink the place at which modern authorship is created, moving it from the geographic confines of the nation to a much less determinate location somewhere in the ether, and from the physical body of the writer to the circuitry of the radio receiver. Second, they cleverly exploit the religious expectations both of their audience and of their producers. And third, they are born from the unprecedented logistical challenge with which the war effort confronted the Allied nations. Overlain with static, Mann's disembodied voice, which he exploited to such great rhetorical effect in his messianic diction, was a direct outcome of the transnational and transmedial processes by which military matériel was shuttled from one end of the world to the other during the early 1940s.

For the Nazis, Mann's broadcasts represented a formidable threat. Joseph Goebbels mentions them no less than five times in his diaries. On April 6, 1942, for example, he caustically notes: "Thomas Mann gave a speech on English radio that was filled with the greatest nonsense that one could possibly imagine. The fact that our enemies dare to praise this putrescent so-called intellectual giant of the German Republic as the spokesperson for the future Germany only proves the general mental aberration on the other side of the Channel."[18] More than a year earlier, in March 1941, his propaganda ministry had already instructed all German newspapers aimed primarily at an educated audience to "polemically attack the speeches by Thomas Mann that are being broadcast over the British radio."[19] Nazi jamming stations also targeted the BBC above and beyond all other foreign radio transmitters, and the German Service features prominently in the court documents of those unfortunate men and women who were tried for listening to "enemy broadcasts."[20] Anecdotal evidence suggests that antifascist resistance circles held similarly high opinions of Mann's radio addresses.[21] Large numbers of Germans, finally, claimed to have listened to the BBC when they filled out denazification questionnaires, although their testimony obviously provides an unreliable gauge for what may actually have happened.[22]

Lyons' Red Label Tea

The BBC broadcasts were by far the most prominent venue through which Thomas Mann maintained a disembodied presence inside the Reich even after the outbreak of the Second World War. This is not to say that the written word did not play any part in keeping his memory alive. For example, over the course of the 1930s and early 1940s, half a dozen *Tarnschriften* were produced of Thomas Mann's political works, including complete copies of his *Exchange of Letters*, as well as "The Coming Victory of Democracy." *Tarnschriften* were camouflaged publications, frequently disguised as street maps, tourist brochures, or other utilitarian examples of print culture, that were smuggled into Nazi Germany for propaganda purposes. By far the largest proportion—roughly 80 percent, by one scholarly estimate—of these writings was produced by Communist sources, and Thomas Mann's presence in the pamphlets once again attests to the high esteem in which he was held by the Popular Front.[23]

Uniformly, the text of the Thomas Mann *Tarnschriften* was copied faithfully from the original sources, and the brochures do not feature any additional commentary.[24] The appeal of these documents to the modern examiner thus lies in their physical qualities, and specifically in their ephemeral nature. To name but one example, in 1938 unidentified sources smuggled copies of Mann's essay "German Education" (originally written as a preface for Erika Mann's book *School for Barbarians*) into the Reich as leaflets hidden in bags of Lyons' Red Label Tea (figure 5.3). As chance would have it, the color scheme of the tea bags (red, black, and creamy white) exactly mirrored that of the dust jacket of *School for Barbarians*, which showed a pile of books being burned and advertised an "Introduction by Thomas Mann" in such a way that the name of Erika's father seemed to hover directly above the flames. It was as if the *Tarnschrift* had given a second life to Mann's work after its original destruction at the hands of the Nazis.

Other *Tarnschriften* were more conventional in format. Sometime around 1941, for example, unknown agents produced a clandestine printing of Mann's 1939 essay "This War" (figure 5.4). The cover page praises Mann as the author of "world famous" works and as the heir of the "German humanistic tradition begun by Goethe"—two epithets that resemble praises heaped on him in America, but acquired a political logic of their own within

FIGURE 5.3. *Tarnschrift* of Thomas Mann's "German Education" disseminated in bag of Lyons' Red Label Tea, 1938. *Tarnschriften*, Rare Book Collection, New York Public Library. Astor, Lenox and Tilden Foundations.

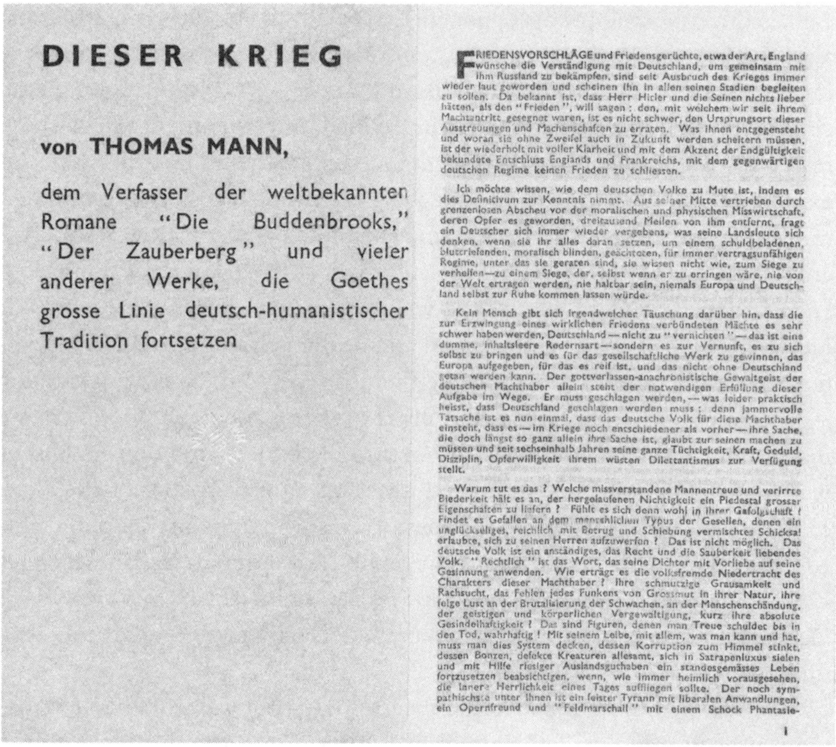

DIESER KRIEG

von THOMAS MANN,

dem Verfasser der weltbekannten Romane "Die Buddenbrooks," "Der Zauberberg" und vieler anderer Werke, die Goethes grosse Linie deutsch-humanistischer Tradition fortsetzen

FRIEDENSVORSCHLÄGE und Friedensgerüchte, etwa der Art, England wünsche die Verständigung mit Deutschland, um gemeinsam mit ihm Russland zu bekämpfen, sind seit Ausbruch des Krieges immer wieder laut geworden und scheinen ihn in allen seinen Stadien begleiten zu sollen. Da bekannt ist, dass Herr Hitler und die Seinen nichts lieber hätten, als den "Frieden", will sagen: den, mit welchem wir seit ihrem Machtantritt gesegnet waren, ist es nicht schwer, den Ursprungsort dieser Ausstreuungen und Machenschaften zu erraten. Was ihnen entgegensteht und woran sie ohne Zweifel auch in Zukunft werden scheitern müssen, ist der wiederholt mit voller Klarheit und mit dem Akzent der Endgültigkeit bekundete Entschluss Englands und Frankreichs, mit dem gegenwärtigen deutschen Regime keinen Frieden zu schliessen.

Ich möchte wissen, wie dem deutschen Volke zu Mute ist, indem es dies Definitivum zur Kenntnis nimmt. Aus seiner Mitte vertrieben durch grenzenlosen Abscheu vor der moralischen und physischen Misswirtschaft, deren Opfer es geworden, dreitausend Meilen von ihm entfernt, fragt ein Deutscher sich immer wieder vergebens, was seine Landsleute sich denken, wenn sie ihr alles daran setzen, um einem schuldbeladenen, blutriefenden, moralisch blinden, geächteten, für immer vertragsunfähigen Regime, unter das sie geraten sind, zu wissen nicht wie, zum Siege zu verhelfen—zu einem Siege, der, selbst wenn er zu erringen wäre, nie von der Welt ertragen werden, nie haltbar sein, niemals Europa und Deutschland selbst zur Ruhe kommen lassen würde.

Kein Mensch gibt sich irgendwelcher Täuschung darüber hin, dass die zur Erzwingung eines wirklichen Friedens verbündeten Mächte es sehr schwer haben werden, Deutschland—nicht zu "vernichten",—das ist eine dumme, inhaltsleere Redensart—sondern es zur Vernunft, es zu sich selbst zu bringen und so für das gesellschaftliche Werk zu gewinnen, das Europa aufgegeben, für das es reif ist, und das nicht ohne Deutschland getan werden kann. Der gottverlassen-anachronistische Gewaltgeist der deutschen Machthaber allein steht der notwendigen Erfüllung dieser Aufgabe im Wege. Er muss geschlagen werden,—was leider praktisch heisst, dass Deutschland geschlagen werden muss; denn jammervolle Tatsache ist es nun einmal, dass das deutsche Volk für diese Machthaber einsteht, dass es—im Kriege noch entschiedener als vorher—ihre Sache, die doch längst so ganz allein ihre Sache ist, glaubt zur seinen machen zu müssen und seit sechseinhalb Jahren seine ganze Tüchtigkeit, Kraft, Geduld, Disziplin, Opferwilligkeit ihrem wüsten Dilettantismus zur Verfügung stellt.

Warum tut es das? Welche missverstandene Mannentreue und verirrte Biederkeit hält es an, der hergelaufenen Nichtigkeit ein Piedestal grosser Eigenschaften zu liefern? Fühlt es sich denn wohl in ihrer Gefolgschaft? Findet es Gefallen an dem menschlichen Typus der Gesellen, denen ein unglückseliges, reichlich mit Betrug und Schiebung vermischtes Schicksal erlaubte, sich zu seinen Herren aufzuwerfen? Das ist nicht möglich. Das deutsche Volk ist ein anständiges, das Recht und die Sauberkeit liebendes Volk. "Rechtlich" ist das Wort, das seine Dichter mit Vorliebe auf seine Gesinnung anwenden. Wie erträgt es die volksfremde Niedertracht des Charakters dieser Machthaber? Ihre schmutzige Grausamkeit und Rachsucht, das Fehlen jedes Funkens von Grossmut in ihrer Natur, ihre feige Lust an der Brutalisierung der Schwachen, an der Menschenschändung, der geistigen und körperlichen Vergewaltigung, kurz ihre absolute Gesindelhaftigkeit? Das sind Figuren, denen man Treue schuldet bis in den Tod, wahrhaftig! Mit seinem Leibe, mit allem, was man kann und hat, muss man dies System decken, dessen Korruption zum Himmel stinkt, dessen Bonzen, defekte Kreaturen allesamt, sich in Satrapenluxus siehen und mit Hilfe riesiger Auslandsguthaben ein standesgemässes Leben fortzusetzen beabsichtigen, wenn, wie immer heimlich vorausgesehen, die innere Herrlichkeit eines Tages auffliegen sollte. Der noch sympathischste unter ihnen ist ein feiser Tyrann mit liberalen Anwandlungen, ein Opernfreund und "Feldmarschall" mit einem Schock Phantasie-

FIGURE 5.4. *Tarnschrift* of Thomas Mann's "This War," ca. 1941. Thomas-Mann-Archiv, ETH Zurich.

the censorship regime of the Third Reich. Mann's covert readers would furthermore have been struck by the abject incongruity between this flimsy, unassuming leaflet and its author's exalted status during the times of the Weimar Republic. Robert Musil famously satirized Mann as a *Großschriftsteller*, a term that can ambiguously refer not only to a writer who is "great," but more importantly, also to one who is "large"—large in sales, large in public influence, large in personality.[25] The antifascist *Tarnschriften* were the exact opposite of all this, featuring, as they did, mere fragments of a formerly expansive oeuvre and consigning them to the hidden recesses of some of the smallest, most disposable, and most quotidian objects imaginable, such as tea bags or seed packets. Mann himself saw matters slightly differently, of course. In a 1939 address to the American Booksellers Association he proclaimed: "If today, the book plays a lamentable role [in Germany], it is because of the terrorism of a regime which misuses the word and has robbed it of all power to inspire confidence. One does not want to read the approved trash. However, for the work which has arisen in freedom—for the translated literature—there is a zealous demand" (MSL, 1888; *GW*, 13:434).

It is thus not true (as his opponents especially would be prone to argue after the Second World War) that Mann was entirely absent from Germany for the majority of the Nazi reign. Both Mann's voice and his writings still circulated, even if in drastically circumscribed and ephemeral form. These residues, furthermore, were more than simple diminutions of what had existed before the time of the Reich. They were transformations, even transfigurations. An authorial personality built on physical charisma and embodied "Germanness" was changed into an ethereal voice speaking from an indeterminate place beyond the walls built by tyranny. An oeuvre built on intellectual grandeur and physical amplitude was fragmented into splinters that could nevertheless insinuate themselves into the most unassuming aspects of everyday life. And a carefully choreographed publication strategy masterminded by an ambitious author and his no-less-ambitious publisher was replaced by the anonymous and unassuming productions of the *Tarnschriften* distributors. Collectively, these transformations prefigured a new role for Thomas Mann in the postwar republic of letters: a role in which his authority would come from abroad and be determined by factors over which Germans themselves had little influence, and which they at times barely even understood.

Thomas Mann himself became increasingly cognizant of this development over the course of the war years. Already in his 1939 address to the booksellers of America, he boldly asserted that publishers and writers alike were now charged with the task of clarifying "for themselves and the world the meaning of their existence" (MSL, 1886; GW, 13:430). The sources of authority on which publishers and writers alike depended were up for renegotiation. Mann was lucky that throughout his time in the United States he could depend on the friendship of two extraordinary publishers: Alfred A. Knopf for the American market and Gottfried Bermann Fischer for the continental European one. Over the course of the decade that stretched from 1936 to 1945, Bermann Fischer too was discovering that the social role of a publisher was rapidly changing in a world altered by war. His success in navigating the resulting challenges contributed greatly to Mann's lasting significance.

Gottfried Bermann Fischer

Gottfried Bermann Fischer was born as Gottfried Bermann in the Silesian town of Gleiwitz in 1897. In 1926, he married Brigitte Fischer, the oldest daughter of Samuel Fischer, founder of one of Germany's most esteemed publishing houses for modern literature. Bermann Fischer was thirty years old when he took over as managing director of the family business, and still only in his mid-thirties when he inherited the company upon his father-in-law's death in 1934.[26]

The S. Fischer Verlag had had a strongly European orientation from the very beginning, and was especially famous for its list of contemporary Scandinavian authors, such as Henrik Ibsen, Jens Peter Jacobsen, Georg Brandes, and Alexander Kielland. Under its new managing director, however, the publishing house became international in a legal sense as well. In 1932, anticipating future harassment from the Nazis, Bermann Fischer founded a shell company in Switzerland, the Corporation for Publishing Rights (AG für Verlagsrechte).[27] After Hitler took power, all contracts with authors liable to cause offense with German authorities, including such big names as Alfred Döblin, Hugo von Hofmannsthal, Annette Kolb, Arthur Schnitzler, and also Thomas Mann, were routed through Switzerland, from where they were then leased back for a nominal fee to the Fischer publishing house.[28]

By 1935 it was clear to Bermann Fischer and his wife that their position as perhaps the most prominent Jewish publishers in Nazi Germany was no longer tenable. Since they knew the authorities would hardly allow them to relocate the entire company with its considerable financial assets to a foreign country, they worked out a compromise with the Reichsschrifttumskammer, the Nazi agency responsible for literature and the book trade. The firm was split in two, with all rights to authors whom the Nazis considered sufficiently "Aryan" remaining in Berlin. This "Aryanized" publishing house would retain the name "S. Fischer" and be led by Bermann Fischer's trusted second-in-command, Peter Suhrkamp.[29] The rights to all authors whom the Nazis deemed offensive, as well as the physical inventory pertaining to these authors (almost eight hundred thousand printed copies in total), would be transferred over to Gottfried Bermann Fischer, who was simultaneously given permission to emigrate.[30] The Bermann Fischers originally intended to move to Switzerland. When the Swiss authorities turned down their settlement request due to the intervention of a rival company, they emigrated to Vienna instead, where the Bermann-Fischer Verlag opened up its doors in early 1936. Decades later, Bermann Fischer would identify the Swiss refusal as a blessing in disguise, claiming that he would not have been able to "establish the global independent publishing house into which the S. Fischer Verlag developed" in the "restrictive circumstances conjured up by the war" in Switzerland.[31] He also argued that the emigration, and the increasing difficulties of selling books in the Reich, acted as a remarkable incentive to internationalize his company, "for as long as we could sell books in Germany, the business there attracted most of our attention. But the sales figures that we could achieve in England, in Czechoslovakia, in Hungary and in Poland were remarkable. It was highly remunerative to develop our relationship with the local book trade in all those countries where the exiled publishing houses held a monopoly on German books."[32] Indeed, within a few months, the new Viennese publishing house received more orders from without the Reich than it did from within.[33]

Following the 1938 Anschluss, Bermann Fischer and his wife were once again forced to relocate, eventually finding a home in neutral Sweden thanks to the help of their Scandinavian publisher friend Tor Bonnier.[34] Thomas Mann, it must unfortunately be said, did little to reduce the existential anxiety his publishers experienced during this period. Beset by doubts about Bermann Fischer's continuing ability to represent him, he on several occasions hinted that he would welcome the dissolution of their contractual bonds. Bermann Fischer simply turned a deaf ear to these innuendos, however, and eventually Mann reversed course. The two men remained friends and allies for the rest of Mann's life—even if of an occasionally rather strained sort. (In his 1994 memoirs, Bermann Fischer describes the bond connecting him to his most famous author as an "authoritarian friendship.")[35]

Between 1938 and 1948, Mann's German-language books were thus published by the Bermann-Fischer Verlag in Stockholm. Because Mann's books had been banned in the Reich in 1936 and because the outbreak of the Second World War closed off a steadily increasing number of markets in Holland and in eastern Europe, they were sold primarily in Switzerland for the majority of this period. The actual circumstances of their production were far more complicated than this description suggests. For in April of 1940, the Nazis invaded Norway, and Mann's publisher began to fear for the safety of his family. The Bermann Fischers emigrated to the United States, where they eventually settled into a house in Connecticut and an office in New York City thanks to the help of yet another publisher, Alfred Harcourt of Harcourt, Brace & Co. Henceforth, the contractual end of the business and all author correspondence would be handled from the United States, while the actual book production took place in Sweden—this at a time when correspondence between the two continents sometimes took as long as three months to reach its destination. Since there were very few German-speaking typesetters in Stockholm, a fair amount of the page proofing and typesetting was also outsourced to Holland prior to the Nazi invasion of May 1940. The paper for the books was generally procured in Switzerland. Here, Bermann Fischer benefited from a reciprocal arrangement between Sweden and the Third Reich, which allowed either country to ferry goods across the territory of the other in sealed freight cars. The paper was thus shuttled back and forth between Switzerland and Sweden as part of the very same arrangement that also allowed the Nazis to transport arms from occupied Denmark to occupied Norway.[36]

Once the books had finally been printed, they often went through a similarly circuitous journey to get to their points of sale. It might be tempting to imagine the world as divided into two spheres: one in which Thomas Mann's novels could be sold, and one in which they couldn't. The reality was more complex. For instance, there were large German-speaking populations in Nazi-aligned Italy, Hungary, and Romania—countries in which the author had never been outlawed.[37] In order to supply these countries, Bermann Fischer joined forced with two other exiled publishing houses, De Lange and Querido, and founded the Central Distributing Company (*Zentralauslieferung*), headquartered in Amsterdam, which in turn brokered contracts with companies such as Literaria in Romania, or Nakladna Kniizara Breyer in Yugoslavia.[38] Once the Second World War broke out and Holland was occupied by the Nazis, this work became even more complicated and consumed a considerable amount of the Bermann-Fischer Verlag's scarce resources.

Shipping books from continental Europe to the large emigrant community in London proved to be similarly difficult, given that the North Sea and the air above it were a battlefield. And there were legal obstacles in addition to political and military ones. Following the invasion of Holland, for example, Bermann Fischer was able to rescue twelve thousand books from Amsterdam, moving them to Sweden just in the nick of time. His plan was to sell them in Switzerland. Unfortunately, Switzerland and Holland had signed a trade agreement according to which payment for all Dutch goods sold on Swiss soil had to be sent back to Holland (and thus straight into the arms of the Nazis) instead of to any third country. Bermann Fischer was forced to sell his books at a steep discount in South America instead (*Br. GBF*, 275).

Thomas Mann repeatedly pressed his German publisher to consolidate the various parts of his operation in America. He wasn't alone in believing that the United States might soon replace Europe as the most important market for German-language books. In a 1939 article in the Chicago socialist newspaper *Volksfront*, for example, Otto Sattler, the president of the German-American League for Culture (*Deutsch-Amerikanischer Kulturverband*) wrote that "now, however, when many of the best German writers have found their new homeland in this country, the German-language press together with these writers should do everything possible to interest the German-American in German literature; and that with the help of those publishers who have also come to these shores. Our German literature can become a world center for Germans in many lands."[39] Bermann Fischer was more cautious. He certainly recognized that there was a market for German literature in the United States, and consequently opened up a printing facility in America that produced as many as five thousand copies of certain titles.[40] But he also patiently explained to his star author that the main avenues of distribution still lay in Europe and that it was indispensable to retain a publishing presence there. It was simply not feasible to ship an entire print run across the Atlantic, especially given the reality of submarine warfare (*Br. GBF*, 275).

To illustrate all these difficulties, consider the hypothetical example of a German-speaking book lover in Copenhagen, who decided to place an order for the two Thomas Mann volumes that Bermann Fischer advertised in his 1938 Christmas catalog: the essay collection *Europe Beware!* and the brochure *This Peace*, containing the author's commentary on the Munich Agreement, at which Neville Chamberlain signed away the Sudetenland. *Europe, Beware!* would have been printed in Stockholm, with typesetting done in Amsterdam on paper most likely imported from Switzerland. From there, the book would have been shipped to Denmark and distributed by the Danish company Boghandel Børge Boesen, pursuant to contracts negotiated with the Central Distributing Company located, once again, in Amsterdam. *This Peace* would have been printed in New Jersey, at Hadden Craftsmen Inc., upon commission from Longmans, Green & Co., a close business associate of Bermann Fischer's whose physical premises also housed the Alliance Book Corporation (ABC), which in turn distributed the Bermann-Fischer volumes in North America. The loose leaves printed at Hadden would then have been shipped to Amsterdam for binding, from whence they would have been brought to Scandinavia by the Stockholm-based Importbokhandeln and forwarded to Børge Boesen in Denmark.[41]

Thomas Mann was thoroughly aware of all these difficulties and reflected upon them in his letters and diaries. In March 1942, for example, busily at work on *Joseph the Provider*, the author wrote to his friend Hermann Hesse that he was resolved "for the present to forego the remnants of the European 'market.' In the present state of communications, it is quite impossible to have a book that is the least bit subtle printed over there" (*HM*, 88; *Br. HH*, 149). Bermann Fischer persuaded him otherwise, however, and in February 1943 Mann sent the finished manuscript to his publisher with the remark,

> Please acknowledge receipt and let me know how you plan to send it on to Europe. It seems we must abide by our agreement to print the book in Stockholm. It will be difficult for me to forego correcting the proofs, and it is doubtful that we'll get an error-free first edition. . . .

For now, the idea that the still valuable remnants of the European market will be open to the book is important to me, and we will probably produce an edition for the US by photographic means, as we did for *Lotte in Weimar*. I would like to hear your estimate of how long it will take until the German edition appears in Europe and over here. (*Br. GBF*, 318)

Three months later, Bermann Fischer's wife wrote to Mann to inform him that "this morning we received the happy news that your manuscript has safely passed over the burning battlefields of Europe and has landed in Sweden, where it will go to the print shop as soon as possible" (*Br. GBF*, 329). Indeed, the Swedish presses produced no less than five editions of *Joseph the Provider* before the end of that year, most of which would have been delivered by freight car to Switzerland. In the United States, however, paper shortages delayed the photomechanical reprint of the novel until July of the following year, which meant that its publication actually followed that of the English translation by Helen Tracy Lowe-Porter. Given these harrowing circumstances, it is easy to see that when Mann claimed that he took "more joy in the 1,800 German copies that have been published in America than in the 200,000 English ones" (*Br.*, 2:392), he was not necessarily expressing a preference for the original versions over the translations. He was mostly expressing relief that a fiendishly difficult publishing endeavor had finally been carried through to a happy conclusion.[42]

The story of *Joseph the Provider* crossing by plane over the "burning battlefields of Europe" recalls the BBC's earlier plans to send phonograph copies of Mann's broadcast speeches to England via bomber. Here as there, the transmission of information was irrevocably altered by the material and logistical challenges of a new form of globalization brought about by war. Gottfried Bermann Fischer's great accomplishment lay in the imaginative energy with which he rose to this situation. It had not always been this way. As late as 1936, when he had already emigrated to Vienna, he wrote to Thomas Mann, "When we were still in Germany, we [émigrés] formed a united, albeit silent, front. Out here we are nothing, apart from a few individuals who stand out by virtue of their personal achievements, and who thereby represent the lost Germany. But only a few are capable of that. I plan to serve you to the best of my abilities. Others may lead the battle from abroad. Let them do it" (*Br. GBF*, 120). As it turned out, Bermann Fischer would lead the battle himself. Over the course of the next decade, his publishing house developed into a finely honed enterprise that was uniquely adapted to the age of military strife and ideally positioned to succeed in the postwar order.

The Republic of Letters at War

Globalization was not an entirely new factor in the book trade, of course. John B. Hench, for example, has pointed out that the title pages of British books produced shortly before the Second World War regularly featured imprint statements such as "Oxford • New York • Bombay • Karachi." British publishers far outpaced their German counterparts in terms of international reach. Roughly a third of all British book production during the late 1930s was destined for export, a survey by the Publishers' Association found, with some companies reaching figures as high as 60 percent.[43] But this was a different kind of globalization from the one experienced by the Bermann-Fischer Verlag, for it came about in alignment with, rather than in opposition to, state power. The books, manuscripts, and business letters that shuttled back and forth between Oxford, Bombay, and Karachi were carried on the same ships that transported imperial troops, colonial administrators, and large numbers of voluntary migrants. The gunboats that the crews piloting these ships espied on the horizon were out on patrol to protect the trade vessels, not to torpedo them.

By contrast, the globalization experienced by Gottfried Bermann Fischer was a globalization of necessity, through which the literary world tried to offer up resistance to the overwhelming counterforce of German state power.[44] Sweden, Holland, and Switzerland, the three countries involved in the physical production of Bermann Fischer's books for the European market, formed a triumvirate of minor nations, in constant danger of being overrun by the Nazi war machine. The employees in these locations lived in perpetual fear for their lives, and the possibility of sabotage by German spies was real. The supply and distribution chains were threatened by bombers, submarines, and shifting battlefronts. Even the neutral governments that harbored the production facilities viewed them with a wary eye. The Swedish government especially would no doubt have been glad to be rid of the Bermann-Fischer Verlag. Exile, furthermore, required resourcefulness, and forced Bermann Fischer to keep his finger on the pulse of industry developments. During the first third of the century, the S. Fischer Verlag had indisputably been one of the most innovative publishing houses in the world, serving as an example not only to Alfred A. Knopf but also to Alfred Harcourt, who showed his gratitude by providing Bermann Fischer with his first office space in Manhattan. But now, Bermann Fischer realized, the tables had turned, and German publishers had much to learn from America. He immediately set about studying US innovations, most importantly the newly invented paperback, which Robert de Graff of Pocket Books had popularized in America in

1939.[45] Once the Second World War came to an end, the Bermann-Fischer Verlag embarked upon a paperback series of its own, which Thomas Mann, responding to a newspaper query in 1954, would come to praise as a remarkable contribution to the "democratization of the book" (*GW*, 10:935).

Thomas Mann's attempts to uncouple German cultural authority from the institutions of the Nazi state were thus matched on a business level by the actions of his publisher. The Bermann-Fischer Verlag was a proudly and self-consciously German publishing house, its colophon with the two black horses no less representative than Thomas Mann's suits and ties. And as was the case with Mann, the conditions of exile strengthened rather than weakened this representative authority, for they separated the company not only from the Nazi bureaucracy but also from the ideology of blood and soil. A book published by the Bermann-Fischer Verlag was "German" not because of the people who had made it or the place where it had gone to print, but on account of the cultural symbolism of which it partook. This redefinition was an important advantage, as the end of the war brought total institutional collapse throughout much of central Europe and a need to rethink national identity that struck Axis and Allied powers alike.

The British especially were slow to understand that 1945 spelled not only the end of the Reich but in many ways also that of the empire, and with it the end of the British publishing trade as the most important force in international letters. No less astute an observer than Rebecca West could still remark, in 1944, that the "demand for books [in liberated Europe] will necessarily be addressed to the United States and to Great Britain," and that among these choices "the responsibility lies the more heavily on Great Britain, because, on the whole, the Continental public would rather take their reading from us than from America."[46] She could not have been more wrong. Not only did American publishers quickly leave their British counterparts in the dust; Gottfried Bermann Fischer had also been working hard to ensure that German voices would have their say in the future republic of letters.

As institutionally savvy as Bermann Fischer may have been, however, during the decade from 1936 to 1945 it was still effectively impossible to connect the books that he published with the audience that needed them most, the audience inside the Reich. The various attempts by Mann and his publisher to do so invariably have a tragicomic air about them. In May of 1939, for example, Mann tried to recruit his colleague Franz Werfel for a series of "24 brochures, written by representatives of the German spirit *for the Germans*" that he planned to simply mail to the Reich from America in editions of five thousand copies each, presumably using the old distribution lists of the S. Fischer Verlag (*Br. Au.*, 516). Needless to say, this endeavor, which took place in the immediate wake of Mann's address to the American Booksellers Association, in which he had expressed his conviction that the Germans were hungering for books published abroad, was stillborn.

A similar attempt to use postal networks for book distribution brought actual harm upon Mann's publisher. Sometime in 1939, Bermann Fischer— then living in Stockholm—was approached by a Mr. Alfred Rickmann, who turned out to be the local undercover agent of the British Secret Service. Rickmann persuaded the publisher to give him the names and addresses of twenty thousand former customers in the Reich. These were to receive copies of Thomas Mann's *Exchange of Letters*, the document that had established his anti-Nazi credentials in America. The Secret Service intended to smuggle them into Germany on Swedish vessels and then post them in the mail.[47] Unfortunately, a German agent got wind of the operation, and when the Swedish police intercepted the report that he sent back to his handler, they arrested both Rickmann and Bermann Fischer in an attempt to deescalate the situation.[48] Bermann Fischer, who had already made arrangements to emigrate to America prior to this affair, spent a few days in prison and was then able to leave the country by the skin of his teeth.

Even if direct distribution into the Reich proved impossible, Bermann Fischer throughout the war years published works by Thomas Mann that were consciously aimed at a European audience living under the long shadow of fascism. Arguably the most important of these was the aforementioned essay collection *Europe Beware!*, which appeared toward the close of 1938. It contained seven political essays that Mann had written over the course of the last eight years, among them two contributions from his American period: the lecture "The Coming Victory of Democracy," with which he had toured the United States earlier that year, and the essay "This Peace" (retitled "The Height of the Moment"), which Bermann Fischer also published as an independent volume that same fall. Attentive readers who turned to the volume in the early 1940s would have discovered foreshadowings of the same prophetic diction that Mann so systematically employed in his BBC broadcasts. Thus, "This Peace" culminates with the rousing appeal from the Christmas story according to Luke: "Have no fear!" (*GW*, 12:845; Fürchtet euch nicht!).

Europe, Beware! was followed by several smaller pamphlets over the coming years that kept interested European readers apprised of Thomas Mann's major utterances in America. Arguably more important from a symbolic point of view, however, was the publication of a reprint of *The Magic Mountain* as part of the so-called Stockholm Edition of the Works of Thomas Mann in 1939. The Stockholm Edition was conceived as a grand gesture by the Bermann-Fischer company: an unmistakable announcement that the distribution of Mann's works would continue even under the threat of Nazism. The first book to appear in the new series was Mann's recently released novel *Lotte in Weimar*. When he followed it up with *The Magic Mountain* just a few weeks later, Bermann Fischer showed that he was committed to keeping in print the very same volumes that had been outlawed by the Nazis.

Buyers of the new edition were in for a surprise, however. Opening the book in search of its famous preface, in which the narrator embarks upon a theoretical excursus concerning the vagaries of modern storytelling, these readers would instead have been greeted by the English salutation "Gentlemen!" (MoM, 41; GW, 11:602). What had happened, in short, was that Bermann Fischer, knowing that the European public had for years been fed an inaccurate impression of Thomas Mann by the Nazi press, had decided to open the volume with a modified version of "The Making of *The Magic Mountain*," the address which Mann had delivered at Princeton University earlier that year.

Mann had, of course, written this lecture at a deeply significant point of his career. Princeton's offer to serve as a lecturer in the humanities during the 1938–39 academic year provided the final impetus for him and his family to leave Europe behind for the New World. Asked to reexamine a novel he had written more than a decade and a half earlier, Mann used the occasion to familiarize himself with what some of his most astute American critics had had to say about the work, and gave extensive credit to them over the course of the lecture. In reading the new preface, Bermann Fischer's European customers were thus not only addressed as if they themselves were American students but also confronted with the unmistakable implication that American interpretations of the work were now what really mattered.

Bermann Fischer's experiences and publications during the late 1930s and early 1940s reinforce some basic points already illustrated by Mann's BBC addresses and give a further contextual frame to them. The bonfires that the Nazis built in the 1930s did not simply divide the world into two parts, one where forbidden books circulated and one where they did not. The truth was much more complex. The borders between the fascist world and the nonfascist were porous, as there were markets that were technically under Axis control but in which books banned in Nazi Germany could nevertheless legally be distributed. The very notion of a "German market" shifted as well. Prior to the 1930s, publishers would almost uniformly have understood this market in national terms. But now there were large German émigré communities in places all over the world (in Zurich, Stockholm, and London, as well as Istanbul, Shanghai, and Buenos Aires) to which Bermann Fischer could and did successfully market. As a result of these new efforts, the presentation of Mann's works shifted as well.

More importantly, however, the logistics of publishing were also irrevocably altered. The BBC addresses were propaganda broadcasts; with the end of the war, they came to a conclusion, and Mann never again took to the ether in a systematic fashion. The *Tarnschriften* and clandestine reprints were haphazard efforts mostly carried out by political agents who had no larger interest in the future of books or of literature. Bermann Fischer, on the other hand, was a forward-thinking and adventurous entrepreneur who would come to preside over what was arguably the most prestigious publishing house in Germany during the postwar period. The way in which the Stockholm Edition was produced—with the manuscript collected in one country, the typesetting done in another, the printing in yet a third, and the final product shipped to booksellers at the other end of the earth—was highly unusual in the early 1940s but would become routine over the following decades. And in blazing a trail for the globalized bookselling business of the future, Bermann Fischer also codified a fairly novel self-understanding for the publishers themselves. His success owed comparatively little to the intervention of state agents but much to collaborations with other booksellers, whether they be Tor Bonnier in Stockholm, Alfred Harcourt in New York, or Emanuel Querido in Amsterdam. Much as Thomas Mann unmoored the concept of representative authorship from its national anchorage and set it in opposition to political power, so Bermann Fischer carved out an independent space for literary publishing.

Toward "Cosmopolitan Germanness"

So far this chapter has focused mostly on the ways in which the physical and logistical vicissitudes of wartime altered the reception of Thomas Mann on the European continent. But Mann himself was a fully conscious participant in this larger process, and the various essays and addresses that he wrote during the war document an ongoing shift in his self-perception as a representative author.

Mann had come to understand and consciously present himself as a "European" writer over the course of the 1920s. There had, to be sure, been traces of a cosmopolitan stance even in his nationalist writings of the previous decade, captured mainly by his conviction that Germany's greatest cultural glories lay in the sphere of music, and thus in an art form that could be easily transported across national borders. But during the years of the Weimar Republic, abstract philosophical rumination gave way to concrete action and to a practical conception of a European literary sphere in which individual writers would act as reporters from, and ambassadors for, their home countries. The essay "Europe Beware!," which first appeared in 1935 and would later lend its title to the 1938 Bermann-Fischer volume, is perhaps the last great outcome of this interwar mindset. Originally written as an address to the International Committee on Intellectual Cooperation in Paris (an associate organization of the League of Nations, and a forerunner to the modern-day UNICEF), the text was quickly reprinted in Swiss, French, and Austrian newspapers. In it Mann quotes at length from the Spanish philosopher José Ortega y Gasset, and describes the modern "spirit of the masses" displayed by the fascist rabble as the greatest threat to contemporary civilization. It is palpably an address written by one member of a cosmopolitan elite to other members of his tribe, a report from Germany that at the same time assumes the sympathetic ear of likeminded European listeners.

Once he settled in America, however, Mann's outlook began to change. He now developed a different understanding of the relationship between nation-state and European community. In the 1939 essay "This War," for example, he declared in no uncertain terms that the outbreak of the Second World War would mean "the epoch-making abandonment of a principle to which Europe with fatal conservatism still adheres. . . : the principle of non-interference, which lies behind the concept of the absolute sovereignty of the national states" (OD, 213; GW, 12:887). The concept of the sovereignty of nations, he continued, had irrevocably served its course and would now have to yield to one of two rivaling conceptions: on the one hand, the imperial ambitions of the Nazis, and on the other, the vision of an "adherence of the European states to a commonwealth" in which "national character" and "social equality" would be equally cultivated (OD, 217; GW, 12:890).

Later readers of Mann's wartime essays have often noted the ways in which such formulations anticipate future debates surrounding the European Union.[49] Just as interesting, however, is the change in Mann's conception of representative authorship that they imply. In 1941 Mann published an important essay, "Germany's Guilt and Mission," in the émigré journal Decision, edited by his oldest son Klaus. In it he declared,

There is a growing realization that nationalism has seen its day, that the age of national states and national culture is rapidly nearing its end, and that this war, which sunders minds rather than nations, is the instrument of their dissolution. A world situation that brings to America all of German literature that counts, as well as all of Italian physics and all the more important representatives of European music. . . —does such a world situation still entitle us to speak of national states and national cultures? (GM, 10; *GW*, 12:904)

Emigration, the essay goes on to proclaim, in words copied from the 1940 lecture on "The War and the Future," is no longer an aberrant condition, but rather a foreshadowing of a future in which national sovereignty has become meaningless.

The phrase "nationalism has seen its day, [and] the age of national states and national culture is rapidly nearing its end" represents a transparent allusion to Goethe's famous declaration on world literature: "national literature is now a rather unmeaning term; the epoch of world literature is at hand."[50] The reference is not altogether surprising, given that the *Conversations with Eckermann*, in which the Goethe quote occurs, had been one of Mann's primary source materials for the novel *Lotte in Weimar*, which he had completed less than two years earlier.[51] Mann was, in other words, for perhaps the first time in his life thinking of himself not merely as the ambassador of a nation-state to a world community, but rather principally as a member of that larger community as such. Gone, furthermore, is any of Mann's old political romanticism, which defined the universal element in German culture primarily through its musicality and its lyrical inwardness. In its place, we find a level-headed realism about the ways in which modern technological means have affected the creation and distribution of cultural works: "We live in a mechanized, wide-awake and energetic age of the masses, and Germany is one of the nations best adapted to such an age. To expect it to remain an island of lyric poetry and philosophical speculation, cherishing the tender flow of romance amid such a world, is a foolish and unwarranted assumption" (GM, 11; *GW*, 12:906).

Mann's new stance represented a break not only from his own former positions but also from his then-fashionable public image in America, where he was celebrated as a spokesperson for his nation. His essays and addresses of the coming years, and especially of the time following the Battle of Stalingrad in February 1943, when it became clear to the world that Nazi Germany would probably lose the war, are largely concerned with finding an explicitly cosmopolitan voice. This shift in self-presentation also constitutes one of the main differences between Mann's itinerant lectures of 1938–43 and his addresses to the Library of Congress, most of which were held at later dates.

Take, for example, his Library of Congress address of October 13, 1943. This lecture—somewhat confusingly called "The War and the Future," but not identical with the earlier lecture script of that name—incorporates and greatly expands upon Mann's German radio address of June 27, 1943, which was broadcast less than two weeks after the Allied invasion of Lampedusa. Throughout the opening section of this lecture, Mann does not address his audience as a German writer at all, but rather as a committed European, who consistently uses the first person plural to refer to those nations presently struggling under the yoke of the Third Reich. With remarkable foresight, he envisions a postwar political order in which nation-states have greatly diminished in importance and are now mere provinces in the transnational empires of global superpowers: "It may well be that we Europeans will only play the part of 'Graeculi' in the Roman world of power that will arise out of this war, whose capitals will be Washington, London, and Moscow; but the diminutive role should not decrease our justifiable pride in our old homeland. . . . I say: all honor to the peoples of Europe. They are our allies, and they deserve to be treated as our allies" (LC, 26–27; GW, 12:920–21). Mann's American listeners would have been well within their rights to ask some questions about the circumstances under which Mann was arrogating this new position. What gave him the right to speak for "us Europeans"? Whom exactly did he mean when he called the peoples of Europe "our" allies?

These questions would only have been amplified for Mann's audience back in Germany. His radio address of June 27 begins with the words, "German Listeners! We Europeans should be proud of our old Europe, even when we are about to assume the citizenship of the New World" (GW, 11:1075). What, his listeners might have asked themselves, was the connection between the invocation of "Germans" in the first sentence and of "Europeans" in the second? And was the "we" in the second sentence an exclusive or an inclusive one? Was Mann reporting on the feelings of the American émigrés, as he had done on several occasions in the past? Or was he trying to encompass his listeners back in the Reich, those Germans who had shown however modest an amount of courage by tuning in to an enemy station? An English-language address that had been broadcast several months earlier by the Voice of America raises similar questions. There, Mann begins by saying, "European listeners! I speak to you as one of you, as a German who has always considered himself a European, who knew your countries and cultures and who was deeply convinced that the political and economic conditions of Europe were outdated, this division into arbitrarily bordered states and sovereignties" (GW, 13:747). If Mann really considered himself to be a European, why did he also insist on his identity as a German, given the reality of the Nazi oppression experienced everywhere on the continent? And what gave him the authority to make such sweeping pronouncements on political and economic matters, when his own expertise was clearly confined to the cultural sphere?

Mann's changing self-perception as a writer should be understood as a direct consequence of the changing ways in which his works were distributed on the European continent throughout the Second World War. Once the advancing armies of the Third Reich made promotional appearances impossible, Mann's representative claims lacked any bodily basis. The author now spoke to his audience via radio transmissions styled as if they had been handed down from somewhere up on high. His written words appeared on ephemeral objects such as leaflets or tea bags, which lacked any definitive provenance. The distribution of his books, such as it still was possible, was greatly hindered by the vicissitudes of wartime. The only thing that could still be stated with absolute certainty was that Mann now spoke to his German audience from somewhere beyond the walls erected by tyranny. Is it surprising that he himself struggled to put it into any more definitive terms?

Mann's final radio address over the BBC, broadcast on December 30, 1945, is perhaps the most compelling illustration of this struggle. *"And where is Germany?"* Mann asks rhetorically, "where might it be found, even in a geographical sense? How might one return to a fatherland that no longer exists as a unity? That has been torn into occupational zones that no longer know one another?" (*GW*, 12:745; emphasis in original). Mann's emphatic question "And where is Germany?" can once again be read as a reference to Weimar Classicism and to Goethe and Schiller's joint pronouncement in the *Xenias*:

> Germany? But where is it? I don't know how to find the country.
> Where the learned one begins, the political one ends.[52]

Just as Goethe and Schiller 150 years earlier had contrasted the fragmented political state of the Holy Roman Empire with the wider sphere of German culture, so Mann now explicitly challenged the notion that representative claims to "Germanness" could only arise from within the various occupational zones, and thus from the heart of the former Reich. His addresses, he now informed his listeners, had almost certainly had a larger influence on the "tormented hearts" in "subjugated Europe" (*GW*, 13:745) than they had had in Germany proper. Why, then, should he not continue to represent Germanic culture abroad?

Simultaneously, however, Mann also made clear that in taking on this role he would not be acting as an ambassador to a foreign country. Without the active support of the Allied Powers, German culture would not have survived the years of the Nazi terror; it was, therefore, now as much a property of the world as it was of the German-speaking people. This is why Mann again invoked the line about exile having become something different from what it once was, something that "tends towards the dissolution of the nation and the unification of the world" (*GW*, 13:747). And this is also why he now spoke of himself as a representative of "cosmopolitan Germanness" (*Weltdeutschtum*). Mann's claim, in so many words, was that the global literary community now had a larger say in defining what counted as "German" than the merely national voices back home. It was an audacious proposal but also one that in its lofty abstraction ignored that it, too, would have to be implemented in concrete material terms. To many Germans these terms would look like nothing short of victor's justice.

Interlude IV: *Joseph the Provider* (1944)

Mann's increasingly spectral presence on the European continent during the early 1940s precipitated a crisis of confidence in the United States as well. The author was already well into his sixties when the Second World War broke out, and he had never thought of himself as anything else but a German writer. Publicly, he unflaggingly reiterated his confidence that the Nazis would be defeated. But privately, he entertained doubts whether he would ever see the country of his birth again, and increasingly, he was not even sure he wanted to.

The logical response to this internal crisis was to become a US citizen. Mann and his wife had taken out their first papers in 1938 and completed the naturalization process in 1944. Although the outcome of their application was never in any real doubt (behind the scenes, Mann's powerful patron Agnes E. Meyer had intervened with the State Department to fast-track their immigration visas), the process was nevertheless freighted with considerable anxieties. This was especially true since the legal benefits of citizenship seemed far from guaranteed. Following the attack on Pearl Harbor, the US government had begun with the large-scale internment of Japanese American citizens. Who was to say it would not implement a similar measure for German Americans?

Mann's anxieties had a notable influence on his fiction. Nowhere is this clearer than in *Joseph the Provider*, the fourth volume of the Joseph tetralogy, on which he began working in August 1940, almost four years after *Joseph in Egypt* had been published in German. The author liked to joke that the "California sky, so like the Egyptian, smiled on my work" (*J*, xiii; *GW*, 11:679), and many a reader since then has suspected that the satirical depiction of the Egyptian "monkey state" was aimed at the Hollywood high society amid which the Manns now moved. In a 1948 preface for an edition collecting all four *Joseph* novels in one volume, Mann admitted that the final volume of the tetralogy had been written "in America from the first word to the last" and that it had "received its share of the spirit of the country" (*J*, xiii; *GW*, 11:679).

English loan words as well as colloquialisms that are unidiomatic in German are scattered throughout *Joseph the Provider* and serve as a symptom of this influence. For example, a minor character uses the English word *lunch* (*J*, 929; *GKFA*, 8.1:1475), then still highly unusual in the German language, to inform Joseph that Pharaoh's court has relocated to another room for its repast. On another occasion, Pharaoh takes leave of his wife with the words *so lange* (*J*, 964; *GKFA*, 8.1:1531), a literal translation of the English locution *so long* (Lowe-Porter, with her usual love of excess, renders this as "adieu and au revoir"). Hans Rudolf Vaget has pointed out that these Anglicisms would multiply in Mann's later works, such as the novels *Doctor Faustus* and *The Holy Sinner*, and that they therefore point to his increasing acculturation in America.[1] Given Mann's general meticulousness, as well as the fact that it was his habit to read all his compositions out loud to his German-speaking friends and family, it seems improbable that these should be mere idiomatic lapses, however. More likely, they are signs pointing to an intentional linguistic game, a form of pastiche through which Mann half-mockingly appropriated the idiom he heard around him every day.

Most explicitly, *Joseph the Provider* pays homage to America through the extended descriptions of Joseph's administrative measures, through which he reforms Egyptian society and stores up the spoils of the seven rich years for use during the seven lean ones. As Mann's smarter readers figured out right away, and as the author confirmed in his 1948 preface, these administrative reforms resemble those of the New Deal. Joseph inaugurates a gargantuan public works project to better harness the Nile, paralleling the mission of the Tennessee Valley Authority. He raises taxes on the wealthy, just as Franklin Delano Roosevelt did, and he creates an Egyptian version of America's new social security system.[2]

Unsurprisingly, given the nature of the biblical source material, Joseph's administrative measures are described as unqualified successes, and this part of the novel thus reads as an extended paean to American society, and especially to its president. Mann had met Roosevelt personally on three different occasions—twice at the White House, and once during a ceremonial dinner at the Gridiron Club in Washington, DC—and he felt a deep personal admiration for the man, whom he regarded as a kind of Manichean counterpart to Hitler. During the 1944 electoral season, he even campaigned for Roosevelt with a speech at a fundraising event in Bel Air. When the president died, Mann wrote a moving elegy for the Jewish-German journal *Aufbau*, and he actively supported political candidates who continued the New Deal legacy, such as the Democratic candidate for the US Senate, Will Rogers Jr., in 1946.

Despite all these affirmative components, *Joseph the Provider* does not by any means take an unambiguously positive stance toward the United States. The same uncertainties that the exile experience introduced to Mann's private reflections on his future, as well as to his literary language, also find a correlative in plot and subject matter. As Ehrhard Bahr has argued, adopting a phrase from Theodor W. Adorno's *Minima Moralia*, *Joseph the Provider* may be read as an extended reflection on the "damaged life" produced by exile.[3] Although Joseph, owing to the young age at which he is sold into Egyptian slavery, has a notably easier time adapting to the customs of his new home than his literary creator did, Mann's narrator nevertheless notes that his "conformance" is always tempered by a certain "silent reservation" (*J*, 638–39; *GKFA*, 8.1:992). And of course Joseph's story in Egypt is hardly one of continuous success. He is thrown into prison for a crime he did not commit, much as Mann needed to fear internment despite his impeccable antifascist credentials. He is forced to mingle with courtiers, much as Mann was passed around at American society parties that frequently bored him. When his Egyptian wife, who was betrothed to him in an arranged marriage, bears him two sons, he calls them Manasse and Ephraim—names which, as the narrator informs us, mean "God has made me forget all my connections and my father's house" (*J*, 1009; *GKFA*, 8.1:1603) and "God has made me to grow in the land of my banishment" (*J*, 1013; *GKFA*, 8.1:1610). In sum, the narrator informs us, Joseph "had not forgotten at all but had always in his mind what he said he had forgotten" (*J*, 1012; *GKFA*, 8.1:1609).

Given the overt allusions to America that are woven into the novel, one might expect that *Joseph the Provider* would have eclipsed the acclaim even of *Joseph in Egypt*. This assumption would not be entirely accurate, however. It is true that the Book-of-the-Month Club once again chose Mann's new novel as one of its monthly selections and thereby guaranteed its commercial success. But the overall sales figures (roughly two hundred thousand copies sold) remained behind those of *Joseph in Egypt*, despite the fact that the club had expanded its subscriber base in the six intervening years. More importantly, the critical reception of Mann's new novel was decidedly mixed. Although the author's old allies, like Henry Seidel Canby in the *Book-of-the-Month Club News*, or Agnes E. Meyer in the *Washington Post*, continued to sing his praises, other important critics turned away from him. Harry Levin, writing for the *New Republic*, presented a review (more fully analyzed in the final chapter of this book) that was outwardly glowing, but upon closer inspection actually killed its subject with a thousand cuts and gave advance warning of Levin's decisive break with Mann three years later. Even more devastatingly, Hamilton Basso, in the pages of the *New Yorker*, called the *Joseph* novels a "highly condimented and exotically garnished dish" and declared that he liked "the Genesis version better."[4] Mann, who was a loyal subscriber to the *New Yorker*, was greatly discouraged by the review, which also alleged that he had delivered nothing more than an updated version of *Tonio Kröger* "in Egyptian Dress" (*Tb.*, July 24, 1944). He might have been even more downtrodden had he learned that Edmund Wilson, the chief literary critic for the *New Yorker*, had supposedly declined the opportunity to review the volume himself.[5]

The vicissitudes of the international book market may partly have been to blame for the bad reception. As is related in the preceding chapter, Mann had finished his novel in February 1943, just a few days after the conclusion of the Battle of Stalingrad, the turning point of the Second World War. A German edition destined for the European market was released later that same year. In America, however, the declining pace of Mann's translator Helen Tracy Lowe-Porter kept *Joseph the Provider* out of bookstores until the summer of 1944, shortly after D-Day. This not only meant that the final *Joseph* novel appeared after the first publication of Mann's Moses story *The Tables of the Law* (even though Mann had written this tale after completing his giant tetralogy); it also meant that world history had changed decisively in the time since the author had put down his pen.

The fact that *The Tables of the Law* was published prior to *Joseph the Provider* meant that the book was, to at least some extent, evaluated in the light of the shorter tale, rather than vice versa. And since the Moses story hardly ranked among Mann's greatest achievements, reviewers might have been forgiven when they approached yet another Mannian excursion into biblical subject matter within the span of one year with a certain amount of trepidation. More importantly, the success of the intervening D-Day operation meant that the outcome of the war was now all but decided, even though a year of bloody fighting still lay ahead. This raised an important question: With Hitler's inevitable defeat drawing nearer every day, what was to be the new social role of the author who had once been acclaimed as the führer's "most intimate enemy"?

Mann's lecturing success during the years immediately preceding Pearl Harbor had come at a time when the United States was as yet uncertain of its role in the new world order brought about by the rise of European fascism. To many Americans, isolationism seemed a valid strategy, certainly no less plausible than military interventionism. What Mann contributed during those years was a sense that an intellectually coherent opposition to fascism was possible, and that American cultural life might be the ideal place in which such opposition could come into being. Against fascism's totalizing political calculus, Mann pitted the notion of a "human totality" that he saw most strongly expressed in the liberal democratic tradition and in the Judeo-Christian heritage, two founding pillars of US republican identity. Mann praised and utilized distinctive features of this identity—the country's town hall forums, ivy-clad university campuses, freely circulating journals of ideas, and its Library of Congress—to strengthen this vision of a cultural, intellectual opposition to fascism.

Related to this larger endeavor was Mann's steadfast belief that mythical thinking and tribal beliefs—the source of fascism's power over the European peoples—could be "humanized" or at least "repurposed" to serve the cause of democracy. In the original manuscript draft for his 1943 Library of Congress lecture on the *Joseph* novels, he makes this quite clear (the passage was dropped from the American lecture script):

> The term "myth" now suffers from ill repute—think only of the title that the "philosopher" of German fascism, Rosenberg, Hitler's preceptor, gave to his evil textbook. Myth has been misused as a tool for obscurantist counterrevolutions too often in the past few decades, and therefore it is not surprising that a mythical novel like *Joseph* would initially raise the suspicion that its author was part of this murky current. But this suspicion proved to be untenable, and upon closer examination the readers of the novel recognized that within it myth was being repurposed in a way that nobody had previously thought possible. (*GW*, 11:658).

This attempt to "repurpose" myth for antifascist ends was, as we saw earlier, also a central strategy of the American Popular Front, from the adoration of Lincoln to the cult of the "common man" in the late 1930s and early 1940s. For a time in US history, the *Joseph* novels were celebrated because, with their numerous self-reflexive asides, they seemed to lay an intellectual foundation and justification for this mythic obsession. At the same time, their subject matter helped strengthen America's understanding of itself as a Judeo-Christian nation that was at war with godless fascism.

Mann's attempt to create a kind of mythical precursor for the New Deal in *Joseph the Provider* fits in perfectly with this more general historical tendency. By the summer of 1944, the time for politically inspired mythopoetics and for intellectual attempts to justify the fight against fascism was irrevocably over, however. The names of generals, such as Dwight D. Eisenhower, George S. Patton, or Omar Bradley, had found a central place in the American pantheon of heroes, and the destiny of the United States to be the leader of what would soon come to be known as the "free world" seemed abundantly clear, no longer in need of intellectual disputation. With the Third Army on the march, who still needed novelists to lead the charge against fascism?

In his Library of Congress lecture, Mann took his own stab at a martial idiom when he claimed that his cycle represented "an action similar to the one when over the course of a battle a gun that has been seized from the enemy is pointed in the other direction" (*GW*, 11:658). The reality looked much more prosaic. It is true that the Manns were invited to the White House and that senior government officials flocked to his lectures at the Library of Congress. Some of these officials even expressed their appreciation of Mann in official eulogies at celebratory occasions. But when push came to shove, more pragmatic influences always prevailed.

The critical failure of *Joseph the Provider* must largely be understood in light of these word historical developments. Most of the critics who took Mann to task did so because they regarded the novel as overly static and ponderous. Hamilton Basso, in the *New Yorker*, was again particularly cutting, writing that "while I share the general opinion that he is one of the greatest living writers, I also find him an extremely clumsy one who at times comes very close to being one of the greatest living bores."[6] William Phillips, in a generally appreciative review for the *Nation*, noted that "this concluding volume of the tetralogy is marred by many dreary passages of spiritual rumination" and added that Mann "has overrun his subject."[7] But perhaps most instructive is an anonymous review in *Time* magazine, which tries hard to sell *Joseph the Provider* as a "masterpiece" but nevertheless continually relapses into admissions that it is perhaps a little long-winded for the present moment. "Few readers will want to know all of Mann's retelling of the story, the resuscitation of Egyptian and Hebrew thought and customs with which he surrounds it, the lessons for the modern world he derives from it. But no contemporary reader can afford not to know what is in Thomas Mann's version of the life of Joseph."[8] That Mann's novel cycle might contain lessons for the modern world derived from ancient myth was undisputed. But what reader in an age of rapidly advancing armies had the patience to read a work that the magazine in the same context described as "so slow-paced and philosophical that it seems static"? *Time* made sure to also point out that Mann had turned sixty-nine on D-Day. He was an old man, it was clear for all to see.

The Marxist critic Fredric Jameson once asserted that the marginal status of the *Joseph* tetralogy within the literary canon owes a lot to the fact that its attempt to serve as an allegorical summary of the New Deal remains incomprehensible in our present neoliberal age.[9] But in reality, the decline of the *Joseph* novels began at a time when the New Deal was still alive and well, and was precipitated by literary critics who for the most part were sympathetic to Roosevelt's agenda. The narrative of this decline points instead to the historic limitations of Mann's strategy to place himself in opposition to the Nazi regime, and by extension also to the limitations of the world republic of letters. When fascism was still new in the world (or at least new in the American understanding of that world), an intellectual like Thomas Mann could command the spellbound attention of a broad populace because he promised answers to questions that nobody had had to ask before. Fascism, with its claim that sovereignty derives from the collective will of the people rather than from the ballot box, and is better represented by a charismatic leader figure than by parliamentarians, sundered the political field as Americans had known it. In the face of such cataclysm, the supposition that a different field—the field of literature—might step in to fill the breach did not look so very implausible. But in the end, military and political might reasserted their dominance and moved in a direction owing very little to Mann's guidance. In the face of this inexorable march, the author's attempts to give programmatic support for Roosevelt's policies no longer came across as radical or original.

CHAPTER 6

The Loyal American Subject

From a juridical point of view, Thomas Mann isn't German anymore. Other emigrants also acquired different citizenships; they all now find themselves in the same disagreeable position. Thomas Mann as a loyal American subject, that is the strange idea we have to comprehend.

—Otto Flake, "The Case of Thomas Mann," December 1945

When Thomas Mann appeared in the auditorium, a friend who sat behind me said proudly: "Lieutenant General Mann!"

—Informational newsletter of the Jewish Club of 1933 (Los Angeles), February 1951

Sometime in the chaotic months that followed the collapse of Nazi Germany, a sixteen-year-old boy named Hans Magnus Enzensberger stole a box of books from the American soldiers stationed in his tiny hometown in Bavaria. The theft alone would hardly be remarkable, if it weren't for the two additional facts that Enzensberger would grow up to become one of the most important poets of postwar Germany and that he would later remember his treasure raid as an important step in his early literary acculturation. Enzensberger's box full of paperbacks contained titles by Ernest Hemingway, William Faulkner, and F. Scott Fitzgerald—authors who would have a lasting impact on him and many other German intellectuals of his generation. This wasn't the most important find, however, for as he recalled in 1985, "my hoard contained other treasures: there were English translations of a Thomas Mann novel (I forget which one) and of Kafka's *Trial*, books nobody in Nazi Germany had ever read. The American Army, in other words, not only gave me a crash course in American civilization, it also provided me with a first and tantalizing glimpse of my very own literature, the best part of which had been banned for 12 years."[1]

Enzensberger's memory, it turns out, was not entirely accurate. We know from his vivid description of the books that he stole, with their "thick, oblong" format and their "covers rather in the style of movie posters," that they were Armed Services Editions (ASE) paperbacks, and thus part of a special imprint created for the entertainment of American troops. The ASE, however, never encompassed a translation of Kafka's *Trial*, and the only Mann volume included among the more than one thousand different titles was a copy of his *Selected Short Stories*.[2] Furthermore, it is unlikely that other imprints of these texts would somehow have ended up in Enzensberger's box, since the Psychological Warfare Division of the US Army closely supervised the shipment of books to Europe, and was not exactly known for any particular affinity with modern German literature.[3] But these errors of recollection only strengthen Enzensberger's main point, which is that the twelve years of the Nazi terror created a hole in Germany's collective literary history—a hole that the American occupiers gladly filled with editions that they themselves had approved. The success of their endeavor is demonstrated by the fact that Enzensberger quite naturally attributes his first encounters with Mann and with Kafka, the twin literary giants of the early twentieth century, to the influence of the US Army, even though it is more than likely he discovered them elsewhere.

In their attempt to distribute literature to occupied Europe, the Americans were driven by commercial as well as by political considerations. The Second World War had upended the global economy, and the publishing industry was no exception in this regard. Thomas Mann was ideally situated to benefit from these developments. Securely established both as a leading citizen of the world republic of letters and as an outspoken enemy of Hitler, he was exactly the kind of author the Americans were hoping to promote in Germany. It is perhaps not altogether surprising, then, that some of Mann's former compatriots wondered whether the famous author really spoke for them at all and accused him of having become thoroughly Americanized. In the debates that ensued, struggles over literary prestige and representation became entangled in debates over far graver matters, such as the questions of German guilt and of who was entitled to pronounce judgment over it.

Many other Germans—sixteen-year-old Hans Magnus Enzensberger among them—were above all glad to be given new reading matter after years of censorship, paper shortages, and aerial bombardments that destroyed a large number of civilian presses. For these Germans, both the US Army and the Bermann-Fischer Verlag, which continued to publish from abroad until 1949, became valuable avenues through which they could reimagine their own broken literary heritage. Thomas Mann, that most German of modern authors, was now indisputably also a part of American (and through it of global) literary culture. His commercial success and his literary reputation were partly, if not predominantly, determined by factors that had nothing to do with the responses of German readers at all.

The Great Controversy

The contentious post-war reception of Thomas Mann was set into motion during the final days of the conflict, when Elmer Davis, the head of the Office of War Information, approached the author with the request to create a radio broadcast addressing the imminent German surrender (*Br. AM*, 626). Inspired by a photo news story on the liberation of the concentration camps Bergen-Belsen and Buchenwald that he had read in *Time* magazine, Mann chose to devote his broadcast to the question of German guilt for the atrocities that had been committed within them. It was the first public reckoning by a German with the horrors of the Holocaust.

The address, which Mann titled "The Camps," was broadcast by the Voice of America on May 8, 1945, the day after Germany's unconditional surrender. In the United States, the *Nation* published it as "Address to the German People." Within days, transcripts of Mann's broadcast started to circulate in various German newspapers, including, most importantly, in the *Bayerische Landeszeitung*, which gave it the unauthorized title "Thomas Mann on German Guilt." Indeed, Mann did not mince words on this topic, informing his listeners that "every German—everyone who speaks German, writes German, has lived as a German—is affected by this shameful exposure. It is not a small clique of criminals who are involved; hundreds of thousands of a so-called German élite—men, youths, and brutish women—committed these misdeeds in morbid lust under the influence of the insane doctrines of National Socialism" (AGP 535, *GW*, 12:951).

Unsurprisingly, Mann's judgment met with strong opposition from his many unrepentant countrymen. A certain Johann Franz Gottlieb Grosser, who had served as a press officer for the Wehrmacht, organized the most consequential response and fanned a debate that has come to be known as "the Great Controversy" in historical circles.[4] Crucially, Grosser did not write to Mann himself. Instead, he convinced a much more prominent author, Walter von Molo, to pen an open letter. Von Molo was joined shortly after by another well-known writer, Frank Thieß (whether Thieß acted independently or also on the urging of Grosser is not known).

By making von Molo and Thieß the public faces of the response to Thomas Mann, the reactionary forces in postwar Germany were able to deflect attention away from the central points that had been raised by the famous author. Instead, the debate became centered on the question what preconditions a writer might have to fulfill in order to pronounce judgment on the German people. Both von Molo and Thieß were members of the so-called Inner Emigration; that is, they had stayed in Germany and more or less (mostly less) successfully tried to keep their distance from the Nazis. As such, they both argued that Mann could not possibly understand the true situation in Germany as long as he remained in the United States. Specifically, he would be unable to comprehend the suffering of the German people in their bombed-out cities. Thieß even went a step further, claiming that to remain in Germany during the Nazi reign had been the true act of courage. By fleeing into the ostensible comforts of a celebrity existence in the United States (Thieß spoke of "box seats in foreign parts"), Mann had instead abandoned his country.[5]

The moral contradictions and deficiencies of this position are so self-evident that they do not require much further elucidation. Mann's opponents in the Great Controversy compromised themselves by painting the suffering of the German people (real as it undoubtedly was) as commensurable with the genocidal mass murder of the Holocaust. They were also blind to the suffering caused by emigration and exile, and they greatly exaggerated their own distance from the actions of the Nazi regime. What is less often noted, however, is that the Great Controversy also was a disguised struggle over the future of publishing in postwar Germany. Professional considerations thus joined, and frequently overshadowed, moral arguments.

Leonore Krenzlin offers a sanguine account of this particular aspect of the debate. The German émigrés like Mann were not just moral beacons; they were also professional writers who had spent the war years "stockpiling" a surplus of antifascist writings that they were now hoping to deploy on German soil.[6] In this endeavor, they knew they would be assured of the help of the US government, as well as of crucial institutions in the world republic of letters, such as the International PEN Club, which had evicted its German member organization in 1934 and instead recognized a refugee organization called the German Group of International PEN under the leadership of Mann's older brother, Heinrich. The authors of the Inner Emigration, by contrast, knew that their own publishing connections and the comparative fame they enjoyed with a German audience would quickly fade if émigré writers were allowed to reestablish themselves within Germany.

Both von Molo and Thieß were exceptionally well-positioned to understand the stakes of this competition. Von Molo had chaired the Section for Literary Arts of the Prussian Academy of the Arts during the closing years of the Weimar Republic, and jockeyed for a similar position in postwar Germany. Frank Thieß had comparable ambitions and would eventually rise to the position of vice president of the German Academy for Language and Literature. His attacks against Mann, furthermore, may have also resulted from personal jealousy, for Thieß must to some extent have regarded Mann as his own shadowy doppelganger. Though Thieß was fifteen years younger, his reception history in the United States imitated that of the more famous author to a remarkable extent. Three of Thieß's novels appeared in English translation during the years of the Weimar Republic, all published by Alfred A. Knopf and all translated by Helen Tracy Lowe-Porter.[7] The same institutions of the middlebrow press that promoted Mann to a US audience also promoted Thieß, sometimes in the same articles. Thieß also occasionally contributed essays to American journals during the 1920s, and was the first person to publish an article on Thomas Mann in the *Saturday Review of Literature*. When Thieß looked at Mann, he must therefore have seen a man who had had a successful career that might have been open to Thieß as well, had he only had the courage to break with the Nazis in 1933. Instead, the American press now turned away from him, and in 1947, the *Saturday Review* would even refer to him as a "collaborator."[8]

The open letters by von Molo and Thieß provoked a response from Mann, which the author himself called simply "Letter to Germany," but which was published back in his native country under the provocative title "Why I Will Not Come Back to Germany." Unfortunately, it hardly rises to the intellectual heights of his most insightful political pronouncements. It contains several ill-considered lines, among them a blanket condemnation of all books published in Germany during the Nazi reign, which Mann claims were marked by the "smell of blood and shame" and therefore deserved to be "pulped" (*GKFA*, 19.1:76). Leaving aside the fact that Mann had been quite happy to see his own books published in the Reich between 1933 and 1936, this bold attack also played into his opponents' hands when they tried to shift attention away from the German guilt question. Mann further made the rhetorical mistake of drawing attention to his American citizenship, as well as to the fact that two of his sons (Klaus and Golo) were serving in the US Armed Forces (*GKFA*, 19.1:75). Needless to say, this hardly strengthened his credibility as an impartial arbiter in the eyes of the Inner Emigration.

Otto Flake's attack on Mann as a "loyal American subject" was written in the aftermath of this second intervention and is clearly marked by it. In shifting the argument against Mann to "juridical" grounds, Flake eagerly exploited the weak spot in Mann's own defense. Unlike the murky philosophical question whether a writer who has spent the better part of a decade in exile can still claim to represent his country, the legal test of citizenship is clear-cut. Arguments that centered on Mann's US citizenship could thus easily be used to drum up consent on what actually were unrelated matters. Flake's use of the term "loyal subject" (Untertan) is even more revealing. For one is never a "subject" of a nation-state, only of an empire. For Flake, then, the true conflict wasn't even between a victorious nation-state and a defeated one. It existed instead between a valorized national community and a malignant empire plotting to swallow it both in territory and in culture.

Within the immediate context of the postwar period, Grosser, von Molo, Thieß, and Flake emerged as the undeniable victors of the Great Controversy. A survey on the question "Would you like to see Thomas Mann return to Germany?" that the American military authorities conducted among academics and other intellectuals in Bavaria during the summer of 1947 returned unambiguous results in the negative.[9] Perhaps even more disconcerting is the fact that several respondents welcomed a return of émigré intellectuals in general, but not of Thomas Mann in particular. The aftereffects of this victory would color the opinions of an entire generation of German readers and, as Hans Rudolf Vaget has shown, can be detected even in the works of contemporary critics who admire Mann as a literary figure but regard him as hopelessly naive from a political point of view.[10]

With the benefit of hindsight and critical detachment, however, it is readily apparent that the attempts to denigrate the legitimacy of the returning émigré writers were compromised from the start by the actual conditions that obtained in the postwar German public sphere. The efforts of von Molo and his ilk assumed the existence of a neutral space where ideas could do battle and where the authors of the Inner Emigration might prove the superiority of their arguments over those of the émigré faction. But in reality no such neutral space existed. The central documents of the debate were published in newspapers such as the *Bayerische Landeszeitung* and the *Augsburger Anzeiger* (Mann), the *Hessische Post* (von Molo), the *Münchner Zeitung* (Thieß), and the *Badener Tageblatt* (Flake), before being widely reprinted under different titles. But while these names all have a venerable ring to them, the papers had, in fact, been founded only weeks earlier by the US Armed Forces in an attempt to fill the information vacuum that resulted from the German collapse. The frequent reprints similarly do not attest to any kind of vigorous debate but instead illustrate the media policies of the US Army, which took a limited number of approved stories, varied headlines, typefaces, and sometimes minor details of language, and thereby supplied an ever-expanding number of papers throughout the American Zone of Occupation, even generating the illusion of a diversity of perspectives.[11] Similarly, Mann might not even have taken note of the arguments that had been launched against him if the Office of War Information hadn't sent him a copy of von Molo's letter via military courier (*Tb.*, August 10, 1945).

The very existence of a "Great Controversy" is incontrovertible proof, in other words, of the fact that the Allies, and with them the émigrés, had already won it. Indeed, the sole reason that Molo, Thieß, Flake, and others were even given a forum in the American zone of occupation appears to be that Hans Habe, the Austrian émigré journalist who supervised newspaper production as an officer in the Psychological Warfare Division, made a personal decision to deflect attention away from the guilt question in order to win the German people as reliable allies in the coming fight against Communism.[12]

Ultimately, the Great Controversy thus provides us with an example of global publishing interests and global literary reputations overriding mere national interests. True, the "global" impulses in this case were exclusively American, and the hateful missives of Flake and his ilk were clearly successful in convincing an older population that the whole debate was merely another attempt at American cultural conquest. The example of Hans Magnus Enzensberger shows, however, that younger Germans were quite receptive to international influences as they reexamined their own national literary tradition. Tellingly, it never occurred to Enzensberger to consider Mann as an "American" author in the way his older contemporaries were urging him to do. Instead, he quite naturally accepted Mann as the missing link in a cultural tradition that was banished from the territory of the Third Reich but found a home on foreign soil during the years of the Nazi terror.

Germany and the Germans

At the precise moment at which the Great Controversy was unfolding in Germany, Mann's fame as "Hitler's most intimate enemy" ascended to one last height back in America. His lecture "Germany and the Germans," given on May 29, 1945 at the Coolidge Auditorium of the Library of Congress, was the third of the annual addresses that Mann was contractually obligated to deliver as a consultant in German literature. The occasion was a grand affair as always, and the guest roster included such illustrious names as the former vice president Henry A. Wallace, the journalist Walter Lippmann, and Elmer Davis, the chief of the Office of War Information. Less than four weeks after the German surrender, the Washington establishment was thus turning out for what would prove to be a kind of farewell salute to Mann. The author did not disappoint, for "Germany and the Germans" was not only the most important pronouncement on his country that Mann had written since his emigration to America (he himself acknowledged as much in his diary entry of March 18, 1945), but also turned out to be an extremely topical address. It was as explosive in its relevance for contemporary events as it was historically and philosophically far-reaching.

Mann's early antifascist writings, stretching roughly from the *Exchange of Letters* to his itinerant lecture scripts, had been concerned first and foremost with strengthening democracy and positing art as a legitimate counterforce to totalitarian politics. In the face of the totalitarian demand that all spiritual aspects of life surrender to political calculation, Mann had challenged his listeners to see politics itself as a spiritual and thus deeply "human" activity, not at all alien to the life of the artist. At the same time, he had recognized, in his essay "Brother Hitler," that the aestheticization of politics was an important characteristic of Nazi spectacle as well, and that the artist's craft could become exceedingly dangerous if it veered into nihilism or decadence.

In the second phase of his antifascist activism, a phase that encompassed his radio broadcasts to Europe, his essay "Germany's Guilt and Mission," as well as the 1943 Library of Congress Lecture "The War and the Future," Mann turned to the question of what it meant to be German at a time when Germany itself was waging war upon the world. In ever more certain terms, Mann turned away from the notion that territorial sovereignty played any important role in preserving a national cultural tradition. To hold on to this notion would have meant conceding representative authority to the Nazis, and it also would have meant acknowledging that the Nazi war machine had been successful in reducing most of the other European cultures to mere slave status in relation to the German one. Instead, Mann postulated that genuine German culture, having been driven out of its native country by the Nazis, had found a home in the world, and that as a result, German national literature was now indistinguishable from world literature.

Once the defeat of the Third Reich came into view, Mann turned to issues that he had previously addressed only in a fragmentary way: the origins of Nazism and the question of collective German guilt. A letter that he wrote to Agnes E. Meyer in November 1944 documents that he knew what a grave and difficult task this would be. "I have," he wrote, "the definite feeling that I can no longer remain silent concerning the German question" (*Br. AM*, 602). Listeners who had read "Brother Hitler" back in 1939 or the "Address to the German People," which the *Nation* printed less than three weeks before Mann took to the lectern at the Library of Congress, would have already been able to guess at the basic thrust of the author's thoughts. In the earlier essay, Mann had acknowledged that he could see troubling similarities between himself and the Nazi dictator, while in the later he had declared that "even the German who escaped in ample time from the realm of National Socialist leadership . . . is ashamed in the depths of his soul for the things that were possible in the land of his fathers and his masters" (AGP, 535; GW, 12:951).

Mann was hardly inclined, in other words, to think of the German people as divided into two camps: one that had succumbed to the seduction of the Nazis and one that had managed to remain morally aloof from it. This uncompromising stance formed perhaps the most important difference between his position and that of the majority of the other émigré intellectuals. In 1940, it had led to his irreconcilable break with the German Academy of Prince Hubertus zu Löwenstein, and as recently as 1943, it had caused major unrest within the exile community, when Mann at the very last moment withdrew his signature from a collective statement in support of the Allied war effort that had been launched by Marxist intellectuals because it simultaneously insisted on the "necessity to firmly differentiate between the Hitler regime as well as those who are loyal to it on the one hand, and the German people on the other" (Br. AM, 983).

"Germany and the Germans" is essentially Mann's attempt to vindicate his position and to explain why he nevertheless does not believe in an indiscriminate punishment of the German people, as it was then being advocated by the British diplomat Robert Vansittart, 1st Baron Vansittart or by the US secretary of the treasury, Henry Morgenthau. Its central thesis is unmistakably clear: "there are *not* two Germanys, a good one and a bad one, but only one, whose best turned into evil through devilish cunning. Wicked Germany is merely good Germany gone astray, good Germany in misfortune, in guilt, and ruin. For that reason it is quite impossible for one born there simply to renounce the wicked guilty Germany and to declare: 'I am the good, the noble, the just Germany in the white robe; I leave it to you to exterminate the wicked one" (LC, 64; GW, 11:1146). In order to defend this statement, Mann invokes all the rhetorical and conceptual moves that he had borrowed from conservative theorists of fascism one decade earlier and put to use in his lectures of the war years: he constructs a grand narrative, uses religious metaphors, and focuses on cultural factors to the exclusion of economic or political ones. But the argumentative logic of "Germany and the Germans" is far more stringent, and Mann's examples are far more concrete than any he had mustered on earlier occasions. A key portion of the lecture is given over to a detailed analysis of Martin Luther, whom Mann praises as a "gigantic incarnation of the German spirit" and as a "tremendously great man, great in the most German manner" (LC, 52–53; GW, 11:1132–33). He "reconstituted the Church," "saved Christianity," "created the German language," "tremendously promoted the freedom of research, of criticism, and of philosophic speculation," "advanced the cause of European democracy," and, according to Mann, laid the foundations for modern psychology (*LC*, 53; *GW*, 11:1133–34). In all this, he represents the very best of Germany.

Luther's achievements also contain within them the seeds of their own undoing and the starting point for all that is most wicked about Germany. His efforts on behalf of the German language went hand in hand with a pronounced tendency toward intemperate invectives. His campaign against the Roman Catholic Church was driven by a provincial mindset. But most importantly, his efforts to promote a personal relationship between man and God resulted in an entirely spiritual understanding of human freedom: one that promoted intellectual inquiry, for example, but did not encompass the right to possess property or the popular franchise. In Mann's terms, Luther "was a liberating hero—but in the German style, for he knew nothing of liberty" (*LC*, 53; *GW*, 11:1133). The most devastating consequence of this was the "berserk fury" (*LC*, 55; *GW*, 11:1136) that the Protestant reformer directed against the Great Peasants' Revolt of 1524, when he instructed the German princes that they could enter into heaven by butchering the rebellious commoners who were threatening the established social order.

Much of "Germany and the Germans" is devoted to tracing this fundamental duality illustrated by Luther through five centuries of German history. Mann also paints a vivid picture of how the spiritual atmosphere of the Protestant Reformation can still be vividly felt in twentieth-century Germany, using his hometown of Lübeck as an example. One of the most striking passages of the essay, however, comes prior to any of this, and immediately follows the section on Luther. Over the course of just two manuscript pages—no more than five minutes of speaking time—Mann sketches a portrait of Luther's contemporary, the sculptor and woodcarver Tilman Riemenschneider. The passage is arresting in part because Mann otherwise paid little attention to the visual arts. But it is also conceptually important because Mann presents Riemenschneider, who publicly spoke out against the suppression of the Peasants' Revolt, was tortured, and lost his career as a result, as a positive counterexample to Luther. "Such men we had in Germany too, at all times," Mann concludes. "But they are not the specifically and monumentally German type" (*LC*, 55; *GW*, 11:1135). And yet, by the start of the twentieth century, Riemenschneider's wood carvings, which had once languished in obscurity, were again recognized as some of the greatest artistic achievements of the Reformation period.

"Germany and the Germans" can be read as Mann's definitive statement on the question of German culpability in the crimes of Nazism. Nazism, the lecture asserts, was not a historical accident. Instead, the fundamental traits of the Nazi mindset can be traced back at least five hundred years, to the Protestant Reformation and the outgoing Middle Ages. The Holocaust, too, and the invectives of Goebbels and Julius Streicher, have roots in the tremendous verbal and intellectual brutality with which Luther reacted to the Peasants' Revolt. As such, all of Germany and all of the Germans must bear a portion of the guilt that accrues from the Holocaust. To believe, as Mann's Marxist contemporaries did, that Nazism was something that was imposed upon the majority of the German people against their will, or that it was the result of highly specific conditions in the larger development of capitalist societies, was simply naive.

Guilt, however, is not the same thing as culpability. And although Mann made clear, in his radio address "The Camps," that the Nazi crimes were possible only because of active support or tacit assent of hundreds of thousands of people, he also believed that there were those Germans who—like Tilman Riemenschneider in the sixteenth century—had shown the courage to do what was right, and who were therefore not individually culpable for the Nazi crimes. It is possible, however, to feel guilty even for something for which one bears no personal culpability. Indeed, it may be necessary to do so, if one recognizes that only accidental circumstances prevented one from committing a crime. Mann's willingness to say, "Not a word of all that I have just told you about Germany . . . came out of alien, cool, objective knowledge, it is all within me" (LC, 64–65; GW, 11:1146), forms the most important difference between him and the hypocrisy of the Inner Emigration. It also differentiates his stance from that of many other emigrants, who believed that the circumstances of their exile or their political convictions elevated them above criticism.

Given its tremendous importance both as an intellectual document and as a personal testament, "Germany and the Germans" received surprisingly little publicity in the months after it was first delivered as a lecture. In America, the Yale Review published a nearly complete version of the manuscript in December 1945; excerpts from the lecture were reprinted by Time magazine under the misleading title of "Germany: Hunter and Hunted" the following month. In Germany, Gottfried Bermann Fischer published Mann's original wording in his house magazine Neue Rundschau in October 1945. The essay never achieved the same kind of impact that Mann's more polemical pieces of the time did, and even today there is a surprising dearth of critical treatments of its argument.[13] As a proxy for its place in the discourses about Germany that dominated at the time, however, we need to look only at Bertolt Brecht's reaction to Mann's decision to withdraw his signature from the public appeal launched by the émigré Marxists. He wrote a scathing satirical poem titled "When the Nobel Prize Winner Thomas Mann Gave the Americans and British the Right to Punish the German People for Ten Years for the Crimes of the Hitler Regime." Wide swaths of Germans on both left and right were simply unwilling to follow Thomas Mann's arguments that decoupled universal guilt from individual culpability.[14] For them, Mann's suggestion that all of his countrymen examine their consciences turned the famous author into a willing lackey of the Allied military powers.

The New World Bookshelf

By the summer of 1945, when the members of the so-called Inner Emigration launched their polemics against Mann, and when the first copies of "Germany and the Germans" were making their way to the press, a quite different class of readers had already settled on an answer to the question whether the author's embrace of American culture had permanently sullied his reputation. This alternative story of a postwar response to Thomas Mann begins on December 15, 1944, when Gottfried Bermann Fischer wrote to his friend to inform him that the Bermann-Fischer Verlag was

> going to print for the War Department twenty-four titles of our books; 10,000 copies each as a first printing but more may follow.
>
> The books will not appear on the open market. They are to be made available only to a special class of German-speaking persons now residing in this country whose reading matter is furnished by the War Department. (That is the explanation I have been authorized to give). (Br. GBF, 373)

The sense of a cloak-and-dagger intrigue is palpable, not least because this is one of the few letters that Bermann Fischer wrote to Mann in English. The "special class of German-speaking persons" whose reading matter was to be furnished by the War Department turned out to comprise the roughly four hundred thousand German prisoners of war that the US government was then interning in 511 camps all across the country.[15]

The Roosevelt administration embraced political reeducation efforts only very late in the war. From May 1942 (when the first group of thirty-one German POWs arrived in the United States) until about September 1944, the prisoners were viewed exclusively as a source of physical labor, not as an intellectual resource to be developed. This neglect was partly due to the military's belief that relentless strategic bombing would destroy Nazi morale more effectively than books ever could, and partly due to the sociologist Talcott Parsons's warnings that misapplied propaganda measures might actually tilt the prisoners toward Communism rather than democracy.[16] There was also some debate as to whether the Geneva Conventions allowed for political reeducation efforts. By the mid-1940s, however, stories about camp mutinies, fights between Nazi and anti-Nazi factions among the prisoners, and even suicides among the inmates had started to surface in the US press.[17] At the same time, American intellectuals such as Archibald MacLeish, Dorothy Canfield Fisher, and Stephen Vincent Benét were increasingly successful in their efforts to convince the American public that books deserved a part in the war against fascism. After Dorothy Thompson took up the matter with Eleanor Roosevelt, the president finally instructed the provost marshal general to develop a program through which German POWs might be exposed to literature.

The Office of the Provost Marshal General (OPMG) eventually alighted on article 17 of the Geneva Conventions, which states that "so far as possible, belligerents shall encourage intellectual diversions and sports organized by prisoners of war." The military interpreted this clause to mean that as long as the reeducation materials were of an entertaining and at least modestly intellectual nature and as long as prisoners consumed them voluntarily, there would not be any issues. Initially, the demand for such materials was filled by providing camp librarians with the catalogs of second-hand book dealers specializing in German-language texts. This proved to be a disaster, however. The book traders soon realized that they could make easy money off the government by raising their prices, and each of the thousands of books that were ordered had to be cumbersomely inspected for possibly subversive content.[18] The OPMG concluded that if it wanted the reeducation campaign to be successful, it had better provide the materials itself.

The result of this realization was another one of the era's characteristic cooperations between the military and the publishing sector. Three entities were involved in producing the so-called Bücherreihe Neue Welt, or New World Bookshelf: the military's Infantry Journal, which handled printing and distribution, Penguin Books USA, which supervised layout and book design, and the Bermann-Fischer Verlag, which provided the rights to all but one of the twenty-four works that were eventually printed in editions of up to fifty thousand copies each.[19] All three partners benefited in equal measure from the arrangement. The OPMG got the books that it wanted; Penguin Books deepened its ties to the military, for which it was already producing a series of educational paperbacks; and Bermann Fischer gained valuable connections to the US government, as well as a head start over his competitors when it came to planning for the postwar market. In his memoirs, the publisher describes the New World Bookshelf as a trial run for his Fischer Bücherei series of pocket books, which he introduced to the German market in 1952.[20]

Because the OPMG was afraid that there might be a backlash if prisoners perceived the new books as being in any way associated with the US government, both the *Infantry Journal* and Penguin Books remained silent partners in the publishing endeavor. This meant that the copyright page of each title in the New World Bookshelf bore the colophon only of the Bermann-Fischer Verlag, along with the somewhat ambiguous statement that this was a "reprint, with kind permission." Bermann Fischer must have been pleased. It established his publishing house as a global power and put his name before thousands of young Germans who were here, much like Hans Magnus Enzensberger would be in a short while, exposed to a literature they hardly knew existed. It is probably not a coincidence that the colophon Bermann Fischer chose for the edition was not the one with the two black horses that he usually used during his exile years, but rather a modified version of the old S. Fischer logo depicting a fisherman with net. It was an image of quality that some of the older soldiers might conceivably still have remembered—as well as a harbinger of the one to which the company would return following the war. The name of the book series as a whole was similarly symbolic. The phrase "new world" in "New World Bookshelf" gestured at once toward America and toward a world without Nazism, clearly establishing the Bermann-Fischer Verlag as an entity that was invested in both (figure 6.1).

Bermann Fischer was initially asked to choose forty titles from his extensive catalog and submit them for approval to the Special Projects Division (SPD), a newly formed entity within the OPMG charged with supervising all reeducation efforts. The list comprised a mix of works by German-language authors along with some translations to which Bermann Fischer held the worldwide German rights, most notably perhaps Ernest Hemingway's *For Whom the Bell Tolls* and Joseph Conrad's *The Corsair*. At SPD headquarters in Manhattan, the Harvard professor Howard Mumford Jones, who had joined the unit as its chief literary expert, carefully vetted the selections. Like most humanistically trained American academics of his generation (he was born in 1892), Jones had cut his spurs during the 1920s and 1930s discussing the merits of the newly formed Great Books curricula and debating Van Wyck Brooks's thesis that American culture was cleft in two between the "lowbrows" and the "highbrows"—or, as Jones helpfully clarified for the readers of the *New York Times*, between "Hollywood" and the "intellectual advance guard."[21]

Generally speaking, Jones believed in the educational values of a literature that treads the middle ground between these paths, although he updated the humanistic optimism of the 1920s for the harsher reality of the 1940s by expressing doubt about the notion that books were particularly effective

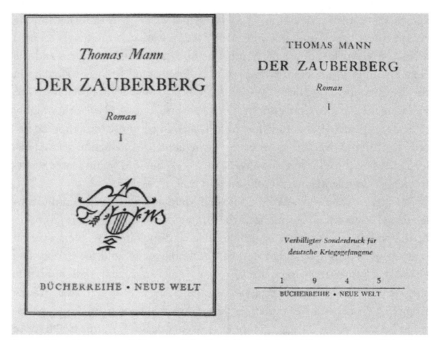

FIGURE 6.1.   Slip cover and title page of *The Magic Mountain* in the Bücherreihe Neue Welt, 1945. Author's personal collection, with permission by S. Fischer Verlag.

vehicles for the promotion of intercultural understanding. Readers, so he believed, invariably approach literature with certain culturally (and more specifically nationally) conditioned presuppositions. In the present instance, this meant that German readers could hardly be trusted to set their prejudices aside when they approached American novels; the matter was made only worse by the fact that contemporary American democracy had developed no adequate "mythology" to counteract that of Nazi Germany.[22]

Jones's personal prejudices perhaps explain why comparatively few American authors were represented among the twenty-four titles the SPD ultimately chose from Bermann Fischer's initial list. The majority of authors were German, and only two of them were represented by more than one book: Franz Werfel (with *The Song of Bernadette*, as well as *The Forty Days of Musa Dagh*, divided over two volumes) and Thomas Mann (with *Europe Beware!*, *Lotte in Weimar*, and *The Magic Mountain*, also divided over two volumes). A 1945 memo that is preserved in the National Archives justifies the inclusion of *The Magic Mountain* in the following terms: "The most important novel by the greatest living German author, who exiled himself because of his disliking of the Nazis. This particular work recommends itself by the famous long-drawn conversations between a defendant and a critic on the values of western civilization."[23] As far as blurbs go, it is hardly a ringing endorsement. But it does document why Mann was so strongly represented in the New World Bookshelf. Mann was both a famous anti-Nazi and the very epitome of someone who provided "intellectual" content cloaked in the diverting form of a novel. With him, nobody could accuse the OPMG of violating the Geneva Conventions. Furthermore, Jones and the other highly educated officers who worked for the SPD almost certainly remembered not only the Knopf advertising campaign of the late 1920s, which had so relentlessly stressed the educational value of the work, but also Mann's later efforts to create a democratic mythology to rival that of fascism.

The titles of the New World Bookshelf were delivered to the commissaries of POW camps all throughout the United States during the final weeks of the war. In a move once again intended to dispel any possible suspicion that these were propaganda treatises, the books were sold for twenty-five cents each rather than merely given away. They immediately flew off the shelves. "The response to the *Buecherreihe Neue Welt* at our two Branch Camps of Grady and Altheimer, Arkansas, are beyond our fondest expectations," reported one camp. "Grady expressed a desire for almost 600 more and Altheimer for about 400 more. They are being widely read and passed around."[24] The comments by camp inmates that the SPD passed on to its superiors in the OPMG were similarly fulsome.

Perhaps the best indication of the appeal that these cheap paperbacks held for their target audience, however, is given by the fact that many of their owners later rebound them in sometimes elaborate hardcovers. The literary critic B. Venkat Mani has recently drawn attention to what he calls "bibliomigrancy": that is, the process by which the contours of the world republic of letters are altered through the physical journeys of books.[25] The Thomas Mann volumes from the New World Bookshelf provide a prime illustration of this dynamic. They became the prize possessions of soldiers who eventually returned to German homes in which all literature had been destroyed, either because of bombs or because of flight and resettlement. Carefully rebound and presumably often reached for whenever "father told stories about the war" (to invoke a German idiom), these books would have acquired a special kind of representative function in which German intellect was invariably mediated through a particularly formative German American encounter.

Learning to Read Again

As with Mann's radio broadcasts over the BBC or the *Tarnschriften* of his works that were smuggled into the Reich, the medium through which this cultural transfer took place was thus arguably more important than the content of the messages that were conveyed. As the focal point of formative experiences, the books themselves became the agents of a new kind of Thomas Mann reception. This does not mean that the volumes weren't read or eagerly discussed. Of course, the vast majority of conscripts in the German army had no advanced literary schooling. But leaving aside the motivating powers of boredom and homesickness, the mere numbers involved— almost four hundred thousand potential readers for a print run of at most fifty thousand copies—strongly suggest that works such as *The Magic Mountain* would have found a grateful and receptive audience. The letters to the editor that were printed in the POW newspaper *Der Ruf* (*The Call*) document how many academics there were among the prisoners, and how eager they were to discuss intellectual matters.

Among these contributions one in particular stands out. The October 1, 1945, issue of *Der Ruf* contained a special tribute section dedicated to Thomas Mann. Among the pieces printed therein was an open letter titled "*The Magic Mountain* and Imprisonment during Wartime" by a certain Dr. Wolfgang Hildebrandt, a resident of Camp Como, Mississippi. It is worth quoting from extensively. "Dear Mr. Thomas Mann," the writer begins,

> Allow me to express my gratitude for something that has been weighing upon me for a long time now. I am writing to you from those circles that have so often been the subject of your writing and have never stopped being your readers, namely the German middle classes [das deutsche Bürgertum]. My aim is to show you that even in the last few years your voice was never silent for us, and that you now speak to us more than ever. My gratitude encompasses you and your entire work, but more than anything it concerns the book to which all of our love belongs, namely *The Magic Mountain*.[26]

Hildebrandt goes on to describe how he carried a copy of Mann's work wherever he went during the course of the war, going so far as to call it his "most cherished possession." He does not content himself with reminiscences, however, but also claims that "the truly magical effect of the novel consists in the fact that the German POW discovers his own destiny, his own story told on its pages." For "even the most courageous soldier, who has done his military duty until the very end, will not only be crestfallen when he is taken prisoner. The strange circumstances of the new situation will also express themselves in feelings of a different kind, a never before experienced joy and hope," much as Hans Castorp experiences when he first arrives at the Berghof sanatorium. Furthermore, "thanks to the Geneva Conventions of

1929. . . our life as prisoners no more resembles 'a Bagno or a Siberian mine' than does Hans Castorp's residence [in the Berghof]; in both cases we are dealing with a place of 'hermetic pedagogy' that includes the possibility of truly remarkable intellectual experiences." This "hermetic pedagogy" consists of a new perspective not only on world literature but also of Germany's place within it: "The American imprisonment opened for us the path to the Western world, which had so long been buried for us. The books issued by the American publishers sufficed to demonstrate for us that the intellectual center of this world lies in the United States. The spatial distance from home, finally, gave us the necessary vantage point to once again situate Germany within this Western world."[27]

Hildebrandt may well have had ulterior motives in thus flattering his American prison guards. Nevertheless, his letter advances an internally coherent and genuinely original interpretation of Mann's most famous novel. This interpretation would have been impossible if that novel had not been mediated for him by the US Army and by life in Camp Como. And it forms a stark contrast to the chorus of visceral rejection that Thomas Mann had to endure from intellectuals back in Germany during the very weeks in which *Der Ruf* published Hildebrandt's letter. In his diary for September 21, 1945, Mann, to whom the SPD regularly forwarded copies of the paper, noted that reading the tribute section put together by the POWs had been "salutary after the disgusting experiences of the last days" (*Tb.*, September 21, 1945).

Mann was not alone in recognizing that *Der Ruf* might potentially serve as a bridge into a brighter postwar future. Earlier that same month, Bermann Fischer had paid a visit to Fort Kearny, Rhode Island, where the newspaper was produced. Known internally as the "Idea Factory," Fort Kearny was a model camp for which the assistant head of the SPD, Captain Walter Schoenstedt, had hand-selected roughly eighty reliably anti-Nazi intellectuals. Upon arrival in Rhode Island, the inmates discarded their military ranks, elected their own "committee of governors," and produced educational materials for their fellow prisoners.[28] Bermann Fischer was especially surprised to discover that virtually all the inmates had listened to Thomas Mann's radio broadcasts into occupied Europe and asked him questions about them, a fact that he immediately communicated to the author (*Br. GBF*, 410–11).

Bermann Fischer was there to meet a certain Curt Vinz, a former employee of the Eugen Diederichs publishing house, which had been one of S. Fischer's closest rivals in the market for high quality literature during the days of the Weimar Republic. Vinz now handled the correspondence between Bermann Fischer and the OPMG. Bermann Fischer hoped that Vinz, with his bill of ideological clean health from the American authorities, might serve as his representative in Berlin and help him reopen his former firm. Although nothing ultimately came of this endeavor, the contact would prove valuable in the future, for in 1946 Vinz founded a firm of his own in Munich, the Nymphenburger Verlagsbuchhandlung. Nor was Vinz the only figure of future industry importance to reside in Fort Kearny. Among the editors of *Der Ruf* were two middle-aged soldiers by the names of Alfred Andersch and Hans Werner Richter. Two years later they would go on to found the most influential West German literary circle, the Gruppe 47 (Group 47).[29] At least some of the links connecting the major players of the postwar German publishing industry were forged in America, in other words, amid a process of active reflection on Thomas Mann and his literary legacy.

Alfred Andersch would in later years develop an extremely complex relationship with Mann's literary legacy. During his time in America, he had a more straightforwardly instrumental relationship to the famous author. Prior to his arrival at Fort Kearny, Andersch spent some time at Fort Hunt, Virginia, a secret military installation where POWs with suspected anti-Nazi leanings were sent for further screening. His conversations with his cellmate there were recorded and transcribed for further examination. The transcripts reveal that Andersch was fond of boasting of his supposed acquaintance with Mann (whom in reality he had met only once, at a public reading) and of claiming that the famous author might help him, if only he could somehow be notified of what was happening to his younger colleague.[30]

Perhaps Andersch was driven by similarly strategic considerations once he took over as editor of *Der Ruf.* Whatever the case may be, however, his tenure at Fort Kearny was marked by consistent and exuberant praises of Thomas Mann. Especially noteworthy in this regard is a detailed and remarkably informed report on "Germany and the Germans" that was published only a few months after Mann delivered his lecture. Overall, Mann's name ranks second in frequency only to Martin Niemöller's among the anti-Nazi intellectuals discussed in the paper.

Perhaps Andersch's most important statement concerning Mann, however, comes in a tribute that he penned on the occasion of the famous author's seventieth birthday, which had taken place in June 1945. There Andersch says, "What we know for sure is that we owe a debt to [Mann]: not through declamations of our admiration and love, but through the adoption of a very simple stance. This stance will be achieved through reading *Buddenbrooks*, *The Magic Mountain*, the *Joseph* trilogy [sic] and his political essays. In this way, we can achieve the mentality that he once promoted at the end of a speech at the University of Munich, when he said that we must learn to read again."[31] "Learning to read again" is precisely what the POWs did, thanks to the help of the New World Bookshelf and the editorial guidance provided by Camp Como.

The Armed Services Editions

Numerous as they may have been, the prisoners of war of course represented a small audience compared to the overall German population. The vast majority of Thomas Mann's former compatriots did not reencounter his books until they became available again in Germany.

As Hans Magnus Enzensberger's recollections illustrate, one important medium for such an encounter during the weeks and months immediately following the war was the US Army, and in particular the imprint of books that had been specifically created for the diversion of American soldiers, the Armed Services Editions. The ASE were the brainchild of the Council on Books in Wartime (CBW), a publishing industry initiative that came into being during the spring of 1942 and worked closely with the propaganda wing of the US government, the Office of Facts and Figures (soon to be renamed the Office of War Information). Its now-famous slogan, coined by its first chairman, W. W. Norton, was "Books are weapons in the war of ideas." Although the executive committee of the CBW was made up almost exclusively of representatives from publishing houses, the council received the formal endorsement of a number of allied organizations, including the American Library Association, the Authors League of America, and the PEN American Center.[32] In many ways, then, it represented the intellectual wing of the propaganda and psychological warfare effort.

Domestically, most Americans would have been familiar with the CBW through its sponsorship of numerous radio programs, of which *They Burned the Books* was far and away the most successful. Arguably more important than any of these domestic propaganda efforts, however, was the CBW's introduction of what a contemporary source called "the greatest mass publishing enterprise of all history"; namely, the Armed Services Editions.[33] The military had recognized as early as 1940 that the mass mobilizations upon which it was about to embark rendered the existing opportunities for intellectual diversion and education provided by the Army Library Service completely inadequate. It initially tried to remedy this problem through volunteer book drives spearheaded by the so-called Victory Book Campaign. This proved to be a dissatisfactory solution for reasons similar to the ones that resulted in the failure of the early book purchases in POW camps: the books, which soon swelled to over eighteen million, all needed to be screened before distribution, and as campaign volunteers soon discovered, callous Americans found a way to use the system to their advantage—in this case by ridding their bookshelves of hopelessly outdated textbooks and other materials that no soldier would possibly want to read.[34] The solution was simple: the CBW would print its own books and sell them to the US Army for distribution at greatly reduced prices.[35] A few publishers were initially skeptical of this scheme, but the vast majority of them soon came around to the opinion of the broadcaster H. V. Kaltenborn, who proclaimed in 1944 that "America's publishers have cooperated in an experiment that will for the first time make us a nation of book readers!"[36]

Between 1943 and 1947, 1,322 titles were produced under the ASE imprint, accounting for a mind-blowing total of 122,951,031 copies. The series far outpaced any of its rivals, such as the Fighting Forces series, which the *Infantry Journal* produced in conjunction with Penguin Books (a collaboration that also laid the foundation for the Bücherreihe Neue Welt). The ASE were not ordinary books; they were printed on lightweight paper on rotary presses normally used for magazines and catalogs, which otherwise would have sat idle during the war years. Designed to fit into a GI's front pocket, the pages were printed "four up" and then cut. This resulted in the characteristic oblong format remembered by Hans Magnus Enzensberger. Each title had a colorful cover that generally also featured a photo of the original book that was being reprinted (figure 6.2). The ASE were clearly marked for exclu-

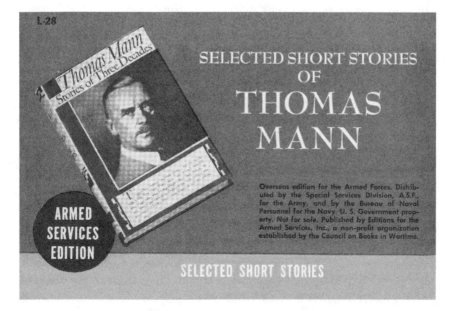

FIGURE 6.2. Armed Services Edition of *Selected Short Stories of Thomas Mann*, 1944. Author's personal collection.

sive distribution overseas, a provision meant to allay publishers' fears that they might undercut the domestic market. At the same time, their cover design provided a tantalizing glimpse at the literary bounty that would await soldiers (who were, after all, potential future customers) upon their return stateside.

Given the nature of the intended audience, the ASE offerings encompassed a remarkably wide spectrum of literature, ranging from pulp fiction to William Faulkner. If both the range of titles and their delivery mechanism seem vaguely reminiscent of the Book-of-the-Month Club, then this is not a coincidence. Amy Loveman, who also managed the business end of the club's selection activities, served on the council's advisory committee, while club judge (and *Saturday Review* editor) Henry Seidel Canby acted as a liaison between the CBW and the Office of War Information. The Armed Services Editions, then, exported middlebrow values and assumptions to a new target audience created by the vicissitudes of war, much as the Bücherreihe Neue Welt had done thanks to its editor Howard Mumford Jones.

Virtually all major American publishing houses provided titles to the series, and needless to say, so did Knopf. Willa Cather, Joseph Conrad, Vachel Lindsay, and W. Somerset Maugham were just some of his authors to be represented in the ASEs, most with multiple titles (Conrad received five, Maugham six). Thomas Mann was represented with *Selected Short Stories*. His title is unusual in that it is a condensed version of *Stories of Three Decades*; both the CBW's advisory council and the military ordinarily eschewed cuts to the books that they published because they were at pains to avoid any suspicion of censorship.

Selected Short Stories was published in an edition of 100,000, of which 76,000 were earmarked for distribution to the army, 20,000 for distribution to the navy, and 4,000 for distribution to American prisoners of war via the intercession of the YMCA.[37] The American soldiers appear not to have been particularly smitten by the book. While the authors of the ASE's most popular titles (especially female authors) sometimes received as many as a thousand fan letters from servicemen, neither the Knopf archives nor the records of the CBW at Princeton University contain any such letters to Mann. What the CBW records do contain, however, are several letters that were written during the closing stages of the war by enterprising soldiers who were trying to collect the ASE and recognized the potential value of the Mann contribution. These soldiers actively complained about being unable to get a hold of *Selected Short Stories*.[38] The question thus naturally arises: what happened to all of these books, given that they were printed in exactly the same numbers as the other ASE produced at that stage of the war?

It is extremely unlikely that American infantrymen would have simply thrown them away, even if they did not find them to their liking. Every study of the ASE stresses how dear they were to the typical soldier and how GIs would happily toss virtually all their other gear before they got rid of a book. In the words of one corporal, "The books are read until they're so dirty you can't see the print. To heave one in the garbage can would be tantamount to striking your grandmother."[39] The evident unpopularity of *Selected Short Stories*, together with the fact that Mann was a German author, makes it all the more likely that a disproportionately large number of his books would have been traded away by US troops as they invaded Austria and Germany. American soldiers frequently used their books as gifts and barter items once they settled into their new role as an occupying force, and the ASE were eagerly received by Germans who had been starved of reading matter during the final years of the war.[40] The lasting impact of this particular example of bibliomigrancy is perhaps best illustrated by the fact that the Rowohlt Verlag, one of the first German publishing houses to reopen after the war and the first to issue a paperback series, adopted the idea of printing on rotary presses from the ASE.

The German readers who turned to *Selected Short Stories* would have discovered a different Thomas Mann than they remembered from the days before the war. For one thing, they would have been confronted with a biographical summary informing them that Mann "considers the United States, the classic ground of democracy, the center to which Western culture is shifting for 'the duration of the present European dark age'" (*SS*, 480). The volume also came adorned with multiple back-cover blurbs by Clifton Fadiman, perhaps the quintessential American middlebrow critic. Fadiman describes *Death in Venice*, the novella about which so much ideological hay had been made in the days during and after the First World war, as "surely the most beautiful long short story ever written," softening not only its content but also subsuming it into a quintessentially American genre, the short story. "A Man and His Dog" is described as "one of the finest of modern dog stories" and "Mario the Magician" as "the most searching indictment of current domination-ideals penned in our time" (*SS*, back cover).

Selected Short Stories was not the only possible occasion on which German readers during the months and years immediately following the war would have encountered an explicitly "American" Thomas Mann. Between 1945 and 1949, Mann's physical presence in Germany was confined to his books, and these books more often than not bore strong reminders of his American existence. Gottfried Bermann Fischer was a principal source of these reminders. (In a letter to Bruno Walter written in May 1943, Mann jokingly compared his publisher to a general when he wrote that he had decided to begin working on another project so that "Bermann might enter through the Brandenburg Gate with four unknown novels from my hand" [*Br.*, 2:311].) To commemorate Mann's seventieth birthday on June 6, 1945, Bermann Fischer published a special edition of his legendary in-house journal *Neue Rundschau*, which he had had to abandon when he left Germany. The edition, naturally enough, was devoted to his most famous author. The dedicatory preface contains the following pathos-laden remarks:

> Then [after the seizure of power] a new voice arose, the voice of Thomas Mann. And the world listened. What had previously appeared a mere mass of uprooted existences suddenly gained a name and an expression. Emigration, up until then a rather disreputable word, suddenly had a visible, admired, and estimable representation. Everyone could appeal to it and was surrounded by the luster of its aura.
>
> If there still exists a German literature today, if there still exists a tradition that sustains the spiritual and moral values of a Germany that once meant something to the world, then this is to a high degree because of Thomas Mann, because of his work, and because of his attitude, his moral and human existence.
>
> The "nation of poets and thinkers" pronounced judgment over itself in May of 1933 on Opera Square, when it permitted the book burnings to take place. Ever since that day there no longer exists an intellectual Germany that would be bound to that country's national borders.
>
> The true Germany in a higher sense is formed by those who left their country for the sake of freedom and justice, who suffered in the concentration camps, and who today fight against "Germany" as Americans or under the British flag.[41]

Bermann-Fischer's dedication not only unambiguously takes sides with the literary émigrés but also emphasizes Thomas Mann's claims toward representativeness. Reinforcing Mann's own rhetorical claims, it detaches the spiritual and cultural Germany from the territorial one and goes so far as to propose that the "true Germany in a higher sense" might actually be found under a foreign flag. The German readers who weren't scared off by these strong words and flipped the page would then have found almost two hundred pages filled mostly with tributes to Thomas Mann, some by fellow émigrés, such as Lion Feuchtwanger or Bruno Walter, but many also by the Americans who had helped shape his career in the United States: his publisher Alfred A. Knopf, his translator Helen Tracy Lowe-Porter, his patron

Agnes E. Meyer, his supporters in the academy Frank Aydelotte and Anna Jacobson. In order to recognize Thomas Mann (and thereby to recognize the "true" Germany), so Bermann Fischer was unapologetically suggesting, it would henceforth also be necessary to acknowledge American voices.

Bermann Fischer contributed other reminders of the exile period to the physical books that he published during the postwar years. In early 1948, Bermann Fischer and his former associate Peter Suhrkamp jointly created the first Thomas Mann volume to be printed on German soil in over a decade, a new edition of his selected stories. The book jacket read,

> The rights to this edition were transferred to the Suhrkamp publishing house (formerly S. Fischer) by the Bermann-Fischer Verlag. The two firms, which were created in the wake of the forcible dissolution of the S. Fischer publishing house in Berlin in 1936, have since then worked separately from one another. . . . The authors of the Bermann-Fischer Verlag and the Bermann-Fischer firm itself have waived their claims to material compensation in order to restore the continuity of German literature.[42]

Even before delving into the actual content of the volume, Mann's German readers would therefore have been reminded of the fractious history of German publishing, and of the author's special place within it.

Of course, after a decade of censorship, the content of Thomas Mann's more recent works held surprises as well. *Lotte in Weimar*, with its confident claim on a new form of representative authorship, was first published in an edition meant specifically for the German market in 1947. The first complete version of the *Joseph* tetralogy, with its attack on the fascist mob mentality and its praise of New Deal democracy, appeared in 1949. Readers who managed to get a hold of the Bermann-Fischer edition of *The Magic Mountain* would, furthermore, have been confronted with the same American preface to which Bermann-Fischer's customers outside the Reich had already been privy since 1939. There, Mann's German readers, some of whom would have been forcibly marched through Buchenwald or Dachau by US soldiers only months earlier, would have encountered the following passage in which Mann praises the interpretation of the Jewish American critic Howard Nemerov:

> Hans Castorp is a searcher after the Holy Grail. You would never have thought it when you read his story. . . . Perhaps you will read the book again from this point of view. . . . You will find [the Grail] in the chapter called "Snow," where Hans Castorp, lost on the perilous heights,

dreams his dream of humanity. If he does not find the Grail, yet he divines it, in his deathly dream, before he is snatched downwards from his heights into the European catastrophe. It is the idea of the human being, the conception of a future humanity that has passed through and survived the profoundest knowledge of disease and death. The Grail is a mystery, but humanity is a mystery too. For man himself is a mystery, and all humanity rests upon reverence before the mystery that is man. (MoM, 45; GW, 11:616–17)

Thomas Mann obviously did not yet envision the Holocaust when he referred to the "European catastrophe" or spoke of the "profoundest knowledge of disease and death" in 1939. His remarks were oriented backward, toward the previous world war. But just as Wolfgang Hildebrandt, the German POW who reread *The Magic Mountain* during his time in the United States, discovered new significance in what he assumed to be a thoroughly familiar work, so the Germans who opened his novel in the years following 1945 would have been primed for a new intellectual experience. It was one thing to dismiss the author of essays such as "The Camps" as a mere American propagandist, especially since the US military indisputably had a hand in placing these publications in front of a German readership. Because of Bermann Fischer's mediation, however, and more specifically because of his decision to preface the novel with a lecture originally intended for American college students, those same readers were given an entirely new perspective on their own literary tradition, which put it into dialogue with what had come to pass in recent years.

Conversations with Riemer

The German struggles to satisfactorily place Thomas Mann within their own broken literary tradition reached a high point over the summer of 1946. Starting in May of that year, a number of intellectually ambitious magazines printed a short text titled "From Goethe's Conversations with Riemer." Though only four paragraphs long, the piece appeared to be ominously prescient about recent history. Perhaps most damningly, the great poet was supposed to have said about his countrymen,

That they hate clarity is not right. That they do not know the charm of truth, lamentable indeed. That they so love cloudy vapouring and berserker excesses, repulsive; wretched that they abandon themselves credulously to every fanatic scoundrel who speaks to their baser qualities, confirms them in their vices, teaches them nationality means barbarism and isolation. To themselves they seem great and glorious only when they have gambled away all that they had worth having. Then they look with jaundiced eyes on those whom foreigners love and respect, seeing in them the true Germany. (GG, 70)[43]

The precise source of this quotation was somewhat nebulous. In some instances, the passage was attributed to the volume *Goethe's Conversations without Eckermann*, a 1929 compilation edited by the noted scholar Flodoard Freiherr von Biedermann. Regardless, the text proved popular among prodemocratic intellectuals in postwar Germany. It first appeared in the *Frankfurter Hefte*, a journal with a left-leaning Catholic editorial line. Next it was picked up by the student newspaper of the University of Hamburg, the *Hamburger Akademische Rundschau*, which had been founded by Karl Ludwig Schneider, a member of the White Rose anti-Nazi resistance group. From there it leapt to the literary journal *Das goldene Tor*, which had been founded by the émigré author Alfred Döblin to support political reeducation efforts in the French zone of occupation. After a few weeks, prominent intellectuals began quoting from the text, giving it a far wider dissemination than it would have reached via journals and magazines alone. Johannes R. Becher, a Communist poet who would go on to become the first minister for culture of the German Democratic Republic, used it in one of his speeches. And the liberal economist Wilhelm Röpke made effective use of it on the closing page of his book *The German Question*, one of the earliest attempts to come to terms with Nazism to be published in postwar Europe.[44]

The literary fad collapsed as quickly as it had started, however. The text, as magazine after magazine was forced to admit in a series of humiliating retractions, was a forgery. Even more embarrassingly, the source of the forgery wasn't all that hard to track down, for the quotations had simply been cobbled together from Thomas Mann's 1939 Goethe novel *Lotte in Weimar*. The affair led to a process of soul-searching. How was it possible that a nation that was fond of declaring itself the "country of poets and thinkers" had fallen for a hoax involving the most famous German poet who ever lived? Why did nobody bother to cross-check the quotation against its ostensible source, a widely disseminated work by a renowned scholar? And why did nobody recognize the true source of the quotations, given Mann's status as a giant of contemporary literature?

The *Hamburger Akademische Rundschau* conducted an inquiry into these questions. It had the most at stake; it was the most academic venue in which the fake quotations had appeared and was doubly humiliated by the fact that it had printed a long review of *Lotte in Weimar* in the very same issue in which it published the ostensible "Conversations with Riemer." The original source that had started the whole affair, it was now revealed, was a typewritten sheet of paper that had already circulated among opponents of the Nazis prior to the downfall of the regime. Doubtlessly, the *Hamburger Akademische Rundschau* conceded, it had been prepared without malice and was simply an example of a *Tarnschrift*: a clever way of smuggling Mann's critical words into the Third Reich by means of a fake attribution to Goethe.[45] The exact same strategy had, in fact, been used on other occasions, for example when Mann's letter to the dean of the University of Bonn was inserted into the fake collection *Letters by Classic German Authors (Briefe deutscher Klassiker)*. And why had the forgery not been spotted earlier? Goethe's conversations, the inquiry suggested, had fallen out of wider knowledge during the Nazi period, and even so popular a volume as the one produced by von Biedermann was difficult to get a hold of considering that so many libraries had been destroyed by the war. *Lotte in Weimar*, finally, had been outlawed by the Nazis and was only now finding a wider audience in Germany.

The affair rattled German intellectuals enough that a small publishing house seized the opportunity to print up a slim compilation of what Goethe had actually said about his compatriots.[46] And the Leipzig-based Insel Verlag reissued the *Conversations without Eckermann*, presumably driven by similar motivations. The whole affair perfectly encapsulates the fragile state of German intellectual life during the years immediately following the war, when an entire country discovered that it was unmoored from its cultural tradition. The problem wasn't just that the Nazis had corrupted central ideas of the German classical legacy. It was also that twelve years of totalitarian domination and six years of total war had destroyed the material substrate through which traditions perpetuate themselves: the libraries, critical editions, and reference works that give a culture literary substance.

The Goethe affair did have one more serious epilogue, and it is this epilogue that completes the triangle between Thomas Mann, the Germans, and the Allied occupiers that forms the subject of this chapter. During the summer of 1946, over the course of which the hoax unfolded, the newspaper headlines in Germany were dominated by the Nuremberg trials, the first and most important set of which were about to draw to a close. A member of the British prosecutorial team working on the trial must have come across either the original *Tarnschrift* reprinting Mann's words or—more likely—one of the articles then circulating in the German press. A translation into English was prepared (poorly, and introducing several errors), and on July 27, the chief prosecutor for the United Kingdom, Sir Hartley Shawcross, read excerpts from it into the trial record during his closing argument. Commenting

THE LOYAL AMERICAN SUBJECT 229

specifically on the murder of Jewish civilians by SS death squads, Shawcross stated,

> Years ago, Goethe said of the German people that fate "would strike them because they betrayed themselves and did not want to be what they are. It is sad that they do not know the charm of truth, that mist, smoke, and berserk immoderation are so dear to them, pathetic that they ingenuously submit to any mad scoundrel who appears to their lowest instinct, who confirms them in their vices and teaches them to conceive nationalism as isolation and brutality." With what a voice of prophecy he spoke—for these are the mad scoundrels who did those very things.[47]

He concluded his argument by expressing the wish that "those other words of Goethe be translated into fact, not only, as we must hope, of the German people but of the whole community of man: ' . . . thus ought the German people to behave; giving and receiving from the world, their hearts open to every fruitful source of wonder, great through understanding and love, through mediation and the spirit—thus ought they to be; that is their destiny.' "[48]

The *Times* of London printed excerpts from Shawcross's closing argument, including the first of the ostensible Goethe quotes, on July 29, from whence the hoax spread in the English-language press as well. But only a few days later, Eugen Kogon broke the news of the true source of the quotation in the pages of the *Frankfurter Hefte*, and suddenly the Allied prosecutors found themselves in the uncomfortable situation of appearing to have distorted history for transparent ideological reasons. After all, Thomas Mann's propaganda activities for the BBC were well-known in Germany. The British ambassador to the United States consequently sent a nervous letter to Thomas Mann in which he asked whether there was any chance that the words were perhaps Goethe's after all, or at least those of a later historical figure. Mann wrote back to say, "It is true, the quoted words do not appear literally in Goethe's writings or conversations; but they were conceived and formulated strictly in his spirit and although he never spoke them, he might well have done so" (GKFA, 9.2:170–71).

This explanation seems to have satisfied the British government, although the affair continued to fester for several months. As late as October 1946, Mann was forced to send a correction to the newspaper the *German American*, which had again printed the relevant excerpts from Shawcross's speech. "My attempt to play God has created quite a confusion," he wrote. "I am pleased when people who quote Goethe quote *my* Goethe. But out of respect for truth and scientific accuracy, I must try to ensure that it doesn't become habitual" (*GKFA*, 19.1:166). In Germany, however, Mann's critics weren't quite so easily appeased. Debates about Mann's literary methods in *Lotte in Weimar* continued for many years thereafter, and as late as 1965, conservative newspapers tried to make hay out of the fact that Mann had supposedly "forged Goethe quotes for anti-German purposes" (*GKFA*, 9.2:171).

The wording of Mann's responses to the ambassador and to the *German American* demonstrates that he secretly enjoyed the confusion his Goethe mimicry had caused. But much more was at stake here than a mere joke. For after all, the central artistic purpose of *Lotte in Weimar* had been to show that a literary "tradition" is forged by those who receive it. The "Goethe" who figures as the protagonist of the novel is a literary amalgam created from quotations, cultural commonplaces, and later observations by critics and biographers. The point of this exercise was not to create a kind of simulacrum whose accuracy might be compared by holding it up to the "real" Goethe. The point was, rather, to show that knowledge of such a "real" Goethe was unavailable to his posthumous recipients, who by necessity had to base their judgments on a similar amalgam of sources. For Mann, this insight was an essential pillar that supported his representative aspirations. For it proved that "tradition" couldn't be confined to a single language or a single territory. As soon as commentators in other parts of the world started issuing opinions on a literary figure, those opinions, too, would become a part of the larger tradition.

In the years following the Second World War, Germans had to confront the fact that their recent historical experience had left them with a deeply disturbed relationship to their own cultural inheritance. Twelve years of Nazi terror had brutally stunted that inheritance within Germany. At the same time, it had given rise to new expressions of it in the wider world. Henceforth, "German culture" would be unthinkable as an island unto itself, cut off from the larger global community. It was, instead, a province within a world republic of letters. Conservative voices may have decried this as a form of imperialism, with Thomas Mann as a loyal subject. But in reality he was merely what voices from the United States had declared him to be for a number of years: the first citizen of a republic of letters created largely through novel means of global literary dissemination.

Interlude V: *Doctor Faustus* (1948)

Doctor Faustus: The Life of the German Composer Adrian Leverkühn, as Told by a Friend is not only the most ambitious work of literature that Thomas Mann wrote during his American exile but also the one most explicitly concerned with the fate of the artist under conditions of totalitarian domination. Begun in May 1943 and completed in January 1947 (the first German-language edition was published later that same year; the first American edition, in 1948), the composition of *Doctor Faustus* overlapped with the death throes of the Third Reich, the Nuremberg trials, and the partition of Germany. If *Joseph in Egypt* and *Lotte in Weimar* were works in which Mann tried to define a conceptual base from which an émigré artist might attack his own government, and if *The Tables of the Law* and *Joseph the Provider* were literary examples of such attacks, then *Doctor Faustus* is a novel of reckoning.

The literary consequences of fascist Germany's defeat are probed nowhere else as trenchantly as in the novel's epilogue. There, Mann's narrator, Serenus Zeitblom, reflects on the situation in Germany immediately subsequent to the Second World War. It is a country in which, in his words, "the monstrous national perversion which then held the Continent, and more than the Continent, in its grip, has celebrated its orgies down to the bitter end" (*DF*, 504; *GKFA*, 10.1:730). In such a country, Zeitblom thinks, it might finally be possible again to publish a work such as his, a work that is openly critical not only of Nazism but also of German artistic and intellectual life over the prior half decade. But "those evil men willed that Germany be destroyed down to the ground; and one dares not hope it could very soon be capable of any sort of cultural activity, even the printing of a book." "In actual fact," Zeitblom concludes, "I have sometimes pondered ways and means of sending these pages to America, in order that they might first be laid before the public in an English translation." His ambitions are clouded, however, by the "thought of the essentially foreign impression my book must make in that cultural climate and coupled with it the dismaying prospect that its translation into English must turn out, at least in some all too radically German parts, to be an impossibility" (*DF*, 504; *GKFA*, 10.1:730).

Unlike Zeitblom, Mann himself could rest assured that his book would be published in America. But the worries expressed by his character were nevertheless also his own. Now that the war was over, Mann's former audience in Germany was available to him again. Indeed, Gottfried Bermann Fischer made aggressive moves to reestablish his company in the country of his birth. When attempts to sell the Stockholm edition of *Doctor Faustus* in Germany proved logistically difficult, and when attempts to reopen the old headquarters of the S. Fischer Verlag in Berlin came to naught, Berman Fischer simply licensed the novel to his old business associate Peter Suhrkamp. But could a novel written primarily with a German audience in mind still appeal to an international readership, now that such stark divisions in cultural life were opening up between the defeated Reich and the victorious Allied powers?

The problem was both intellectual and linguistic in nature, for Mann still believed modern Nazism to be a phenomenon whose roots reached back centuries, and as a result had written part of his novel in the idiom of the Reformation period. Helen Tracy Lowe-Porter struggled mightily to find an appropriate English counterpart for these passages and drafted a somewhat plaintive translator's preface in which she highlighted the difficulties she had faced. Mann, upon reading a draft version of this preface, instantly mobilized and urged her to also stress the appeal his novel might hold for an international audience: "[it may be] a book that is painfully preoccupied with the German fate and character, and whose language also burrows deeply into the German past, but it is also a decidedly international work that has a lot to say about the general fate of Occidental culture." Ever the savvy businessman, he continued, "all this explains why the original edition has caused tremors on the European continent that none of my other books has been able to provoke—in Switzerland and in the Nordic countries especially, but also in France and now increasingly in Germany. Translations are already being planned into French, Italian, Swedish, Czech, and Hungarian" (*DüD*, 3:156).

It is safe to say that US readers didn't react with quite the same excitement as their European counterparts. *Doctor Faustus* once again sold over two hundred thousand copies, buoyed by the ever-supportive Book-of-the-Month Club, as well as by reliably glowing reviews by the likes of Clifton Fadiman ("one of the most astonishing novels of our time") and of Claude Hill in the pages of the *Saturday Review* ("the book floats like a gigantic intellect-laden vessel in the shallow waters of current world literature").[1] But the overall critical reception was tepid, much as it had been for *Joseph the Provider*. Hamilton Basso, who had already done so much damage with his review of the last *Joseph* novel, called the new work a "thick, heavy pudding that it is hard to get one's teeth into," while Harry Levin, writing for the *New York Times*, announced that Lowe-Porter's doubts about her own abilities as a translator were "well grounded."[2]

Much of the seemingly inexhaustible stream of critical commentary that has been devoted to *Doctor Faustus* over the course of the past seventy years is concerned with the topic of German guilt and mentions Mann's anxieties about remaining apprehensible to an international audience only in passing, if at all. But what if we moved this question front and center, and treated *Doctor Faustus* as a text concerned not only with the darker undercurrents of German history but also with the place of the writer in an increasingly global world republic of letters? This second topic is closely tied up with another question; namely, Mann's contentious relationship with literary modernism.

In February 1942, roughly a year before he began work on *Doctor Faustus*, Mann read Harry Levin's seminal study *James Joyce: A Critical Introduction*. Mann had first taken jealous note of his Irish contemporary in 1929 (*GKFA*, 23.1:417), and now that entire books were being devoted to Joyce begrudgingly acknowledged him as "a brother" (*Tb.*, February 20, 1942). Over the course of the next few years, however, as not only Joyce's but also Kafka's star ascended ever higher, a certain amount of panic set in. Mann now feared that he would be eclipsed by authors who cultivated a more advanced style than he did, and that his more or less "realist" technique would come to be regarded as old-fashioned.[3]

Doctor Faustus can be seen as a response to this development. In his *Story of a Novel*, Mann claims that his late work was no less a "novel to end all novels" (Levin's description of *Ulysses*) than anything written by his Irish rival (*SN*, 91; *GW*, 11:205). And of course *Doctor Faustus* is the story of an avant-garde composer who pioneers an explicitly "modernist" style that is, in fact, a thinly veiled copy of Arnold Schoenberg's twelve-tone system. The influence of Mann's musical advisor, Theodor W. Adorno, also hangs heavily over the text. There has thus always been a strong critical current that focuses on the ostensibly avant-garde elements of the novel, including no shortage of readings that try to interpret the work as itself an example of a "strict" or "serial" style, in which the shape of individual episodes is determined by larger systemic exigencies.[4] Other critics have not been so sure. Hans Rudolf Vaget, for example, points out how carefully Mann disguised ostensibly "modernist" techniques, such as montage, in order to create a readable text.[5] And Rüdiger Görner, who has offered perhaps the most comprehensive analysis of Mann's "late style," dismisses any attempts to connect the author to the literary avant-garde as "erroneous."[6]

Very little attention has so far been paid to the subject area that is the main focus of this book, however—Thomas Mann's attempt to blaze a new path to global literary relevance by setting himself in opposition to the Nazi government. Mann's contentious relationship with modernist aesthetics should be evaluated in light of this larger project, which in turn is intimately tied to his quest to remain relevant to an international audience, not just to readers back in his native Germany.

Any reading of *Doctor Faustus* must sooner or later come to terms with the fact that there are multiple layers of artistic creation and literary narration at work in the text. The first of these layers is the one that centers on Adrian Leverkühn, the composer whose life's story provides the main subject matter of the novel. Adrian is the creator of numerous avant-garde compositions, as well as an accomplished theoretician of modernist music. In addition to all this, he is also to a certain extent his own autobiographer, for many key moments in his life can be reconstructed only through documents from his own hand. Central among these is the record of his conversation with the devil, which may just be a syphilitic hallucination, or even just a bad joke, and which is written in the Reformation idiom that gave Lowe-Porter so much trouble. The second layer is the one that centers on Serenus Zeitblom, the narrator of the novel. Serenus, too, is an artist of sorts, for he is the "friend" mentioned in the subtitle, and he mixes his own recollections of Adrian with the available documentary evidence to create a coherent biography that may nevertheless be partially fictional. In addition, Serenus is extremely loquacious about the circumstances under which he composes his work, and as a result we learn quite a bit about his own biography as well.

To these two layers, which any reader of Mann's novel will instantly recognize, we can add a third. This third layer is the life of Thomas Mann, the author who created both Serenus Zeitblom and Adrian Leverkühn, and who himself struggled to achieve a specific tone and artistic purpose. To mix fictional and historical, textual, and contextual elements in this fashion may seem at first sight to run contrary to all basic procedures of responsible literary criticism. But then we might remember two things. The first is that Mann himself scattered clues throughout the novel that invite the reader to draw parallels between his fictional characters and their creator. Zeitblom and Mann, for example, begin their respective projects in the same week in May 1943, and for a while their compositions progress in tandem with one another, although Zeitblom wraps up his biography in 1945, while Mann took until 1947 to complete his novel.[7] Leverkühn and Mann share biographical similarities as well; for instance, they both embark upon formative artistic residencies in Italy. The second thing to remember is that Mann, shortly after completing *Doctor Faustus*, took the unprecedented step of writing a companion work in which he recounted the compositional history of his late masterpiece in great detail. The German subtitle of this work, which has come to be known in English as *The Story of a Novel*, is *Roman eines Romans*, or "novel of a novel."[8] The boundaries between fact and fiction are thus blurry in the case of *Doctor Faustus*.

Adrian Leverkühn, as was already mentioned, can be seen as the archetype of the avant-garde artist, a type that Mann regarded with some jealousy, but also suspicion. Avant-garde art, in *Doctor Faustus*, is never treated as a mere formal experiment, however, but always also as a social project. Fairly early in the novel, for example, a young Leverkühn, inspired by the lectures of his American music teacher Wendell Kretzschmar, tells Zeitblom of his ambition to reverse the "secularization of art, its separation from divine service" (*DF*, 59; *GKFA*, 10.1:90).[9] Art, in other words, is supposed to perform a cultic function again, and to enter into the "service of a higher union, which did not need to be, as it once was, the Church" (*DF*, 60; *GKFA*, 10.1:91). He also identifies Ludwig van Beethoven as the composer who more than anybody else led art into its current condition of cultic estrangement, its "elevation into the individual and culturally self-purposive" (*DF*, 60; *GKFA*, 10.1:91). He thereby signals to the attentive reader that these are not merely immature musings but ideas that will preoccupy Leverkühn until the day of his descent into madness, when he proclaims his ultimate goal to be "to take back the Ninth Symphony."

Zeitblom responds to Leverkühn's proposal with the panicked cry of "barbarism," to which Leverkühn replies that "barbarism" makes sense as the ostensible antithesis to "culture" only within the worldview propagated by culture itself. The argument, as any careful reader of Nietzsche will have to acknowledge, is valid, but does nothing to dispel the fundamental discomfort many readers will feel at the thought of a postindividual, cultic, and yet non-Christian art. Indeed, while the idea of a cultic postindividualism was central also to many left-wing avant-garde movements during the early twentieth century, Mann leaves no doubts that he wants us to see the affinities between Leverkühn's project and the aesthetics of German fascism. During a subsequent discussion with Zeitblom that takes place during the time of the First World War, for example, Leverkühn uses the word "breakthrough," which Zeitblom himself used a few pages earlier to praise the German war aims, to describe the move from "intellectual coldness into a daring world of new feeling" (*DF*, 321, translation modified; *GKFA*, 10.1:468).

Leverkühn, in sum, can be seen as an extreme illustration of the fundamental congruity between artist and fascist dictator that Mann already postulated in "Brother Hitler." Like the fascist dictator, he is interested in employing aesthetic means not as ends in and of themselves but rather in support of an ulterior communal end. These totalitarian elements, furthermore, are inextricably linked to Leverkühn's musical modernism, which is conceived as a response to Beethoven's attempts to dissolve the boundaries of traditional tonality. Against the resulting musical romanticism, Leverkühn pits the idea of a strict and hierarchical musical system (the twelve-tone row) in which every note is assigned a specific place and function.

Leverkühn's avant-garde project must be contrasted with that of Serenus Zeitblom, the traditional (indeed rather old-fashioned) humanist, who reacts to his friend's musical experimentation with a mixture of fascination and horror. But Zeitblom, too, is an experimental composer, albeit of a literary kind. Far from being the mere "realist" narrator as which many critics from Georg Lukács to the present have categorized him, Zeitblom actually creates before our eyes a complex narrative texture that obeys the four-fold logic of medieval literary interpretation—a logic that American theorists of modernism, such as Clement Greenberg, were just then beginning to apply to literary texts.[10] Viewed through this lens, the story of Leverkühn can be read not only *literally* (as a biography of a specific individual) but also *typologically* (as a modern version of the Faustus myth), *morally* (as a historical account of Germany's descent into fascism), and *anagogically* (as a story about the outcome of five hundred years of German cultural separatism). That Zeitblom himself is aware of these allegorical layers is demonstrated by the incessant remonstrations and disclaimers that he intersperses throughout his text. Regarding the ostensible conversation with the devil, for example (a key passage without which a typological reading of the novel would be far less convincing), Zeitblom says that "the unreasonable demand made upon the reader does not lie at my door and need not trouble me" (*DF*, 251; *GKFA*, 10.1:365). The truth, of course, is precisely the opposite. It is Zeitblom who decides to pass on Leverkühn's recollections of what happened in Italy, and Zeitblom who decides to make them a structurally central feature of his text.

Zeitblom's attempts to use Leverkühn's biography as an allegorical vehicle that would explain not only recent political history but also the German national character directly parallels Mann's own attempts to pit humanist totality against fascist totalitarianism. In his lecture scripts of the 1930s and early 1940s, Mann repeatedly declared that if artists wanted to truly counter the fascist tendency to subordinate all of life to politics, then they would have to think big, toward an art that would encompass all human experience, including politics. This is precisely what Zeitblom does with his allegorical schema. Far from being a mere reactionary trying to contain the avant-garde radicalism of his friend, Zeitblom thus offers an alternate version of what artistic modernism might look like.

His method, however, takes a decided toll on the reader who, in order to understand the moral dimensions of the text (i.e., its analysis of, and warning against, fascism) will also have to struggle through the typological and anagogical layers of the novel. To fully understand what is going on, in other words, readers not only will have to recognize the Faustian elements but also will have to be able to spot and properly place the numerous other allusions to German cultural history, such as the invocation of Martin Luther or of Friedrich Nietzsche. For much of the past two decades, Mann had worked with the biblical Joseph story as an allegorical vehicle, turning, for example, Joseph's tenure in Egypt into a parable of the New Deal. The biblical material was nearly universal in reach, at least in the western world. *Doctor Faustus*, with its decidedly denser and more Germanic texture, was a different story entirely.

This, perhaps, is why Mann decided to add yet another layer to Zeitblom's narration, which consists of the continuous references to the creation of the biographical text. At the beginning of chapter 33, for example, Zeitblom writes, "The time of which I write was for us Germans an era of national collapse, of capitulation, of uprisings due to exhaustion, of helpless surrender into the hands of strangers. The time *in* which I write, which must serve me to set down these recollections here in my silence and solitude, this time has a horribly swollen belly, it carries in its womb a national catastrophe compared with which the defeat of those earlier days seems a moderate misfortune" (*DF*, 336; *GKFA*, 10.1:488). Again and again, through grammatical repetition, lexical parallelism, and evaluative comparison, this passage draws a connection between the mid-1940s—the present day for Mann's implied readership—and the story that Zeitblom is struggling to relate. In so doing, it highlights the contemporary relevance of a complex allegorical tale.

Zeitblom, however, remains a quintessentially Germanic figure. Nobody would mistake the retired high school teacher who holds a PhD and refers to himself as a "scholar and conjuratus of the 'Latin Host'" (*DF*, 3; *GKFA*, 10.1:12) for a member of the American middle classes. The tale that he relates about himself is a specifically German one as well, a story of growing disenchantment with inherited narratives of national identity and of apprehension as to what the future might hold for his fatherland. Non-German Europeans, whose lives had often become tangled up with the crimes of the Nazis in complex ways, might conceivably recognize Zeitblom as a familiar type, even if they did not exactly identify with him. But ordinary Americans?

Mann's "novel of a novel" fixes this gap in address by imposing a further layer, which adds his own experiences in America to the allegorical mill. When the two books are read side by side, *Doctor Faustus* reveals itself to be simultaneously a work about a set of fictional musical compositions written between 1906 and 1930, a fictional biographical narrative written in Germany between 1943 and 1945, and a very real novel written in America between 1943 and 1947. This final layer of the story is entirely relatable to US reader and connects the American war effort, which was entering its final phase as Mann was working on his novel, to everything that Zeitblom has to say.

For Mann, this must have been an attempt to reconcile the two essentially separate lives that he had lived over the course of the last decade: his life as an author of demanding fiction, often with no overtly identifiable relationship to the war against fascism, and his life as a militant public intellectual in America. Through *The Story of a Novel*, Mann's life as a public intellectual became part of the effort to grasp a totalizing account of human experience that he himself saw as literature's only possible answer to fascism. This, incidentally, is presumably also why *The Story of a Novel* opens with a numerical game forecasting the author's own death: the move strengthens the parallel to Leverkühn with his Faustian pact and draws Mann's autobiography closer into the allegorical fabric.

Mann's endeavors proved to be entirely in vain, of course. Far from being recognized as an attempt to bridge the gap between the rapid forward march of contemporary history and the far vaster temporal expanse of epic fiction, *Doctor Faustus* instead acquired the reputation of being a formidable intellectual puzzle box, a textual riddle challenging even the most learned of academic interpreters. Precisely those qualities, in other words, that earned *Doctor Faustus* a lasting place in world literature were also those that obscured Thomas Mann's ongoing struggle with the question of what a global republic of letters should actually look like.

CHAPTER 7

The Isolated World Citizen

The narrative works of Thomas Mann have stood above the fray for a generation. Scholars and exegetes may continue to quarrel about them. But Mann's characters long ago began to live their own life. Generations of future readers will laugh and cry with them. Who cares whether or not the "objective spirit" has forsaken Thomas Mann, or perhaps never even touched him? The greatest moments of his characters will endure forever.

—Arnold Bauer, "Thomas Mann and His Adversaries," March 1949

In an article in The Observer *called "The Isolated World Citizen," Philip Toynbee, an English critic, called the political stance that I've taken for the past 30 years "too good to be true." . . . Young Toynbee is right: my stance has become quietly questionable, especially those things about it that relate to optimism, democracy, faith in humanity—and yes, even to my "world citizenship." My books are hopelessly German.*

—Thomas Mann, "The Artist and Society," 1952

Thomas Mann was not, generally speaking, a superstitious man, but in his autobiographical account of the 1940s, *The Story of a Novel*, he nevertheless reveals that he approached his seventieth birthday, which took place on June 6, 1945, in the firm conviction that it would herald the year in which he would die (*SN*, 1; *GKFA*, 19.1:409). The superstition was not entirely incorrect, for in March 1946, Mann was diagnosed with a carcinoma on his right lung that required immediate surgery. The procedure took place at the University of Chicago hospital, and the famous writer made a complete recovery, henceforth troubled only by a nagging conscience regarding his habit of smoking ten cigarettes a day (*Tb.*, July 14, 1946).

The person who did die around the time of Mann's seventieth birthday was Adolf Hitler, who committed suicide on April 30, 1945. The following day the New York newspaper *PM-Daily* cabled Mann to inquire whether he believed the rumors asserting the death of the führer. His response was as succinct as it was insouciant: "Who cares?" (*EF*, 100; *Br. EK*, 2:80). Inwardly, however, Mann was deeply anxious. When news of Germany's unconditional surrender reached him a week later, he noted in his diaries, "[Is this] day a cause for utmost celebration? I don't exactly feel elated" (*Tb.*, May 7, 1945). Indeed, it was as yet far from certain what these cataclysmic events would portend for the future of the country that the author loved so dearly.

There were people who believed that Mann should play an active part in determining this future. Back in 1944, Agnes E. Meyer's *Washington Post* had tried to bill Mann as the logical choice to become president of a "reborn German republic," a suggestion that the author himself ridiculed, writing back to his patron, "Germany will be under a complete tutelage and need no head at all, only sensible local administrations."[1] Once the war was over, calls to take on a political role also reached Mann from the ruins of the Reich. The *Hannoversche Zeitung* published an editorial in which it wrote that "in the depths of our need we still hope for him."[2] Similar entreaties reached Mann from the Soviet occupied zone, from whence a committee of "victims of fascism" wrote him a public letter to say, "We believe you now have a historic work to accomplish in Germany. We need your help. You belong to us."[3]

Mann was smart enough to realize that these various entreaties had little to do with him and much to do with the political calculations of those who uttered them. The German Communist cadres who had descended upon the Soviet occupied zone had taken careful note of Mann's many pronouncements in favor of democratic socialism, and especially of his Library of Congress address "The War and the Future," in which Mann had expressed his conviction that "the world and everyday life are moving, *nolens volens*, toward a social structure for which the epithet "communistic" is a relatively adequate term" (*LC*, 42; *GW*, 12:937). They were now hoping to score a propaganda coup by luring Mann away from America and into what would eventually become East Germany. The calls from the western zones were driven by similarly impure motives. Many of his supplicants there were merely hoping to better their own standing in the eyes of the Allied powers by establishing a connection to the famous writer. And besides, Mann surmised that were he to come back, his former countrymen would certainly turn on him if he proved incapable of working miracles on their behalf (*Br. AM*, 637).

For a number of reasons, then, the idea of Mann leading postwar Germany on its thorny path back to democracy was utterly illusory. But what, then, would his future role be now that it was no longer necessary to represent the autonomy of German culture against the totalitarian demands of the Nazis? This question would plague Mann for the remainder of his life and lead to the decline of his public reputation in America during the late 1940s and early 1950s. As had been the case in the 1930s, however, Mann's search for a new representative role did not take place in a vacuum. The American cultural landscape was changing as well, and realigning itself in ways that made the once-topical author come to seem superannuated.

Birthday Greetings

This change in the cultural landscape of America is perfectly captured by the remarks that were delivered at a stately dinner in honor of Mann's seventieth birthday at the Waldorf Astoria Hotel in New York on June 25, 1945. Sponsored by the *Nation*, which had published Mann's letter to the dean as well as numerous of his subsequent essays and commentaries, the dinner was a grand affair indeed. It was presided over by Robert E. Sherwood, whose Pulitzer Prize–winning play *There Shall Be No Night* had been one of the prime achievements of the US Popular Front. The honorary speakers were the Supreme Court justice Felix Frankfurter; the secretary of the interior, Harold L. Ickes; and Juan Negrín López, the prime minister of the last Republican government of Spain. Mann was given the opportunity to say a few words as well, and hastened to assert that he never would have agreed to such a lavish celebration if he "had not from the very beginning been allowed to ascribe to it a wholly suprapersonal meaning and purpose—the meaning of a demonstration in honor and in behalf of liberal thought in America" (*ADH*, 20; *GKFA*, 19.1:27).

These remarks were almost painfully accurate. Frankfurter and Ickes may nominally have been there to convey birthday greetings to a famous writer. But as quickly became obvious when they launched into their respective speeches, they were actually preoccupied by another recent event. Franklin Delano Roosevelt had died just two months earlier, and his passing marked the symbolic end of an important phase of US liberalism in which both the Supreme Court justice and the secretary of the interior had played central parts. What was to come next was as yet far from certain.

Frankfurter used the first part of his speech to heap exuberant if rather predictable praises upon Mann. At roughly the halfway mark, however, he issued a more surprising pronouncement. By "crossing the ocean and casting his lot among us," so he asserted, the émigré author had "reinforced [a] truth" that said more about America than it did about Mann as an individual (*ADH*, 10). This truth was that "we are all immigrants" and that proper Americanism would always rest on "completeness of devotion to the Declaration of Independence, the Second Inaugural, and the Four Freedoms," rather than on blood. Frankfurter then posed a rhetorical question that must have seemed a rather incongruous closing point for a birthday address to Thomas Mann: "what is more fitting than that Lincoln should gradually but securely have become the uncontested symbol of America?" (*ADH*, 10).

In drawing such attention to the legacy of Lincoln, and to America as a republic defined by shared civic values rather than by heritage or blood, Frankfurter was almost certainly alluding to the new era of civil rights struggles that had been set into motion by the Second World War. In 1941 Roosevelt had signed Executive Order 8802, prohibiting racial discrimination within the defense industry. Maltreatment of African American citizens nevertheless persisted, leading most famously to the race riots of Detroit and Los Angeles in June 1943. Frankfurter knew that with thousands of black soldiers returning from the war and rightfully demanding recognition for their sacrifices, race relations would have to change in the United States.

Mann's name makes occasional appearances in the records of the civil rights struggles of the 1930s and 1940s. In 1931 he joined a German committee trying to save the so-called Scottsboro Boys (a group of nine African American teenagers accused of raping two white women in Alabama) from the electric chair. And in 1943 he was one of the sponsors of a goodwill program that was broadcast over CBS about a month after the Detroit race riots. Both of these actions were mentioned in the African American press.[4] However, these were tangential activities at best for the author, who signed literally hundreds of proclamations and protest letters throughout this period. His letters and diaries give no indication that he took much note of the racial unrest surrounding him, and he also never mentions African American intellectuals such as Langston Hughes, who crossed his path several times and who, in turn, deeply admired him.[5]

More damning than these personal oversights, however, is that the author's eulogies to American democracy show no awareness whatsoever of the ways in which racial disparities were undermining the ideals of "liberty" and "equality" that Mann so cherished. In his Library of Congress address "The War and the Future," for example, Mann cheerfully proclaims that "a country of America's courageous progressivity . . . gives us the premonitions of this coming world in its equalitarianism," and cites as evidence for his thesis the fact that "the difference in clothing is disappearing more and more" (*LC*, 40; *GW*, 12:935–36). The lecture was delivered less than four months after the so-called Zoot Suit Riots that took place just a few miles from Mann's doorstep in Santa Monica, when Mexican Americans, African Americans, and members of other racial minorities were attacked by white soldiers and policemen precisely for their ostensibly wasteful style of dress. Earlier that same year, Marc M. Moreland, a philosophy professor at the historically black

Morgan State University, had already gone on the offensive in an editorial for the *Arkansas State Press* in which he asked, "Is Thomas Mann serious, or just misinformed, when he speaks of Americanizing the world after the war? I'm sure that Mr. Mann, when he speaks of 'Americanizing the world,' has in mind the basic moral, original promise of the American ideal of democracy being applied to human relationships on earth. But is Mr. Mann so thankful for his own personal refuge as a free spirit in this 'great country' that he doesn't see the practiced ramifications of Americanization?"[6] For these reasons and others, then, Mann was an awkward fit at best for the world that Frankfurter was sketching as arising in the wake of Roosevelt's death.

The second American speaker at Thomas Mann's birthday banquet, Harold L. Ickes, was most famous as one of the principal architects of the New Deal. His left-leaning background is readily apparent in the speech that he gave for Thomas Mann. Noting at the outset that he saw "no occasion to become excited when a man attains the age of seventy," Ickes crammed everything that he had to say about the famous author into one short paragraph, vaguely praising Mann for his "great qualities of leadership that have grown out of his experience and are fortified by intellectual stamina" (*ADH*, 11). He then went on to present his main thesis: "We are going to need these qualities in solving the pressing problems of the world that will continue to crowd in upon us as time passes" (*ADH*, 11). These problems would consist principally of defeating Japan, judging Germany, and figuring out how to make peace with Russia, overruling the "sibilant whispers" of those that are "so devoted to America and American institutions that they stir up suspicions and foment fear and hate of that great nation" (*ADH*, 14). Ickes even went a step further, averring that "so many of the things that are said now about Russia in this country are Goebbelese. It may be true that the songster is dead, but it certainly is not true that the song is over" (*ADH*, 15).

Within the span of just a few months, such outright declarations of sympathy with Communist Russia would become a kiss of death for any US politician; Ickes himself resigned from public office in early 1946. Indeed, such statements were dangerous even in 1945, when Congress elevated the House Un-American Activities Committee (HUAC) from a special investigative entity to a standing committee, charging it with the hunt for Communists within government circles. Nevertheless, Ickes clearly thought at the time of Mann's seventieth birthday that a peaceful coexistence between the capitalist West and Communist Russia was both possible and advisable, and that Mann might prove to be a useful guide to such a future.

If Frankfurter, in his speech, painted multiculturalism and racial equality as the greatest challenge confronting a future America, Ickes, in turn, believed that this challenge lay instead in keeping alive the progressive spirit of the New Deal in an age of hypernationalism and anti-Communism. Both speakers thought that Mann, whether through his status as an immigrant or as a protosocialist thinker, might be able to maintain his representative authority. The reality, however, would prove to be far harsher.

A Dupe and Fellow Traveler

In March 1947 the German émigré journalist Gerhart Eisler, editor-in-chief of the Communist newspaper the *German American*, was summoned in front of HUAC. He was the brother of the composer Hanns Eisler, as well as of Ruth Fischer, who had formerly been a leading figure in the German Communist Party but had been expelled from its ranks over her uncompromising anti-Stalinism. Eisler, a high-ranking spy for the Comintern, refused to testify to HUAC and was found guilty of contempt of Congress. His arrest provoked a declaration of solidarity from numerous prominent intellectuals, among them W. E. B. Du Bois, Arthur Miller, and Dorothy Parker. Mann signed as well, and in doing so set himself in public opposition to the US government for the first time of his life.

The Eisler affair would prove to have far-reaching consequences for cultural life in the United States. While Gerhart Eisler himself eventually fled the country, becoming head of the state radio services of the German Democratic Republic (GDR), his sister Ruth Fischer turned witness for the prosecution and implicated both Gerhart and Hanns in Communist espionage activities. Prior to the ensuing HUAC investigation, Hanns Eisler's scores had twice been nominated for an Oscar. After the investigations, during which he was repeatedly accused of being the chief Soviet agent in Hollywood, his American career lay in ruins. He too returned to Europe, and eventually to the GDR, for which he composed the national anthem.

The Eisler affair set off a Communist witch hunt in the motion picture industry, the most important outcome of which was the HUAC investigation against the so-called Hollywood Ten, a group of screenwriters and directors who were sentenced to prison and then blacklisted after refusing to testify about their alleged membership in the Communist Party USA. Mann, who was on friendly terms with Hanns Eisler, recorded a brief statement for the radio program "Hollywood Fights Back," which was broadcast on November 2, 1947.[7] "I have the honor to expose myself as a hostile witness," he there declared. "Since my arrival in the United States, nine years ago, I've seen a great many Hollywood films. If Communist propaganda has been smuggled into any of them, it must have been most thoroughly hidden." And "spiritual intolerance, political inquisition and declining legal security; and all this in the name of an alleged 'state of emergency,'—that's how it started,—in Germany" (*GKFA*, 19.1:298). The following summer he found even stronger words. At a gathering of the Hollywood Peace Group, he received a standing ovation when he declared that peace with Russia "is not a communist catch-phrase. It is a moral command, a categorical imperative handed down to humanity, which risks self-destruction if it ignores it. A peace conference such as ours is not an un-American activity, but rather serves to restore the honor of America as a nation of well-meaning intelligence" (*GKFA*, 19.1:393). And when the *St. Louis Post-Dispatch* solicited from him and several other prominent émigrés an answer to the question "Has America fulfilled our hopes?," he replied that "while in the United States the preservation of democratic freedom is allegedly the mainspring of all that's being done, our means of defense are sometimes dangerously close to those of the police state" (*GKFA*, 19.1:398).

This rapid concatenation of events and proclamations documents the speed with which American society changed as it launched into the Cold War. In 1943 Mann had still been able to declare (in a gilded auditorium at the Library of Congress and in front of some of the nation's highest-ranking politicians) that the world was moving toward a "communistic" form of life. In early 1947, a sitting cabinet member had used the occasion of Mann's seventieth birthday to declare "peace with Russia" as one of the most pressing challenges confronting America. Yet now, little more than a year later, people were being sent to prison simply for refusing to publicly declare their political convictions, and Mann was drawing public comparisons between the United States and Nazi Germany.

Despite such strong language, neither the FBI nor HUAC at this point took particular interest in what Thomas Mann had to say about McCarthyism.[8] All of this changed in 1949, a year which stands second only to 1937 as a turning point in the author's American fortunes. Two different developments took place that year. The first was that Mann once again was involved in a conference agitating for peace between the United States and Soviet Russia. Hosted at the Waldorf Astoria Hotel in New York, the same place where his seventieth birthday celebration had been held four years earlier, the conference was sponsored by the National Council of Arts, Sciences, and Professions, a group that had originally been founded under the chairmanship of Harold L. Ickes to promote Roosevelt's legacy. It had taken a swerve to the hard left following Ickes's departure, and was now essentially a Stalinist front. Unlike the obscure Hollywood Peace conference of the previous year, the Waldorf Astoria event was a highly prominent affair and has even been called "one of the strangest gatherings in American history."[9] The Cominform sent a number of high-ranking Soviet intellectuals, most notably the composer Dmitry Shostakovich, to America on a propaganda mission. Meanwhile, prominent westerners who were known to be critical of the Soviet Union, such as the philosophers John Dewey and Ernest Nagel, were shut out from the conference. In their stead, the lineup featured speakers such as the playwright Arthur Miller and the composer Aaron Copland, both of whom were known for more Soviet-friendly positions. The US State Department, not to be outdone by such maneuvers, engaged in some manipulative acts of its own, readily granting visas to the speakers from behind the Iron Curtain but withholding them for western European intellectuals who advocated for neutrality between the two emerging superpowers. In so doing, it created the illusion of a Manichean struggle between Communist Russia and the capitalist West.[10]

In order to create legitimacy for the conference, the National Council actively sought out the sponsorship of a number of high-ranking Western intellectuals who stood above suspicion of being Communist pawns. Thomas Mann, who was never one to turn down an invitation to join a political action committee, readily assented to the council's approach. This in turn provoked a heated response from the philosopher Sidney Hook, who wrote Mann several irate letters, copies of which he also included in correspondence with other people whom he was trying to badger out of supporting the Waldorf event.[11] Mann remained unimpressed, referring in his diaries to the "threatening letters by that New York professor" (Tb., March 16, 1949). The following day he instead sent a telegram to the National Council's president, Harlow Shapley, in which he called the conference a "noble and humane enterprise" and reiterated his willing association with the event (GKFA, 19.1:645). Parts of this telegram were read over the radio and also printed in the New York Times. A few days later, Mann even went so far as to lodge a formal protest against the visa denials with the secretary of state, Dean Acheson, though predictably, nothing ever came of this.

The Waldorf Astoria conference descended into a farce and became one of the first true flash points in what eventually would come to be known as the "cultural Cold War." Outside the hotel, a motley mix of American Legion veterans and Catholic nuns picketed the event. Inside, Sidney Hook, who never did manage to obtain an invitation, commandeered a bridal suite from which he oversaw the efforts of an illustrious gathering of the New York anti-Communist left to disrupt the proceedings. From their perch on the tenth floor, Hook's troops descended upon the panels and plenaries below to heckle and ask uncomfortable questions. Things came to a climax when the composer Nicolas Nabokov confronted Shostakovich after the Russian had dutifully read a statement prepared for him by his KGB handlers. Did Shostakovich approve of an article in *Pravda* in which Paul Hindemith, Arnold Schoenberg, and Igor Stravinsky had been labeled as "decadent bourgeois formalists" whose works should under no circumstances be performed in the Soviet Union? A pale Shostakovich muttered that he did, struggling to convey a semblance of conviction. In his memoirs he later admitted he was convinced that he would be shot upon his return home.[12]

Hook's hardline tactics clearly won the battle in the court of popular opinion. The *Daily Mirror* published an article in which it taunted, "But, Thomas Mann—when you were a refugee from Hitler's wrath, this country let you in. You did not go to Soviet Russia for sanctuary. You came here. And you lived here in peace, comfort and prosperity. You plied your trade here in freedom. But we see your name on this list!" The following day, it added, "Thomas Mann is now an American citizen and may say anything he likes, as this is a free country. He apparently finds our freedom distasteful, for otherwise, why would he engage in supporting Soviet Russia's propagandistic war against us?" (*Tb.*, March 26, 1949, n1).

A story in *Life* magazine ridiculing the Waldorf Astoria conference and its participants proved even more damaging than these tabloid attacks. The feature was accompanied by a gallery of fifty prominent Americans who were accused of being "dupes and fellow travelers" who "dress up communist fronts." Among them was Thomas Mann. The author could admittedly claim to be in good company. The list of the accused included the former vice president Henry A. Wallace as well as Albert Einstein, Charlie Chaplin, Langston Hughes, Leonard Bernstein, and many others. Still, this was the same *Life* magazine that, ten years earlier, had run a glowing photo news story on Mann's lecture tours in defense of democracy and that, only five years previously, had printed admiring articles on the Soviet Union and its valiant struggle against Nazi Germany. The shift in public perception was now unmistakable, and Mann's allies among the educated liberal elite found themselves shaken as well. Francis Biddle, who had been the chief judge at the Nuremberg trials, sent Mann a letter asking whether the accusations in *Life* were really true. Mann, who privately confessed himself to be "disgusted and depressed" (*Tb.*, April 2, 1949) by the story, was forced to aver that "I am neither a dupe nor a fellow-traveler and by no means an admirer of the quite malicious present phase of the Russian revolution" (*L*, 412).

The second major event that took place in 1949 was that Mann returned to his native Germany for the first time since 1933. The reason for the trip was the two hundredth anniversary of the birth of Goethe, which brought with it a number of lecturing invitations. The return to Germany was an emotionally charged affair for Mann, who knew that few of his compatriots would welcome him with open arms. While the night train that carried the author and his wife across the border was greeted by a French military honor guard, many ordinary Germans still regarded Mann as, essentially, a traitor who had left his country in its hour of direst need and who was now providing intellectual support to the Allies in their alleged attempts to chastise a suffering nation.[13] The fact that he was once again aligning himself with Goethe was not exactly helpful either. The memories of the Nuremberg trials, when Sir Hartley Shawcross had accidentally attributed a Mann quote to Goethe in his condemnation of the German national character, still rankled.

These details were of little concern to the average American. What did cause dismay in the US press, however, was that Mann accepted lecturing invitations from both the western and the eastern zones of occupation and delivered his "Address in the Goethe Year 1949" both in Frankfurt, the city where Goethe was born, and in Weimar, the town where he had spent much of his life (figure 7.1).[14] The timing of this decision was delicate, to say the least. When Mann visited Weimar on August 1, 1949, the Berlin airlift was still underway, though the Soviet blockade itself had ended three months earlier. Mann did not help his cause when he said, following his lecture "Goethe and

FIGURE 7.1.   Thomas Mann during his visit to Frankfurt am Main in July 1949. Not all Germans were as welcoming of the author as the ones shown in this picture. The LIFE Picture Collection/ Getty Images.

Democracy" at the Library of Congress, that the Soviet agreement to lift the blockade should be interpreted as a "long-range bid for peace."[15] Nor did he win any friends with a travel report that was published in the *New York Times Magazine*, in which he meekly defended his decision not to press for a visit to the Buchenwald concentration camp on the outskirts of Weimar, which had been turned into a Stalinist internment facility (GT, 32; *GKFA*, 19.1:715).

Many US papers carried critical stories about Mann's excursion to the Soviet zone, but the charge against the famous author was led by an émigré journalist named Eugene Tillinger, who published an article called "The Moral Eclipse of Thomas Mann" in the anti-Communist monthly *Plain Talk*. Tillinger defamed Mann as "America's Fellow Traveler No. 1" and spoke of his "avowed championship of the dark forces threatening civilization."[16] *Plain Talk* had a somewhat limited reach, but Tillinger made sure to forward copies of his article to the FBI. Strong circumstantial evidence suggests that the bureau thereafter paid a visit to Luther H. Evans, who had succeeded Archibald MacLeish as librarian of Congress, and made it plain to him that it might be in the library's best interest to steer clear of the increasingly controversial author.[17] Mann's next lecture was quietly cancelled, and although the author continued to serve as a fellow even after his final departure for Europe in 1952, this effectively ended his career as a public intellectual in America.

The Cultural Cold War and the World Republic of Letters

It would be easy to conclude from the foregoing summary that Thomas Mann's fading influence in the United States was due simply to a number of ill-fated pronouncements, as well as to a general shift in American interests from fascism to Communism. The truth is much more complex. For even as official circles turned away from him, Mann's status as a cultural icon continued largely unabated. Perhaps nothing makes this clearer than the fact that the author appeared as one of the sponsors of the Goethe Bicentennial Convocation and Music Festival in Aspen, Colorado, in June 1949 (figure 7.2). Just two months after being blacklisted by *Life* magazine as a Communist "dupe," his photograph was here printed face-to-face with that of the convocation's honorary chairman, former Republican president Herbert Hoover (who was also one of the financial backers of *Plain Talk* magazine, which played such an important role in defaming the author). And though the Aspen bicentennial celebration took place at the exact same time at which Mann's decision to accept the invitation from East Germany was causing international tensions, nobody seems have thought ill of his association with the much more placid affair in Colorado.

FIGURE 7.2. The officers and board of directors of the Goethe Bicentennial Convocation and Music Festival in Aspen, Colorado, June 27–July 16, 1949. Hoover is depicted at top left; Mann, in the bottom row. Image provided by Kai Sina.

Other cultural honors continued to accumulate as well. In 1949 Mann was not only inducted into the American Academy of Arts and Letters but also awarded its Merit Medal. The following year Knopf published *The Thomas Mann Reader*, hoping to cash in on a general vogue for the format that was driven by the GI Bill and the boom in college literature classes.[18] Although the reviews of the volume were generally tepid, the consensus opinion put the blame at the feet of the anthology's editor, Joseph Angell, who had mainly served up snippets from Mann's demanding longer works. The year 1950 also brought a major Thomas Mann retrospective at Yale University, an exhibit which Mann himself called "truly astonishing" (*L*, 430; *Br.*, 3:168). And when the *Saturday Review of Literature* conducted a Christmas poll in order to determine which works of classic literature its readers were most likely to place under their Yuletide trees, Mann was represented by two books, *The Magic Mountain* and *Doctor Faustus*.[19] Clearly, the accusations of being a Communist sympathizer did not hurt him all too much.

What is also true, however, is that Mann was at this point of his life mainly reaping the fruits of former accomplishments. The reviews of his late novels were polite, but also lukewarm. The *Joseph* tetralogy, a monumental work on which Mann had slaved for nearly two decades, vanished from public consciousness with alarming speed. Mann himself took note of the problem, and in a letter to the University of Pittsburgh German professor Klaus W. Jonas complained of a review in the *New Yorker*, which had quipped that anyone looking at *The Thomas Mann Reader* would never believe that its subject was still alive, and which had characterized him as "a major author, alright" but "not *that* major" (*L*, 430; *Br.* 3:168–69).

The diminishing strength of old age may have been partly to blame for all this, but Mann was also suffering from a fundamental realignment in the structure of the world republic of letters. Put in the simplest terms, the very notion of what counted as world literature was changing in dramatic fashion. Mann's younger contemporary, the literature scholar Erich Auerbach, described these changes in his classic essay "The Philology of World Literature," published in 1952. "The *felix culpa* [fortunate accident] of the division of the human race into a profusion of cultures is the precondition of world literature," Auerbach there averred. But "today we are witnessing a homogenization of human life the world over."[20] Such homogenized life essentially came in two flavors: "the Euro-American or the Soviet-Bolshevist pattern."[21] Moreover, "no matter how different from each other these two patterns may be, the distinctions between them are relatively minor when they are compared, in their current forms, with the patterns that underlie the Muslim, South Asian, or Chinese traditions."[22] Ideological standardization according to either capitalist or Bolshevist models was, in other words, replacing the national variations that had previously characterized global literary affairs. For Auerbach, this was a frightening prospect. "Should the human race in the end succeed in surviving the shock of so violent, enormously rapid, and poorly conceived a process of contraction, then we will have to accustom ourselves to the thought that only a single literary culture may survive in this homogenized world," he wrote.[23]

Auerbach's essay offers a near-perfect description of Thomas Mann's predicament in the late 1940s. His ascent to "first citizen in the international republic of letters" had been premised on two principal factors: first, the assumption that art is an autonomous sphere of activity that can flourish only in material and intellectual independence from political parties, state-controlled academies, or propaganda institutes; and second, the assertion that artists nevertheless act as ambassadors of their respective countries within this autonomous sphere. The onset of the Cold War nullified both of these factors. As Auerbach so vividly described, the notion of the republic of letters as a meeting ground of different national traditions was replaced by a competing model in which individual writers instead function as stand-ins for either one of two competing visions of modernity, one capitalist and one Communist.

At the same time, governments began to employ art for propagandistic purposes with a sophistication that far surpassed anything that had been tried in the 1930s and early 1940s. In the West, this actually involved bolstering the notion of an autonomous literary sphere, but only in order to then use this notion to lend ideological support to the system of free-market capitalism, which was similarly built on the notion that "freedom" and "modernity" could most readily be achieved through independence from government interference. (The Soviet Union, of course, with its five-year plans and its rhetoric about the party as the vanguard of the masses, took the exact opposite approach.) Starting around 1950, the CIA and other US government institutions began to take an active hand in shaping what counted as "modern" art. They attempted to promote all those currents premised on the assumption of an underlying autonomy of aesthetic production and to dissuade all practices built upon the notion of a mutual "engagement" between art and politics.[24] Perhaps nowhere is this as readily apparent as in the story of Melvin J. Lasky and his German-language Cold War journal *Der Monat*.

Melvin J. Lasky, *Der Monat*, and the Battle with Georg Lukács

Melvin J. Lasky was one of the most scintillating figures of the cultural Cold War and exerted a profound influence on German-American relations from the late 1940s to his death in 2004. Born in the Bronx, he attended New York's City College, where he at first considered himself a Troskyist but ultimately evolved into a liberal anti-Communist, as did so many of the other New York intellectuals of his generation. After a brief stint as editor of the anti-Stalinist journal the *New Leader*, Lasky was drafted into the army and eventually ended up working for the US military government in Germany under General Lucius D. Clay. Following the end of his service, he remained in Berlin as a German correspondent for the *New Leader* as well as for *Partisan Review*.

Lasky resented what he regarded as the cowardliness of the American authorities in the face of Soviet Communism, and in one famous simile compared Cold War Berlin to a Wild West frontier town, where there were "Indians on the horizon, and you've simply got to have that rifle handy, or [if] not your scalp is gone."[25] By October 1947, he had exhausted his patience with the military government's peace-keeping efforts, and decided to ride into East Berlin like a lone gunslinger. He registered for the First German Writers' Congress, a thinly disguised Soviet propaganda vehicle that was organized by the future culture minister of the GDR, Johannes R. Becher. Lasky's presentation caused a scandal that overshadowed the entire proceedings when, after excoriating the Nazi book burnings to thunderous applause, he turned his attention to the Stalinist censors. "Just imagine," Lasky said, "how humiliating it must be for so significant an artist as Sergei Eisenstein . . . to appear in front of a suspicious politburo every couple of years in order to acknowledge that up to this point he simply had not properly understood the true aesthetic principles underlying socialist art."[26] The auditorium erupted in chaos, and it took moderator Günther Birkenfeld several minutes to restore order and allow Lasky to finish his speech.

Lasky's foray into cultural politics so impressed General Clay that the Allied military government offered the young journalist money to start his own journal, in which he would seek to combat Communism through literary and artistic means. The name for this journal was suggested by Thomas Mann's oldest son Klaus during an informal meeting in April 1948: *Der Monat*, or *The Month*, an appellation chosen because it was as unpretentious as possible and thereby signaled a clean break with the bourgeois periodical culture of prewar Germany.[27] The first issue of *Der Monat* appeared in October 1948, and for the next twenty-three years, it was published from a small office in Berlin-Dahlem. Never profitable, the journal received funding first from the US military government and then, starting in 1953, from the Paris-based Congress for Cultural Freedom (CCF). In 1966 it was revealed that the CCF was a CIA front, and the ensuing scandal contributed to the eventual demise of *Der Monat*.[28]

It is exceedingly likely that Lasky knew where the money for his journal came from, since he stood at the heart of the US cultural warfare networks at the time and was on intimate terms with the driving forces behind the CCF, the American CIA agent Michael Josselson, the émigré Russian composer Nicolas Nabokov, and the French philosopher Denis de Rougemont. These were men who, although coming from a left-of-center intellectual background, passionately thought of themselves as fighting in the front lines of a mortal battle with Communism. They had nothing but scorn for the McCarthyites and their henchmen in the FBI, whom they regarded as primitive zealots and who, in turn, treated the CCF with the greatest suspicion. At the same time, they were proudly aware of having inaugurated a new phase of cultural warfare, a new relationship between state and artist. As Nabokov would later write in his memoirs,

No one before had tried to mobilize intellectuals and artists on a worldwide scale in order to fight an ideological war against oppressors of the mind, or to defend what one called by the hackneyed term "our cultural heritage." This kind of ideological war had so far been the appanage of Stalinists and Nazis. . . . To lead a rational, ice-cold, determinedly intellectual war against Stalinism without falling into the easy Manichean trap of phony righteousness seemed essential to me, especially at a time when in America that ideological war was getting histrionically hysterical and crusaderishly paranoiac.[29]

In order to understand what happened to Thomas Mann's reputation in the early days of the Cold War, it is necessary to look to men like Lasky and Nabokov as well, not just to the FBI or the House Un-American Activities Committee.

Like most American intellectuals of his generation, Lasky was intimately familiar with Mann's major works. He read the famous author in the original German during his City College days (a charming student composition on "Mario and the Magician" survives in the Lasky archives), and he seems to have regarded the exchanges between Naphta and Settembrini in *The Magic Mountain* as a prophetic allegory of the Cold War encounters between Stalinist apologists and neutralist western intellectuals.[30] The fact that Naphta was patterned on the Hungarian intellectual Georg Lukács, a bête noir to Lasky, only strengthened him in these convictions. Lasky's first personal interaction with Mann took place in June 1947, when he attended a PEN Congress in Zurich at which the famous author delivered his lecture "Nietzsche's Philosophy in the Light of Contemporary Events" (figure 7.3). Lasky published a flattering review of the occasion in the *New Leader*, in which he deemed Mann's return to Europe "a cultural phenomenon" and expressed particular pleasure at the fact that the German refused "to offer himself as an official Occupation-line lecturer" for the US Army.[31] Over the next few years, he repeatedly tried to court Thomas Mann, although the efforts weren't reciprocated. When the two men met for a second time, in the summer of 1952, Mann noted in his diaries, "I didn't like Lasky. A lively but narrow-minded fellow, who lives and thinks in his American propaganda bubble and mistakes himself for Hamlet" (*Tb.*, August 17, 1952). Lasky had better luck with Mann's middle son, Golo, who became a regular contributor to *Der Monat* and who frequently vented to him about his father, with whom he was locked in an intense Oedipal struggle.[32]

Such personal differences aside, Lasky made Thomas Mann a focal point of his publishing strategy for *Der Monat* almost immediately. In 1949, the same year in which anti-Communist smear campaigns against the author reached their boiling point in the United States, Lasky's resolutely anti-Stalinist journal printed no fewer than five different contributions by the famous German: a dossier on *Doctor Faustus* that included an excerpt from the novel in the January issue, an excerpt from *The Story of a Novel* as well as Mann's

FIGURE 7.3.   Thomas Mann in conversation with Melvin J. Lasky (left) at the 1947 Zurich PEN Congress. Stars & Stripes/Melvin J. Lasky Archives, Lasky Institute for Transatlantic Studies, University of Munich.

open letter to Arnold Schoenberg in March, the essay "Homage" (about Franz Kafka's novel *The Castle*) in June, and finally "Goethe, the German Miracle" in August. Contributions relating to contemporary literature had been central to the editorial policy of *Der Monat* from day one. However, prior to January 1949, the journal had never devoted sustained attention to contemporary German fiction.[33] *Doctor Faustus* was a logical choice to break this pattern; the novel had been published in German almost two years earlier, but paper shortages had kept it from reaching a wider circulation. Nevertheless, German intellectual circles were abuzz with discussions of Mann's latest work, and Lasky received several unsolicited manuscripts related to the novel. The fact that he rejected all of these submissions without even looking at them suggests that his foray into Mann criticism obeyed its own strategic logic.[34]

Lasky's decision to focus on *Doctor Faustus* was undoubtedly motivated at least in part by an essay that the leading literary theorist of the Warsaw

Pact, Georg Lukács, had published the previous year. Lukács's stated goal in "The Tragedy of Modern Art" had been to treat *Doctor Faustus* as "a novel of the times, as the tragic quintessence of bourgeois culture of the present."[35] This tragedy consists of the increasing alienation of the artist from society, an alienation that, in turn, mirrors the larger alienation from collective social life that afflicts all individuals under conditions of advanced capitalism. For Lukács, Adrian Leverkühn is a Faustus of the "small world," a hero who— unlike Goethe's protagonist—never succeeds in stepping outside his own study and connecting with the world at large. His avant-garde compositions remain self-satisfied formal exercises: symptoms of the fact that in contemporary times the "tragic predicament of modern art" is reflected not only in the biographies of misunderstood artists but also in the "work itself."[36]

Thomas Mann himself, however, manages to escape this tragic predicament because his novel does not repeat the cardinal mistake so regularly committed by other ambitious artists of the modern age, including the fictitious Adrian Leverkühn. This mistake consists of inadequate grounding in the bedrock of history, which for Lukács is the stratum from which any attempt at epic representation must spring. Modern art is the product of an era in which the internal contradictions of capitalism reveal themselves in a series of upheavals and revulsions: the world wars, the Soviet Revolution, the Great Depression, and so on. Most modern artists respond to these upheavals by severing the link "between individual (experienced) and objective (physical and historical) time."[37] Following the lead of Gustave Flaubert in his *Sentimental Education*, in other words, they focus on inner experience because the outside world no longer makes sense. Not so Thomas Mann. His *Doctor Faustus* offers a sustained analysis of contemporary times, the seeming contradictions of which are revealed to be mere symptoms of the continuing decay of the capitalist world. This analysis is offered by Serenus Zeitblom, who thus, in a sense, emerges as the true protagonist of Mann's novel.

Lasky himself never commented on Lukács's essay, and yet the interventions he printed in *Der Monat* can nevertheless be read as a collective response to the piece, and specifically to Lukács's antiformalism. Readers thumbing through the January 1949 issue of *Der Monat* to get to the excerpt from Mann's new novel would have first encountered a programmatic statement by James T. Farrell called "What Does Literature Need?" The essay does not refer to Thomas Mann by name, and it is unlikely that Farrell knew Lasky would use his piece to preface a selection by the German author. The juxtaposition is, furthermore, inherently strange, because Farrell had repeatedly criticized Mann's politics during the 1930s and early 1940s. Nevertheless, Lasky's editorial decision was clearly intentional. "What Does Literature Need?" is essentially an attack on socialist realism and other forms of literature in which an author can succeed "as long as he solemnly pledges himself to a cause and gives as many high-sounding declarations as possible."[38] True literature, by contrast, "does not willingly and obediently follow social forces"; instead, Farrell exhorts artists to "take their own characteristic problems as their starting point."[39]

The battle lines having been drawn in this fashion, Lasky next printed an excerpt from *Doctor Faustus* that encompasses chapters 30 and 31 of the novel, which deal with the outbreak of the First World War. In these chapters, Serenus offers some ruminations of his own concerning the role of art in society, which have nothing to do with the opposition of capitalism and Communism. Instead, he contrasts the days of the Second Empire with those of the Third Reich. The kaiser, so Serenus admits, may have been a "play-actor," that is, somebody who delighted in rituals and ceremonial games with no real grounding in historical circumstances. But these were forgivable errors, for at least art was free under his reign—a notable contrast to the Nazi period, in which "state and culture [are] one" (*DF*, 300; *GKFA*, 10.1:437–38) and in which all art is enlisted to glorify a putative world-historical destiny.

This excerpt from *Doctor Faustus* was followed by a study of the musical elements of the novel written by Mann's brother-in-law Klaus Pringsheim, a composer who had studied under Gustav Mahler. Pringsheim was one of the first critics to point out that Mann, in *Doctor Faustus*, appeared to have found a formalist metaphor by which to capture the spiritual tendencies of the age. Leverkühn's overall project "to take back the Ninth Symphony" can be seen as a succinct evocation of Nazism's antihumanist ambitions. And the twelve-tone row, which forms the greatest achievement of this project, and whose essence consists of the fact that it assigns each note a fixed place within an overall system, corresponds to the political logic of totalitarianism. Contrary to what Lukács had claimed, in other words, the historical relevance of *Doctor Faustus* was to be found not in Zeitblom's attempts to string together a coherent account of the German years between the war, but rather in the formal innovations of Leverkühn's compositions, which make no reference to contemporary politics whatsoever.

For good measure, Lasky rounded out his dossier on *Doctor Faustus* with a short piece by his coeditor Hellmut Jaesrich, who praised the great lengths to which American publishers, translators, and critics had gone to disseminate Mann's new novel even in the face of negative reviews ("in America, translating a book takes roughly the same amount of time as it takes to print one in Germany").[40] He thus made it unmistakably clear that this supposed indictment of western imperialism could never have succeeded without a helping hand from the very cradle of modern capitalism.

Lasky continued his attack two months later, in the March issue of *Der Monat*, which included not only an excerpt from Mann's autobiographical *Story of a Novel* but also a reprint of the exchange of letters between Mann and Arnold Schoenberg that had taken place in the pages of the *Saturday Review of Literature* in January 1949. There, Schoenberg had accused Mann of having stolen his intellectual "property" by making Adrian Leverkühn the inventor of the twelve-tone system, a charge that Mann rebutted.[41] Lukács, who wrote his essay just as Schoenberg was starting to publicly voice misgivings, ridiculed this accusation, claiming that "the originality of the *Faustus* music is not its atonality as such, but the general character of contemporary music as the concentrated expression of intellectual and moral decadence."[42] But for Lasky, the affair itself was the point. At a time when Stalinist aesthetics demanded the subservience of art to the dictates of the party, Lasky was able to present the case of two western modernists who were conducting a spirited fight over the intellectual property rights to their creations. It was a tailor-made illustration of the capitalist approach to aesthetics, which insisted on the putative autonomy of art as a means for shoring up a free-market ideology.

This particular argument was given further force by an incendiary footnote in Arnold Bauer's essay "Thomas Mann and His Adversaries," which was also printed in the March 1949 issue of *Der Monat*. There, Bauer attacked Mann's "false friends" in the Warsaw Pact, and specifically Lukács's rather absurd pronouncement that *Doctor Faustus* represented a "far-reaching spiritual-artistic affirmation" of the "Resolution on Modern Music" issued by the Communist Party of the Soviet Union.[43] Bauer's essay provoked a near-instantaneous response from the East German journal *Aufbau*, which had first printed "The Tragedy of Modern Art," and this in turn generated a counter-statement in the July issue of *Der Monat*. Lasky's proposal that a battle with Communism might be fought by intellectual means had thus come to fruition within half a year of the founding of his journal, and Thomas Mann played an important part in the proceedings.

Harry Levin, Clement Greenberg, and the Ideology of Modernism

Melvin J. Lasky, Nikolas Nabokov, and other cultural Cold Warriors were far from the only people who were fundamentally reshaping the world republic of letters during the late 1940s, of course. In academia as well as in broader

US intellectual life, the years immediately following the Second World War were the period in which "modernism" became a respectable topic of conversation and the subject of many a taxonomic essay—or, to rephrase the same point in the words of Fredric Jameson, the period in which modernism ceased to be a vital spiritual force and instead became an aesthetic "ideology" and lifestyle choice.[44] Thomas Mann played an ambiguous role in this development. Throughout his entire career, he had been celebrated as an exponent of "modern" literature. Because his enormous commercial success aligned him with popular formations against which the new ideology was consciously rebelling, however, he increasingly became a persona non grata to the tastemakers of the new epoch. This is especially clear in the case of two of the most important theorists of modernism active during those years, the Harvard literature professor Harry Levin and the New York art critic Clement Greenberg.

Levin played perhaps a greater part than anybody else during the 1940s in making modernist literature not only socially acceptable but also an object of conscious cultural aspiration on the part of intellectual elites. He almost single-handedly opened up the literature curriculum at Harvard University to include works by twentieth-century poets and writers; his annual class on Joyce, Proust, and Mann was a sensation, prompting Harvard men to "plan their entire course load around it."[45] Levin also regularly published reviews in venues such as the *New York Times*, the *Nation*, or the *New Republic*, while his 1941 volume *James Joyce: A Critical Introduction* was passed around as a one-stop introduction to the man whose name was increasingly becoming synonymous with modernist literature. One of the people in whose hands it ended up was Thomas Mann, who studied it carefully as a substitute for engaging with Joyce's oeuvre directly. What he found there dismayed him profoundly; he already intuited that Joyce's rising star would hasten his own obsolescence.

Although Mann's fears would certainly turn out to be justified, a closer reading of Levin's book nevertheless reveals them to have been a surprising reaction. For throughout *James Joyce: A Critical Introduction*, the German author is treated with respect and repeatedly held up as a favorable counterexample to his younger Irish contemporary. One of Levin's interpretive tics is to cast Mann as a model that Joyce's creative successes resemble, such as when Stephen Dedalus is described as being "like Thomas Mann's outsiders, pressing their noses against the window panes of a bourgeois society from which they feel excluded," or when Joyce's books are characterized as "neither short nor long, but hermetic" "as Mann said of *Der Zauberberg*."[46] Similarly, Levin diagnoses ostensible flaws in Joyce's oeuvre by showing how

Mann tackled a given aesthetic problem differently. Pondering whether the Irishman's "confidence in words was not overweening, whether he was not too articulate to achieve a really profound portrayal of human emotion," for example, Levin draws admiring attention to the scene in *The Magic Mountain* where the dying Peeperkorn's speech is drowned out by the sound of a waterfall.[47]

Levin's 1944 review of *Joseph the Provider* for the *New Republic* was similarly charitable, even if the Harvard critic did not hesitate to scold Mann for his commercial success, which he evidently considered increasingly unbecoming for a modernist master: "One reads of the 'gilding,' when Joseph was welcomed to the court of Egypt and thinks of the official encomiums that the Book-of-the-Month Club is doubtlessly lavishing."[48] By 1948, however, the tide had turned. Levin's review of *Doctor Faustus* for the *New York Times Book Review* was an unapologetic pan of Mann's ambitious late novel, which Levin not only unfavorably compared to Romain Rolland's *Jean-Christophe* but also called a work of "portentous commentary, if not sustained imagination."[49] These charges were, in truth, poorly articulated and even more poorly defended. Levin claimed, for example, that the musical passages of the novel would only appeal to those "who like to read program notes about imaginary compositions," an assessment with which no reasonable critic since has agreed.[50] But they stung nonetheless when Mann stumbled across them, as did the news that Levin had removed him from his influential syllabus, retitling his Harvard class "Joyce, Proust, and Kafka" (*DüD*, 3:227).[51]

Levin's disaffection with Thomas Mann took an essentially twofold form. He believed the German author to be too didactic ("portentous commentary") and above all too Teutonic in his allegorical inclinations. Ignoring completely the fact that *Doctor Faustus* can also be read as a novel about the fate of the modern artist, Levin instead zeroed in on Adrian Leverkühn as an allegorical vehicle for German history. Such a focus cast an unfavorable light on Mann's novel when compared to the works of Franz Kafka, which had been rapidly gaining attention in US critical circles during the late 1940s, where they were rapturously received as attempts at a new and utterly contemporary form of realistic writing.[52] In this way, the postwar "ideology of modernism" ended up positioning itself in exactly the same critical space also occupied by Lasky and the Cold Warriors—in opposition to Georg Lukács's defense of Mann as the last of the bourgeois realists, who had used the biography of Adrian Leverkühn to tell a tale about the origins of Nazism.

A more charitable approach to the question of allegorical narration can be found—perhaps somewhat surprisingly—in an essay by Clement Greenberg that was never published and now survives only in manuscript form. "The

Last of the Fathers: A Consideration of Mann's *Joseph*," was most likely written between 1943 and 1948, since it references neither *Doctor Faustus* nor the one-volume edition of the *Joseph* novels, both of which came out in that latter year. Greenberg was then already securely installed as the leading art critic in America and, toward the beginning of the decade, he had formulated his influential concept of "medium specificity."[53] By this he meant the notion that the primary concern of modern art should be with the artistic medium itself, rather than with any reference to the external world.

Indeed, "The Last of the Fathers" proceeds from the premise that the *Joseph* novels, much like Joyce's *Finnegans Wake*, strive to create a form of literary narration that has been purged as much as possible from the mimetic imperative to depict the outside world: "Art turns in upon itself for lack of sustenance. The novelist feels that the traditional matter of fiction is, at least for the time being, exhausted." The reason for this is to be found "in the face of encroaching science, historicism, relativism."[54] Joyce responds to this crisis of relativism by withdrawing entirely into the unconscious life of the sleeping Earwicker and creating a new formal language through which to refract the exterior world.

So far this is a fairly conventional account of the nature of literary modernism. Greenberg's innovation consists of the fact that he interprets Mann's pivot toward allegorical narratives as a productive response to the same experiential crises also confronted by Joyce, rather than as an attempt to bypass them, as both Lukács and Levin had done. The "real subject" of the *Joseph* novels "was to be the *interpretation* of the story."[55] As Greenberg proposes in a central passage, "The matter of the story is taken as a theme for descant rather than as a narrative to be unfolded. The action is subordinated to the imagination's response to it and to the analogical, anagogical, and historical interpretations placed upon it. Its narrative and dramatic possibilities are not so much exploited as speculated upon."[56]

Here, then, was an approach to literary allegory that saw it as more than just a vehicle to assert historical continuities amid times of radical upheaval. Instead, Greenberg proposed that Mann had responded to the mimetic crisis of literature with a new formal language based on the four-fold allegorical scheme first worked out by medieval theologians (even if the "moral" dimension is missing in Greenberg's enumeration), and had shifted attention from the narrative as such to the intellectual responses that might be built upon it.[57]

This was about as generous an intellectual reception as Mann would ever receive in America during the 1940s and early 1950s. Even Greenberg judges the *Joseph* novels only a qualified success. His application of the four-fold scheme never progresses beyond the historical, and is scathing at that. He identifies Joseph's economic policies as a commentary on the redistributive efforts of the New Deal but correctly points out that in order to make this connection, Mann has to distort the biblical story, where the expropriations of the rich are carried out in the service of an absolutist state, rather than a social democracy. Mann, in other words, is not nearly as profound, or nearly as consistent, a thinker as one would like in such an aesthetic endeavor. Worse yet, his attempts to cram multiple allegorical layers into his text result in humorless and frequently boring digressions—at one point Greenberg uses the word *klatschig* (chatty), a German loan word that sounds suspiciously similar to that better-known Greenbergian term of opprobrium, *kitschig*.[58]

Ultimately, then, the late novels of Thomas Mann proved impossible to assimilate to the new ideology of art that came into being in the 1940s. At the heart of the new ideology stood the assumption that modern art should never explain, should never seek to convince, and above all, should never be about anything other than itself. Novels such as *Joseph the Provider* or *Doctor Faustus*, with their pedagogic digressions, their earnest agendas, and their love of allusion and allegory, simply did not conform to this rubric. As a result, Mann became increasingly marginal to the cultural discussions of the day, and his name makes virtually no appearance in the pages of *Partisan Review* or *Commentary*, the leading US intellectual journals of the 1950s and 1960s.

The Return to Divided Europe

Mann's own activities in America during the last five years of his exile offer little to contradict this narrative of waning influence and creeping obsolescence. He held two more lectures at the Library of Congress in 1947 and 1949 but was never given the chance to deliver his grandly synoptic presentation "My Age" in 1950. Mann's creative energies during those same years were directed toward the novel *The Holy Sinner*, which was published to muted reception in 1951. It did get promoted by the Book-of-the-Month Club, but has never managed to step out of a shadowy place at the outer fringes of the Thomas Mann canon. Short, at times overly playful, and curiously bereft of any of the grand ideas that had animated *Doctor Faustus* or the *Joseph* novels, *The Holy Sinner* seems like a product of old age indeed. Soon after its publication, increasingly disgusted by the rising tide of McCarthyism and the ways in which it threatened to dismantle the legacy of Roosevelt, Mann and his wife decided to move back to Europe. Mistrustful of the two postwar Germanies, they took up residency in Switzerland. For the last three years of his life (he died in 1955 at age 80, killed by an aortic rupture caused by arteriosclerosis), Thomas Mann thus resided just a few miles away from where he had lived prior to his move to the United States: practically within sight of the country to which he felt himself bound by such a strong representative bond, but nevertheless beyond its borders.

It would be a mistake, however, to conclude this story of how Thomas Mann changed the nature of representative authorship with a myopic focus upon the United States. Mann's most consequential innovations—his realization, for example, that the autonomous stance characteristic of modern art confers a political capital of its own, or his insistence that German culture is also shaped by the actions of non-Germans—could never have come about without his exile to America. But those same innovations would have been transient and ultimately meaningless had they also been bound to that nation alone. Mann's return to Europe was more than just a flight from a country that no longer supported him. It was also an attempt to share the experiences of his exile with a continent that once again lay in ruins, much as it had done thirty years earlier, following the First World War.

Between 1947 and 1949 especially, Mann thus returned to the same kinds of sites at which he had lectured over the course of the 1920s: to PEN Clubs in Zurich and London, as well as universities in England and Sweden. He corresponded with newspapers in various European nations (as well as far-away Japan) and dutifully provided copy for the fledgling journal UN World, much as he had associated with the League of Nations during the early 1930s. In his address to the English PEN Club, which he delivered in 1949, shortly before his contentious trip to Frankfurt and Weimar, he drew explicit comparisons between his current activities and those he had performed following the last war. Mann stated that he would cherish forever "the generous kindness with which the assembled colleagues welcomed one who had only just ceased to be an enemy alien" (GKFA, 19.1:662) when he visited England during the 1920s. The phrasing here is suggestive, for of course Mann had never resided in Britain and thus hadn't been an "enemy alien" in the sense given to that term by the Aliens Restriction Act of August 1914. It is likely that his choice of words was instead inflected by his experiences with the Tolan Committee; it thus documents a conflation of the two world wars and of their immediate aftermath.

But if Mann was keen to remind his listeners of his earlier activities on behalf of a pan-European community of letters, then he was equally vocal in his criticism of some of the strategies that had been pursued thirty years earlier. In his address to the English PEN Club, Mann acknowledged that "the idea of organization and corporation in the cultural field is likely to arouse a measure of skepticism" and immediately went on to tell a story of his own endeavors on behalf of the League of Nations: "It is hard to describe the feeling of futility and utter insufficiency which I never failed to derive from the committee's sessions. The academic and cagey spirit that prevailed there proved unforgettably discouraging" (*GKFA*, 19.1:662). Caginess and academic infighting were not the only reasons why Mann was now skeptical of his approach during the 1920s, however. Back in 1926, Mann had written to Ernst Robert Curtius that "the main efforts to achieve an amicable understanding [between France and Germany] will probably have to be made by us [intellectuals]" (*Reg.*, 25/215) rather than by professional politicians and diplomats. Chastened by the ease with which Europe had relapsed into its old antagonisms over the course of the 1930s, Mann now was no longer as confident in the persuading powers of intellectuals. "I am very much cognizant of the critical complexity of the present world situation, and know that we [writers] are incapable of exercising any influence on the state and development of affairs, say, in Eastern Europe" (*GKFA*, 19.1:663), he said.

What, then, should writers and cultural organizations like PEN do instead? Mann had a clear prescription: "All the more seriously . . . ought we to consider ourselves the attentive and vigilant guardians of spiritual freedom and independent thinking and writing in our own sphere. Whenever and wherever in our part of the world, the free spirit is being infringed upon, whenever and wherever it is being reprimanded, punished, and spied upon, we should promptly raise our voice in protest and in warning" (*GKFA*, 19.1:663). The aim to stand up in the face of censorship and state-sponsored violence against writers was, of course, a constitutive part of the institutional identity of PEN. But Mann's reference to "spiritual freedom . . . in our own sphere" also hearkened back to his essays and political speeches of the 1930s, when he first realized that artists could most effectively position themselves in opposition to totalitarian tyranny by emphasizing, rather than downplaying, the necessity for an autonomous place for the artistic producer in contemporary society.

There were other ways in which Mann connected his contemporary public appearances on the European scene to those of thirty years earlier. The lecture "Goethe and Democracy," for example, which Mann premiered at the Library of Congress but then also delivered as the Taylorian Lecture at the University of Oxford in 1949, begins with a brief reference to the various addresses on Goethe with which Mann had toured the continent in the early 1930s, around the time of the one hundredth anniversary of the poet's death. "Frankly," Mann admitted here, "I am not very proud of these contributions, neither of the critical nor even of the artistic absorption in this life and this work. . . . I am not proud of it because it is the absorption of a German in a German phenomenon" (*LC*, 107; *GKFA*, 19.1:606). In lieu of such projects of strictly nationalist philology, Mann now praised the efforts of English-speaking Goethe scholars from Thomas Carlyle to the present, going to almost comical lengths to prove his familiarity with recent academic criticism produced in the British Isles (*LC*, 110–11; *GKFA*, 19.1:611–12).

Such references were motivated by more than just attempted flattery. In the early 1930s, Mann had written essays such as "Goethe's Career as a Writer" in order to give form to his own representative aspirations, which were those of a modern professional, not those of a traditional Germanic poet. Now, toward the end of the 1940s, Mann was doing the same thing, but by drawing attention to different facets of Goethe's significance: his invention of the concept of "world literature," as well as his "supra-German, European character" (*LC*, 108; *GKFA*, 19.1:608). References to these twin aspects can also be found in many other texts of this period, such as Mann's speech before the English PEN Club (*GKFA*, 19.1:662) or a brief address he delivered over the French radio services (*GKFA*, 19.1:649). Mann furthermore went out of his way to assert that he was not merely dealing in intellectual abstractions. Separation from the purely national sphere and immersion in a culture other than one's own could have unquestionably salutary effects on a writer: "The division of my work into a German-language and an English-language half has always seemed absurd to me. On the contrary, my productive labor in foreign parts . . . became a conscious engagement with my language over the years, and provoked the ambition to pull out all the stops of the magnificent organ of our language. I strove to both recapitulate and advance the expressive possibilities of German prose" (*GKFA*, 19.1:672). These arguments formed more than just a collection of platitudes about the international reach of quality literature or about the need for cosmopolitan dispositions in the postwar era. They were, instead, attempts to once again reiterate the fundamental difference between "German culture" and "German political territory," and to simultaneously repurpose a distinction used for invidious ends throughout the nineteenth century as a potent weapon against the totalitarian mindset.

These rhetorical efforts on behalf of a reformed understanding of representative art were completely overshadowed by the scandal caused by his decision to address audiences in both West and East Germany. "I do not recognize any zones of occupation," Mann said during his respective visits, and to many these words appeared at best naive and at worst casually dismissive of the dangers posed by either Communism or imperialism, depending on the ideological perspective of the listener.[59] But during his visit to Weimar, he added a few crucial phrases, asking, "Who else should guarantee and represent German unity if not the independent writer, whose true home is the free German language, untouched by any division into zones of occupation?" (*GKFA*, 19.1:695). Mann was not dismissing political realities, in other words. He was merely disputing that the present political fragmentation had created an all-encompassing, totalizing rift through German culture, much as he had over the past decade disputed the notion that the "synchronization" of all forms of public life in Nazi Germany had put an end to autonomous cultural production. The role of the representative writer should be to demonstrate independence from all such political meddling, for only in resistance to a world in which all facets of human existence are dominated by politics might true humanity flourish.

Mann never crafted a political statement suitable to the Cold War era that might have competed in daring and intellectual rigor with his *Exchange of Letters*, the essay "Brother Hitler," or the address "Germany and the Germans." But neither did he lapse into quietude, as many of his critics have asserted. Sometime in late May or early June 1951, Mann received a petition signed by the family members of seven GDR citizens who were serving draconian prison terms after having been found guilty of collaboration with the Nazis during a series of show trials in the East German town of Waldheim. Mann had received similar petitions before and had usually forwarded them to Johannes R. Becher, the GDR's culture minister, whom he knew from collaborations on literary committees during the 1920s. In this instance, however, the blunt description of the trials—which rarely lasted more than thirty minutes and resulted in death sentences in thirty-two cases—seems to have reminded Mann of the infamous *Volksgerichtshof*, the Nazi tribunal through which "enemies of the people" were sent to concentration camps and execution squads by the thousands.[60] He wrote a letter to Walter Ulbricht, the general secretary of the East German Socialist Unity Party (SED). This letter was dispatched in late June or early July 1951; the fact that Mann commissioned an English translation of the manuscript strongly suggests that he also contemplated publishing it as an open letter, much as he had done fourteen years earlier with his missive to the dean of the philosophical faculty of the University of Bonn.

For reasons that are lost to history, such a publication never took place. Although the manuscript survives in the Thomas Mann archives in Zurich, and although the letter itself (with Ulbricht's personal annotations) was taken to the West when the head of the Thomas Mann Archives of the East German Academy of the Arts fled the GDR in 1957, the document remained largely unknown until the early 1990s. Had it been published during Thomas

Mann's lifetime, it might well have impacted the way we now view his American exile. Instead of the conventional narrative of a meteoric rise and equally swift decline as a public figure in the United States, we might now be talking of a fourteen-year period of uninterrupted courageous activism, bookended by two important open letters: the first directed against the Nazis, the second against the Warsaw Pact.

A central passage in the "Letter to Walter Ulbricht" (which the General Secretary himself duly highlighted) reads, "Communism shares with fascism—this is the truth—a totalitarian conception of the state" (E, 6:213). These were strong words, even if Mann, who was, after all, approaching Ulbricht as a petitioner, immediately softened them by saying: "But communism nevertheless insists, and we are willing to grant, that a world of difference separates its conception of totalitarianism from the fascist one. It has a different ideological background, as well as a different orientation towards the idea of the human, and for this reason it would do well to avoid anything that might give rise to the possibility of an equation or willful confusion between the two." Mann could easily have avoided the loaded term "totalitarianism," and indeed could even have avoided any comparison with Nazi Germany, if his aim had been merely to protest a judicial injustice. That he used the term nevertheless implies that it was somehow important to him—that he believed he could somehow speak to it with an authority that he could not bring to the topic of mere miscarriages of justice.

And indeed, Mann's letter to Ulbricht opens with a paragraph-long reflection on the possibilities and limitations assigned to the artist in modern affairs. Writers, Mann concedes here, are "without power and influence in the real world." But they nevertheless are held in high esteem in the "political and ideological sphere" of men like Ulbricht and are therefore "lifted above" (überheben) any residual worries that they might trouble the powerful by addressing them with personal counsels. Indeed, it appears to be this very dissociation from the realm of practical affairs that enables writers to all the more clearly envision a "humanism that agitates for peace by giving time (and the moral self-development of nations within time) a chance to level the differences that currently separate the two halves of our world, and to sublate them into a higher unity."

In his radio addresses via the BBC German Service, Mann had routinely stylized himself as a messianic figure, speaking on behalf of a Christian ethical tradition brutally abrogated by the Nazis. At the same time, he had turned immateriality and remoteness, two characteristics attaining to his exile experiences, into rhetorical weapons. In the letter to Ulbricht, we can detect an attempt to repurpose these very same strategies for a different rhetorical stance. Here, Mann appears almost like an angel of history, trying to remind Ulbricht that the historical destiny of Communism consists of the fading away of politics in the face of a more encompassing sense of the human, as the writer himself had tried to map it in his foreword to *Measure and Value*.

Mann's efforts were in vain, of course. Although Ulbricht sent out missives both to the deputy head of the Ministry of State Security, Erich Mielke, and to the Soviet cultural administration, no measures on behalf of the prisoners were ever taken. The authoritarian dictators in charge of the GDR were not any more amenable to intervention by writers, no matter how "representative," than the Nazis would have been. But it would be unfair the judge the outcome of Mann's war against the evils of the twentieth century by how many lives it saved or didn't save. Art, unfortunately, rarely holds such interventionist powers. Mann's achievement lies, rather, in a realm that is just as important if admittedly rather less concrete: he made it possible to imagine what a principled literary opposition to totalitarian terror might actually look like.

Conclusion

What, then, is the continuing importance of Thomas Mann to the world republic of letters? Before turning to this question, it is worthwhile to briefly reflect on the place he has occupied in literary history over the past seventy-five years, a period during which his former representative status in the United States was all but forgotten.

Undoubtedly the most important event of this period took place in August 1975, when a small group of lawyers and literary critics assembled in Zurich to break the seals on four parcels wrapped in plain brown packing paper, on which Mann had written, "Daily notes from 1933–1951. Without any literary value, but not to be opened by anybody before 20 years after my death."[1] Mann's diaries revealed his identity as a gay man to the wider world for the first time, and set in motion an inexorable process by which his private life ever more completely came to overshadow his public persona. Henceforth, both Mann's representative strivings and his fictions would, with increasing frequency, be read as elaborately constructed masks the author had put on to redirect the intense pain caused by his repressed personal longings.[2]

Two seminal documents of US intellectual culture that were both published in 1987 document the long-range effects of this shift from the public to the private. The first of these is Allan Bloom's *The Closing of the American Mind*, which in a characteristically polemical passage trots out Mann's *Death in Venice* as an illustration of the dynamics that have led to the supposed decline of the public sphere in the United States. *Death in Venice*, Bloom readily acknowledges, is a complex work in which Mann dramatizes central problems of post-Nietzschean and post-Freudian thought. But none of this matters, because "this is not how it was received by Americans. They were titillated and really took to it as an early manifesto of the sexual-liberation movement."[3] Influenced by accounts of Mann's own tragically repressed sexual longings, so Bloom suggests, readers on America's college campuses adopted his protagonist Aschenbach as a hero, who in death finally discovers the erotic fulfillment that eluded him throughout all his civilizational labors. Making no mention of Mann's valiant attempts to fortify the American public for the fight against fascism, Bloom instead indicts him for having contributed to the destruction of American liberal democracy by promoting an undue emphasis on personal wish fulfillment.

The second document charting this shift in Mann's reception, also published in 1987, was "Pilgrimage," an autobiographical essay by Susan Sontag that appeared in the *New Yorker*.[4] Sontag had been arguably the last major American intellectual to meet Thomas Mann personally, when she visited him in his house in Pacific Palisades in December 1949 as a sixteen-year-old undergraduate at the University of Chicago. To put her unassuming essay in the company of *The Closing of the American Mind* may seem like a bit of a stretch, but "Pilgrimage" is perhaps best approached as the capstone in an aesthetic project that Sontag had been pursuing for the preceding twenty-five years, and with which she fundamentally altered literary culture in the United States. Back in 1964, Sontag had published her groundbreaking essay "Against Interpretation," in which she decisively broke with the mid-century tendency to treat literary fiction as a form of intellectual argument by other means, and famously proposed that "in place of a hermeneutics we need an erotics of art."[5] And ten years later, she wrote *Illness as Metaphor*, in which she warned against the dangers of treating diseases as metaphors of moral ailments. Though the book was inspired by her own struggle with cancer, it acquired a kind of manifesto-like quality during the AIDS epidemic of the 1980s.

Sontag had been a great admirer of Thomas Mann since her early youth, and the literary critic Kai Sina has recently documented what a long shadow the German author cast over her intellectual development.[6] And yet the public reputation that Mann enjoyed in America during the early 1940s, when Sontag first discovered him, can hardly have been compatible with her later aesthetic trajectory. More than perhaps any other writer, Mann had been treated as the author of "intellectual" books that posed hermeneutical riddles to their readers. And more than perhaps any other novel, his *Magic Mountain* epitomized the literary tendency to treat illness as a metaphor. "Pilgrimage" can thus be seen as an attempt to rewrite Sontag's relationship with her intellectual forebear. As Sina shows, Sontag introduced factual errors to her account—errors that must have been intentional, because she had never committed them in earlier attempts to tell the same story and also still possessed her notebooks from 1949. Most importantly, she predates her encounter with Mann to 1947, describing herself as a high-school student rather than an undergraduate. She also neglects to mention that her excursion to Pacific Palisades was preceded by a careful study of Clifton Fadiman's 1943 primer *Reading I've Liked*, which contains several Thomas Mann passages.

The collective effect of these changes is to detach Mann from the cultural networks that had actually conditioned his reception during the 1940s, and of which both Clifton Fadiman and the Great Books course that Robert M. Hutchins had started at the University of Chicago were important exemplars. Instead, Sontag's "pilgrimage" to Pacific Palisades is framed as a kind of spiritual quest, an intimate encounter over tea between a star-struck American intellectual and her world-weary European idol. Once again, the personal vanquishes the public and the political.

Bloom's and Sontag's interventions, diverse as they may otherwise be, at least have the common merit that they are serious attempts to examine the meaning of Mann's literary legacy for contemporary thought. The last thirty years have arguably produced no such sustained interventions. Instead, they have given rise to a veritable cottage industry of biographical studies focused on the author and his family, many of them premised on the notion that the personal tribulations suffered by the Mann family are of greater interest than anything that Mann himself or his children ever wrote. In Germany there are now over twenty such works in print. There has also been a highly successful popular television series, the title of which, *The Manns: The Novel of a Century*, testifies to the way in which life has eclipsed art. In America, meanwhile, the past twenty-five years have brought four full-length biographies of Thomas Mann: not a bad harvest at a time when other prominent German authors would be lucky to receive even one.[7]

The times may well be changing, however. Amid rising currents of authoritarian populism, xenophobic nationalism, and transatlantic insecurity, Thomas Mann's public attempts to position himself in opposition to fascism are interesting again. In a recent editorial in the *New York Times*, for example, David Brooks extols the author of "The Coming Victory of Democracy" as exactly the kind of intellectual our present era needs. Putting a new spin on the old tale about Mann's ostensible struggles to channel his repressed energies into a more productive direction, Brooks writes, "Mann's great contribution is to remind us that democracy is not just about politics; it's about the individual's daily struggle to be better and nobler and to resist the cheap and the superficial."[8]

The political battles of the twenty-first century are unlikely to be won with the rhetoric of the twentieth, however. More importantly, it is possible to advance far more sophisticated arguments about the continuing relevance of Thomas Mann to the intellectual culture of our own day. The parameters that conditioned Mann's rise to the status of literary celebrity and antifascist icon in the United States of the 1930s and 1940s foreshadow developments in the world republic of letters that did not fully come to fruition until after the Second World War, and that continue to affect global literary production in the twenty-first century. In many respects, Thomas Mann was a forerunner for experiences that have become commonplace for writers in our own day, especially those that hail from the periphery of the global literary community. There are at least six different ways in which this is true.

National Representation

First, Thomas Mann instinctively grasped that writers in a globally interconnected world would inevitably come to be marketed as representatives of national literary traditions. At the same time, he realized that such branding always carries the danger of reducing authors to the status of mere mouthpieces for more powerful forces within their home countries, especially national governments. The contemporary world republic of letters remains full of examples in which authors are essentially fêted as delegates of their nations, much like Mann was in America. We see this at the Frankfurt Book Fair, for example, which shines a spotlight on a different country every year. (The 2018 fair, which is about to open as I am writing these lines, features the Republic of Georgia as a guest of honor, and amid receptions showcasing Georgian wine and culinary delicacies, visitors will be invited to discover authors such as Aka Morchiladze or Naira Gelaschwili.) Or we see it in the ongoing fracas surrounding the Booker Prize, and the question whether it should be open to any English-language novel or only those written by citizens of a specific set of nations. Perhaps the best illustration of this dynamic, however, is provided by the world's oldest truly global literary prize, the Nobel.

The annals of the Swedish Academy, which has been awarding the Nobel Prize in Literature since 1901, are full of anxious reflections upon the issue of national representation. In 1913, for example, academy member Verner von

Heidenstam compared the Nobel Committee to "a kind of foreign office" that had allowed the prize to be shared out "country by country."[9] And the following year, amid ever more ominous portents of the war to come, an internal academy report recommended that the Nobel might become "a restraining and counterbalancing influence on the excesses" of nationalism, if only it were awarded properly—for instance by honoring minor nations so as not to further inflate the blustering of the major European powers.[10] (The 1914 prize consequently went to the Swiss author Carl Spitteler.)

In the century that has passed since then, the Nobel has often been compared to the Olympics, or to similar kinds of sporting competition in which athletes compete for their countries. The paradoxes and tensions implicit in this equation are most visible in the case of the two prizes that have been awarded to authors from the People's Republic of China, a country that has striven more than perhaps any other to win recognition in the eyes of the global literary community. As the scholar and translator Julia Lovell has documented, China has engaged in an active quest to win the Nobel Prize in Literature since at least the 1980s, a phenomenon that has even been given its own name—the "Nobel complex" (*Nuobeier qingjie*).[11] Government measures to redress the situation encompass both lobbying efforts and state patronage programs, and were crowned with an ambiguous sort of success in 2000, when the prize was awarded to Gao Xingjian. I say "ambiguous" because from the perspective of the Chinese government this was an unacceptable outcome, since Gao has lived in France since 1987 and became a French citizen in 1998. His novels and plays, furthermore, owe at least as much to European modernist influences (such as Samuel Beckett and Eugène Ionesco) than they do to traditional Chinese literary aesthetics. Worst of all, the literary works cited by the Swedish Academy in its Nobel commendation arguably all express dissident sentiments. The government in Beijing consequently responded to news of the award by denouncing the "political purpose" of the decision and declaring that the prize had lost all legitimacy.[12]

Contrast this with the very different reception afforded to Mo Yan, who in 2012 became China's second Nobel laureate in literature. Unlike Gao, Mo had never sought to actively distance himself from his country of origin or its regime and had gone on record as admiring the aesthetic pronouncements that Mao Zedong had issued in the *Yan'an Forum on Literature and Art* (1942). News of Mo's prize won immediate acclaim from the Chinese government but equally quick condemnation from a number of influential world literary figures, including the Nobel laureate Herta Müller and Salman Rushdie, who in a Facebook post referred to Mo as a "patsy of the regime" and as the "Chinese equivalent of the Soviet Russian apparatchik writer Mikhail Sholokov."[13]

The Swedish Academy also came under attack; the award was widely seen as an attempt to repair relations with the Chinese government that had frayed when the dissident intellectual Lu Xiaobo was awarded the Peace Prize in 2010.

Contemporary authors (especially those from outside Europe or North America), then, seem caught in a double bind. On the one hand, writers who stray too far from officially sanctioned traditions in their countries of origin risk being labeled as traitors and apostates if the international literary community embraces them. Those who play it safe, on the other hand, expose themselves to charges of aesthetic subservience, of being mere "patsies." Thomas Mann, who was simultaneously attacked by the Nazis as a foreign propagandist and by American intellectuals such as James T. Farrell as a German apologist, certainly knew this double bind well.

The Burden of Politics

Of course, not all authors who are accorded "representative" status in the eyes of the world are treated in the same fashion. This too is something that Thomas Mann understood. As we have seen, throughout the 1920s and early 1930s, Mann was far more likely to be fêted in America as a European writer, or as somebody extolling classical humanist values, than as a specifically German figure. Only in the middle of the 1930s, when the US public became increasingly interested in Nazi Germany, and when Mann publicly spoke out against Hitler, did this identification change. And as the interview that he gave on the deck of the *Queen Mary* indicates, this shift was accompanied by surging interest in his political and cultural writings. Soon Mann's role as a commentator on contemporary events competed with, and even overshadowed, his literary reputation. Mann recognized the inevitability of this development, although he inwardly resented it. His diaries are full of anxious remarks about the amount of time his lecture tours took away from his literary activity, for example.

In the contemporary literary marketplace, it is mostly writers from the so-called Third World who are asked to shoulder this kind of political burden. The critic Timothy Brennan, for example, writing in the immediate wake of the fatwa issued against Salman Rushdie in 1989, has pointed out how this affair and its implications for discussions of artistic censorship, the future of Islam, and the state of relations between West and East have completely overshadowed any critical interest in the complex aesthetic structure of *The Satanic Verses*. "The prominence of politics in Third-World fiction," so Brennan concludes, "or rather, our own tendentious projection of politics on to a mythical 'Third World,' is exactly what Western critics find attractive."[14]

By extension, authors from such countries who refuse to engage in politics, or at least to submit to the formal dicta of what Fredric Jameson has called "national allegory" (i.e., to a form of narration in which the fate of individual characters sheds light on that of the entire community), have a much harder time finding success in the literary marketplace.[15]

Of course Germany is not a Third World nation, and Thomas Mann was never perceived in the eyes of the American public as some kind of racial or religious "other." Nevertheless, it is possible to draw a direct line from his own situation to those confronting contemporary writers from the Global South. For as more recent critics working on issues of global literary circulation have pointed out, writers from Africa, the Middle East, or Southeast Asia who are showered with attention by western readers frequently have one thing in common: they hail from places that have recently become of acute geopolitical interest, whether because of civil unrest, invasion by coalition armies in the name of the "War on Terror," or natural disaster. The critic Gloria Fisk, for example, has written about Nobel laureate Orhan Pamuk that his "canonization rests on his ability to render Turkish people and places eminently legible to readers who lack the facility to read his words without a translator or to locate his characters and settings with ease on a map." Pamuk "gains currency," Fisk continues, "from the strategic value of his geographic location, which prompts his readers to gesture towards their anxieties about Islamic terrorism and the wars against it when they describe the greatness of Orhan Pamuk in terms of his goodness as a citizen of the world."[16]

Thomas Mann, writing at a time when the United States was rousing itself from isolationist slumber and reaching for the status of global hegemon, was arguably the first writer in literary history to "gain currency" in precisely this fashion. His novels were praised in America in no small part because of his perceived "goodness as a citizen of the world." It's true that the works Mann wrote during his exile are formally very different from those written by Pamuk or other contemporary writers who benefit from their "geographic location," such as Khaled Hosseini (author of the 2003 novel *The Kite Runner*) or Amitav Ghosh (*Sea of Poppies*, 2008). Neither are they explicitly about Nazism nor do they employ realist aesthetics to tell the story of a people through the lives of individual protagonists (as Mann arguably still had done in his 1901 debut novel *Buddenbrooks*). And yet they too lent themselves to interpretation as national allegories, such as when Sir Hartley Shawcross quoted from *Lotte in Weimar* during the Nuremberg trials or when Harry Levin detected shadows of the Office of Price Administration in *Joseph the Provider* by the newly Americanized Thomas Mann.

Exile as a Transformative Condition

The third way in which Mann prefigured the fate of many a writer in the twenty-first century comes through his status as an émigré, and as somebody who recognized that a foreign reading public had now largely supplanted the domestic one that originally nourished him. Harry Levin, in his 1941 book on James Joyce, acknowledged that "Mann is a more typical and explicit figure than Joyce, possibly because he has worked in a narrower and heavier tradition. He has been exiled by fascism, not philistinism."[17] Indeed, over the course of the latter half of the twentieth century, the case of the writer exiled to a foreign country by violence or persecution would come to seem far more "typical" than that of the avant-garde figure who flees from mere misunderstanding and philistinism. Examples of this category would include Milan Kundera leaving post-1968 Czechoslovakia for Paris, Salman Rushdie relocating to the safety of a guarded compound in London following the Iranian fatwa, or Wole Soyinka taking up residence in New York following the Abacha military coup in Nigeria.

It is important to remember, of course, that exile is first and foremost a personal tragedy, not a mark of aesthetic distinction. And despite the uninterrupted current of political violence that connects Mann's time with our own, the vast majority of successful writers over the past seventy-five years have never experienced displacement of this kind. But what nevertheless renders the exiled writer of the mid-twentieth century a "typical" figure for the present day is that authors like Mann, who were cut off from the personal and professional networks that nourished them during earlier parts of their careers, were forced to adapt to the needs of a new and more international audience in order to survive. In this, they foreshadow conditions also experienced by at least two different sets of contemporary writers: on the one hand, authors like Pamuk or J. M. Coetzee, who were forced to seek international markets after facing insult and slander, but not outright persecution, in their home countries. On the other, those writers who come from national traditions that are simply too small or too destitute to support an author of ambitious literary fiction and thus require a move to some other location, usually a western metropolis.

To a certain extent, this third criterion works in direct opposition to the first one. Western consumers (for it is western consumers, of course, who dictate demands in the "international" book market) tend to prefer literary fare that engages in active dialogue with globally established aesthetic norms. As the critic James English has pointed out, the first Nobel Prize to be awarded to an African author did precisely *not* go to Léopold Sédar Senghor of Senegal, president of his country for the first two decades following its independence, and a strong proponent of authentically African cultural traditions.[18] Instead, it went to Wole Soyinka—no less noteworthy a literary figure, perhaps, but also an author who cast Nigerian subjects into literary forms that were clearly descended from the European modernist idiom. English compares this decision to the Grammy that the United States Recording Academy awarded in the same year to Paul Simon's *Graceland*, an album that repackaged South African rhythms and melodies as "world music."

Unsurprisingly, however, Soyinka himself saw matters differently, and in his Nobel acceptance speech, which he delivered in a traditional Yoruba ceremonial robe, described the award as a "national honor" for Nigeria.[19] The simple lesson here, perhaps, is that the international literary community prefers writers who are recognizably "from somewhere" in their personal demeanor, nonliterary pronouncements, and political activism, but who nevertheless write their poetic works in a globally accessible idiom. Here, too, Mann can be seen as a paradigmatic figure. Unmistakably German in his essays, speeches, and personal interviews, he nevertheless devoted a substantial portion of his time in the United States to rewriting stories drawn from the Old Testament, and thus to materials that would have been instantly recognizable even to US readers that knew nothing at all about German culture.

Stylistic Adaptations

Authors are not merely passive victims in a selection process whereby some writers find acceptance in the eyes of the international community while others falter, however. More often than not, they willingly alter their styles to appeal to a global readership. The critic Rebecca Walkowitz has spoken in this context of "born translated" texts—literary works written in the conscious knowledge that they would primarily be read in translation, and by a far-flung readership.[20] Of the many characteristics of such texts adduced by Walkowitz and like-minded critics, two seem especially noteworthy. First, high literary (as opposed to pulp or genre) fiction that has been born translated tends to contain a metatextual element, in which authors directly reflect on the conditions of their global circulation. "While many books produced today seek to entice or accommodate translation, aiming to increase their audiences and the market-share of their publishers, born-translated works are notable because they highlight the effects of circulation on production," Walkowitz writes. "Not only are they quickly and widely translated, they are also engaged in thinking about that process."[21]

The critic Nergis Ertürk provides a good example of how this process works in her analysis of Orhan Pamuk's novel *Snow* (2002), which features a scene in which the various residents of a provincial Turkish town come together to jointly deliberate how they would like to see themselves represented in a report that Pamuk's journalist-protagonist Ka is about to file for a German newspaper.[22] (The invisible editor of that newspaper, coincidentally, is named Hans Hansen, after a character from Thomas Mann's *Tonio Kröger*.) But more than sixty years before *Snow* was published, Mann himself already employed a very similar dynamic in the seventh chapter of his novel *Lotte in Weimar*, which is, in a sense, all about how autobiographical confessions, second-hand testimony, critical studies, and other sources interlink to create an abiding image of an author entirely by textual means. And only a few years later, he wrote *The Tables of the Law*, his biblical narrative in which Moses is reinvented as an author-hero who struggles to invent an appropriate form through which a written version of the Ten Commandments might be spread to all the peoples of the earth, not just his own.

A second feature of born-translated fiction is that it often (whether consciously or unconsciously) strives for an idiom that will lend itself to easy translation into other languages. The author and translator Tim Parks has been scathing of this tendency. "What seems doomed to disappear" in the new global novel, so he complains, "is the kind of work that revels in the subtle nuances of its own language and literary culture."[23] This, admittedly, is not an accusation that one might ever make against Thomas Mann. His prose toward the end of his exile is not in any way "simpler" or "less subtle" than the kind of writing that he produced during the 1920s, when he was still comfortably ensconced in Germany. Indeed, in many ways a novel like *Doctor Faustus* is more difficult, more Germanic, and more nuanced than anything that Mann wrote before. In particular, the famous conversation with the devil, which is written in the style of the Protestant Reformation, runs directly counter to Walkowitz's observation that many texts to be born in translation consciously erase nuances of idiom and dialect when rendering dialogue between characters. Many of Mann's interlocutors in the American publishing industry—from his translator Helen Tracy Lowe-Porter to the Book-of-the-Month Club judge Dorothy Canfield Fisher to his admiring exegete Clifton Fadiman—were driven to occasional vexation by his stylistic flights of fancy, and yet nobody ever exerted any meaningful pressure on Mann to simplify his prose.

What is also true, however, is that Mann himself was aware of the difficulties presented by his style and responded to these in his authorial practice. Most obvious here are his instructions to Lowe-Porter to cut certain sections of his texts that he did not think would be readily intelligible to an American audience. Nowhere does he give the impression that he regarded these cuts as literary mutilations; he was comfortable with different versions of his works existing for different target audiences, and thus with the creation of what Walkowitz has called "multiples" of his works. As the example of *Joseph the Provider* shows, over time Mann also let American idioms and English loan words creep into his otherwise carefully controlled German. The result was a prose that, even if it had not been created with translatability explicitly in mind, was nevertheless touched by the quotidian reality of an exile existence and gave stylistic testimony to the fact that Mann refused to shut himself off from the English-speaking world.

Literature as Therapy and World Building

The fifth way in which the story of Thomas Mann's American exile foreshadows developments in contemporary literature has less to do with the author's own choices and predispositions than it does with the structural conditions that made his success possible. Each successive stage of Mann's rise to fame in the United States took place amid distinct efforts of ordinary Americans to make sense of their own place in the wider world. First, there were the middlebrow reception networks of the 1920s and early 1930s, which attempted to commodify a vision of European cultural greatness for practical use by American audiences. This was followed by the Popular Front of the mid-1930s, which sought international solidarity under the sign of literary engagement. Then there were the efforts of various organizations ranging from commercial lecturing bureaus to the America First Committee, which helped (and sometimes cajoled) ordinary citizens to form an opinion on how their republic should relate to the world at large during the years immediately preceding Pearl Harbor. This, in turn, was followed by the creation of a military-industrial complex that transformed publishing and aimed to mobilize the American masses for a time of total war. And finally, there was the early Cold War, with its paranoia and anti-Communist hysteria.

The composite story told by these various endeavors to use fiction in an attempt to paint a picture of the world contrasts with some of the more traditional efforts to tell the literary history of this period. Surveys of modernism have often focused on the devotion to purity, honesty, and anticommercialism that created bonds of solidarity among a fairly small segment of the world's writers and readers. Studies of the left-wing avant-garde have, on the other hand, generally focused on political engagement at the expense of other explanatory factors. But reframing the story of Thomas Mann in the ways I endeavor to do in this book not only results in a more democratic explanation for what he meant to ordinary readers in the 1930s and 1940s but also helps us connect his fate to that of later generations of authors.

The critic Timothy Aubry, for example, has spent considerable time reflecting on the ways in which ordinary readers in the twenty-first century utilize fiction to make sense of their lives amid conditions of globalized, late-stage capitalism. In contrast to Gloria Fisk, who describes much of contemporary world literature as an attempt to "market writers to guilty tourists," Aubry speaks of a "therapy" culture and examines the various ways in which literary texts are employed for healing purposes in times of fragmentation, alienation, and financial precarity.[24] One of his case studies concerns Khaled Hosseini's bestselling phenomenon *The Kite Runner* and examines how western readers used this novel of a faraway country to soothe their fears about a rapidly escalating War on Terror. Jim Collins, in his work on popular literary culture in the twenty-first century, similarly stresses how book clubs, online literary communities, and crowd-sourced reviewing platforms not only provide their users with a sense of self-affirmation but also help them make sense of the world.[25]

Agnes E. Meyer's rhapsodic reaction to her reading of *Joseph in Egypt* in the mountains of Wyoming, or Ralph Ellison's imaginative projection of himself into the North German world of *Tonio Kröger* ("I found it impossible not to identify myself with the character," he wrote to Langston Hughes) show that the therapeutic culture discussed by Aubrey existed too in the case of Thomas Mann.[26] And the online communities of the present day were foreshadowed by the Book-of-the-Month Club of the 1930s as well as, for example, the reading coteries that formed in US prisoner-of-war camps, where bored German soldiers engaged with Thomas Mann and learned to relate to the world in an entirely novel fashion. In other words, Mann became a star not only because he was a great writer but also because he was useful to his audience.

Publishing Revolutions

The final way in which we might connect Mann's American years to the present day has to do with his participation in the various publishing revolutions of the mid-twentieth century. As Rebecca Walkowitz has stressed, born-translated fiction is defined by a certain kind of style in combination with a self-aware relationship to novel media and distribution channels. Digital and multimedial texts play an important role in her twenty-first-century story—for example, in her discussion of the collaborative web artists Young-Hae Chang Heavy Industries. So do reflections on the complex copyright regimes that govern the global distribution of literature, and on the multiple language- or country-specific editions of books that now exist simultaneously and in some cases blur the definitions of what counts as an original and what constitutes a translation.

Thomas Mann was not an artist who displayed any interest in multimediality, and he rarely intervened in the physical design of his books. In this he notably differed from many of his modernist contemporaries—for example, from James Joyce, with his doodles and experimental typefaces in *Ulysses* (1922). But it was precisely because, rather than despite, of this laissez-faire attitude that Mann's works experienced the full force of a rapidly evolving global book market. What mattered to Mann first and foremost was that his works reached an audience, an ambition in which he found two eager partners in Alfred A. Knopf and Gottfried Bermann Fischer. At a time when worldwide war shook up the publishing industry, these two entrepreneurs were willing to compromise and innovate to place books into the hands of consumers. Their books were in various ways marked by the chaotic circumstances of their production. Is the Stockholm edition of *The Magic Mountain* a mere reprint or a substantially altered work, for example, given that it added a preface that challenged readers to reinterpret the novel in light of its author's exile experience? Which editions of Mann's works should count as "originals," given that English- and German-language versions often appeared in close temporal proximity, and that during the war years, the US editions inevitably reached more readers by an order of magnitude than the German ones did? If the German-language editions deserve to be privileged, then which ones, given that there sometimes were multiple versions of the same work? Is the 1947 edition of *Doktor Faustus* a German or an American book, given that it was published in Germany but copyrighted in the United States? And is the German-language version of "Brother Hitler" that was published in *Das neue Tage-Buch* really primary to the translated version that came out in *Esquire*, despite the fact that the essay grew out of an American commission, the *Esquire* version slightly preceded the one in *Das neue Tage-Buch*, and *Esquire* also preserved Mann's original title, which *Das neue Tage-Buch* changed without authorization?

Then there were the circuitous journeys that Mann's books—and Mann's voice, recorded for his BBC radio addresses—took to avoid Nazi border posts, submarines, and fighter jets. In a very real sense, works like *Lotte in Weimar* or *Joseph the Provider* modeled a new form of world literature. This new form of literature circulated globally very soon after its original publication and it made its way into the hands of far-flung readers in places such as Shanghai or São Paulo despite the best efforts of governments and militaries to stop it.

Nowadays, large publishing houses are multinational enterprises as a matter of course, and new works by globally famous authors are sometimes released in many editions across multiple languages and countries all on the same day. Word processing and typesetting software, cloud computing, and print-on-demand technology have revolutionized global production and distribution processes just as surely as the freight container and the advent of the modern cargo ship. It is a long journey from the age of total war to the incontrovertibly global economy of the twenty-first century. Mann's manuscripts, which would have passed from his writer's desk in Pacific Palisades to his translator in New Jersey, from there to his publishers' offices in Manhattan, and onward to copyediting, typesetting, and printing on the European continent, before they were finally distributed to a diasporic readership scattered across the globe, nevertheless point the way.

What, then, to repeat the initial question, is the continued relevance of Thomas Mann to the world republic of letters? The answer, quite simply, is that when he took to the deck of the *Queen Mary* to proudly declare his autonomy from Hitler, he cast off his roots in the nineteenth century and modeled a new form of authorship that pointed the way to the twenty-first. Clearly, the circumstances under which this new conception was forged will never be replicated exactly. Thomas Mann's war was a war against totalitarianism, and none of the authorial strategies that he developed over the course of the decade that he fought it make sense without the underlying foil of a society entirely subjected to dehumanizing politics. But the idea that in an age in which demagogues legitimate their crimes by invoking the popular will of the people, artists need to stand up to assert their autonomy—this idea, surely, makes as much sense in our time as it did in Thomas Mann's.

NOTES

Introduction

Bodo Uhse, "Der Entsandte Deutschlands in Amerika," July 23/24, 1939, clipping from an unidentified German-language newspaper, A-I Mat. 10/58, TMA. Four years later, Uhse wrote a second article with the same title and very similar content, reprinted in Klaus Schröter, ed., *Thomas Mann im Urteil seiner Zeit: Dokumente 1891–1955* (Hamburg: Christian Wegner Verlag, 1969), 319–21.

Karl Schwarz, "Thomas Mann: Ein Wächter deutscher Kultur?," *Völkischer Beobachter*, October 25, 1935, reprinted in Schröter, *Thomas Mann im Urteil seiner Zeit*, 258.

1. The footage has unfortunately been lost. Ernst Loewy, *Thomas Mann: Ton- und Filmaufnahmen. Ein Verzeichnis* (Frankfurt am Main: S. Fischer Verlag, 1974), 133. The text of Mann's speech survives, because it was reprinted in the émigré newspaper *Deutsches Volksecho* under the title "A Message to America" (*E*, 4:245–47).

2. "Mann Finds U.S. Sole Peace Hope," *New York Times*, February 22, 1938, 13. On this article, see Volkmar Hansen, "'Where I am, there is Germany': Thomas Manns Interview vom 21. Februar 1938 in New York," in *Textkonstitution bei mündlicher und bei schriftlicher Überlieferung: Basler Editoren-Kolloquium 19.-22. März 1990, Autor- und Werkbezogene Referate*, ed. Martin Stern (Tübingen: Max Niemeyer Verlag, 1991), 176–88.

3. Mann made a note of the former publication, recording in his diaries that "the [open letter] has been given a big spread in the New York *Nation*" (*Tb.*, March 20, 1937), but seems to have missed the much more widely circulated reprint in *Reader's Digest*.

4. Otto Flake, "Der Fall Thomas Mann," *Badener Tageblatt*, December 8, 1945, reprinted in *Die große Kontroverse: Ein Briefwechsel um Deutschland*, ed. J. F. G. Grosser (Hamburg: Nagel, 1963), 53. In rendering the German word *Untertan* as "loyal subject," I am following Helmut Peitsch's English translation of Heinrich Mann's novel of the same name.

5. "Turkish Novelists Orhan Pamuk and Elif Shafak Accused of Being Western Stooges by Pro-government Press," *Guardian*, December 12, 2014, http://www.theguardian.com/books/2014/dec/12/pamuk-shafak-turkish-press-campaign.

6. Or Kashti, "Israel Bans Novel on Arab-Jewish Romance from Schools for Threatening Jewish Identity," *Haaretz*, December 31, 2015, http://www.haaretz.com/israel-news/.premium-1.694620.

7. The text of the Hobart College diploma is quoted in John Franklin White, *Thomas Mann in America: The Rhetorical and Political Experiences of an Exiled Artist* (Ann Arbor: University of Michigan Doctoral Dissertation Series, 1971), 382.

8. Johann Wolfgang von Goethe, *Conversations with Eckermann (1823–1832)*, trans. John Oxenford (San Francisco: North Point, 1984), 132.

9. Pascale Casanova, *The World Republic of Letters*, trans. M. B. DeBevoise (Cambridge, MA: Harvard University Press, 2004), 4.

10. The connection between the two titles would have been immediately obvious to most readers of the *Nation*, since Alfred Dreyfus had died less than two years earlier. European papers made similar connections between Thomas Mann's letter and Zola's manifesto. See, e.g., "Thomas Manns *J'accuse*," *Basler Arbeiter-Zeitung*, February 6, 1937, 3.

11. Jürgen Habermas even avers that the "anticipated interventions of the censors had a stylistically formative influence on Heine's texts." "Geist und Macht: ein deutsches Thema. Heinrich Heine und die Rolle des Intellektuellen in Deutschland," *Das junge Deutschland: Kolloquium zum 150. Jahrestag des Verbots vom 10. Dezember 1835*, ed. Joseph A. Kruse and Bernd Kortländer (Hamburg: Hoffmann und Campe, 1987), 17.

12. Volkmar Zühlsdorff, *Hitler's Exiles: The German Cultural Resistance in America and Europe*, trans. Martin H. Bott (London: Continuum, 2004), 36.

13. Alfred Kantorowicz, *In unserem Lager ist Deutschland: Reden und Aufsätze* (Paris: Éditions du Phoenix, 1936).

14. Quoted in Klaus-Dieter Lehmann, "Foreword: Culture as a Weapon," in Zühlsdorff, *Hitler's Exiles*, xiv.

15. A more literal translation of *Weltdeutschtum* would be "world Germanness" or "global Germanness." I have opted for the present translation because it seems obvious that Mann's coinage was meant to allude to the German word for "cosmopolitanism," *Weltbürgertum*.

16. One can only imagine how such contemporaries might have reacted had they known that Mann had taken the inspiration for the phrase "where I am, there is Germany" from the Jewish poet Karl Wolfskehl, who had written "where I am, there is German spirit" in a poem that their mutual friend Erich Kahler had shown to Mann during the spring of 1937. Friedrich Voit, *Karl Wolfskehl: Leben und Werk im Exil* (Göttingen: Wallstein Verlag, 2005), 161.

17. Eckart Conze, Peter Frei, Peter Hayes, and Moshe Zimmermann, eds., *Das Amt und die Vergangenheit: Deutsche Diplomaten im Dritten Reich und in der Bundesrepublik* (Munich: Blessing, 2010), 85.

18. Thomas Mann to Alfred A. Knopf, June 1939, Koshland Files, box 5, folder 3, HRC.

19. Rebecca Walkowitz, *Born Translated: The Contemporary Novel in an Age of World Literature* (New York: Columbia University Press, 2015).

20. The exact legal formalities applying to this case are described in Irene Nawrocka, "Verlagssitz: Wien, Stockholm, New York, Amsterdam. Der Bermann-Fischer Verlag im Exil (1933–1950)," *Archiv für Geschichte des Buchwesens* 53 (2000): 150.

21. The critic Timothy Aubry has written perceptively about the psychic healing powers of books in *Reading as Therapy: What Contemporary Fiction Does for Middle-Class Americans* (Iowa City: University of Iowa Press, 2011). My approach owes a lot to his work but differs in the sense that my main focus is not on the healing of individual psychic grievances but rather on the need of entire communities of readers to orient themselves in a rapidly changing world transformed by new forms of politics, and ultimately by total war.

22. A recent work on this topic that pays particular attention to Thomas Mann is Wolf Lepenies, *The Seduction of Culture in German History* (Princeton, NJ: Princeton University Press, 2014).

23. Pierre Bourdieu, *The Field of Cultural Production: Essays on Art and Literature*, ed. Randal Johnson (New York: Columbia University Press, 1993).

24. A detailed genealogy of this struggle toward autonomy (modeled on France, but to some extent transferable to the German situation) can be found in the first part of Pierre Bourdieu, *The Rules of Art: Genesis and Structure of the Literary Field*, trans. Susan Emanuel (Palo Alto, CA: Stanford University Press, 1996). An attempt to explicitly apply Bourdieu's theories to Mann's fight for recognition in the German cultural system of the late nineteenth and early twentieth centuries is made by Marius Nied in *Der Weg zu "Geist und Kunst": Thomas Mann und sein Frühwerk unter dem Blickwinkel der Feldtheorie Pierre Bourdieus* (Darmstadt: Büchner-Verlag, 2010).

25. Aaron Jaffe, *Modernism and the Culture of Celebrity* (Cambridge: Cambridge University Press, 2005), 20.

26. On Mann's identification with Germany, see, among many other works, Yahya Elsaghe, *Die imaginäre Nation: Thomas Mann und das "Deutsche"* (Paderborn: Wilhelm Fink Verlag, 2000); Jochen Strobel, *Entzauberung der Nation: Die Repräsentation Deutschlands im Werk Thomas Manns* (Dresden: Thelem Verlag, 2000); and Philipp Gut, *Thomas Manns Idee einer deutschen Kultur* (Frankfurt am Main: S. Fischer Verlag, 2008).

27. Anthony Heilbut, *Thomas Mann: Eros and Literature* (New York: Alfred A. Knopf, 1996), 568.

28. David Trotter, *Literature in the First Media Age: Britain between the Wars* (Cambridge, MA: Harvard University Press, 2013).

29. Theodor W. Adorno, *Minima Moralia: Reflections from Damaged Life*, trans. E. F. N. Jephcott (London: Verso Books, 1974), 33.

1. The Teacher of Germany

Max Rychner, "Literarischer Nobelpreis 1929," *Neue Schweizer Rundschau* (1929), reprinted in *Thomas Mann im Urteil seiner Zeit: Dokumente 1891–1955*, ed. Klaus Schröter (Hamburg: Christian Wegner Verlag, 1969), 170.

Bertolt Brecht, *Große kommentierte Berliner und Frankfurter Ausgabe*, ed. Werner Hecht et. al. (Frankfurt am Main: Suhrkamp Verlag, 1988–2000), 29:211.

1. Quoted in Dieter W. Adolphs, "Thomas Manns Einflussnahme auf die Rezeption seiner Werke in Amerika," *Deutsche Vierteljahrsschrift für Literaturwissenschaft und Geistesgeschichte* 64 (1990): 568.

2. This, at any rate, was the keen hope of no less a formidable antagonist than Joseph Goebbels, who noted in his diary for August 11, 1941, "This run-down and moth-eaten scribbler has undergone so many political metamorphoses since 1914 that he arguably isn't taken seriously anywhere anymore." *Die Tagebücher von Joseph Goebbels* (Munich: Institut für Zeitgeschichte, 2013).

3. Hanns M. Elster, "Offener Brief an Thomas Mann," *Deutsche Stimmen: Halbmonatsschrift* 31 (1919): 64.

4. Jean Améry, "Von den Möglichkeiten geistiger Repräsentanz," *Neue Rund-schau* 86, no. 1 (1975): 45.

5. For a detailed reconstruction of this affair, see Hans Rudolf Vaget, *Seelenzauber: Thomas Mann und die Musik* (Frankfurt am Main: S. Fischer Verlag, 2011), 323–57.

6. Klaus Manger, "Wieland, der klassische Nationalautor," in *Metamorphosen des Dichters: Das Rollenverständnis deutscher Schriftsteller vom Barock bis zur Gegenwart*, ed. Gunter E. Grimm (Frankfurt am Main: Fischer Taschenbuch Verlag, 1992), 67–83.

7. Johann Wolfgang von Goethe, "Response to a Literary Rabble-Rouser," trans. Ellen von Nardroff and Ernest H. von Nardroff, in *The Essential Goethe*, ed. Matthew Bell (Princeton, NJ: Princeton University Press, 2016), 879. Translation modified.

8. Goethe, 880.

9. On Schiller's importance for Thomas Mann's conception of representative authorship, see Hans Rudolf Vaget, "Thomas Mann, Schiller, and the Politics of Literary Self-Fashioning," *Monatshefte* 97, no. 3 (2005): 494–510.

10. Friedrich Schiller, "On Naïve and Sentimental Poetry," trans. Daniel O. Dahlstrohm, in *Essays*, ed. Walter Hinderer and Daniel O. Dahlstrohm (New York: Continuum, 1993), 238.

11. For a general overview of this process, see Wolf Lepenies, "A German Specialty: Poetry and Literature in Opposition," in *Between Literature and Science: The Rise of Sociology* (Cambridge: Cambridge University Press, 1988), 220–33.

12. Peter de Mendelssohn memorably summarizes the German conceptual division between poets, writers, and men of letters as follows: "Poets drink clean water directly from the fountain of life, writers drink from the tap. It's best not to inquire too closely from whence men of letters get their water." *Von deutscher Repräsentanz: Thomas und Heinrich Mann, Hermann Hesse, Gerhart Hauptmann* (Munich: Prestel Verlag, 1984), 171. On the rise of the term *Literat* in the early twentieth century, see Gangolf Hübinger, " 'Journalist' und 'Literat': Vom Bildungsbürger zum Intellektuellen," in *Intellektuelle im deutschen Kaiserreich*, ed. Gangolf Hübinger and Wolfgang J. Mommsen (Frankfurt am Main: S. Fischer Verlag, 1993), 95–110.

13. On the *bohème* as a transitional phase in the functional differentiation of the field of cultural production, see Pierre Bourdieu, *The Rules of Art: Genesis and Structure of the Literary Field*, trans. Susan Emanuel (Palo Alto, CA: Stanford University Press, 1996), 54–57.

14. Quoted in Daniel DiMassa, "Stefan George, Thomas Mann, and the Politics of Homoeroticism," *German Quarterly* 86, no. 3 (Summer 2013): 313.

15. See in this context the detailed analysis in Friedhelm Marx, "Heilige Autorschaft? *Self-Fashioning*-Strategien in der Literatur der Moderne," in *Autorschaft: Positionen und Revisionen*, ed. Heinrich Detering (Stuttgart: Verlag J. B. Metzler, 2002), 107–20.

16. George professed to admire homoerotic attraction as a Platonic force only, and claimed to be repulsed by what he regarded as the sexualized imagery of *Death in Venice*. Mann, on the other hand, regarded the secretive bonds of male friendship holding together George's circle as obstacles to the kind of liberating homoerotic passion that he associated with Whitman and sought to introduce to Germany in the early 1920s. DiMassa, "Stefan George."

17. Pierre Bourdieu, *Distinction: A Social Critique of the Judgment of Taste*, trans. Richard Nice (Cambridge, MA: Harvard University Press, 1984).

18. On this process, see Rüdiger vom Bruch, "Kunst und Kulturkritik in führenden bildungsbürgerlichen Zeitschriften des Kaiserreichs," in *Ideengeschichte und Kunstwissenschaft: Philosophie und bildende Kunst im Kaiserreich*, ed. Ekkehard Mai (Berlin: Gebr. Mann, 1983), 313–47.

19. Pierre Bourdieu speaks in this context of a contrast between the "sub-field of large scale production," governed by economic interests, and the "sub-field of small scale production," governed by elite aspirations. *Rules of Art*, 113–40.

20. *Pan* commissioned a story but, for reasons lost to time, never actually printed one. For more on Thomas Mann's time at *Simplicissimus*, see Heinrich Detering, "Akteur im Literaturbetrieb: Der junge Thomas Mann als Rezensent, Lektor, Redakteur," in *Thomas Mann Jahrbuch* 23 (2010): 27–46.

21. Wilhelm Haefs, "Geist, Geld und Buch: Thomas Manns Aufstieg zum Erfolgsautor im S. Fischer Verlag in der Weimarer Republik," in *Die Erfindung des Schriftstellers Thomas Mann*, ed. Michael Ansel, Hans-Edwin Friedrich, and Gerhard Lauer (Berlin: Walter de Gruyter, 2009), 150.

22. Tim Lörke, "Bürgerlicher Avantgardismus: Thomas Manns mediale Selbstinszenierung im literarischen Feld," *Thomas Mann Jahrbuch* 23 (2010): 61–76.

23. During Mann's American years, his admirer Ida Herz acted as a kind of newspaper cutting service for him, a labor that Mann greatly appreciated even if he grew resentful of the person performing it. Herz's clippings now provide one of the most important collections within the TMA.

24. The group was founded in 1905; Mann joined shortly thereafter. Paul Egon Hübinger, *Thomas Mann, die Universität Bonn und die Zeitgeschichte: Drei Kapitel deutscher Vergangenheit aus dem Leben des Dichters 1905–1955* (Munich: R. Oldenbourg, 1974), 25–27. On Mann's relationship to academic readers of his works, see Steffen Martus, "Die Geistesgeschichte der Gegenwartsliteratur: Wissenschaftliche Aufmerksamkeit für Thomas Mann zwischen 1900 und 1933," in Ansel, Friedrich, and Lauer, *Die Erfindung des Schriftstellers Thomas Mann*, 47–84, and Friedhelm Marx, "'Lauter Professoren und Docenten': Thomas Manns Verhältnis zur Literaturwissenschaft," in the same volume (85–96).

25. Christoph Charle, *Birth of the Intellectuals: 1880–1900*, trans. David Fernbach and G. M. Goshgarian (Cambridge: Polity Press, 2015), 38–39.

26. As Pierre Bourdieu notes,

> Thus, paradoxically, it is the autonomy of the intellectual field that makes possible the inaugural act of a writer who, in the name of norms belonging to the literary field, intervenes in the political field, thus constituting himself as an intellectual. *J'accuse* is the outcome and the fulfillment of a collective process of emancipation that is progressively carried out in the field of cultural production: as a prophetic rupture with the established order, it reasserts against all reasons of state the irreducibility of the values of truth and justice and, at the same stroke, the independence of the guardians of these values from the norms of politics (those of patriotism, for example) and from the constraints of economic life. (*Rules of Art*, 129)

27. Mann's diaries for the period have been lost, but there is no reference to Dreyfus in either his surviving letters or his published writings. On the reception of the Dreyfus affair in imperial Germany, see Gerd Krumeich, "Die Resonanz der Dreyfus-Affäre im Deutschen Reich," in *Intellektuelle im deutschen Kaiserreich*, ed. Gangolf Hübinger and Wolfgang J. Mommsen (Frankfurt am Main: S. Fischer Verlag, 1993), 13–32.

28. Hübinger, "'Journalist' und 'Literat,'" 100.

29. Throughout this book I use "intellect" or "spirit" to translate *Geist*, depending on which choice seems more suitable to any given context.

30. Helmut Koopmann notes that Thomas raged against his brother's "silly glorification of the Dreyfus scandal" as late as 1918 (*Tb.*, December 4, 1918). *Thomas Mann—Heinrich Mann: Die ungleichen Brüder* (Munich: C. H. Beck, 2005), 311.

31. Harden had published Mann's story "The Hungry Ones" in his journal *Die Zukunft* (the same paper that now carried the accusations against the kaiser) in 1903. He was also a good friend of Mann's mother-in-law, Hedwig Pringsheim. Mann's conflicted attitudes toward Harden are documented by his letters to Paul and Carl Ehrenberg of October 22, 1902 (*GKFA*, 21:219), and to Heinrich Mann of December 5, 1905 (*GKFA*, 21:337). For Mann's complex relationship to Maximilian Harden, see Helga Neumann and Manfred Neumann, *Maximilian Harden (1861–1927): Ein unerschrockener deutsch-jüdischer Publizist* (Würzburg: Königshausen & Neumann, 2003), 74–94.

32. On Eulenburg and gay culture, see Robert Beachy, *Gay Berlin: Birthplace of a Modern Identity* (New York: Vintage, 2015), 120–39.

33. The TMA also possesses a manuscript of about three pages that is titled "On Maximilian Harden." It was most likely written in 1916, probably for inclusion in *Reflections of a Nonpolitical Man*, and is not specifically about the Eulenburg affair (Thomas Mann, "On Maximilian Harden," A-I-Mp VIII 134, TMA).

34. For a fuller analysis of Mann's use of the term *Literat*, see Heinrich Detering, "Der Litterat: Inszenierung stigmatisierter Autorschaft im Frühwerk Thomas Manns," in Ansel, Friedrich, and Lauer, *Die Erfindung des Schrifstellers Thomas Mann*, 191–206.

35. Heinrich Mann, "Zola," in *Essays und Publizistik, Oktober 1904 bis Oktober 1918*, ed. Manfred Hahn, Anne Flierl, and Wolfgang Klein (Bielefeld: Aisthesis, 2012), 148.

36. Heinrich Mann, 205.

37. This view, with which once upon a time only a small minority of Mann scholars agreed, has gained increasing traction in recent years. See, e.g., Wolf Lepenies, *The Seduction of Culture in German History* (Princeton, NJ: Princeton University Press, 2014), 27–35, and Hermann Kurzke's critical commentary on *Reflections* in *GKFA*, 13.2:9–144.

38. Peter Sprengel, *Gerhart Hauptmann: Epoche—Werk—Wirkung* (Munich: C. H. Beck, 1984), 226.

39. Jean Améry speaks in this context of Hauptmann's "dramatically emphasized Germanness." "Von den Möglichkeiten geistiger Repräsentanz," 41.

40. Another dirty secret was that Hauptmann didn't even sell all that well anymore, because his insistence on sumptuously printed editions of his works ran counter to developments in the German book market. See in this context Haefs, "Geist Geld und Buch," 129–31.

41. Mann had already tried out and rejected literary neoclassicism in *Death in Venice* where, tellingly, the Apollonian self-presentation of the protagonist crumbles in the face of Dionysian forces. Ritchie Robertson, "Classicism and Its Pitfalls: *Death in Venice*," in *The Cambridge Companion to Thomas Mann*, ed. Ritchie Robertson (Cambridge: Cambridge University Press, 2001), 95–106.

42. Quoted in John C. Thirlwall, "In Another Language," in *In Another Language: A Record of the Thirty-Year Relationship between Thomas Mann and His English Translator, Helen Tracy Lowe-Porter*, ed. John C. Thirlwall (New York: Alfred A. Knopf, 1966), 6.

43. "Thomas Mann's New Novel," *Times Literary Supplement*, March 12, 1925, 170.

44. David Horton, *Thomas Mann in English* (London: Bloomsbury, 2013), 25.

45. A detailed description of one of his lecture tours can be found in Mann's letter to Samuel Fischer of October 4, 1924 (*GKFA*, 22:89).

46. Mann's coeditor for Novels of the World was the German American translator and journalist Herman George Scheffauer, who would also play a part in introducing Mann's works to the United States. For more information on the doomed endeavor, see Stefan Rehm, "'Könnte das Massenhafte, das Massengerechte nicht einmal gut sein?': Thomas Mann und die Massenkultur des Literaturmarktes der Weimarer Republik," *Düsseldorfer Beiträge zur Thomas Mann Forschung* 2 (2011): 199–209.

47. On the difficulties of placing Thomas Mann within the history of modernist literature, see Stefan Börnchen and Claudia Liebrand, eds., *Apokrypher Avantgardismus: Thomas Mann und die klassische Moderne* (Munich: Wilhelm Fink Verlag, 2008), and Tim Lörke and Christian Müller, eds., *Thomas Manns kulturelle Zeitgenossenschaft* (Würzburg: Königshausen & Neumann, 2009).

48. Pascale Casanova, *The World Republic of Letters*, trans. M. B. DeBevoise (Cambridge, MA: Harvard University Press, 2004), 4.

49. For a longer discussion of these quotations in the context of Thomas Mann's developing self-understanding as a representative writer, see Doerte Bischoff, "Repräsentanten für Europa? Thomas und Heinrich Mann als Grenz-Gänger eines Europa-Diskurses in ihren Essays 1914–1933," in *Suchbild Europa: Künstlerische Konzepte der Moderne*, ed. Jürgen Wertheimer (Amsterdam: Rodopi, 1995), 25, 26.

50. George C. Schoolfield, "Thomas Mann und Fredrik Böök," in *Deutsche Weltliteratur: Von Goethe bis Ingeborg Bachmann. Festgabe für J. Allan Pfeffer*, ed. Klaus W. Jonas (Tübingen: Max Niemeyer Verlag, 1972), 158–88.

51. On the history of the Section for Poetic Art in the Prussian Academy of the Arts, and on Mann's role within it, see Inge Jens, *Dichter zwischen links und rechts: Die Geschichte der Sektion für Dichtkunst an der Preußischen Akademie der Künste, dargestellt nach den Dokumenten* (Leipzig: Gustav Kiepenhauer, 1994).

52. The Swiss author Max Frisch, for example, described hearing Thomas Mann deliver a lecture at the University of Zurich during the mid-1930s with the following words:

> Of course the man up there on the podium spoke out against Hitler, that's what we were waiting for, that's what we wanted to hear, but he talked about how the University of Bonn had stripped him, Thomas Mann, of his honorary doctorate, and young as I was I thought, "good God, doesn't this guy have other problems?" For after all, at that time we already knew about Dachau, . . . and so there he was, this Nobel laureate and what have you, there he stood and talked about how he had lost an honorary doctorate from the University of Bonn—at this time, at this hour!

Quoted in Katrin Bedenig, "Max Frisch und Thomas Mann: Ihr Weg zu engagierten Staatsbürgern von den Anfängen bis 1947," in *Max Frisch: Sein Weg im Kontext der europäischen Literatur seiner Zeit*, ed. Régine Battison and Margit Unser (Würzburg: Königshausen & Neumann, 2012), 55.

53. In this they were different from the French tradition of the *grandes écoles*, for example.

54. Mann's ecstatic joy when he received word of the award is documented in *D*, 64; *Tb.*, August 4, 1919.

2. The Greatest Living Man of Letters

M. E. S., Thomas Mann, *Nobel Prize Winner of 1929: A Critical Estimate* (New York: Alfred A. Knopf, 1930), 5.

"Vladimir Nabokov," *USA: The Novel*, NET National Educational Television, February 3, 1965, transcript in "Why Nabokov Detests Freud," *New York Times*, January 30, 1966, 346.

1. H. L. Mencken and George Jean Nathan, "Répétition Générale," *Smart Set* 63, no. 1 (1920): 50.

2. For a general overview of Thomas Mann's changing attitudes toward the United States, see Hans-Rudolf Vaget, *Thomas Mann, der Amerikaner. Leben und Werk im amerikanischen Exil 1938–1952* (Frankfurt am Main: S. Fischer Verlag, 2011), 29–66.

3. "Notes on Contributors," *Dial*, December 1922, back cover. M. E. S., *Thomas Mann*, 6.

4. Dorothy Thompson, "The Most Eminent Living Man of Letters," *New York Herald Tribune*, June 10, 1934, G1–2.

5. "Great Mann," *Time*, June 11, 1934, 81–85.

6. Ludwig Lewisohn, "Thomas Mann," *English Journal* 22, no. 7 (September 1933): 528; Archibald MacLeish, lecture introduction (1947), quoted in Donald Prater, *Thomas Mann: A Life* (New York: Oxford University Press, 1995), 376; Henry Seidel Canby, "The Dean of Novelists Recounts a Famous Medieval Tale of Romance, Sin, and Expiation," *Book-of-the-Month Club News*, September 1951, 1–5.

7. James L. Ford, "The Tidal Wave of Books," *New York Tribune*, August 13, 1922, A1.

8. Joan Shelley Rubin, *The Making of Middlebrow Culture* (Chapel Hill: University of North Carolina Press, 1992), 148–208.

9. "Why Nabokov Detests Freud," 346. Emphasis in original.

10. For an explicit comparison of the aesthetics and biographical trajectories of Mann and Nabokov, see Joseph Horowitz, *Artists in Exile: How Refugees from Twentieth-Century War and Revolution Transformed the American Performing Arts* (New York: Harper Collins, 2008), 401–7.

11. For a case study of popular interest in a difficult literary text, see Kevin Birmingham, *The Most Dangerous Book: The Battle for James Joyce's "Ulysses"* (New York: Penguin, 2014). For an exploration of the cult of celebrity surrounding modernist authors, see Aaron Jaffe, *Modernism and the Culture of Celebrity* (Cambridge: Cambridge University Press, 2005).

12. One can still find traces of this conception in the worldview of Thomas Mann's American patron Agnes E. Meyer, who spoke about her proximity to Mann as a struggle for "goodness, purity, and the eternal" (Br. AM, 485).

13. Rubin, *Making of Middlebrow Culture*, 6.

14. "Roosevelt Bars the Hyphenated," *New York Times*, October 13, 1915, 5.

15. In the final years before the First World War, the United States was home to roughly ten million German Americans, many of them first-generation immigrants who still spoke German at home and maintained strong ties to their country of origin.

16. Jeffrey Sammons, in his book-length study of The German Classics, describes the edition as belonging to a series of "anxious and often ineffective efforts to repair relations" between two countries drifting apart. *Kuno Francke's Edition of "The German Classics" (1913–15): A Critical and Historical Overview* (New York: Peter Lang, 2009), 7.

17. Julius Petersen, "The Contemporary Short Story," trans. William Guild Howard, in *The German Classics of the Nineteenth and Twentieth Centuries*, ed. Kuno Francke, vol. 19, ed. Julius Petersen (New York: German Publication Society, 1914 [1915]), xi.

18. Charles Francis Horne, *The Great Events of the Great War*, vol. 3 (New York: J. J. Little & Ives, 1920), 34.

19. See Erik Kirschbaum, *Burning Beethoven: The Eradication of German Culture in the United States during World War One* (New York: Berlinica, 2014).

20. Van Wyck Brooks, *America's Coming-of-Age* (New York: B. W. Huebsch, 1915), 7.

21. Brooks, 6.

22. Brooks, 7–8.

23. Brooks, 7.

24. For more on Brooks's understanding of highbrow and lowbrow culture, see Casey Nelson Blake, *Beloved Community: The Cultural Criticism of Randolph Bourne, Van Wyck Brooks, Waldo Frank, & Lewis Mumford* (Chapel Hill: University of North Carolina Press, 1990), 115–17. Margaret Widdemer's coinage of the term "middlebrow" and the subsequent changes in its meaning are discussed in Rubin, *Making of Middlebrow Culture*, xii–xv.

25. The shadowy presence of *Faust II* in these lines is just one of several examples by which Thomas Mann pays an indirect homage to Goethe in the story. See in this context Eckart Goebel, "Tierische Transzendenz: Herr und Hund," in *Apokrypher Avantgardismus: Thomas Mann und die klassische Moderne*, ed. Stefan Börnchen and Claudia Liebrand (Munich: Wilhelm Fink Verlag, 2008), 307–27.

26. David Blackbourn, *The Conquest of Nature: Water, Landscape, and the Making of Modern Germany* (New York: W. W. Norton, 2006).

27. Randolph Bourne, "Transnational America," *Atlantic Monthly*, July 1916, 90.

28. Bourne, 92.

29. Bourne, 95.

30. Quoted in Michael Kammen, *The Lively Arts: Gilbert Seldes and the Transformation of Cultural Criticism in the United States* (New York: Oxford University Press, 1996), 63.

31. Alec W. G. Randall, "Main Currents in Contemporary German Literature," *Dial*, April 1921, 422.

32. The reference to "odd jobs" (Gelegenheitsarbeiten) is from Hans Wysling, "'German Letters': Thomas Manns Briefe an The Dial (1922–28)," in *Dokumente*

und Untersuchungen: Beiträge zur Thomas-Mann-Forschung, ed. Hans Wysling (Bern: Francke Verlag, 1974), 13.

33. Quoted in Fred Hobson, *H. L. Mencken: A Life* (Baltimore: Johns Hopkins University Press, 1994), 251.

34. Klaus Mann, *The Turning Point: Thirty-Five Years in This Century* (New York: L. B. Fischer, 1942), 137. Klaus likely told his father about his admiration of Mencken, for Thomas Mann mentions his name in a minor essay written in 1929. During the 1930s and 1940s, Mencken and Mann would occasionally run into one another on social occasions, but the encounters seem to have left no deeper impression on the German author.

35. Alfred A. Knopf, "For Henry with Love," *Atlantic Monthly*, May 1959, 50–54.

36. For a perceptive reading of these efforts, see Peter Lancelot Mallios, *Our Conrad: Constituting American Modernity* (Stanford, CA: Stanford University Press, 2010), 64–87.

37. Hans Rudolf Vaget provides an extensive analysis of Janet Flanner's profile of Mann for the *New Yorker* in *Thomas Mann, der Amerikaner*, 322–28. The title of Flanner's story, "Goethe in Hollywood," neatly encapsulates the main source of US interest in the author: the unusual juxtaposition between European cultural sophistication and the fast-paced, highly materialistic American social life.

38. Catherine Turner, *Marketing Modernism Between the Two World Wars* (Amherst: University of Massachusetts Press, 2003), 83.

39. Alfred A. Knopf, "On Publishing Thomas Mann," *American Pen: An International Quarterly of Writing* 7, no. 3 (1975): 2.

40. Jeffrey B. Berlin, "On the Making of *The Magic Mountain*: The Unpublished Correspondence of Thomas Mann, Alfred A. Knopf, and H. T. Lowe-Porter," *Seminar* 28, no. 4 (1992): 283–84. See also Alfred A. Knopf, unpublished memoir, Alfred A. Knopf Files, box 610, folder 2, HRC.

41. George Stevens, "Foothills of the *Magic Mountain*," *Saturday Review of Literature*, November 11, 1933, 257. The evidence suggests that Mann was a willing participant in this marketing strategy. Dieter W. Adolphs, "Thomas Manns Einflussnahme auf die Rezeption seiner Werke in Amerika," *Deutsche Vierteljahrsschrift für Literaturwissenschaft und Geistesgeschichte* 64 (1990): 566.

42. David Horton, *Thomas Mann in English* (London: Bloomsbury, 2013), 33.

43. Turner, *Marketing Modernism*, 89.

44. Quoted in Turner, 91; M. E. S., *Thomas Mann*, 15–16.

45. Knopf had carefully studied Thayer's framing of Mann in his little magazine and would later call him "a young man of taste and means." Knopf, "On Publishing Thomas Mann," 3.

46. Ad copy from the *New York Times Book Review* for May 15, 1927, quoted in Turner, *Marketing Modernism*, 103.

47. Both New York and national newspapers devoted extensive coverage to the event, emphasizing its glamorous nature. The *Saturday Review of Literature*, for example, printed the full text of Mann's dinner address and ran four different features on the visit, including a photo spread and a list of the wines served at the speaker's table.

48. See, e.g., Alfred A. Knopf to Fiorello H. La Guardia, May 14, 1934, Koshland Files, box 5, folder 4, HRC.

49. Arthur Hays Sulzberger to Alfred A. Knopf, May 8, 1934, Koshland Files, box 5, folder 4, HRC.

50. Thomas Mann to Alfred A. Knopf, June 1939, Koshland Files, box 5, folder 3, HRC.

51. Mann's reservations about Lowe-Porter's gender may have been driven by secret fears that a woman would be less likely to pick up on the many homoerotic undertones in his stories, rather than by outright misogyny. Frederick A. Lubich has shown that these fears were not unfounded, since Lowe-Porter did indeed remove many sexual innuendos from Mann's fiction through either ignorance or prudishness—most likely a mixture of both. "Thomas Mann's Sexual Politics—Lost in Translation," *Comparative Literature Studies* 31 (1994): 104–27.

52. Alfred A. Knopf to Thomas Mann, April 17, 1925, Koshland Files, box 2, folder 5, HRC.

53. Alfred A. Knopf to Thomas Mann, May 18, 1925, Koshland Files, box 2, folder 5, HRC. The relevant passage reads,

> Dear Mr. Mann,
> I have just had a cable from your London publisher which reads: Disapprove Scheffauer Strongly Support Porter Very Willing Share Translation Cots [sic] If Latter. Under the circumstances I really don't know just what to say, as my own inclination is very much to agree with Mr. Secker, for whose literary judgment I have always had the highest respect.

Also in the same folder is a letter from Knopf to Mann dated May 6, to which Berlin refers as "not extant" in "On the Making" (303). In it, Knopf makes some concessions and acknowledges that he might agree to Scheffauer as translator after all, provided Mann could insure that Scheffauer would accept the salary of four dollars per thousand words that Knopf offered. Whether Mann relayed the offer is not known; at any rate the matter became moot with Scheffauer's death in 1927.

54. Kenneth Burke, "Thomas Mann and André Gide," in *Counter-Statement* (Berkeley: University of California Press, 1931), 92–106.

55. For a detailed overview of the storied relationship between Knopf, Mann, and Lowe-Porter, see the essays by Berlin as well as by Berlin and Herz in the bibliography.

56. See, e.g., Richard Winston, "On Translating Thomas Mann," *American Pen: An International Quarterly of Writing* 7, no. 3 (1975): 15–22; Lubich, "Thomas Mann's Sexual Politics"; Timothy Buck, "Loyalty and Licence: Thomas Mann's Fiction in English Translation," *Modern Language Review* 91, no. 4 (1996): 898–921; Timothy Buck, "Mann in English," in *The Cambridge Companion to Thomas Mann*, ed. Ritchie Robertson (Cambridge: Cambridge University Press, 2001), 235–48; Horton, *Thomas Mann in English*; Tobias Boes, "Aschenbach Crosses the Waters: Reading Death in Venice in America," *Modernism/modernity* 21, no. 2 (2014): 429–45. Knopf and Lowe-Porter's monopoly on the English-language market lasted until the late 1980s, when a number of new translations were published. There are now roughly half a dozen different collections of Mann's short stories available, all by different translators, while most of his major novels were retranslated to admirable effect by John E. Woods starting in the 1990s.

57. "H. T. Lowe-Porter, Translator, Dead," *New York Times*, 27 April, 1963, 25.

58. Helen Tracy Lowe-Porter, "On Translating Thomas Mann," in *In Another Language: A Record of the Thirty-Year Relationship between Thomas Mann and His English Translator, Helen Tracy Lowe-Porter*, ed. John C. Thirlwall (New York: Alfred A. Knopf, 1966), 204.

59. Lowe-Porter, 182.

60. On Lowe-Porter and Belloc, see John C. Thirlwall, "In Another Language," in *In Another Language*, 57. On Lowe-Porter and Wilamowitz-Moellendorf, see Boes, "Aschenbach Crosses the Waters," 437–38.

61. Lowe-Porter, "On Translating Thomas Mann," 181.

62. Horton, *Thomas Mann in English*, 121.

63. For an exemplary study of this process, see Dorrit Cohn, "The Second Author of Der Tod in Venedig," in *Probleme der Moderne: Studien zur deutschen Literatur von Nietzsche bis Brecht*, ed. Benjamin Bennett, Anton Kaes, and William J. Lillyman (Tübingen: Max Niemeyer Verlag, 1983), 223–45. For more on the grammatical manifestations of Mann's ironic style, see Horton, *Thomas Mann in English*, 111–15.

64. Erich Heller, *Thomas Mann: The Ironic German* (London: Secker & Warburg, 1958), 103. Note Heller's sartorial metaphor. If Mann's works are "draped" already in the original German, rather than just in translation, then what exactly are we to expect behind all that fabric?

65. T. J. Reed, *Thomas Mann: The Uses of Tradition* (Oxford: Oxford University Press, 1973), 2.

66. Oliver Jahraus, "Die Geburt des Klassikers aus dem Tod der Figur: Autorschaft diesseits und jenseits des Textes Der Tod in Venedig von Thomas Mann," in *Die Erfindung des Schriftstellers Thomas Mann*, ed. Michael Ansel, Hans-Edwin Friedrich, and Gerhard Lauer (Berlin: Walter de Gruyter, 2009), 219.

67. The publisher George Doran enthusiastically declared in a 1921 interview with the *New York Herald* that "never in the history of literature in America has there been such an increase in the number of readers, or, as this may or may not indicate, so widespread an interest in all kinds of books. . . . The sales of our serious books furnish the best proof of the remarkable change in the wants of book buyers." Quoted in John William Tebbel, *A History of Book Publishing in the United States*, vol. 3, *The Golden Age between Two Wars 1920–1940* (New York: R. R. Bowker, 1978), 45.

68. May Lamberton Becker, "Reader's Guide," *Saturday Review of Literature*, April 30, 1927, 793.

69. Ernest Boyd, "Translations," *Saturday Review of Literature*, December 26, 1925, 441–42.

70. Frank Thieß, "German Literature of Today," *Saturday Review of Literature*, May 9, 1925, 745. For more on Thieß, see chapter 6.

71. Rebecca West, "Notes on Three Novels," *Saturday Review of Literature*, October 17, 1925, 207–8.

72. "Some Personal Choices," *Saturday Review of Literature*, December 3, 1927, 410.

73. Aldo Sorani, "A Letter from Italy," *Saturday Review of Literature*, August 1, 1925, 13.

74. Olga Marx, "German Literature of Today," *Saturday Review of Literature*, February 6, 1926, 545; Pierre Loving, "Thomas Mann," *Saturday Review of Literature*,

May 22, 1926, 809; J. C. "An Answer to 'One Question,'" *Saturday Review of Literature*, July 7, 1934, 792.

75. For a thorough study of the Book-of-the-Month Club, see Janice Radway, *A Feeling for Books: The Book-of-the-Month Club, Literary Taste, and Middle-Class Desire* (Chapel Hill: University of North Carolina Press, 1999).

76. A detailed account of the state of the US book industry during the time of the Great Depression can be found in Orion Howard Cheney, *Economic Survey of the Book Industry, 1930–1931* (New York: National Association of Book Publishers, 1931), 233–50.

77. Charles Lee, *The Hidden Public: The Story of the Book-of-the-Month Club* (Westport, CT: Praeger, 1973), 12.

78. Quoted in Thirlwall, "In Another Language," 30.

79. Lee, *Hidden Public*, 88. The enormous influence of the Book-of-the-Month Club is illustrated by the fact that the size of the average print run for a commercial book in the mid-1930s was about seventeen thousand copies; and in the mid-1940s, about sixty-five thousand copies. Tebbel, *History of Book Publishing*, 662.

80. The chosen titles were *Stories of Three Decades* in 1936, *Joseph in Egypt* in 1938, *Joseph the Provider* in 1944, *Doctor Faustus* in 1948, and *The Holy Sinner* in 1951. Of the five, the first two were distributed as "dividends," that is, promotional enticements for regular club purchasers. In addition, the club also "recommended" three further Mann titles to its readership: *This Peace* and *Royal Highness* in 1939, and *The Beloved Returns: Lotte in Weimar* in 1940.

81. Henry Seidel Canby, "Joseph the Provider, by Thomas Mann," *Book-of-the-Month Club News*, July 1944, 4.

82. Clifton Fadiman, "Doctor Faustus: A Profound Novel by Thomas Mann, Nobel Prize Winner and 'Perhaps the Age's Greatest Writer,'" *Book-of-the-Month Club News*, November 1948, 3.

83. The most popular German authors other than Mann were Erich Maria Remarque, Franz Werfel, and Stefan Zweig, who each had three titles chosen.

84. "Nymph," *Saturday Review of Literature*, May 8, 1937, 8.

85. Henry Seidel Canby, "The Threatening Thirties," *Saturday Review of Literature*, May 22, 1937, 4, 14.

Interlude I

1. Henry Seidel Canby, "The First Puritan," *Saturday Review of Literature*, February 26, 1938, 5; Clifton Fadiman, "Thomas Mann," *New Yorker*, February 26, 1938, 58.

2. Malcolm Cowley, "Second Thoughts on 'Joseph,'" *New Republic*, March 23, 1938, 199.

3. William Troy, "Thomas Mann," *Partisan Review*, June 1938, 24.

4. [Dwight Macdonald], "This Quarter: Reflections on a Non-political Man," *Partisan Review*, Fall 1938, 16. The editorial is unsigned, but the manuscript survives among Macdonald's personal papers.

5. William Phillips, "Thomas Mann: Humanism in Exile," *Partisan Review*, May 1938, 8.

6. Todd Kontje, *Thomas Mann's World: Empire, Race, and the Jewish Question* (Ann Arbor: University of Michigan Press, 2011), 125. I borrow Kontje's translation of Mann's words.

7. Dieter Borchmeyer, "'Zurück zum Anfang aller Dinge': Mythos und Religion in Thomas Manns *Josephsromanen*," *Thomas Mann Jahrbuch* 11 (1998): 9–30.

8. For representative criticism in this vein that focuses primarily on Mann's fiction, see, e.g., Christoph Schwöbel, *Die Religion des Zauberers: Theologisches in den großen Romanen Thomas Manns* (Tübingen: Mohr Siebeck, 2008), and Niklaus Peter and Thomas Sprecher, eds., *Der Ungläubige Thomas: Zur Religion in Thomas Manns Romanen* (Frankfurt am Main: Vittorio Klostermann, 2012). For criticism that focuses instead on Mann's aesthetic and political writings, see especially Heinrich Detering, "Das Werk und die Gnade: Zu Religion und Kunstreligion in der Poetik Thomas Manns," in Peter and Sprecher, *Der Ungläubige Thomas*, 149–66, and Heinrich Detering, *Thomas Manns amerikanische Religion: Theologie, Politik und Literatur im kalifornischen Exil* (Frankfurt am Main: S. Fischer Verlag, 2012).

9. Franklin D. Roosevelt, "Fireside Chat: September 3, 1939," The American Presidency Project, https://www.presidency.ucsb.edu/node/209990.

10. National Conference of Christians and Jews, *Toward Brotherhood: Annual Report 1942 of the President of the National Conference of Christians and Jews* (New York: NCCJ, 1942), 19.

11. John Hyde Preston, "Searching for Roots in America," *Harper's*, October 1937, 490.

12. Quoted in James Woodress, *Willa Cather: A Literary Life* (Lincoln: University of Nebraska Press, 1987), 472. Cather herself expressed her admiration for the *Joseph* novels in a short review essay, "The Birth of Personality," *Saturday Review of Literature*, June 6, 1936, 3–4.

13. Fadiman, "Thomas Mann," 58.

14. Canby, "First Puritan," 5.

3. The First Citizen of the International Republic of Letters

Dorothy Thompson, "To Thomas Mann: An Appreciation," *New York Herald Tribune*, April 14, 1937, 21.

Br. GBF, 109.

1. If Mann's daughter Erika is to be believed, this did not stop Hermann Göring from boasting, after his arrest by the Americans, that "a German of Thomas Mann's stature could certainly have been adapted to the Third Reich," if only *he* had been tasked with this job. Hermann Kurzke, *Thomas Mann: Life as a Work of Art*, trans. Leslie Willson (Princeton, NJ: Princeton University Press, 2002), 497.

2. Mann's decision to put revenue over principles led to a bitter quarrel with his two oldest children, Erika and Klaus. "Whom can we still count on if those whom we trusted the most abandon us for the sake of the 'German market'?" Klaus wrote to Stefan Zweig in September 1933. This quote, together with a longer discussion of Mann's silence, can be found in Kurzke, 376–80.

3. "Weit klüger ist's dem Vaterland entsagen, / Als unter einem kindischen Geschlechte / Das Joch des blinden Pöbelhasses tragen." I quote the translation by Reginald Bancroft Cooke in *The Sonnets of Karl August Georg Max Graf von Platen-Hallermünde* (Boston: Richard G. Badger, 1923), 129.

4. Mann's path to US citizenship is described in great detail by Hans Rudolf Vaget in *Thomas Mann, der Amerikaner: Leben und Werk im amerikanischen Exil 1938–1952* (Frankfurt am Main: S. Fischer Verlag, 2011), 59–66.

5. Hans Rudolf Vaget, "Introduction," in *Thomas Mann's "The Magic Mountain": A Casebook*, ed. Hans Rudolf Vaget (New York: Oxford University Press, 2008), 4.

6. David Ewen, "Thomas Mann Talks of the Nazi State," *New York Times*, September 10, 1933, 2xx.

7. Harry Slochower, "An Open Letter to Thomas Mann," *New Republic*, June 27, 1934, 185.

8. "Cartwheel Girl," *Time*, June 12, 1939, 47–51.

9. Thus the actual text of the Harvard citation, which appeared in Latin on the diploma and which Mann then translated into German in a slightly different form for his *Exchange of Letters*. Citation for Honorary Degree to Thomas Mann, Conant Files, box 27, HUA.

10. Quoted in John Franklin White, *Thomas Mann in America: The Rhetorical and Political Experiences of an Exiled Artist* (Ann Arbor: University of Michigan Doctoral Dissertation Series, 1971), 382.

11. Quoted in White, 383.

12. The correspondence between Harvard and Mann is in the Conant Files, box 34, HUA.

13. "Striking Scenes and Personalities at Brilliant Harvard Commencement," *Boston Post*, June 21, 1935, 15.

14. Quoted in "Training Leaders: A Test for Colleges," *New York Times Magazine*, June 16, 1935, 3, 15.

15. Kenneth B. Murdock to James B. Conant, November 19, 1935, Conant Files, box 34, HUA.

16. Unsigned letter to George R. Agassiz, January 10, 1935, Conant Files, box 34, HUA.

17. "Striking Scenes and Personalities," 15.

18. Roger W. Smith '07, telegram to James B. Conant, June 20, 1935, and Edward N. Wright 3rd '11 to James B. Conant, June 28, 1935, Conant Files, box 34, HUA.

19. Jerome D. Greene to Delcevare King '95, June 18, 1935, Conant Files, box 34, HUA.

20. My summary of the Hanfstaengl episode is greatly indebted to the research of three previous scholars: Reginald Phelps, "Thomas Mann, LLD, Harvard, and the Third Reich," *Harvard Magazine*, July/August 1986, 65–68; Peter Conradi, *Hitler's Piano Player: The Rise and Fall of Ernst Hanfstaengl, Confidant of Hitler, Ally of FDR* (New York: Carroll and Graf, 2004); and especially the comprehensive account in Vaget, *Thomas Mann, der Amerikaner*, 301–8.

21. The historian Stephen H. Norwood has argued that such study-abroad programs at elite universities were deliberately targeted by the Nazis as a way of recruiting influential supporters in the United States. *The Third Reich in the Ivory Tower: Complicity and Conflict on American Campuses* (New York: Cambridge University Press, 2009), 133–57. The original sum of the "Hanfstaengl bequest" was to be one thousand dollars, an amount which Hanfstaengl multiplied ten-fold when he again made

the offer two years later, as part of an alumni donations drive in connection with the Harvard tercentennial. At that time the State Department sent a confidential memo to Conant confirming what every reasonable person would have already suspected: that Hanfstaengl himself did not possess the financial resources to make such a large bequest and that the offer must therefore have been channeled through him by the German government. William Phillips to James B. Conant, March 13, 1936, Conant Files, box 58, HUA.

22. Vaget, *Thomas Mann, der Amerikaner*, 305. On Harvard's anti-Semitism and comfortable relationship with Nazism during the 1930s, see Norwood, *Third Reich*, 36–74.

23. "Harvard Has Most Colorful Class Day," *Boston Post*, June 21, 1934, 8–9.

24. Quoted in Conradi, *Hitler's Piano Player*, 158.

25. James B. Conant, address delivered at the Harvard Alumni Association exercises in Sever Quadrangle, June 21, 1934, Conant Files, box 4, HUA.

26. Clipping from *Boston Herald*, June 18, 1934, HUC 6934, HUA.

27. Seddon L. Etherton to James B. Conant, March 20, 1936, Conant Files, box 58, HUA.

28. Morris Dickstein, *Dancing in the Dark: A Cultural History of the Great Depression* (New York: Norton, 2009), 22.

29. Serge Guilbaut, *How New York Stole the Idea of Modern Art: Abstract Expressionism, Freedom, and the Cold War*, trans. Arthur Goldhammer (Chicago: University of Chicago Press, 1983), 17–18.

30. For a detailed treatment of Mann's contradictory views, see Manfred Görtemaker, *Thomas Mann und die Politik* (Frankfurt am Main: S. Fischer Verlag, 2005).

31. On Thomas Mann's efforts for the German People's Front, see Ursula Langkau-Alex, *Deutsche Volksfront 1932–39*, vol. 2 (Berlin: Akademie Verlag, 2004), 450–52.

32. Lewis Mumford, "Opening Address," in *Artists against War and Fascism: Papers of the First American Artists' Congress*, ed. Matthew Baigell and Julia Williams (New Brunswick, NJ: Rutgers University Press, 1986), 64.

33. Quoted in "Congress," *Time*, December 27, 1937, 18. The full message of Mann's telegram can be found in *Tb.*, December 2, 1937.

34. Mann did offer a direct repudiation of his earlier stance in a 1939 address to the PEN World Congress of Writers, presumably because he knew that many members of his audience there would have read *Reflections* carefully. In this address he acknowledged, "Only in my riper years have I seen and come to admit that there cannot be a clear distinction between the intellectual and the political. I see now that it was a mistake for a German citizen to believe that a man could be cultured and non-political" (*GW*, 13:680).

35. James T. Farrell, "Thomas Mann's Manifesto against Fascism," *New York Herald Tribune*, December 21, 1938, 14. Farrell presents a longer critique of Mann that is explicitly linked to an argument about Popular Front strategy in "Literature and Ideology," *New International* 8, no. 4 (May 1942): 107–11.

36. Michael Denning, *The Cultural Front: The Laboring of American Culture in the Twentieth Century* (London: Verso, 1998), 4.

37. For more on *There Shall Be No Night* and its place in American culture during the final days before Pearl Harbor, see Ichiro Takayoshi, *American Writers and the*

Approach of World War II, 1935–1941: A Literary History (New York: Cambridge University Press, 2015), 41–42.

38. For a detailed examination of this surging interest, see Takayoshi.

39. Denning, *Cultural Front*, 12.

40. Kenneth Burke, "Thomas Mann and André Gide," in *Counter-Statement* (Berkeley: University of California Press, 1931), 105.

41. Kenneth Burke, "Fraught with Freight," *New Republic*, January 10, 1934, 257.

42. Kenneth Burke, "Revolutionary Symbolism in America," in *The First American Writers' Congress*, ed. Henry Hart (New York: International Publishers, 1935), 89–90.

43. Ann George and Jack Selzer, "What Happened at the First American Writers' Congress? Kenneth Burke's 'Revolutionary Symbolism in America,'" *Rhetoric Society Quarterly* 33, no. 2 (Spring 2003): 47–66.

44. On Copland's relationship to the Popular Front, see Alex Ross, *The Rest is Noise: Listening to the Twentieth Century* (New York: Farrar, Straus and Giroux, 2008), 269–77.

45. Menno ter Braak, "Emigranten-Literatur," *Das neue Tage-Buch* 2, no. 52 (December 1934): 1245.

46. For a detailed overview of the publication and reception history of *Measure and Value*, see Thomas Baltensweiler, *Mass und Wert: Die Exilzeitschrift von Thomas Mann und Konrad Falke* (Bern: Peter Lang, 1996). For its position within the larger landscape of émigré publishing, see Hans-Albert Walter, *Deutsche Exilliteratur 1933– 1950*, vol. 4, *Exilpresse* (Stuttgart: J. B. Metzlersche Verlagsbuchhandlung, 1978).

47. Upon receiving offprints of the *Post* article, Mann politely complimented Meyer on the "utmost precision" and "flawless English" of her rendition (*Br. AM*, 87). This didn't prevent Alfred A. Knopf from commissioning a new translation by Helen Tracy Lowe-Porter when he included the essay in the 1942 volume *Order of the Day*. For simplicity's sake, the following quotations will all be from the Lowe-Porter translation.

48. The literary critic Tim Lörke has shown that this position is actually contained in embryonic form in *Reflections of a Nonpolitical Man* and then developed in Mann's political essays of the 1920s. *Die Verteidigung der Kultur: Mythos und Musik als Medien der Gegenmoderne* (Würzburg: Königshausen & Neumann, 2010), 131–49.

49. Lörke speaks in this context of a move from a "utopic" to a "heterotopic" social vision (121, 149).

50. Fritz Erpenbeck, "Preface," *Das Wort* 2, no. 11 (November 1937): 6.

51. Ernst Bloch, "Thomas Manns Manifest," *Neue Weltbühne*, September 9, 1937, 1157.

52. "Thomas Mann Charts Course for New German Magazine," *Washington Post*, August 15, 1937, B1; "Mann Strikes Out at Nazi Concepts," *New York Times*, August 15, 1937, N6.

53. Steven Marcus, "Humanities from Classics to Cultural Studies: Notes towards the History of an Idea," *Daedalus* 135, no. 2 (Spring 2006): 18.

54. Marcus, 17–19. The origins of the Special Program in the Humanities in a disciplinary crisis triggered by the professionalization of the social sciences are made especially clear in early promotional materials for the program preserved in the Princeton University Archives. An undated program brochure speaks of humanists

who "were in need of help" in finding how their various courses of study "could be enriched and enlivened by the understanding of [their] ramifications in other fields." And a memo by Princeton dean Radcliffe Heermance explicitly calls the Special Program the humanities equivalent to the social scientific School of Public and International Affairs. "The Divisional Program in the Humanities," [probably 1942], Council of Humanities Records, box 2, PUA.

55. For confirmation that this was indeed perceived as a stated policy goal of the program, see "Mann, Exile, Will Teach at Princeton," clipping from *Philadelphia Evening Ledger*, n.d., n.p., Thomas Mann File, PUA.

56. Quoted in Herbert Lehnert, "Thomas Mann in Princeton," *Germanic Review* 39, no. 1 (1964): 21. A capsule biography of Mann, prepared at the same time and probably intended for use in the convocation program, also repeats the phrase "first citizen in the international republic of letters" coined by Hobart College. Untitled biographical summary, [probably spring 1939], Thomas Mann File, PUA.

57. For further details on Mann's lectures at Princeton, see Hans Rudolf Vaget, "The Best of Worlds: Thomas Mann in Princeton," *Princeton University Library Chronicle* 75, no. 1 (2013): 9–37, and James N. Bade, ed., *"On Myself" and Other Princeton Lectures* (Frankfurt am Main: Peter Lang, 1996), 9–21.

58. Ruth B. Bottigheimer, "One Hundred and Fifty Years of German at Princeton: A Descriptive Account," in *Teaching German in America: Prolegomena to a History*, ed. David P. Benseler, Walter F. W. Lohnes, and Valters Nollendorfs (Madison: University of Wisconsin Press, 1988), 90–93.

59. Among other studies on this subject, see Susan L. Pentlin, "German Teachers' Reaction to the Third Reich, 1933–1939," in Benseler, Lohnes, and Nollendorfs, *Teaching German in America*, 228–52.

60. Bottigheimer, "One Hundred and Fifty Years," 91. The frosty attitude of the Germanic division is also indicated by the brevity of the congratulatory letter it sent to the famous visitor on the occasion of his sixty-fifth birthday in 1940. Princeton Germanic Division to Thomas Mann, June 1940, Thomas Mann File, PUA.

61. Henry J. Schmidt, "Interview with Hermann J. Weigand (1892–1985)," in Benseler, Lohnes, and Nollendorfs, *Teaching German in America*, 285–92.

62. Hermann Weigand, *Thomas Mann's Novel "Der Zauberberg": A Study* (New York: D. Appleton–Century Company, 1933), 100.

63. Harry Slochower's treatment of *The Magic Mountain* in *Three Ways of Modern Man* (New York: International Publishers, 1937) offers an example of this tendency that is concurrent to Weigand's study. Mann read the chapter in manuscript form in 1935 and noted his displeasure (*Tb.*, July 30, 1935).

64. That Mann's mistrust was at least somewhat justified is humorously demonstrated by a feature on him that ran in the commencement issue of the Hobart College student newspaper, the *Hobart Herald*, a few weeks before the dignitaries of that college declared him to be the "first citizen of the international republic of letters." There, Mann is described as an "ear-wiggling, cane-swinging, scotch-and-soda drinker" who likes "to have his wife, a Brazilian pianist [*sic*], bring him his slippers, and 'load the new gramaphone [*sic*] with Brahms.'" "Thomas Mann Will Be Phi Beta Kappa Speaker for Graduates," *Hobart Herald*, May 4, 1939, 1.

65. This was not the only time Mann was involved in humorous confusions concerning academic ranks. In a feature story on the author, Janet Flanner insinuated

that Mann had made his literary bequest to Yale University in no small part because he had mistaken Joseph W. Angell, the ambitious Yale graduate student who had first approached him with the suggestion, with James R. Angell, the president of Yale University. "Goethe in Hollywood," *New Yorker*, December 13, 1941, 41. Vaget, who examines the question in *Thomas Mann, der Amerikaner*, finds Flanner's argument plausible (312).

66. Howard Nemerov, "The Quester Hero: Myth as Universal Symbol in the Works of Thomas Mann," (undergraduate thesis, Harvard University, 1939), 19–22.

67. For a reading of the essay in this light, see Michael Bell, *Literature, Modernism, and Myth: Belief and Responsibility in the Twentieth Century* (Cambridge: Cambridge University Press, 1997), 161–65.

68. See in this context Gene R. Pendleton and Linda L. Williams, "Themes of Exile in Thomas Mann's 'Voyage with Don Quixote,'" *Cervantes* 21, no. 2 (2001): 77–78.

Interlude II

1. Agnes E. Meyer, "A New Novel by Thomas Mann: *The Beloved Returns*," *New York Times Book Review*, August 25, 1940, 23; Clifton Fadiman, "Mann on Goethe," *New Yorker*, August 31, 1940, 44. An extensive survey of the American reception can be found in Werner Frizen's excellent commentary on *Lotte in Weimar* (GKFA, 9.2:134–41).

2. The Swiss critic Yahya Elsaghe goes so far as to claim that "only five copies of the English translation reissued in 1990 have been sold in Great Britain." "*Lotte in Weimar*," in *The Cambridge Companion to Thomas Mann*, ed. Ritchie Robertson (New York: Cambridge University Press, 2002), 198. In Elsaghe's subsequent book *Thomas Mann und die kleinen Unterschiede: Zur erzählenden Imagination des Anderen* (Vienna: Böhlau, 2004), this somewhat astonishing proposition recurs in slightly toned-down form (336), though in neither case does Elsaghe offer a source for it.

3. Meyer, "New Novel by Thomas Mann," 1, 23.

4. Alfred A. Knopf, "*The Beloved Returns*, by Thomas Mann," signed testimonial for an advertisement in *New York Times Book Review*, August 25, 1940, 13.

5. This sentence was missing in both the first German and the first American printing of the novel, most likely because of a transcription error from the manuscript.

6. For an early occurrence of this metaphor, see M. W. S., "Reunion in Weimar," *Christian Science Monitor*, September 7, 1940, 18.

7. Rudolf Brettschneider, "Die Entdeckung des Wälsungenblut," *Die Bücherstube* (October 1920): 110–12.

8. Todd Kontje speaks in this context of Thomas Mann's tendency toward "symbolic autobiography." "Thomas Mann's 'Wälsungenblut': The Married Artist and the 'Jewish Question,'" *PMLA* 123, no. 1 (January 2008): 111.

9. The connection between the stream-of-consciousness style of *Lotte in Weimar* and the works of James Joyce was first made by Georg Lukács in "Franz Kafka or Thomas Mann?," in *The Meaning of Contemporary Realism*, trans. John and Necke Mander (London: Merlin Press, 1963), 47–48. It influentially recurs in Franco Moretti, *Modern Epic: The World System from Goethe to García Márquez*, trans. Quintin Hoare

(London: Verso, 1996), 172. Mann documents his anxieties about Joyce most explicitly in the eighth chapter of *The Story of a Novel: The Genesis of "Doctor Faustus"* (*SN*, 91; *GKFA* 19.1:474–75).

10. Werner Frizen, the editor of volume devoted to *Lotte in Weimar* in the ongoing critical edition of Mann's works, the *Große kommentierte Frankfurter Ausgabe*, deserves a lot of the credit in this regard. Tellingly, his commentary on the work is much longer than the novel itself.

4. Hitler's Most Intimate Enemy

Günther Anders, "Germany in Exile," *New Republic*, May 5, 1937, 392–93.

Sicherheitsdienst des Reichsführers SS, "Meldungen aus dem Reich," quoted in Martina Hoffschulte, *"Deutsche Hörer!" Thomas Manns Rundfunkreden (1940 bis 1945) im Werkkontext* (Münster: Telos Verlag, 2003), 61.

1. Quoted in Erich A. Frey, "Thomas Mann and His Friends before the Tolan Committee," in *Exile: The Writer's Experience*, ed. John M. Spalek and Robert F. Bell (Chapel Hill: University of North Carolina Press, 1982), 215.

2. A detailed treatment of Mann's interactions with President Roosevelt can be found in Hans Rudolf Vaget, *Thomas Mann, der Amerikaner: Leben und Werk im amerikanischen Exil 1938–1952* (Frankfurt am Main: S. Fischer Verlag, 2011), 67–156. While the 1935 visit was a more or less accidental one, arranged at the last minute by Hendrik Willem van Loon, a mutual acquaintance of the Manns' and the Roosevelts', Vaget speculates (108–9) that the second invitation was proffered in tacit support of Mann's activities as a wartime propagandist.

3. Memorandum by the OSS employee Emmy C. Rado to DeWitt Poole, head of the OSS Foreign Nationalities Branch, December 12, 1943, quoted in Alexander Stephan, *Im Visier des FBI: Deutsche Exilschriftsteller in den Akten amerikanischer Geheimdienste* (Stuttgart: Verlag J. B. Metzler, 1995), 111.

4. Heike Bungert, "Deutsche Emigranten im Amerikanischen Kalkül: Die Regierung in Washington, Thomas Mann, und die Gründung eines Emigrantenkomitees 1943," *Vierteljahresschrift für Zeitgeschichte* 46, no. 2 (1998): 253–68.

5. On the benefits and perils of such a broad comparative approach, see Wolfgang Schivelbusch, *Three New Deals: Reflections on Roosevelt's America, Mussolini's Italy, and Hitler's Germany, 1933–1939* (New York: Picador, 2007), especially the third chapter, which is explicitly devoted to art and propaganda.

6. Privately, Mann was much more critical. In a letter to Ludwig Marcuse, for example, he castigated the hypocritical American attitude that demanded loyalty from the Japanese "enemy aliens," yet denied them their basic rights (*Br.*, 2:251).

7. For more on Mann's house on San Remo Drive, see Alex Ross, "Will Thomas Mann's House Be Demolished?" *New Yorker*, August 18, 2016, http://www.new yorker.com/culture/cultural-comment/will-thomas-manns-house-be-demolished. The answer to Ross's question turns out to be no. In November of 2016, the German government purchased Mann's former residence for thirteen million dollars, and recently opened it as a residential center for artists and intellectuals engaged in German-American cultural dialogue.

8. See, e.g., Ehrhard Bahr, *Weimar on the Pacific: German Exile Culture in Los Angeles and the Crisis of Modernism* (Berkeley: University of California Press, 2008).

9. "Los Angeles Metropolitan Area during World War II," California State Military Museums, updated January 20, 2019, http://www.militarymuseum.org/LAWWII.html.

10. Paul V. C. Whitney, "Distinguished Exile Speaks Here Tonight," *Deseret News*, March 21, 1938, 1.

11. Max Domarus, ed., *Hitler. Reden und Proklamationen 1932–1945*, vol. 2 (Würzburg: Süddeutscher Verlag, 1965), 1669.

12. Mann's decision to make this pivot may have been influenced by positive experiences with a photographer for *Life* magazine, who met him in Tulsa to shoot material for a story on his American lecture tour. For the resulting article, see Marquis Childs, "Thomas Mann: Germany's Foremost Literary Exile Speaks Now for Freedom and Democracy in America," *Life*, April 17, 1939, 56–59, 74–76.

13. For a detailed analysis of the complex genesis and publication history of the essay, see Paolo Panizzo, "Künstler, Genie und Demagoge: Thomas Manns Essay 'Bruder Hitler,'" in *Thomas Manns kulturelle Zeitgenossenschaft*, ed. Tim Lörke and Christian Müller (Würzburg: Königshausen & Neumann, 2009), 13–27.

14. Mann also emphasized the "literary importance" of this essay in a letter to Bermann Fischer (*Br. GBF*, 186–87). For an essay attuned to the stylistic dimension, see Reinhold Niebuhr, "Mann's Political Essays," *Nation*, November 28, 1942, 582–84.

15. The incongruity between Mann's style and the ordinary fare served up by *Esquire* magazine was noted by contemporary reviewers. See, e.g., Henry Smith, "Thomas Mann Says Democracy Will Win," *Dallas Morning News*, August 7, 1938, 9.

16. For several examples, see O. K. Werckmeister, "Hitler the Artist," *Critical Inquiry* 23, no. 3 (Winter 1997): 270–97.

17. Mann's thesis that a degenerate Wagnerism formed an essential, rather than merely incidental, part of Hitler's character and political thinking has recently been developed at much greater length by Hans Rudolf Vaget in *"Wehvolles Erbe": Richard Wagner in Deutschland: Hitler, Knappertsbusch, Mann* (Frankfurt am Main: S. Fischer Verlag, 2017).

18. Hermann Kurzke rightly points to a structural similarity between "Brother Hitler" and Nietzsche's essay "The Case of Wagner." Having earlier (in *The Birth of Tragedy*) diagnosed a fundamental parallel between philosophy and Wagnerian spectacle, Nietzsche in this later essay sought to wean philosophy from the Wagnerian influence and open the way toward a healthier future. "'Bruder' Hitler. Thomas Mann und das Dritte Reich," *Schopenhauer-Jahrbuch* 71 (1990): 125–35.

19. On Thomas Mann at the microphone, see Donald Prater, *Thomas Mann: A Life* (New York: Oxford University Press, 1995), 47.

20. Jochen Hieber, "Der audiovisuelle Urknall unserer Literatur: Thomas Mann im Tonfilm, " *Frankfurter Allgemeine Zeitung*, September 20, 2014, http://www.faz.net/-hp7-7trqj.

21. Detailed information about Thomas Mann's lecture tours can be found in Hans Wißkirchen, "Gegen Hitler: Thomas Manns mediale Strategien auf dem Weg zum Repräsentanten des anderen Deutschland," *Thomas Mann Jahrbuch* 23 (2011): 77–90, and Vaget, *Thomas Mann, der Amerikaner*, 219–66.

22. Harold Ross, "From Captain to Private," *New Yorker*, October 17, 1942, 17.

23. The estimate of Mann's royalties is taken from Childs, "Thomas Mann," 75.

24. "Authors to the Road," *Time*, December 27, 1937, 49.

25. For a cease-and-desist letter by Knopf addressed to Chicago-area booksellers who were carrying pirated lecture transcripts, see Koshland Files, box 4, folder 5, HRC. The same archive also contains an inquiry by a representative of the Hollywood producer Harold Hurley, who wanted to print fifty thousand copies of one of Mann's lectures at his own expense. George Oppenheimer to Alfred A. Knopf, April 12, 1939, Koshland Files, box 2, folder 6, HRC.

26. Childs, "Thomas Mann," 76. On the endorsement by Eleanor Roosevelt, see Ines Robb, "Mrs. Roosevelt Holds Peace Hope," *Cleveland Plain Dealer*, September 28, 1939, 8.

27. Quoted in Donald M. Scott, "The Popular Lecture and the Creation of a Public in Mid-Nineteenth-Century America," *Journal of American History* 66, no. 4 (1980): 791.

28. Jan Loomis, *Pacific Palisades* (Charleston, SC: Arcadia Publishing, 2009), 8.

29. Erika Mann, "Lecturer's Lot," *Liberty Magazine*, March 24, 1945, 24.

30. Erika Mann, 62.

31. Scott, "Popular Lecture," 795.

32. "Bikes for Bookman," *Cleveland Plain Dealer*, May 1, 1938, 32-A.

33. See, e.g., "Big Audience Hears Lecture of Dr. Mann," *Seattle Daily Times*, March 30, 1939, 27.

34. Charles Poore, "Books of the Times," *New York Times*, July 2, 1939, 11.

35. Scott, "Popular Lecture," 808.

36. Charlotte M. Canning, *The Most American Thing in America: Circuit Chautauqua as Performance* (Iowa City: University of Iowa Press, 2007), 21.

37. Tom F. Wright, "Introduction," in *The Cosmopolitan Lyceum: Lecture Culture and the Globe in Nineteenth-Century America*, ed. Tom F. Wright (Amherst: University of Massachusetts Press, 2013), 2.

38. Promotional brochure quoted in Canning, *Most American Thing*, 16.

39. See, e.g., the report in the *Chicago Tribune* of March 16, 1939, quoted in John Franklin White, *Thomas Mann in America: The Rhetorical and Political Experiences of an Exiled Artist* (Ann Arbor: University of Michigan Doctoral Dissertation Series, 1971), 277.

40. This printed essay should not be confused with the lecture, also called "The War and the Future," that Mann delivered in October of 1943 at the Library of Congress, which was later published in the *Atlantic Monthly* as "What Is German?"

41. "20,000 in Garden Cheer for Czechs," *New York Times*, September 26, 1938, 4.

42. Newsreel footage of the German American Bund rally in Madison Square Garden can be found in Emily Buder, "When 20,000 American Nazis Descended upon New York City," *Atlantic*, October 10, 2017, https://www.theatlantic.com/video/index/542499/marshall-curry-nazi-rally-madison-square-garden-1939/.

43. The first academic studies on these enemies of liberalism appeared even before the Second World War. See, e.g., Alfred McClung Lee and Elizabeth Briant Lee, *The Fine Art of Propaganda: A Study of Father Coughlin's Speeches* (New York: Institute for Propaganda Analysis, 1939). Probably the most influential work on this topic was written by two German émigrés: Leo Löwenthal and Norbert Guterman, *Prophets of Deceit: A Study of the Techniques of the American Agitator* (New York: Harper and Brothers, 1949).

44. Quoted in White, *Thomas Mann in America*, 296.

45. Quoted in White, 235.

46. Bruno Frank, untitled lecture script, n.d., Edward G. Robinson collection, box 29, folder 30, USC.

47. Gladys Lloyd Robinson, "Thomas Mann in Hollywood," *Script*, April 9, 1938, 6.

48. Christine Ann Colgan, "Warner Brothers' Crusade against the Third Reich: A Study of Anti-Nazi Activism and Film Production, 1933 to 1941" (PhD diss., University of Southern California, 1985), 225–27.

49. The fact that these names have been recovered from obscurity for Thomas Mann studies is largely the accomplishment of Hans Rudolf Vaget. On Mann and Erich Kahler, see "Erich Kahler, Thomas Mann und Deutschland: Eine Miszelle zum *Doktor Faustus*," in *Ethik und Ästhetik: Werke und Werte in der Literatur vom 18. Bis zum 20. Jahrhundert*, ed. Richard Fisher (Frankfurt am Main: Peter Lang, 1995), 509–18, and *Thomas Mann, der Amerikaner*, 447–58. On Mann and Peter Viereck, see *Thomas Mann, der Amerikaner*, 338–41. This volume also briefly treats Borgese's intellectual relationship to Thomas Mann (271–74). For a more extensive examination, see Giovanni di Stefano, "'Italienische Optik, furios behauptet': Giuseppe Antonio Borgese—der schwierige Schwiegersohn," *Thomas Mann Jahrbuch* 8 (1995)· 139–165. On Mann and Rauschning, see Hoffschulte, *"Deutsche Hörer!,"* 89–90.

50. Hermann Rauschning, *The Revolution of Nihilism*, trans. E. W. Dickes (New York: Alliance Book Corporation, 1939), vii.

51. Peter Viereck, *Metapolitics: From the Romantics to Hitler* (New York: Alfred A. Knopf, 1941), 5.

52. Erich Kahler, *Der Deutsche Charakter in der Geschichte Europas* (Zurich: Europa-Verlag, 1937), 9.

53. Rauschning, *Revolution of Nihilism*, xii; Giuseppe Antonio Borgese, *Goliath: The March of Fascism* (Kirkwood, NY: Vail-Ballou Press, 1937), 3.

54. On this point, see especially Hans Rudolf Vaget, "Deutsche Einheit und Nationale Identität: Zur Genealogie der gegenwärtigen Deutschland-Debatte am Beispiel von Thomas Mann," *Literaturwissenschaftliches Jahrbuch der Görres-Gesellschaft* 33 (1992): 277–98.

55. Mark Greif, *The Age of the Crisis of Man: Thought and Fiction in America, 1933–1973* (Princeton, NJ: Princeton University Press, 2015), 33–34 (on Rauschning), 45–46 (on Kahler).

56. On the "responsible liberalism" label, see Richard Wightman Fox, "Tragedy, Responsibility, and the American Intellectual, 1925–1950," in *Lewis Mumford: Public Intellectual*, ed. Thomas P. Hughes and Agatha C. Hughes (New York: Oxford University Press, 1990), 323–37.

57. The quotation is from Lewis Mumford's treatment of *The Magic Mountain* in *The Condition of Man*, excerpted as *"The Magic Mountain,"* in *The Stature of Thomas Mann*, ed. Charles Neider (New York: New Directions, 1947), 150–55. Niebuhr's review of *Order of the Day* is mentioned in the previous chapter; I touch on MacLeish's remarks about Mann below and on Waldo Frank's review of *Joseph the Provider* in the fourth literary interlude in this book.

58. Their arguments for a self-assertive democracy that would engage openly with fascism and totalitarianism, as well as their willingness to enlist in government service, brings the responsible liberals into close proximity to a number of other intellectuals of the time, whom the émigré legal scholar Karl Loewenstein (another

close friend of Thomas Mann's) subsumed under the name "militant democrats." What distinguished the responsible liberals from the militant democrats, however, was their focus on a tragic view of life and on aesthetics as an important medium of self-expression. By contrast, most of the militant democrats were technocrats. The distinction between the two groups resulted in diametrically opposed paths during the Cold War. On militant democracy in general and on Loewenstein in particular, see Udi Greenberg, *The Weimar Century: German Émigrés and the Ideological Foundations of the Cold War* (Princeton, NJ: Princeton University Press, 2014), 169–210, as well as Daniel Bessner and Udi Greenberg "The Weimar Analogy," *Jacobin*, December 17, 2016, https://www.jacobinmag.com/2016/12/trump-hitler-germany-fascism-weimar-democracy/.

59. Archibald MacLeish, "The Irresponsibles," in *A Time to Speak: The Selected Prose of Archibald MacLeish* (Boston: Houghton Mifflin, 1941), 103.

60. Lewis Mumford, *My Works and Days: A Personal Chronicle* (New York: Harcourt Brace Jovanovic, 1979), 391.

61. For a reading of the declaration as a conservative document, see Adi Gordon and Udi Greenberg, "*The City of Man*, European Émigrés, and the Genesis of Postwar Conservative Thought," *Religions* 3 (2012): 681–98. For a reading of it as a liberal document, see Paul Michael Lützeler, "Visionaries in Exile: Broch's Cooperation with G. A. Borgese and Hannah Arendt," in *Hermann Broch: Visionary in Exile: The 2001 Yale Symposium*, ed. Paul Michael Lützeler (Rochester, NY: Camden House, 2003), 67–88.

62. Herbert Agar, Frank Aydelotte, G. A. Borgese, et. al., *The City of Man: A Declaration on World Democracy* (New York: Viking Press, 1941), 30.

63. Agar, Aydelotte, Borgese, et. al., 17–18.

64. Agar, Aydelotte, Borgese, et. al., 60.

65. On the drama surrounding the confirmation hearings, see Scott Donaldson, *Archibald MacLeish: An American Life* (Boston: Houghton Mifflin, 1992), 290–301.

66. There are multiple accounts of Putnam's time as a librarian, the most comprehensive of which is Jane Rosenberg, *The Nation's Great Library: Herbert Putnam and the Library of Congress* (Champaign: University of Illinois Press, 1993).

67. Donaldson, *Archibald MacLeish*, 319.

68. Lucy Salamanca, *Fortress of Freedom: The Story of the Library of Congress* (Philadelphia: J. B. Lippincott, 1942).

69. MacLeish fully articulated this vision in an internal memo, "Objectives of the Library of Congress," published in David C. Mearns, *The Story up to Now: The Library of Congress, 1800–1946* (Washington, DC: Library of Congress, 1947), 211–13.

70. Archibald MacLeish, "Foreword," in Salamanca, *Fortress of Freedom*, 11.

71. Archibald MacLeish, "Libraries in the Contemporary Crisis," in *A Time to Speak*, 122–23.

72. Archibald MacLeish, "The Librarian and the Democratic Process," in *A Time to Speak*, 145.

73. Dorothy Canfield Fisher to Archibald MacLeish, December 1, 1939, Archibald MacLeish Papers, Dorothy Canfield Fisher folder, LOC.

74. Luther H. Evans to H. H. Fisher, September 18, 1945, Central File, box 771, folder Fellows 1, LOC.

75. Donaldson, *Archibald MacLeish*, 327.

76. The correspondence pertaining to these searches can be found scattered throughout the Central File, boxes 18, 770, 771, LOC.

77. "Fellowship Programs of the Library of Congress," May 17, 1944, Central File, box 770, folder 7.1, LOC.

78. Detailed information on Mann's employment at the library can be found in Kurt S. Maier, "A Fellowship in German Literature: Thomas Mann, Agnes Meyer, and Archibald MacLeish," *Quarterly Journal of the Library of Congress* 36, no. 4 (Fall 1979): 385–400.

79. On rumors in the press and the embarrassment they caused both Mann and MacLeish, see Maier, 390.

Interlude III

1. For two examples of these opposing critical tendencies, see Herbert Lehnert, "Thomas Manns Erzählung 'Das Gesetz' und andere erzählerische Nachspiele im Rahmen des Gesamtwerkes," *Deutsche Vierteljahresschrift* 43 (1969): 515–43, and Fredrick A. Lubich, " 'Fascinating Fascism': Thomas Manns 'Das Gesetz' und seine Selbst-de-Montage als Moses-Hitler," *German Studies Review* 14, no. 3 (1991): 553–73.

2. Quoted in Kurt S. Maier, "A Fellowship in German Literature: Thomas Mann, Agnes Meyer, and Archibald MacLeish," *Quarterly Journal of the Library of Congress* 36, no. 4 (Fall 1979): 391.

3. Hermann Rauschning, "Preface: A Conversation with Hitler," in *The Ten Commandments: Ten Short Novels of Hitler's War against the Moral Code*, ed. Arnim L. Robinson (New York: Simon and Schuster, 1943), xiii. Nowadays, most historians regard Rauschning's Hitler quotes as fakes.

4. "Briefly Noted: *The Ten Commandments*," *New Yorker*, January 1, 1944, 59.

5. Hans Rudolf Vaget, *Thomas Mann: Kommentar zu sämtlichen Erzählungen* (Munich: Winkler, 1984), 275.

6. For an overview of this literary tradition, see, among other available sources, Theodore Ziolkowski, *Uses and Abuses of Moses: Literary Representations since the Enlightenment* (Notre Dame, IN: University of Notre Dame Press, 2016).

7. See Herbert Robinson Marbury, *Pillars of Cloud and Fire: The Politics of Exodus in African American Biblical Interpretation* (New York: NYU Press, 2015).

8. Zora Neale Hurston, *Moses, Man of the Mountain* (New York: Lippincott, 1939), xxi-xxii. Capitalization in original.

9. Hurston, 1.

10. See, e.g., the contemporary review by Dorothy Donnelly, "Pulling the Lion's Teeth," *Commonweal*, September 7, 1945, 503–4.

11. Barbara Johnson, *Moses and Multiculturalism* (Berkeley: University of California Press, 2010).

12. For a detailed exploration of Mann's scriptural studies and the ways in which his narrative innovations play with the theological knowledge of his time, see Käte Hamburger, *Thomas Mann: "Das Gesetz"* (Frankfurt am Main: Ullstein, 1964), 58–112.

13. Further context for this quote is given by Jan Assmann, "Mose gegen Hitler: Die Zehn Gebote als antifaschistisches Manifest," *Thomas Mann Jahrbuch* 28 (2015): 47–61.

5. A Blooming Flower

Langston Hughes, "Madrid's Flowers Hoist Blooms to Meet Raining Fascist Bombs," *Baltimore Afro-American*, November 27, 1937, 1.

K. H., "Bücher in dieser Zeit. Gespräch mit Gottfried Bermann Fischer," *Der Aufbau*, December 20, 1940, 7.

1. United States Holocaust Museum, "Fighting the Fires of Hate: America and the Nazi Book Burnings," accessed March 20, 2019, https://www.ushmm.org/exhibition/book-burning/burning.php.

2. Stephen Vincent Benét, "They Burned the Books," *Saturday Review of Literature*, May 8, 1943, 4–5.

3. "2,000 Writers Assist in Winning the War," *New York Times*, January 9, 1943, 11.

4. Quoted in Matthew Fishburn, *Burning Books* (New York: Palgrave Macmillan, 2008), 107. For more on the Council on Books in Wartime, see John B. Hench, *Books as Weapons: Propaganda, Publishing, and the Battle for Global Markets in the Era of World War II* (Ithaca, NY: Cornell University Press, 2010).

5. The enormous reach of these addresses, rarely discussed in the critical literature, is pointed out in Sonja Valentin, *"Steine in Hitlers Fenster": Thomas Manns Radiosendungen "Deutsche Hörer!" 1940–1945* (Göttingen: Wallstein Verlag, 2015), 263n20.

6. The following summary of Thomas Mann's cooperation with the BBC is derived primarily from the detailed reports by J. F. Slattery in "Thomas Mann und die B.B.C.: Die Bedingungen ihrer Zusammenarbeit 1940–1945," *Thomas Mann Jahrbuch* 5 (1992): 142–170, and "Erika Mann und die BBC 1940–1943," *Thomas Mann Jahrbuch* 12 (1999): 309–47.

7. Erika Mann, unpublished letter to Patrick S. Smith, quoted in Slattery, "Erika Mann und die BBC," 314.

8. Conrad Pütter, *Rundfunk gegen das "Dritte Reich": Ein Handbuch* (Munich: KG Saur, 1986), 94.

9. BBC transmissions were initially via shortwave radio, which would have penetrated farther into Europe. Since the most common German radio set, the *Volksempfänger*, lacked a shortwave receiver and could often only be tuned to Nazi-approved stations, the BBC added medium-wave and long-wave transmitters starting in 1943. BBC broadcasts often also included instructions on how to modify radio sets to enable shortwave reception. For more on the technical background, see Bernhard Wittek, *Der britische Ätherkrieg gegen das Dritte Reich: Die deutschsprachigen Kriegssendungen der British Broadcasting Corporation* (Münster: Verlag C. J. Fahle, 1962).

10. Lindley M. Fraser, unpublished manuscript for talk delivered at the Royal Institute of International Affairs, London, October 1, 1942, quoted in J. F. Slattery, "'Oskar Zuversichtlich': A German Response to British Radio Propaganda during World War II," *Historical Journal of Film, Radio and Television* 12, no. 1 (1992): 69–85.

11. Reinhold Niebuhr, "Mann Speaks to Germany," *Nation*, February 13, 1943, 244.

12. Bernd Hamacher, "Die Poesie im Krieg: Thomas Manns Radiosendungen *Deutsche Hörer!* als Ernstfall der Literatur," *Thomas Mann Jahrbuch* 13 (2000): 66–74. See also the supplemental remarks in Bernd Hamacher, "Thomas Manns Medientheologie: Medien und Masken," in *Autorinszenierungen: Autorschaft und Literarisches Werk im Kontext der Medien*, ed. Christine Künzel and Jörg Schönert (Würzburg: Königshausen & Neumann, 2007), 75–77.

13. Melissa Dinsman, *Modernism at the Microphone: Radio, Propaganda, and Literary Aesthetics during World War II* (London: Bloomsbury Academic, 2015), 154–65.

14. One year prior to this, Knopf had used the same image for the dust jacket of *Order of the Day*, the collection of Mann's political essays and lecture transcripts. The floating heads might therefore also be read as a nod toward the three cities and regions to which he returned more than any others on his journeys as the "itinerant lecturer of democracy": New York, the upper Midwest, and Los Angeles.

15. Erika Mann, unpublished telegram to Thomas Mann, July 11, 1941, quoted in Slattery, "Thomas Mann und die B.B.C.," 162.

16. Cyril Conner, unpublished memo to Leonard Miall, July 11, 1941, quoted in Slattery, "Thomas Mann und die B.B.C.," 162.

17. Edward Tangye Lean, unpublished memo to the European Programmes Executive, quoted in Slattery, "Thomas Mann und die B.B.C.," 152.

18. Joseph Goebbels, *Die Tagebücher von Joseph Goebbels* (Munich: Institut für Zeitgeschichte, 2013).

19. Quoted in Winfrid Halder, *Exilrufe nach Deutschland: Die Rundfunkreden von Thomas Mann, Paul Tillich und Johannes R. Becher 1940–1945* (Berlin: LIT-Verlag, 2002), 304.

20. Pütter, *Rundfunk gegen das "Dritte Reich,"* 95.

21. See the discussion of testimony by the resistance fighter Robert Mohren (303) and of the social democratic paper-in-exile the *New Leader* (306) in Valentin, *Steine in Hitlers Fenster*.

22. See the documents collected by Martina Hoffschulte, *"Deutsche Hörer!" Thomas Manns Rundfunkreden (1940 bis 1945) im Werkkontext* (Münster: Telos Verlag, 2003), 362.

23. Heinz Gittik, *Illegale Antifaschistische Tarnschriften 1933–1945* (Frankfurt am Main: Röderberg Verlag, 1971), 15. The same volume also contains a bibliography of all known *Tarnschriften*, including those by Thomas Mann.

24. That said, on at least one occasion a critical essay devoting sustained attention to Thomas Mann was smuggled into the Reich in tomato seed packages. Gustav Regler, "Der letzte Appell," *Tarnschriften*, Rare Book Collection, box 1, NYPL.

25. For a detailed discussion of Musil's notion of the *Großschriftsteller* and its applicability to Thomas Mann, see Michael Ansel, Hans-Edwin Friedrich, and Gerhard Lauer, "Hybride Repräsentanz: Zu den Bedingungen einer Erfindung," in *Die Erfindung des Schriftstellers Thomas Mann*, ed. Michael Ansel, Hans-Edwin Friedrich, and Gerhard Lauer (Berlin: Walter de Gruyter, 2009), 1–3.

26. All biographical details are adapted from Gottfried Bermann Fischer, *Bedroht—Bewahrt: Weg eines Verlegers* (Frankfurt am Main: S. Fischer Verlag, 1967); Gottfried Bermann Fischer, *Wanderer durch ein Jahrhundert* (Frankfurt am Main: S. Fischer Verlag, 1994); and Brigitte Bermann Fischer, *My European Heritage: Life among Great Men of Letters*, trans. Harry Zohn (Boston: Branden, 1987).

27. Bermann Fischer, *Wanderer*, 98. The chronology here is contested. As Volker Dahm points out, the *AG für Verlagsrechte* wasn't fully incorporated until 1936. *Das jüdische Buch im Dritten Reich* (Munich: C. H. Beck, 1993), 135.

28. A full account of the process by which authors' intellectual property was saved from the hands of the Nazis is given in Irene Nawrocka, "Verlagssitz: Wien,

Stockholm, New York, Amsterdam. Der Bermann-Fischer Verlag im Exil (1933–1950)," *Archiv für Geschichte des Buchwesens* 53 (2000): 71–81.

29. By government decree, Suhrkamp was forced to change the name of the new company to "Suhrkamp Publishing House, Formerly S. Fischer" in 1942, and to just "Suhrkamp Publishing House" in 1943.

30. The exact modalities of this transaction are traced in Nawrocka, "Verlagssitz," 31–46.

31. Bermann Fischer, *Bedroht—Bewahrt*, 122.

32. Bermann Fischer, 132.

33. Nawrocka, "Verlagssitz," 115.

34. Technically speaking, it would be more correct to say that Bonnier purchased the Bermann-Fischer Verlag outright, since he bought 51 percent of the stocks in a Swedish holding company, the Aktiebolag, and then hired Bermann Fischer as an executive director. However, Bonnier never interfered with any editorial or business decisions by his German associate, except insofar as to have him sign a contract that forbade Bermann Fischer to start additional publishing houses dealing with German literature. Nawrocka, "Verlagssitz," 88.

35. Bermann Fischer, *Wanderer*, 240.

36. Bermann Fischer, *Bedroht-Bewahrt*, 165.

37. On Italy, Hungary, and Romania as markets for Bermann Fischer, see Nawrocka, "Verlagssitz," 167.

38. Nawrocka, 111.

39. Quoted in Robert E. Cazden, *German Exile Literature in America, 1933–1950: A History of the Free German Press and Book Trade* (Chicago: American Library Association, 1970), 93.

40. He also founded the English-language L. B. Fischer Publishing Corporation, which issued, among many other titles, Erika Mann's *A Gang of Ten* and Klaus Mann's *The Turning Point* (both 1942). It never published any books by Thomas Mann, since Alfred A. Knopf held the exclusive rights to Mann's American editions.

41. These scenarios are reconstructed following information given in Nawrocka, "Verlagssitz," 110–18.

42. Cazden offers an earlier, though less complete, account of this story. *German Exile Literature*, 99–100.

43. Hench, *Books as Weapons*, 198–99.

44. This fact would have been especially apparent in the years between 1938 and 1940, when there were two Bermann-Fischer publishing houses: the one in Stockholm that was actually run by the eponymous publisher, and the one in Vienna, which the Nazis had seized and which they now used to sell off the remaining physical inventory that Bermann Fischer had been able to take with him to Austria. For more on this, see Nawrocka, "Verlagssitz," 92.

45. John William Tebbel, *A History of Book Publishing in the United States*, vol. 3, *The Golden Age between Two Wars, 1920–1940* (New York: R. R. Bowker, 1978), 7. The paperback was introduced to Great Britain two years earlier, by Penguin Books.

46. Rebecca West, "Books for Liberated Europe," *English-Speaking World: Journal of the English-Speaking Union* 26 (December 1943–January 1944): 4. John B. Hench analyzes this remarkable essay at great length from the point of view of publishing competition between the United States and Britain. As he notes, US authorities are

likely to have paid close attention to West's remarks, which were excerpted at length in *Publisher's Weekly*. *Books as Weapons*, 76.

47. Bermann Fischer, *Bedroht—Bewahrt*, 202.

48. Bermann Fischer, 278–80.

49. See, e.g., Paul Michael Lützeler, *Die Schriftsteller und Europa: Von der Romantik bis zur Gegenwart* (Baden-Baden: Nomos, 1998), and Hans Rudolf Vaget, "Deutsche Einheit und Nationale Identität: Zur Genealogie der gegenwärtigen Deutschland-Debatte am Beispiel von Thomas Mann," *Literaturwissenschaftliches Jahrbuch der Görres-Gesellschaft* 33 (1992): 277–98.

50. Johann Wolfgang von Goethe, *Conversations with Eckermann (1823–1832)*, trans. John Oxenford (San Francisco: North Point, 1984), 132.

51. Mann also invokes the Goethean notion of world literature directly in "The Problem of Freedom," an address he delivered in 1939 to International PEN in Stockholm (*GW*, 11:955).

52. Johann Wolfgang von Goethe and Friedrich Schiller, "Das deutsche Reich," in Johann Wolfgang von Goethe, *Werke*, 143 vols. (Weimar: 1897–1919), I, 5.1:218.

Interlude IV

1. Hans Rudolf Vaget, *Thomas Mann, der Amerikaner: Leben und Werk im amerikanischen Exil 1938–1952* (Frankfurt am Main: S. Fischer Verlag, 2011), 151.

2. A detailed summary of Joseph's various administrative measures that also compares formulations from the novels with ones drawn from Roosevelt's speeches can be found in John-Thomas Siehoff, "Josephs 'New Deal': Franklin Delano Roosevelts Politik in Thomas Manns *Joseph der Ernährer*," *New German Review* 11 (1995): 74–88.

3. Ehrhard Bahr, "Exil als 'beschädigtes Leben': Thomas Mann und sein Roman *Joseph, der Ernährer*," in *Exilerfahrung und Konstruktionen von Identität, 1933 bis 1945*, ed. Hans Otto Horch and Hanni Mittelmann (Berlin: Walter de Gruyter, 2013), 245–55.

4. Hamilton Basso, "Tonio Kröger in Egyptian Dress," *New Yorker*, July 22, 1944, 53.

5. The rumor about Edmund Wilson turning down the chance to review Mann's novel is related in Charles Neider, "Thomas Mann's Joseph Myth," *New Mexico Quarterly* 14, no. 3 (1944): 286.

6. Basso, "Tonio Kröger in Egyptian Dress," 53.

7. William Phillips, "The One and the Many," *Nation*, July 22, 1944, 47.

8. "Masterpiece," *Time*, July 3, 1944, 90.

9. Fredric Jameson, "Allegory and History: On Rereading Doctor Faustus," in *The Modernist Papers* (London: Verso, 2007), 113.

6. The Loyal American Subject

Otto Flake, "Der Fall Thomas Mann," *Badener Tageblatt*, December 8, 1945, reprinted in *Die große Kontroverse: Ein Briefwechsel um Deutschland*, ed. Johannes F. G. Grosser (Hamburg: Nagel, 1963), 53.

Quoted in John Franklin White, *Thomas Mann in America: The Rhetorical and Political Experiences of an Exiled Artist* (Ann Arbor: University of Michigan Doctoral Dissertation Series, 1971), 108.

1. Hans Magnus Enzensberger, "Mann, Kafka, and the Katzenjammer Kids," *New York Times Book Review*, November 17, 1985, 37.

2. A complete listing of ASE titles can be found in Molly Guptill Manning, *When Books Went to War: The Stories That Helped Us Win World War II* (Boston: Houghton Mifflin Harcourt, 2014), 202–32.

3. For a full account of the operations of the Psychological Warfare Division of the Supreme Headquarters Allied Expeditionary Force, see John B. Hench, *Books as Weapons: Propaganda, Publishing, and the Battle for Global Markets in the Era of World War II* (Ithaca, NY: Cornell University Press, 2010), 151–77.

4. My account in the following paragraphs is greatly indebted to Leonore Krenzlin, "Geschichte des Scheiterns—Geschichte des Lernens? Überlegungen zur Lage während und nach der 'Großen Kontroverse' und zur Motivation ihrer Akteure," in *Fremdes Heimatland: Remigration und literarisches Leben nach 1945*, ed. Irmela von der Lühe and Claus-Dieter Krohn (Göttingen: Wallstein Verlag, 2005), 57–70.

5. Frank Thieß, "Die innere Emigration," in *Die grosse Kontroverse: Ein Briefwechsel um Deutschland*, ed. J. F. G. Grosser (Hamburg: Nagel Verlag, 1963), 24.

6. Krenzlin, "Geschichte des Scheiterns," 60. Her metaphor is clearly not an exaggeration. On Bermann Fischer's methodical efforts—begun as early as late 1943 and propelled by capital infusions from his Swedish publishing partner, Tor Bonnier—to prepare for the postwar German market, see Irene Nawrocka, "Verlagssitz: Wien, Stockholm, New York, Amsterdam. Der Bermann-Fischer Verlag im Exil (1933–1950)," *Archiv für Geschichte des Buchwesens* 53 (2000): 161, 169–70.

7. In her autobiographical reflections, Helen Tracy Lowe-Porter would later call these Thieß novels "mediocre" works that she "did not in the least want to translate at all." Since these remarks were made after the Great Controversy, however, it is not clear whether they reflect her actual opinions of the 1920s. "On Translating Thomas Mann," in *In Another Language: A Record of the Thirty-Year Relationship between Thomas Mann and His English Translator, Helen Tracy Lowe-Porter*, ed. John C. Thirlwall (New York: Alfred A. Knopf, 1966), 188.

8. Leo Lania, "Time Out from Terror," *Saturday Review of Literature*, July 26, 1947, 29.

9. Jost Hermand and Wigand Lange, eds., *"Wollt ihr Thomas Mann wiederhaben?" Deutschland und die Emigranten* (Hamburg: Europäische Verlagsanstalt, 1999).

10. Hans Rudolf Vaget, *Thomas Mann, der Amerikaner: Leben und Werk im amerikanischen Exil 1938–1952* (Frankfurt am Main: S. Fischer Verlag, 2011), 495–502.

11. For a detailed treatment of American involvement with German newspapers in the months following the war, see Harold Hurwitz, *Die Stunde Null der Deutschen Presse* (Cologne: Verlag Wissenschaft und Politik, 1972).

12. This, at any rate, is the conclusion reached by Krenzlin. "Geschichte des Scheiterns," 63. For further details on Hans Habe's involvement with the Great Controversy, see his autobiography, *Ich stelle mich: Meine Lebensgeschichte* (Vienna: Desch, 1955).

13. Two recent works that deal with the lecture at length are Vaget, *Thomas Mann, der Amerikaner*, 464–78, and Manfred Görtemaker, *Thomas Mann und die Politik* (Frankfurt am Main: S. Fischer Verlag, 2005), 161–75.

14. For more context on the rivalry between Brecht and Mann, see Helmut Koopmann, "Bertolt Brecht und Thomas Mann: Eine repräsentative Gegnerschaft," *Heinrich-Mann-Jahrbuch* 13 (1995): 101–26.

15. For a list of POW camps in America and an analysis of the number of prisoners, see Arnold Krammer, *Nazi Prisoners of War in America* (New York: Stein & Day, 1979), 268–72.

16. Ron Robin, *The Barbed-Wire College: Reeducating German POWs in the United States during World War II* (Princeton, NJ: Princeton University Press, 1995), 18–22. A concise summary of the circumstances leading to the military's cooperation with Gottfried Bermann Fischer can also be found in Hench, *Books as Weapons*, 115–21.

17. Krammer, *Nazi Prisoners of War*, 194.

18. Robin, *Barbed-Wire College*, 92.

19. The exact print run of the New World Bookshelf is difficult to determine. The figure of fifty thousand copies each derives from the recollections of Curt Vinz, a German POW who was involved in the production of the series. Bermann Fischer himself speaks only of an initial print run of ten thousand copies each, followed by a second print run of fifteen thousand copies each. Friedrich Pfäfflin and Ingrid Kussmaul, *S. Fischer, Verlag: Von der Gründung bis zur Rückkehr aus dem Exil* (Stuttgart: Deutsche Schillergesellschaft, 1985), 619. The only volume in the series for which rights were not provided by Bermann Fischer was the first, Stephen Vincent Benét's *Amerika*, which had been commissioned specially for the occasion by the Office of War Information.

20. Gottfried Bermann Fischer, *Bedroht—Bewahrt: Weg eines Verlegers* (Frankfurt am Main: S. Fischer Verlag, 1967), 241.

21. Howard Mumford Jones, "Writers and American Values," *New York Times Book Review*, August 5, 1945, 2. For more on Jones and his contributions to the SPD, see Robin, *Barbed-Wire College*, 97–98.

22. Howard Mumford Jones, "Patriotism—But How?," *Atlantic Monthly*, November 1938, 585–92.

23. Quoted in Hench, *Books as Weapons*, 122–23. For more on the OPMG's justifications of its selections, see also Robin, *Barbed-Wire College*, 99–105.

24. Quoted in Robin, *Barbed-Wire College*, 105.

25. B. Venkat Mani, *Recoding World Literature: Libraries, Print Culture, and Germany's Pact with Books* (New York: Fordham University Press, 2017), 10.

26. Wolfgang Hildebrandt, "Zauberberg und Kriegsgefangenschaft: Offener Brief an Thomas Mann," *Der Ruf*, October 1, 1945, 4.

27. Hildebrandt, 4.

28. For a comprehensive treatment of the "Idea Factory," and of its leader Captain Walter Schoenstedt, see Robin, *Barbed-Wire College*, 59–68.

29. For more on this connection, see Aaron D. Horton, *German POWs, "Der Ruf," and the Genesis of Group 47: The Political Journey of Alfred Andersch and Hans Werner Richter* (Madison, NJ: Fairleigh Dickinson University Press, 2014).

30. Horton, 47.

31. Alfred Andersch, "Thomas Mann," *Der Ruf*, July 1, 1945, 4. I am freely adapting the translation of this passage in Horton, *German POWs*, 69.

32. Robert O. Ballou, *A History of the Council on Books in Wartime, 1942–1946* (New York: Country Life Press, 1946), 5. See also Hench, *Books as Weapons*, 45–50.

33. Lewis Gannett, "Books," in *While You Were Gone: A Report on Wartime Life in the United States* (New York: Simon & Schuster, 1946), 460, quoted in Hench, *Books as Weapons*, 52.

34. For the history of the campaign and other early attempts to get books to the troops, see Guptill Manning, *When Books Went to War*, 24–58.

35. On the history of the Armed Services Editions, see principally John Y. Cole, ed. *Books in Action: The Armed Services Editions* (Washington, DC: Library of Congress, 1984), as well as Hench, *Books as Weapons*, 51–54.

36. Quoted in Yoni Appelbaum, "Publishers Gave Away 122,951,031 Books during World War II," *Atlantic*, September 10, 2014, https://www.theatlantic.com/business/archive/2014/09/publishers-gave-away-122951031-books-during-world-war-ii/379893/.

37. "Army and Navy Contracts," 1944, Council on Books in Wartime Records, box 29, PUA.

38. See, e.g., the letters by Private N. Miller, January 29, 1945, Corporal Arno Gruen, February 1945, and Private Carl Aimone, May 30, 1946, Council on Books in Wartime Records, box 31, PUA.

39. Quoted in George Hutchinson, *Facing the Abyss: American Literature and Culture in the 1940s* (New York: Columbia University Press, 2018), 23.

40. Martin Meyer, "American Literature in Germany and Its Reception in the Political Context of the Postwar Years," trans. Sally E. Robertson, in *The United States and Germany in the Era of the Cold War: A Handbook*, vol. 1, *1945–1968*, ed. Detlef Junker (Cambridge: Cambridge University Press, 2004), 426.

41. Gottfried Bermann Fischer, "Zueignung zum 6. Juni 1945," in "Thomas Mann," special issue, *Neue Rundschau*, June 6, 1945, 1.

42. Bermann-Fischer, *Bedroht—Bewahrt*, 295.

43. The English translation is taken from *BR*, 330. The version that was circulated in 1946 introduces several minor grammatical and lexical changes to Mann's original (*GKFA*, 9.1:327) that do not, however, significantly affect the translation.

44. The main relay stops of this literary transmission are summarized in Hans H. Bockwitz, "Ein Goethegespräch," *Der Zwiebelfisch: Zeitschrift über Bücher, Kunst und Kultur* 25, no. 7 (1947): 14–15.

45. Gerhard Alexander, "Geschichte einer Mystifikation," *Hamburger Akademische Rundschau* 1, no. 4 (1946/47): 148–49.

46. Hans-J. Weitz, ed., *Johann Wolfgang von Goethe: Die Deutschen* (Konstanz: Südverlag, 1949). The editor's postscript to this collection confirms that the volume was inspired by the Goethe hoax.

47. *Trial of the Major War Criminals before the International Military Tribunal, Nuremberg, 14 November 1945–1 October 1946* (Nuremberg: International Military Tribunal, 1947), 29:527.

48. *Trial of the Major War Criminals*, 29:528.

Interlude V

1. Clifton Fadiman, "*Doctor Faustus*: A Profound Novel by Thomas Mann, Nobel Prize Winner and Perhaps the Age's Greatest Writer," *Book-of-the-Month Club News*, October 1948, 4; Claude Hill, "Mirror of the German Soul: Thomas Mann Closes an Account," *Saturday Review of Literature*, October 30, 1948, 11.

2. Hamilton Basso, "A New Deal with the Old Nick," *New Yorker*, October 30, 1948, 106; Harry Levin, "Doctor Mann versus a Teutonic Mephisto," *New York Times Book Review*, October 31, 1948, 5.

3. For more on the changing literary tastes of the 1940s, see the following chapter. For an overview of Mann's vexatious relationship with Joyce, see Hans Rudolf Vaget, "Mann, Joyce, and the Question of Modernism in *Doctor Faustus*," in *Thomas Mann's "Doctor Faustus": A Novel at the Margins of Modernism*, ed. Herbert Lehnert and Peter C. Pfeiffer (Columbia, SC: Camden House, 1991), 167–92.

4. Perhaps the most successful example of such a reading is the one offered by Gunilla Bergsten, *Thomas Manns Doktor Faustus: Untersuchungen zu den Quellen und zur Struktur des Romans* (Tübingen: Max Niemeyer, 1974). Fredric Jameson's analysis in "Allegory and History: On Rereading *Doktor Faustus*" also fits into this broad pattern. *The Modernist Papers* (London: Verso, 2007), 113–36.

5. Vaget, "Mann, Joyce."

6. Rüdiger Görner, *Thomas Mann: Der Zauberer des Letzten* (Zurich: Artemis & Winkler, 2005), 9.

7. Zeitblom tells us on the opening page of the novel that he begins work on his narrative on May 27, 1943, four days after Mann himself commenced writing *Doctor Faustus*. There is good reason to believe that Mann merely got his dates confused, however, and some editions of the novel change the line to have Zeitblom start on the exact same day as his creator. See the editorial commentary by Ruprecht Wimmer and Stephan Stachorski in *GKFA*, 9.2:9–59.

8. The idea of treating Mann's *Story of a Novel* as a kind of narrative extension of *Doctor Faustus* is developed at much greater length by Luca Crescenzi in "Masken: Zu den Strategien der Selbstbiografik im *Doktor Faustus* und in der *Entstehung des Doktor Faustus*," *Thomas Mann Jahrbuch* 30 (2017): 87–98.

9. I owe this example, and the one in the following paragraph, to Herbert Lehnert's insightful analysis in his "Introduction," in Lehnert and Pfeiffer, *Thomas Mann's "Doctor Faustus,"* 9–11.

10. Greenberg speculates on medieval typology as a characteristic feature of modernist literature in his essay "The Last of the Fathers," analyzed in greater detail in the following chapter.

7. The Isolated World Citizen

Arnold Bauer, "Thomas Mann und seine Widersacher," *Der Monat* 6 (March 1949): 75.

GW, 10:398. I have been unable to verify the authenticity of the Toynbee quote. Toynbee was a frequent contributor to the *Observer*, but no article called "The Isolated World Citizen" seems to exist. The citation given in the critical apparatus of *GW* does not match the *Observer*'s own volume and page numbering scheme.

1. Quoted in Donald Prater, *Thomas Mann: A Life* (New York: Oxford University Press, 1995), 356.

2. Quoted in Hermann Kurzke, *Thomas Mann: Life as a Work of Art*, trans. Leslie Willson (Princeton, NJ: Princeton University Press, 2002), 498.

3. Quoted in Kurzke, 498, and Prater, *Thomas Mann*, 382.

4. See, e.g., "Scottsboro Protest by Russia, Germany," *Negro World*, July 11, 1931, 8, and "Goodwill Program over CBS," *New York Age*, July 24, 1943, 10. Both these articles were syndicated and appeared in African American newspapers throughout the country.

5. Mann and Hughes shared a stage at the Third American Writers' Congress in 1939 and served on the editorial board for the journal *Common Ground* in the 1940s. Hughes's admiration for the German author is documented, among other things, by the fact that when he wanted to support the young Ralph Ellison on his trajectory to becoming a writer, he did so by sending him a stack of Thomas Mann volumes. Arnold Rampersad, *Ralph Ellison: A Biography* (New York: Vintage, 2008), 91.

6. Marc. M. Moreland, "Conversation Piece," *Arkansas State Press*, January 8, 1943, 6.

7. Mann's involvement in the Eisler affair is analyzed in Hans Rudolf Vaget, *Thomas Mann, der Amerikaner: Leben und Werk im amerikanischen Exil 1938–1952* (Frankfurt am Main: S. Fischer Verlag, 2011), 376–87. I owe many of the quotes and citations in the following paragraphs to this work.

8. Thomas Mann's record with the FBI is described in Hans Rudolf Vaget, "Vorzeitiger Antifaschismus und andere unamerikanische Umtriebe," in *Horizonte: Festschrift für Herbert Lehnert, zum 65. Geburtstag*, ed. Hannelore Mundt, Egon Schwarz, and William J. Lillyman (Tübingen: Max Niemeyer Verlag, 1990), 173–204, and Alexander Stephan, *Im Visier des FBI: Deutsche Exilschriftsteller in den Akten amerikanischer Geheimdienste* (Stuttgart: Verlag J. B. Metzler, 1995), 121–27. A summary of the findings can also be found in Vaget, *Thomas Mann, der Amerikaner*, 387–411.

9. Michael Warner, "Origins of the Congress of Cultural Freedom, 1949–50," *Studies in Intelligence* 38, no. 5 (1995): 90.

10. The Waldorf Astoria conference has spawned an extensive body of scholarly literature. The most informed account is that of Michael Warner, quoted above, which draws heavily on classified government sources. However, since it was produced during Warner's tenure as an official historian for the CIA and underwent a process of redaction prior to publication, its objectivity cannot be independently verified. My own narrative here relies greatly on Frances Stonor Saunders, *Who Paid the Piper? The CIA and the Cultural Cold War* (London: Granta Books, 1999), 45–56.

11. See the letters to Algernon D. Black, Thomas Mann, and Louis I. Newman dated March 7–14, 1949, in *Letters of Sidney Hook: Democracy, Communism, and the Cold War*, ed. Edward S. Shapiro (London: Routledge, 1995), 120–25.

12. Stonor Saunders, *Who Paid the Piper?*, 50–51.

13. For the honor guard, see Prater, *Thomas Mann*, 415.

14. The US press would presumably have devoted greater attention to the actual contents of the lecture had Mann not at the very last minute struck a passage in which he speculated that Goethe, were he alive, would probably have cast his lot with the Soviet Union rather than with the United States (*E*, 6:454–55).

15. "Mann Sees Soviet Bidding for Peace," *New York Times*, May 6, 1949, 23.

16. Eugene Tillinger, "The Moral Eclipse of Thomas Mann," *Plain Talk* 4, no. 3 (December 1949): 53.

17. The Tillinger campaign and its aftereffects with the FBI are analyzed by Hans Rudolf Vaget in *Thomas Mann, der Amerikaner*, 401–9.

18. The professional journal the *German Quarterly* had already published an evaluative overview of the availability of Thomas Mann stories in various standard anthologies in 1945. Marianne Zerner, "Thomas Mann in Standard English Anthologies," *German Quarterly* 18, no. 4 (November 1945): 178–88.

19. "SRL Reader Poll: From the Subscribing Santas," *Saturday Review of Literature*, December 2, 1950, 48.

20. Erich Auerbach, "The Philology of World Literature," trans. Jane O. Newman, in *Time, History, and Literature: Selected Essays of Erich Auerbach*, ed. James I. Porter (Princeton, NJ: Princeton University Press, 2014), 253.

21. Auerbach, 253.

22. Auerbach, 254.

23. Auerbach, 254.

24. Two fairly recent historical overviews of this process that focus on the CIA and other institutional actors are Stonor Saunders, *Who Paid the Piper?*, and Giles Scott-Smith, *The Politics of Apolitical Culture: The Congress for Cultural Freedom, the CIA and Post-war American Hegemony* (London: Routledge, 2002). The classic overview of how the new aesthetic ideology affected the fine arts is provided in Serge Guilbaut, *How New York Stole the Idea of Modern Art: Abstract Expressionism, Freedom, and the Cold War*, trans. Arthur Goldhammer (Chicago: University of Chicago Press, 1983). For an attempt at a similarly comprehensive treatment for the sphere of literature, see Greg Barnhisel, *Cold War Modernists: Art, Literature, and American Cultural Diplomacy* (New York: Columbia University Press, 2015).

25. Quoted in Stonor Saunders, *Who Paid the Piper?*, 28.

26. Ursula Reinhold, Dieter Schlenstedt, and Horst Tanneberger, *Erster Deutscher Schriftstellerkongreß, 4.–8. Oktober 1947: Protokoll und Doumente* (Berlin: Aufbau-Verlag, 1997), 300. For an English account of the Writers' Congress, and of Lasky's involvement in it, see Sean A. Forner, *German Intellectuals and the Challenge of Democratic Renewal: Culture and Politics after 1945* (Cambridge: Cambridge University Press, 2014).

27. Marko Martin, *Orwell, Koestler und all die anderen: Melvin J. Lasky und "Der Monat"* (Asendorf: MUT Verlag, 1999), 23–24.

28. On Lasky's connections to the CCF see Stonor Saunders, *Who Paid the Piper?*, and Giles Scott-Smith, "'A Radical Democratic Political Offensive': Melvin J. Lasky, *Der Monat*, and the Congress for Cultural Freedom," *Journal of Contemporary History* 35, no. 2 (April 2000): 263–80.

29. Quoted in Stonor-Saunders, *Who Paid the Piper?*, 100.

30. See, e.g., Melvin J. Lasky, *Utopia & Revolution: On the Origins of a Metaphor* (Chicago: University of Chicago Press, 1976), 53.

31. Melvin J. Lasky, "Mann and Nietzsche," *New Leader*, August 16, 1947, 11. A shortened version of this article was published in German as "Thomas Mann und Friedrich Nietzsche," *Der Tagesspiegel*, November 12, 1947, 9–10.

32. Lasky's relationships with various members of the Mann family are described in Friedrich Albrecht, *Klaus Mann, der Mittler: Studien aus vier Jahrzehnten* (Bern: Peter Lang, 2009), 236–41.

33. The impression that this made on a young German readership is documented in a testimonial by the German publisher Wolf Jobst Siedler, who enthused that Lasky's journal was "a window to the world for us who had grown up in the Third Reich. . . . Previously forbidden names and debates were carried out in *Der Monat*. . . .

All that impressed me greatly: the return of the twenties and thirties, the texts by Thomas Mann, Hermann Hesse, Hans Sahl, and the way in which they were linked to the debates of the present." Quoted in Martin, *Orwell, Koestler*, 26.

34. See, e.g., Lasky's correspondence with Jürgen von Kempski, *Der Monat* Papers, box 3, folder 1, UCL, or with Dr. Albrecht Knaus, *Der Monat* Papers, box 3, folder 2, UCL.

35. Georg Lukács, "The Tragedy of Modern Art," in *Essays on Thomas Mann*, trans. Stanley Mitchell (London: Merlin Press, 1964), 69.

36. Lukács, 67.

37. Lukács, 79.

38. James T. Farrell, "Was braucht die Literatur?" *Der Monat* 4 (January 1949): 67. My translation. I have been unable to track down the English original of this piece. The *Monat* archives contain a request for copyright clearance for a Farrell essay called "The Needs of American Literature," which was supposedly published in the *Monthly Review*, but no such essay seems to exist. *Der Monat* Papers, box 73, folder 7, UCL.

39. Farrell, "Was braucht die Literatur?," 69, 66.

40. Hellmut Jaesrich, "Doktor Faustus in Amerika," *Der Monat* 4 (January 1949): 92.

41. Arnold Schoenberg and Thomas Mann, " 'Doctor Faustus' Schoenberg?," letters to the editor, *Saturday Review of Literature*, January 1, 1949, 22–23, reprinted in German with a brief unsigned commentary as "Der Eigentliche: Die Dissonanzen zwischen Arnold Schoenberg und Thomas Mann," *Der Monat* 4 (March 1949): 76–78.

42. Lukács, "Tragedy of Modern Art," 68.

43. Arnold Bauer, "Thomas Mann und seine Widersacher," 75; Lukács, "Tragedy of Modern Art," 71–72.

44. Fredric Jameson, *A Singular Modernity: Essay on the Ontology of the Present* (London: Verso, 2002), especially 161–65.

45. "Harry Levin, Critic, Is Dead at 81," *New York Times*, June 1, 1994, B9.

46. Harry Levin, *James Joyce: A Critical Introduction* (New York: New Directions, 1941), 49, 156.

47. Levin, 97.

48. Levin, "From Ur to OPA," *New Republic*, July 10, 1944, 49.

49. Harry Levin, "Doctor Mann versus a Teutonic Mephisto," *New York Times Book Review*, October 31, 1948, 5.

50. Levin, 5.

51. In a short article published the previous year, Harry Levin had written about Kafka's works that "the dryness of their irony, the clairvoyance of their imagery, and the limpidity of their prose have scarcely been equaled by any contemporary using his language—certainly not by Thomas Mann." "Metacriticism," *Yale Review* 36, no. 2 (Winter 1947): 354.

52. On the rise of this distinctively American strand of Kafka criticism during the 1940s, see Jürgen Born, "Kafka in America: His Growing Reputation during the Forties," in *The Fortunes of German Writers in America*, ed. Wolfgang Elfe, James Hardin, and Gunther Holst (Columbia: University of South Carolina Press, 1992), 121–30. The view that Kafka's stories resisted reduction to allegory was central to Levin's criticism. See, e.g., "Metacriticism," 355, and "On the Dissemination of Realism," *TriQuarterly* 11 (Winter 1968): 163–78.

53. Clement Greenberg, "Towards a Newer Laokoön," *Partisan Review*, July–August 1940, 296–310.

54. Clement Greenberg, "The Last of the Fathers: A Consideration of Mann's Joseph," 1, Clement Greenberg Papers, box 24, folder 13, GRI.

55. Greenberg, 2. My emphasis.

56. Greenberg, 4.

57. No wonder, then, that Fredric Jameson, the Marxist critic who has done more than any other to bridge the gap between Lukács and aesthetic formalism, has also eagerly adopted the four-fold allegorical scheme for his own writings on Mann. "Allegory and History: On Rereading *Doktor Faustus*," in *The Modernist Papers* (London: Verso, 2007), 113–36.

58. Greenberg, "Last of the Fathers," 9. See also in this context Clement Greenberg, "Avant-Garde and Kitsch," *Partisan Review* 6, Fall 1939, 34–49.

59. See in this context Hans Rudolf Vaget, "Deutsche Einheit und Nationale Identität: Zur Genealogie der gegenwärtigen Deutschland-Debatte am Beispiel von Thomas Mann," *Literaturwissenschaftliches Jahrbuch der Görres-Gesellschaft* 33 (1992): 277–98.

60. For more on the historical background of Mann's letter, see *Tb.*, June 10, 1951, n3.

Conclusion

1. Peter de Mendelssohn, "Vorbemerkungen des Herausgebers," in *Thomas Mann: Tagebücher 1933–1934*, ed. Peter de Mendelssohn (Frankfurt am Main: S. Fischer, 1977), xiv.

2. As Walter Delabar puts it, "Thomas Mann's life [has become] the primary source, while his literary texts [have become] a secondary source used to illuminate the life." "Der Autor als Repräsentant, Thomas Mann als Star: Aufstieg und Niedergang der öffentlichen Funktion des Autors im 20. Jahrhundert," in *Schriftsteller-Inszenierungen*, ed. Gunter E. Grimm and Christian Schärf (Bielefeld: Aisthesis, 2008), 100.

3. Alan Bloom, *The Closing of the American Mind* (New York: Simon & Schuster, 1987), 231.

4. Susan Sontag, "Pilgrimage," *New Yorker*, December 21, 1987, 38–54.

5. Susan Sontag, "Against Interpretation," in *Against Interpretation and Other Essays* (New York: Picador, 1966), 14.

6. Kai Sina, *Susan Sontag und Thomas Mann* (Göttingen: Wallstein Verlag, 2017).

7. Ronald Hayman, *Thomas Mann: A Biography* (New York: Scribner, 1995); Donald Prater, *Thomas Mann: A Life* (New York: Oxford University Press, 1995); Anthony Heilbut, *Thomas Mann: Eros and Literature* (New York: Alfred A. Knopf, 1996); Hermann Kurzke, *Thomas Mann: Life as a Work of Art*, trans. Leslie Willson (Princeton, NJ: Princeton University Press, 2002). Kurzke's book was translated from the German. There has also been a biography of Mann's two oldest children. Andrea Weiss, *In the Shadow of the Magic Mountain: The Erika and Klaus Mann Story* (Chicago: University of Chicago Press, 2008).

8. David Brooks, "The Glory of Democracy," *New York Times*, December 15, 2017, A31.

9. Quoted in Kjell Espmark, *The Nobel Prize in Literature: A Study of the Criteria behind the Choices* (Boston: G. K. Hall, 1991), 29.

10. Quoted in Espmark, 30.

11. Julia Lovell, *The Politics of Cultural Capital: China's Quest for a Nobel Prize in Literature* (Honolulu: University of Hawai'i Press, 2006), 3.

12. Quoted in Lovell, 1.

13. David Daley, "Rushdie: Mo Yan is a 'Patsy of the Regime,'" *Salon*, December 7, 2012, https://www.salon.com/2012/12/07/rushdie_mo_yan_is_a_patsy_of_the_regime/.

14. Timothy Brennan, *Salman Rushdie and the Third World: Myths of the Nation* (New York: Palgrave McMillan, 1989), 38.

15. Fredric Jameson, "Third-World Literature in the Age of Multinational Capitalism," *Social Text* 15 (Autumn 1986): 65–88.

16. Gloria Fisk, *Orhan Pamuk and the Good of World Literature* (New York: Columbia University Press, 2018), 2.

17. Harry Levin, *James Joyce: A Critical Introduction* (New York: New Directions, 1941), 212.

18. James English, *The Economy of Prestige: Prizes, Awards, and the Circulation of Cultural Value* (Cambridge, MA: Harvard University Press, 2008), 300.

19. Quoted in English, 303.

20. Rebecca Walkowitz, *Born Translated: The Contemporary Novel in an Age of World Literature* (New York: Columbia University Press, 2015).

21. Walkowitz, 6.

22. Nergis Ertürk, "Those Outside the Scene: *Snow* in the World Republic of Letters," *New Literary History* 41, no. 3 (2010): 633–51.

23. Tim Parks, "The Dull New Global Novel," *New York Review of Books Daily*, February 9, 2010, https://www.nybooks.com/daily/2010/02/09/the-dull-new-global-novel/.

24. Timothy Aubry, *Reading as Therapy: What Contemporary Fiction Does for Middle-Class Americans* (Iowa City: University of Iowa Press, 2011); Fisk, *Orhan Pamuk*, 146.

25. Jim Collins, *Bring on the Books for Everybody: How Literary Culture Became Popular Culture* (Durham, NC: Duke University Press, 2010).

26. Quoted in Arnold Rampersad, *Ralph Ellison: A Biography* (New York: Vintage, 2007), 91.

BIBLIOGRAPHY

"2,000 Writers Assist in Winning the War." *New York Times*, January 9, 1943, 11.

"20,000 in Garden Cheer for Czechs." *New York Times*, September 26, 1938, 4.

Adolphs, Dieter W. "Thomas Manns Einflussnahme auf die Rezeption seiner Werke in Amerika." *Deutsche Vierteljahrsschrift für Literaturwissenschaft und Geistesgeschichte* 64 (1990): 560–82.

Adorno, Theodor. *Minima Moralia: Reflections from Damaged Life.* Translated by E. F. N. Jephcott. London: Verso Books, 1974.

Agar, Herbert, Frank Aydelotte, G. A. Borgese, et. al. *The City of Man: A Declaration on World Democracy.* New York: Viking Press, 1941.

Albrecht, Friedrich. *Klaus Mann, der Mittler: Studien aus vier Jahrzehnten.* Bern: Peter Lang, 2009.

Alexander, Gerhard. "Geschichte einer Mystifikation." *Hamburger Akademische Rundschau* 1, no. 4 (1946/47): 148–49.

Améry, Jean. "Von den Möglichkeiten geistiger Repräsentanz." *Neue Rundschau* 86, no. 1 (1975): 38–49.

Anders, Günther. "Germany in Exile." *New Republic*, May 5, 1937, 392–93.

Andersch, Alfred. "Thomas Mann," *Der Ruf*, July 1, 1945, 4.

Ansel, Michael, Hans-Edwin Friedrich, and Gerhard Lauer. "Hybride Repräsentanz: Zu den Bedingungen einer Erfindung." In Ansel, Friedrich, and Lauer, *Die Erfindung des Schriftstellers Thomas Mann*, 1–34.

Ansel, Michael, Hans-Edwin Friedrich, and Gerhard Lauer, eds. *Die Erfindung des Schriftstellers Thomas Mann.* Berlin: Walter de Gruyter, 2009.

Appelbaum, Yoni. "Publishers Gave Away 122,951,031 Books during World War II." *Atlantic*, September 10, 2014. https://www.theatlantic.com/business/archive/2014/09/publishers-gave-away-122951031-books-during-world-war-ii/379893/.

Assmann, Jan. "Mose gegen Hitler: Die Zehn Gebote als antifaschistisches Manifest." *Thomas Mann Jahrbuch* 28 (2015): 47–61.

Aubry, Timothy. *Reading as Therapy: What Contemporary Fiction Does for Middle-Class Americans.* Iowa City: University of Iowa Press, 2011.

Auerbach, Erich. "The Philology of World Literature." Translated by Jane O. Newman. In *Time, History, and Literature: Selected Essays of Erich Auerbach*, edited by James I. Porter, 253–65. Princeton, NJ: Princeton University Press, 2014.

"Authors to the Road." *Time*, December 27, 1937, 49.

Bade, James N., ed. *"On Myself" and Other Princeton Lectures.* Frankfurt am Main: Peter Lang, 1996.

Bahr, Ehrhard. "Exil als 'beschädigtes Leben': Thomas Mann und sein Roman *Joseph, der Ernährer.*" In *Exilerfahrung und Konstruktionen von Identität, 1933 bis 1945,* edited by Hans Otto Horch and Hanni Mittelmann, 245–55. Berlin: Walter de Gruyter, 2013.

———. *Weimar on the Pacific: German Exile Culture in Los Angeles and the Crisis of Modernism.* Berkeley: University of California Press, 2008.

Ballou, Robert O. *A History of the Council on Books in Wartime, 1942–1946.* New York: Country Life Press, 1946.

Baltensweiler, Thomas. *Mass und Wert: Die Exilzeitschrift von Thomas Mann und Konrad Falke.* Bern: Peter Lang, 1996.

Barnhisel, Greg. *Cold War Modernists: Art, Literature, and American Cultural Diplomacy.* New York: Columbia University Press, 2015.

Basso, Hamilton. "A New Deal with the Old Nick." *New Yorker,* October 30, 1948, 106–7.

———. "Tonio Kröger in Egyptian Dress." *New Yorker,* July 22, 1944, 53–57.

Bauer, Arnold. "Thomas Mann und seine Widersacher." *Der Monat* 6 (March 1949): 68–75.

Beachy, Robert. *Gay Berlin: Birthplace of a Modern Identity.* New York: Vintage, 2015.

Becker, May Lamberton. "Reader's Guide." *Saturday Review of Literature,* April 30, 1927, 793.

Bedenig, Katrin. "Max Frisch und Thomas Mann: Ihr Weg zu engagierten Staatsbürgern von den Anfängen bis 1947." In *Max Frisch: Sein Weg im Kontext der europäischen Literatur seiner Zeit,* edited by Régine Battison and Margit Unser, 43–68. Würzburg: Königshausen & Neumann, 2012.

Bell, Michael. *Literature, Modernism, and Myth: Belief and Responsibility in the Twentieth Century.* Cambridge: Cambridge University Press, 1997.

Benét, Stephen Vincent. "They Burned the Books." *Saturday Review of Literature,* May 8, 1943, 4–6.

Benseler, David P., Walter F. W. Lohnes, and Valters Nollendorfs, eds. *Teaching German in America: Prolegomena to a History.* Madison: University of Wisconsin Press, 1988.

Bergsten, Gunilla. *Thomas Manns Doktor Faustus: Untersuchungen zu den Quellen und zur Struktur des Romans.* Tübingen: Max Niemeyer, 1974.

Berlin, Jeffrey B. "Additional Reflections on Thomas Mann as a Letter-Writer: With the Unpublished Correspondence of Thomas Mann, Alfred A. Knopf, and H. T. Lowe-Porter about the Genesis of *Doctor Faustus, The Black Swan,* and *Confessions of Felix Krull—Confidence Man: The Early Years.*" *Oxford German Studies* 34, no. 2 (2005): 123–57.

———. "'Ihr Gedanke, dieser Äußerung in Amerika noch etwas weitere Publizität zu verschaffen, ist mir sehr sympathisch': Thomas Mann's Unpublished Correspondence from 5 January 1936 to 3 May 1936 with Alfred A. Knopf and H. T. Lowe-Porter." *Euphorion* 95 (2001): 197–210.

———. "On the Making of *The Magic Mountain*: The Unpublished Correspondence of Thomas Mann, Alfred A. Knopf, and H. T. Lowe-Porter." *Seminar* 28, no. 4 (1992): 283–320.

———. "On the Nature of Letter: Thomas Mann's Unpublished Correspondence with His American Publisher and Translator, and Unpublished Letters about the Writing of *Doctor Faustus*." *European Journal of English Studies* 9, no. 1 (2005): 61–73.

Berlin, Jeffrey B. and Julius Herz. "'Ein Lese- und Bilderbuch von Menschen': Unpublished Letters of Thomas Mann, Alfred A. Knopf, and H. T. Lowe-Porter, 1929–34, with Special Reference to the *Joseph*-Novels." *Seminar* 30, no. 3 (1994): 227–75.

Bermann Fischer, Brigitte. *My European Heritage: Life among Great Men of Letters*. Translated by Harry Zohn. Boston: Branden, 1987.

Bermann Fischer, Gottfried. *Bedroht—Bewahrt: Weg eines Verlegers*. Frankfurt am Main: S. Fischer Verlag, 1967.

———. *Wanderer durch ein Jahrhundert*. Frankfurt am Main: S. Fischer Verlag, 1994.

———. "Zueignung zum 6. Juni 1945." In "Thomas Mann," special issue, *Neue Rundschau*, June 6, 1945, 1.

Bessner, Daniel, and Udi Greenberg. "The Weimar Analogy." *Jacobin*, December 17, 2016. https://www.jacobinmag.com/2016/12/trump-hitler-germany-fascism-weimar-democracy/.

"Big Audience Hears Lecture of Dr. Mann." *Seattle Daily Times*, March 30, 1939, 27.

"Bikes for Bookman." *Cleveland Plain Dealer*, May 1, 1938, 32-A.

Birmingham, Kevin. *The Most Dangerous Book: The Battle for James Joyce's "Ulysses."* New York: Penguin, 2014.

Bischoff, Doerte. "Repräsentanten für Europa? Thomas und Heinrich Mann als Grenz-Gänger eines Europa-Diskurses in ihren Essays 1914–1933." In *Suchbild Europa: Künstlerische Konzepte der Moderne*, edited by Jürgen Wertheimer, 18–37. Amsterdam: Rodopi, 1995.

Blackbourne, David. *The Conquest of Nature: Water, Landscape, and the Making of Modern Germany*. New York: W. W. Norton, 2006.

Blake, Casey Nelson. *Beloved Community: The Cultural Criticism of Randolph Bourne, Van Wyck Brooks, Waldo Frank, & Lewis Mumford*. Chapel Hill: University of North Carolina Press, 1990.

Bloch, Ernst. "Thomas Manns Manifest." *Neue Weltbühne*, September 9, 1937, 1152–58.

Bloom, Allan. *The Closing of the American Mind*. New York: Simon & Schuster, 1987.

Bockwitz, Hans H. "Ein Goethegespräch." *Der Zwiebelfisch: Zeitschrift über Bücher, Kunst und Kultur* 25, no. 7 (1947): 14–15.

Boes, Tobias. "Aschenbach Crosses the Waters: Reading *Death in Venice* in America." *Modernism/modernity* 21, no. 2 (2014): 429–45.

Börnchen, Stefan, and Claudia Liebrand, eds. *Apokrypher Avantgardismus: Thomas Mann und die klassische Moderne*. Munich: Wilhelm Fink Verlag, 2008.

Borchmeyer, Dieter. "'Zurück zum Anfang aller Dinge': Mythos und Religion in Thomas Manns *Josephsromanen*." *Thomas Mann Jahrbuch* 11 (1998): 9–30.

Borgese, Giuseppe Antonio. *Goliath: The March of Fascism*. Kirkwood, NY: Vail-Ballou Press, 1937.

Born, Jürgen. "Kafka in America: His Growing Reputation during the Forties." In *The Fortunes of German Writers in America*, edited by Wolfgang Elfe, James Hardin, and Gunther Holst, 121–30. Columbia: University of South Carolina Press, 1992.

Bottigheimer, Ruth B. "One Hundred and Fifty Years of German at Princeton: A Descriptive Account." In Benseler, Lohnes, and Nollendorfs, *Teaching German in America*, 90–93.

Bourdieu, Pierre. *Distinction: A Social Critique of the Judgment of Taste*. Translated by Richard Nice. Cambridge, MA: Harvard University Press, 1984.

——. *The Field of Cultural Production: Essays on Art and Literature*. Edited by Randal Johnson. New York: Columbia University Press, 1993.

——. *The Rules of Art: Genesis and Structure of the Literary Field*. Translated by Susan Emanuel. Palo Alto, CA: Stanford University Press, 1996.

Boyd, Ernest. "Translations." *Saturday Review of Literature*, December 26, 1925, 441–42.

Bourne, Randolph. "Transnational America." *Atlantic Monthly*, July 1916, 86–97.

Brecht, Bertolt. *Große kommentierte Berliner und Frankfurter Ausgabe*. Edited by Werner Hecht et. al. 30 volumes. Frankfurt am Main: Suhrkamp Verlag, 1988–2000.

Brennan, Timothy. *Salman Rushdie and the Third World: Myths of the Nation*. New York: Palgrave McMillan, 1989.

Brettschneider, Rudolf. "Die Entdeckung des Wälsungenblut." *Die Bücherstube*, October 1920, 110–12.

"Briefly Noted: *The Ten Commandments*." *New Yorker*, January 1, 1944, 59–60.

Brooks, David. "The Glory of Democracy." *New York Times*, December 15, 2017, A31.

Brooks, Van Wyck. *America's Coming-of-Age*. New York: B. W. Huebsch, 1915.

Bruch, Rüdiger vom. "Kunst und Kulturkritik in führenden bildungsbürgerlichen Zeitschriften des Kaiserreichs." In *Ideengeschichte und Kunstwissenschaft: Philosophie und bildende Kunst im Kaiserreich*, edited by Ekkehard Mai, 313–47. Berlin: Gebr. Mann, 1983.

Buck, Timothy. "Loyalty and Licence: Thomas Mann's Fiction in English Translation." *Modern Language Review* 91, no. 4 (1996): 898–921.

——. "Mann in English." In Robertson, *Cambridge Companion to Thomas Mann*, 235–48.

Buder, Emily. "When 20,000 American Nazis Descended upon New York City." *Atlantic*, October 10, 2017. https://www.theatlantic.com/video/index/542499/marshall-curry-nazi-rally-madison-square-garden-1939/.

Bungert, Heike. "Deutsche Emigranten im Amerikanischen Kalkül: Die Regierung in Washington, Thomas Mann, und die Gründung eines Emigrantenkomitees 1943." *Vierteljahresschrift für Zeitgeschichte* 46, no. 2 (1998): 253–68.

Burke, Kenneth. "Fraught with Freight." *New Republic*, January 10, 1934, 257.

——. "Revolutionary Symbolism in America." In *The First American Writers' Congress*, edited by Henry Hart, 89–90. New York: International Publishers, 1935.

——. "Thomas Mann and André Gide." In *Counter-Statement*, 92–106. Berkeley: University of California Press, 1931.

Canby, Henry Seidel. "The Dean of Novelists Recounts a Famous Medieval Tale of Romance, Sin, and Expiation." *Book-of-the-Month Club News*, September 1951, 1–5.

——. "The First Puritan." *Saturday Review of Literature*, February 26, 1938, 5.

——. "*Joseph the Provider*, by Thomas Mann." *Book-of-the-Month Club News*, July 1944, 3–5.

——. "The Threatening Thirties." *Saturday Review of Literature*, May 22, 1937, 4, 14.

Canning, Charlotte M. *The Most American Thing in America: Circuit Chautauqua as Performance*. Iowa City: University of Iowa Press, 2007.

——. "Cartwheel Girl," *Time*, June 12, 1939, 47–51.

Casanova, Pascale. *The World Republic of Letters*. Translated by M. B. DeBevoise. Cambridge, MA: Harvard University Press, 2004.

Cather, Willa. "The Birth of Personality." *Saturday Review of Literature*, June 6, 1936, 3–4.

Cazden, Robert E. *German Exile Literature in America, 1933–1950: A History of the Free German Press and Book Trade*. Chicago: American Library Association, 1970.

Charle, Christoph. *Birth of the Intellectuals: 1880–1900*. Translated by David Fernbach and G. M. Goshgarian. Cambridge: Polity Press, 2015.

Cheney, Orion Howard. *Economic Survey of the Book Industry, 1930–1931*. New York: National Association of Book Publishers, 1931.

Childs, Marquis. "Thomas Mann: Germany's Foremost Literary Exile Speaks Now for Freedom and Democracy in America." *Life*, April 17, 1939, 56–59, 74–76.

Cohn, Dorrit. "The Second Author of *Der Tod in Venedig*." In *Probleme der Moderne: Studien zur deutschen Literatur von Nietzsche bis Brecht*, edited by Benjamin Bennet, Anton Kaes, and William J. Lillyman, 223–45. Tübingen: Max Niemeyer Verlag, 1983.

Cole, John Y., ed. *Books in Action: The Armed Services Editions*. Washington, DC: Library of Congress, 1984.

Colgan, Christine Ann. "Warner Brothers' Crusade against the Third Reich: A Study of Anti-Nazi Activism and Film Production, 1933 to 1941." PhD diss., University of Southern California, 1985.

Collins, Jim. *Bring on the Books for Everybody: How Literary Culture Became Popular Culture*. Durham, NC: Duke University Press, 2010.

——. "Congress." *Time*, December 27, 1937, 18.

Conradi, Peter. *Hitler's Piano Player: The Rise and Fall of Ernst Hanfstaengl, Confidant of Hitler, Ally of FDR*. New York: Carroll and Graf, 2004.

Conze, Eckart, Peter Frei, Peter Hayes, and Moshe Zimmermann, eds. *Das Amt und die Vergangenheit: Deutsche Diplomaten im Dritten Reich und in der Bundesrepublik*. Munich: Blessing, 2010.

Cowley, Malcolm. "Second Thoughts on 'Joseph.'" *New Republic*, March 23, 1938, 198–99.

Creszenzi, Luca. "Masken: Zu den Strategien der Selbstbiografik im *Doktor Faustus* und in der *Entstehung des Doktor Faustus*." *Thomas Mann Jahrbuch* 30 (2017): 87–98.

Dahm, Volker. *Das jüdische Buch im Dritten Reich*. Munich: C. H. Beck, 1993.

Daley, David. "Rushdie: Mo Yan is a 'Patsy of the Regime.'" *Salon*, December 7, 2012. https://www.salon.com/2012/12/07/rushdie_mo_yan_is_a_patsy_of_the_regime/.

Delabar, Walter. "Der Autor als Repräsentant, Thomas Mann als Star: Aufstieg und Niedergang der öffentlichen Funktion des Autors im 20. Jahrhundert." In *Schriftsteller-Inszenierungen*, edited by Gunter E. Grimm and Christian Schärf, 87–102. Bielefeld: Aisthesis, 2008.

Denning, Michael. *The Cultural Front: The Laboring of American Culture in the Twentieth Century*. London: Verso, 1998.

Detering, Heinrich. "Akteur im Literaturbetrieb: Der junge Thomas Mann als Rezensent, Lektor, Redakteur." *Thomas Mann Jahrbuch* 23 (2010): 27–46.

——. "Der Litterat: Inszenierung stigmatisierter Autorschaft im Frühwerk Thomas Manns." In Ansel, Friedrich, and Lauer, *Die Erfindung des Schriftstellers Thomas Mann*, 191–206.

——. *Thomas Manns amerikanische Religion: Theologie, Politik und Literatur im kalifornischen Exil.* Frankfurt am Main: S. Fischer Verlag, 2012.

——. "Das Werk und die Gnade: Zu Religion und Kunstreligion in der Poetik Thomas Manns." In Peter and Sprecher, *Der Ungläubige Thomas*, 149–66.

Dickstein, Morris. *Dancing in the Dark: A Cultural History of the Great Depression.* New York: Norton, 2009.

DiMassa, Daniel. "Stefan George, Thomas Mann, and the Politics of Homoeroticism." *German Quarterly* 86, no. 3 (Summer 2013): 311–33.

Dinsman, Melissa. *Modernism at the Microphone: Radio, Propaganda, and Literary Aesthetics during World War II.* London: Bloomsbury Academic, 2015.

di Stefano, Giovanni. "'Italienische Optik, furios behauptet': Giuseppe Antonio Borgese—der schwierige Schwiegersohn." *Thomas Mann Jahrbuch* 8 (1995): 139–65.

Domarus, Max, ed. *Hitler. Reden und Proklamationen 1932–1945.* Vol. 2. Würzburg: Süddeutscher Verlag, 1965.

Donaldson, Scott. *Archibald MacLeish: An American Life.* Boston: Houghton Mifflin, 1992.

Donnelly, Dorothy. "Pulling the Lion's Teeth." *Commonweal*, September 7, 1945, 503–4.

"Der Eigentliche: Die Dissonanzen zwischen Arnold Schoenberg und Thomas Mann." *Der Monat* 4 (March 1949): 76–78.

Elsaghe, Yahya. *Die imaginäre Nation: Thomas Mann und das "Deutsche."* Paderborn: Wilhelm Fink Verlag, 2000.

——. "*Lotte in Weimar.*" In Robertson, *Cambridge Companion to Thomas Mann*, 185–98.

——. *Thomas Mann und die kleinen Unterschiede: Zur erzählenden Imagination des Anderen.* Vienna: Böhlau, 2004.

Elster, Hanns M. "Offener Brief an Thomas Mann." *Deutsche Stimmen: Halbmonatsschrift* 31 (1919): 60–64.

English, James. *The Economy of Prestige: Prizes, Awards, and the Circulation of Cultural Value.* Cambridge, MA: Harvard University Press, 2008.

Enzensberger, Hans Magnus. "Mann, Kafka, and the Katzenjammer Kids." *New York Times Book Review*, November 17, 1985, 37.

Erpenbeck, Fritz. "Preface." *Das Wort* 2, no. 11 (November 1937): 3–7.

Ertürk, Nergis. "Those Outside the Scene: *Snow* in the World Republic of Letters." *New Literary History* 41, no. 3 (2010): 633–51.

Espmark, Kjell. *The Nobel Prize in Literature: A Study of the Criteria behind the Choices.* Boston: G. K. Hall, 1991.

Ewen, David. "Thomas Mann Talks of the Nazi State." *New York Times*, September 10, 1933, 2xx.

Farrell, James T. "Literature and Ideology." *New International* 8, no. 4 (May 1942): 107–11.

——. "Thomas Mann's Manifesto against Fascism." *New York Herald Tribune*, December 21, 1938, 14.

——. "Was braucht die Literatur?" *Der Monat* 4 (January 1949): 66–71.

Fadiman, Clifton. "*Doctor Faustus*: A Profound Novel by Thomas Mann, Nobel Prize Winner and Perhaps the Age's Greatest Writer." *Book-of-the-Month Club News*, October 1948, 3–5.

———. "Thomas Mann." *New Yorker*, February 26, 1938, 58–62.

———. "Mann on Goethe." *New Yorker*, August 31, 1940, 44–45.

Fishburn, Matthew. *Burning Books*. New York: Palgrave Macmillan, 2008.

Fisk, Gloria. *Orhan Pamuk and the Good of World Literature*. New York: Columbia University Press, 2018.

Flake, Otto. "Der Fall Thomas Mann." *Badener Tageblatt*, December 8, 1945. Reprinted in Grosser, *Die grosse Kontroverse*, 51–56.

Flanner, Janet. "Goethe in Hollywood." *New Yorker*, December 13, 1941, 31–42, and December 20, 1941, 22–35.

Ford, James L. "The Tidal Wave of Books." *New York Tribune*, August 13, 1922, A1.

Forner, Sean A. *German Intellectuals and the Challenge of Democratic Renewal: Culture and Politics after 1945*. Cambridge: Cambridge University Press, 2014.

Foucault, Michel. "What Is an Author?" In *Aesthetics, Method, and Epistemology: The Essential Works of Foucault, 1954–1984*, vol. 2, edited by James Faubion, 205–22. London: Penguin, 1998.

Fox, Richard Wightman. "Tragedy, Responsibility, and the American Intellectual, 1925–1950." In *Lewis Mumford: Public Intellectual*, edited by Thomas P. Hughes and Agatha C. Hughes, 323–37. New York: Oxford University Press, 1990.

Franco, Jean. *The Decline and Fall of the Lettered City: Latin America in the Cold War*. Cambridge, MA: Harvard University Press, 2002.

Frey, Erich A. "Thomas Mann and His Friends before the Tolan Committee." In *Exile: The Writer's Experience*, edited by John M. Spalek and Robert F. Bell, 203–17. Chapel Hill: University of North Carolina Press. 1982.

Gannett, Lewis. "Books." In *While You Were Gone: A Report on Wartime Life in the United States*. New York: Simon & Schuster, 1946.

George, Ann, and Jack Selzer. "What Happened at the First American Writers' Congress? Kenneth Burke's 'Revolutionary Symbolism in America.'" *Rhetoric Society Quarterly* 33, no. 2 (Spring 2003): 47–66.

Gittik, Heinz. *Illegale Antifaschistische Tarnschriften 1933–1945*. Frankfurt am Main: Röderberg Verlag, 1971.

Goebbels, Joseph. *Die Tagebücher von Joseph Goebbels*. Munich: Institut für Zeitgeschichte, 2013.

Goebel, Eckart. "Tierische Transzendenz: *Herr und Hund*." In Börnchen and Liebrand, *Apokrypher Avantgardismus*, 307–27.

Goethe, Johann Wolfgang von. *Conversations with Eckermann (1823–1832)*. Translated by John Oxenford. San Francisco: North Point, 1984.

———. "Das deutsche Reich," in *Werke*. 143 volumes. Weimar: 1897–1919, I, 5.1:218.

———. "Response to a Literary Rabble-Rouser." Translated by Ellen von Nardroff and Ernest H. von Nardroff. In *The Essential Goethe*, edited by Matthew Bell, 878–81. Princeton, NJ: Princeton University Press, 2016.

"Goodwill Program over CBS." *New York Age*, July 24, 1943, 10.

Gordon, Adi, and Udi Greenberg. "*The City of Man*, European Émigrés, and the Genesis of Postwar Conservative Thought." *Religions* 3 (2012): 681–98.

Görner, Rüdiger. *Thomas Mann: Der Zauberer des Letzten*. Zurich: Artemis & Winkler, 2005.

Görtemaker, Manfred. *Thomas Mann und die Politik*. Frankfurt am Main: S. Fischer Verlag, 2005.

"Great Mann." *Time*, June 11, 1934, 81–85.

Greenberg, Clement. "Avant-Garde and Kitsch." *Partisan Review*, Fall 1939, 34–49.

———. "The Last of the Fathers: A Consideration of Mann's *Joseph*." Clement Greenberg Papers, box 24, folder 13, GRI.

———. "Towards a Newer Laokoön." *Partisan Review*, July–August 1940, 296–310.

Greenberg, Udi. *The Weimar Century: German Émigrés and the Ideological Foundations of the Cold War*. Princeton, NJ: Princeton University Press, 2014.

Greif, Mark. *The Age of the Crisis of Man: Thought and Fiction in America, 1933–1973*. Princeton, NJ: Princeton University Press, 2015.

Grosser, J. F. G. *Die grosse Kontroverse: Ein Briefwechsel um Deutschland*. Hamburg: Nagel, 1963.

Guilbaut, Serge. *How New York Stole the Idea of Modern Art: Abstract Expressionism, Freedom, and the Cold War*. Translated by Arthur Goldhammer. Chicago: University of Chicago Press, 1983.

Guptill Manning, Molly. *When Books Went to War: The Stories That Helped Us Win World War II*. Boston: Houghton Mifflin Harcourt, 2014.

Gut, Philipp. *Thomas Manns Idee einer deutschen Kultur*. Frankfurt am Main: S. Fischer Verlag, 2008.

Habe, Hans. *Ich stelle mich: Meine Lebensgeschichte*. Vienna: Desch, 1955.

Habermas, Jürgen. "Geist und Macht: ein deutsches Thema. Heinrich Heine und die Rolle des Intellektuellen in Deutschland." In *Das junge Deutschland: Kolloquium zum 150. Jahrestag des Verbots vom 10. Dezember 1835*, edited by Joseph A. Kruse and Bernd Kortländer, 15–38. Hamburg: Hoffmann und Campe, 1987.

Haefs, Wilhelm. "Geist, Geld und Buch: Thomas Manns Aufstieg zum Erfolgsautor im S. Fischer Verlag in der Weimarer Republik." In Ansel, Friedrich, and Lauer, *Die Erfindung des Schriftstellers Thomas Mann*, 123–59.

Halder, Winfrid. *Exilrufe nach Deutschland: Die Rundfunkreden von Thomas Mann, Paul Tillich und Johannes R. Becher 1940–1945*. Berlin: LIT-Verlag, 2002.

Hamacher, Bernd. "Die Poesie im Krieg: Thomas Manns Radiosendungen *Deutsche Hörer!* als Ernstfall der Literatur." *Thomas Mann Jahrbuch* 13 (2000): 57–74.

———. "Thomas Manns Medientheologie: Medien und Masken." In *Autorinszenierungen: Autorschaft und Literarisches Werk im Kontext der Medien*, edited by Christine Künzel and Jörg Schönert, 55–77. Würzburg: Königshausen & Neumann, 2007.

Hamburger, Käte. *Thomas Mann: "Das Gesetz."* Frankfurt am Main: Ullstein, 1964.

Hansen, Volkmar. " 'Where I am, there is Germany': Thomas Manns Interview vom 21. Februar 1938 in New York." In *Textkonstitution bei mündlicher und bei schriftlicher Überlieferung: Basler Editoren-Kolloquium 19.-22. März 1990, Autor- und Werkbezogene Referate*, edited by Martin Stern, 176–88. Tübingen: Max Niemeyer Verlag, 1991.

"Harry Levin, Critic, Is Dead at 81." *New York Times*, June 1, 1994, B9.

"Harvard Has Most Colorful Class Day." *Boston Post*, June 21, 1934, 8–9.

Hayman, Ronald. *Thomas Mann: A Life.* New York: Scribner, 1995.

Heilbut, Anthony. *Thomas Mann: Eros and Literature.* New York: Alfred A. Knopf, 1996.

Heller, Erich. *Thomas Mann: The Ironic German.* London: Secker & Warburg, 1958.

Hench, John B. *Books as Weapons: Propaganda, Publishing, and the Battle for Global Markets in the Era of World War II.* Ithaca, NY: Cornell University Press, 2010.

Hermand, Jost, and Wigand Lange, eds. *"Wollt ihr Thomas Mann wiederhaben?" Deutschland und die Emigranten.* Hamburg: Europäische Verlagsanstalt, 1999.

Hieber, Jochen. "Der audiovisuelle Urknall unserer Literatur: Thomas Mann im Tonfilm." *Frankfurter Allgemeine Zeitung,* September 20, 2014. http://www.faz.net/-hp7-7trqj.

Hildebrandt, Wolfgang. "Zauberberg und Kriegsgefangenschaft: Offener Brief an Thomas Mann." *Der Ruf,* October 1, 1945, 4.

Hill, Claude. "Mirror of the German Soul: Thomas Mann Closes an Account." *Saturday Review of Literature,* October 30, 1948, 11–13, 37.

Hobson, Fred. *H. L. Mencken: A Life.* Baltimore: Johns Hopkins University Press, 1994.

Hoffschulte, Martina. *"Deutsche Hörer!" Thomas Manns Rundfunkreden (1940 bis 1945) im Werkkontext.* Münster: Telos Verlag, 2003.

Hook, Sidney. *Letters of Sidney Hook: Democracy, Communism, and the Cold War.* Edited by Edward S. Shapiro. London: Routledge, 1995.

Horne, Charles Francis. *The Great Events of the Great War.* 7 vols. New York: J. J. Little & Ives, 1920.

Horowitz, Joseph. *Artists in Exile: How Refugees from Twentieth-Century War and Revolution Transformed the American Performing Arts.* New York: Harper Collins, 2008.

Horton, Aaron D. *German POWs, "Der Ruf," and the Genesis of Group 47: The Political Journey of Alfred Andersch and Hans Werner Richter.* Madison, NJ: Fairleigh Dickinson University Press, 2014.

Horton, David. *Thomas Mann in English.* London: Bloomsbury, 2013.

"H. T. Lowe-Porter, Translator, Dead." *New York Times,* 27 April, 1963, 25.

Hübinger, Gangolf. "'Journalist' und 'Literat': Vom Bildungsbürger zum Intellektuellen." In Hübinger and Mommsen, *Intellektuelle im deutschen Kaiserreich,* 95–110.

Hübinger, Gangolf, and Wolfgang J. Mommsen, eds. *Intellektuelle im deutschen Kaiserreich.* Frankfurt am Main: S. Fischer Verlag, 1993.

Hübinger, Paul Egon. *Thomas Mann, die Universität Bonn und die Zeitgeschichte: Drei Kapitel deutscher Vergangenheit aus dem Leben des Dichters 1905–1955.* Munich: R. Oldenbourg, 1974.

Hughes, Langston. "Madrid's Flowers Hoist Blooms to Meet Raining Fascist Bombs." *Baltimore Afro-American,* November 27, 1937, 1.

Hurston, Zora Neale. *Moses, Man of the Mountain.* New York: Lippincott, 1939.

Hurwitz, Harold. *Die Stunde Null der Deutschen Presse.* Cologne: Verlag Wissenschaft und Politik, 1972.

Hutchinson, George. *Facing the Abyss: American Literature and Culture in the 1940s.* New York: Columbia University Press, 2018.

Jaesrich, Hellmut. "Doktor Faustus in Amerika." *Der Monat* 4 (January 1949): 92–94.

Jaffe, Aaron. *Modernism and the Culture of Celebrity.* Cambridge: Cambridge University Press, 2005.

Jahraus, Oliver. "Die Geburt des Klassikers aus dem Tod der Figur: Autorschaft diesseits und jenseits des Textes *Der Tod in Venedig* von Thomas Mann. In Ansel, Friedrich, and Lauer, *Die Erfindung des Schriftstellers Thomas Mann*, 219–36.

Jameson, Fredric. "Allegory and History: On Rereading *Doktor Faustus*." In *The Modernist Papers*, 113–36. London: Verso, 2007.

——. *A Singular Modernity: Essay on the Ontology of the Present*. London: Verso, 2002.

——. "Third-World Literature in the Age of Multinational Capitalism." *Social Text* 15 (Autumn 1986): 65–88.

J. C. "An Answer to 'One Question.'" *Saturday Review of Literature*, July 7, 1934, 792.

Jens, Inge. *Dichter zwischen links und rechts: Die Geschichte der Sektion für Dichtkunst an der Preußischen Akademie der Künste, dargestellt nach den Dokumenten*. Leipzig: Gustav Kiepenhauer, 1994.

Johnson, Barbara. *Moses and Multiculturalism*. Berkeley: University of California Press, 2010.

Jones, Howard Mumford. "Patriotism—But How?" *Atlantic Monthly*, November 1938, 585–92.

——. "Writers and American Values." *New York Times Book Review*, August 5, 1945, 2.

Kahler, Erich. *Der Deutsche Charakter in der Geschichte Europas*. Zurich: Europa-Verlag, 1937.

Kammen, Michael. *The Lively Arts: Gilbert Seldes and the Transformation of Cultural Criticism in the United States*. New York: Oxford University Press, 1996.

Kantorowicz, Alfred. *In unserem Lager ist Deutschland: Reden und Aufsätze*. Paris: Éditions du Phoenix, 1936.

Kashti, Or. "Israel Bans Novel on Arab-Jewish Romance from Schools for Threatening Jewish Identity." *Haaretz*, December 31, 2015. http://www.haaretz.com/israel-news/.premium-1.694620.

K. H. "Bücher in dieser Zeit: Gespräch mit Gottfried Bermann Fischer." *Der Aufbau*, December 20, 1940, 7.

Kirschbaum, Erik. *Burning Beethoven: The Eradication of German Culture in the United States during World War One*. New York: Berlinica, 2014.

Knopf, Alfred A. "*The Beloved Returns*, by Thomas Mann." Signed testimonial for an advertisement in *New York Times Book Review*, August 25, 1940, 13.

——. "For Henry with Love." *Atlantic Monthly* May 1959, 50–54.

——. "On Publishing Thomas Mann." *American Pen: An International Quarterly of Writing* 7, no. 3 (1975): 1–9.

Kontje, Todd. "Thomas Mann's 'Wälsungenblut': The Married Artist and the 'Jewish Question.'" *PMLA* 123, no. 1 (January 2008): 109–24.

——. *Thomas Mann's World: Empire, Race, and the Jewish Question*. Ann Arbor: University of Michigan Press, 2011.

Koopmann, Helmut. "Bertolt Brecht und Thomas Mann: Eine repräsentative Gegnerschaft." *Heinrich-Mann-Jahrbuch* 13 (1995): 101–26.

——. *Thomas Mann—Heinrich Mann: Die ungleichen Brüder*. Munich: C. H. Beck, 2005.

Krammer, Arnold. *Nazi Prisoners of War in America*. New York: Stein & Day, 1979.

Krenzlin, Leonore. "Geschichte des Scheiterns—Geschichte des Lernens? Überlegungen zur Lage während und nach der 'Großen Kontroverse' und zur Motivation ihrer Akteure." In *Fremdes Heimatland: Remigration und literarisches Leben nach 1945*, edited by Irmela von der Lühe and Claus-Dieter Krohn, 57–70. Göttingen: Wallstein Verlag, 2005.

Krumeich, Gerd. "Die Resonanz der Dreyfus-Affäre im Deutschen Reich." In Hübinger and Mommsen, *Intellektuelle im deutschen Kaiserreich*, 13–32.

Kurzke, Hermann. "'Bruder' Hitler. Thomas Mann und das Dritte Reich." *Schopenhauer-Jahrbuch* 71 (1990): 125–35.

——. *Thomas Mann: Life as a Work of Art*. Translated by Leslie Willson. Princeton, NJ: Princeton University Press, 2002.

Langkau-Alex, Ursula. *Deutsche Volksfront 1932–39*. Vol. 2. Berlin: Akademie Verlag, 2004.

Lania, Leo. "Time Out from Terror." *Saturday Review of Literature*, July 26, 1947, 7–8, 28–29.

Lasky, Melvin J. "Mann and Nietzsche." *New Leader*, August 16, 1947, 11.

——. "Thomas Mann und Friedrich Nietzsche." *Der Tagesspiegel*, November 12, 1947, 9–10.

——. *Utopia & Revolution: On the Origins of a Metaphor*. Chicago: University of Chicago Press, 1976.

Lee, Alfred McClung, and Elizabeth Briant Lee. *The Fine Art of Propaganda: A Study of Father Coughlin's Speeches*. New York: Institute for Propaganda Analysis, 1939.

Lee, Charles. *The Hidden Public: The Story of the Book-of-the-Month Club*. Westport, CT: Praeger, 1973.

Lehmann, Klaus-Dieter. "Foreword: Culture as a Weapon." In Zühlsdorff, *Hitler's Exiles*, x–xv.

Lehnert, Herbert. "Introduction." In Lehnert and Pfeiffer, *Thomas Mann's "Doctor Faustus,"* 1–15.

——. "Thomas Mann in Princeton." *Germanic Review* 39, no. 1 (1964): 15–32.

——. "Thomas Manns Erzählung 'Das Gesetz' und andere erzählerische Nachspiele im Rahmen des Gesamtwerkes." *Deutsche Vierteljahresschrift* 43 (1969): 515–43.

Lehnert, Herbert, and Peter C. Pfeiffer, eds. *Thomas Mann's "Doctor Faustus": A Novel at the Margins of Modernism*. Columbia, SC: Camden House, 1991.

Lepenies, Wolf. "A German Specialty: Poetry and Literature in Opposition." In *Between Literature and Science: The Rise of Sociology*, 220–33. Cambridge: Cambridge University Press, 1988.

——. *The Seduction of Culture in German History*. Princeton, NJ: Princeton University Press, 2014.

Levin, Harry. "Doctor Mann versus a Teutonic Mephisto." *New York Times Book Review*, October 31, 1948, 5.

——. *James Joyce: A Critical Introduction*. New York: New Directions, 1941.

——. "Mann: From Ur to OPA." *New Republic*, July 10, 1944, 49–50.

——. "Metacriticism." *Yale Review* 36, no. 2 (Winter 1947): 354–56.

——. "On the Dissemination of Realism." *TriQuarterly* 11 (Winter 1968): 163–78.

Lewisohn, Ludwig. "Thomas Mann." *English Journal* 22, no. 7 (September 1933): 527–35.

Loewy, Ernst. *Thomas Mann: Ton- und Filmaufnahmen. Ein Verzeichnis*. Frankfurt am Main: S. Fischer Verlag, 1974.

Loomis, Jan. *Pacific Palisades*. Charleston, SC: Arcadia Publishing, 2009.

Lörke, Tim. "Bürgerlicher Avantgardismus: Thomas Manns mediale Selbstinszenierung im literarischen Feld." *Thomas Mann Jahrbuch* 23 (2010): 61–76.

———. *Die Verteidigung der Kultur: Mythos und Musik als Medien der Gegenmoderne*. Würzburg: Königshausen & Neumann, 2010.

Lörke, Tim, and Christian Müller, eds. *Thomas Manns kulturelle Zeitgenossenschaft*. Würzburg: Königshausen & Neumann, 2009.

"Los Angeles Metropolitan Area during World War II." California State Military Museums, updated January 20, 2019. http://www.militarymuseum.org/LAWWII.html.

Lovell, Julia. *The Politics of Cultural Capital: China's Quest for a Nobel Prize in Literature*. Honolulu: University of Hawai'i Press, 2006.

Loving, Pierre. "Thomas Mann." *Saturday Review of Literature*, May 22, 1926, 809.

Löwenthal, Leo, and Norbert Guterman. *Prophets of Deceit: A Study of the Techniques of the American Agitator*. New York: Harper and Brothers, 1949.

Lowe-Porter, Helen Tracy. "On Translating Thomas Mann." In Thirlwall, *In Another Language*, 178–209.

Lubich, Frederick A. "'Fascinating Fascism': Thomas Manns 'Das Gesetz' und seine Selbst-de-Montage als Moses-Hitler." *German Studies Review* 14, no. 3 (1991): 553–73.

———. "Thomas Mann's Sexual Politics–Lost in Translation." *Comparative Literature Studies* 31 (1994): 104–27.

Lukács, Georg. "Franz Kafka or Thomas Mann?" In *The Meaning of Contemporary Realism*, translated by John and Necke Mander, 47–92. London: Merlin Press, 1963.

———. "The Tragedy of Modern Art." In *Essays on Thomas Mann*, translated by Stanley Mitchell, 47–97. London: Merlin Press, 1964.

Lützeler, Paul Michael. *Die Schriftsteller und Europa: Von der Romantik bis zur Gegenwart*. Baden-Baden: Nomos, 1998.

———. "Visionaries in Exile: Broch's Cooperation with G. A. Borgese and Hannah Arendt." In *Hermann Broch: Visionary in Exile. The 2001 Yale Symposium*, edited by Paul Michael Lützeler, 67–88. Rochester, NY: Camden House, 2003.

Macdonald, Dwight. "Masscult and Midcult." *Partisan Review*, Spring 1960, 589–631.

[Macdonald, Dwight]. "This Quarter: Reflections on a Non-political Man." *Partisan Review*, Fall 1938, 14–16.

MacLeish, Archibald. "Foreword." In Salamanca, *Fortress of Freedom*, 9–11.

———. "The Irresponsibles." In *A Time to Speak*, 103–21.

———. "The Librarian and the Democratic Process." In *A Time to Speak*, 144–51.

———. "Libraries in the Contemporary Crisis." In *A Time to Speak*, 122–30.

———. "Objectives of the Library of Congress." In *The Story up to Now: The Library of Congress, 1800–1946*, by David C. Mearns, 211–13. Washington, DC: Library of Congress, 1947.

———. *A Time to Speak: The Selected Prose of Archibald MacLeish*. Boston: Houghton Mifflin, 1941.

Maier, Kurt S. "A Fellowship in German Literature: Thomas Mann, Agnes Meyer, and Archibald MacLeish." *Quarterly Journal of the Library of Congress* 36, no. 4 (Fall 1979): 385–400.

Mallios, Peter Lancelot. *Our Conrad: Constituting American Modernity*. Stanford, CA: Stanford University Press, 2010.

Manger, Klaus. "Wieland, der klassische Nationalautor." In *Metamorphosen des Dichters: Das Rollenverständnis deutscher Schriftsteller vom Barock bis zur Gegenwart*, edited by Gunter E. Grimm, 67–83. Frankfurt am Main: Fischer Taschenbuch Verlag, 1992.

Mani, B. Venkat. *Recoding World Literature: Libraries, Print Culture, and Germany's Pact with Books*. New York: Fordham University Press, 2017.

Mann, Erika. "Lecturer's Lot." *Liberty Magazine*, March 24, 1945, 24–25, 61–62.

Mann, Heinrich. "Zola." In *Essays und Publizistik, Oktober 1904 bis Oktober 1918*, edited by Manfred Hahn, Anne Flierl, and Wolfgang Klein, 148–209. Bielefeld: Aisthesis, 2012.

Mann, Klaus. *The Turning Point: Thirty-Five Years in This Century*. New York: L. B. Fischer, 1942.

"Mann Finds U.S. Sole Peace Hope." *New York Times*, February 22, 1938, 13.

"Mann Sees Soviet Bidding for Peace." *New York Times*, May 6, 1949, 23.

"Mann Strikes Out at Nazi Concepts." *New York Times*, August 15, 1937, N1, N6.

Marbury, Herbert Robinson. *Pillars of Cloud and Fire: The Politics of Exodus in African American Biblical Interpretation*. New York: NYU Press, 2015.

Marcus, Steven. "Humanities from Classics to Cultural Studies: Notes towards the History of an Idea." *Daedalus* 135, no. 2 (Spring 2006): 17–19.

Martin, Marko. *Orwell, Koestler und all die anderen: Melvin J. Lasky und "Der Monat."* Asendorf: MUT Verlag, 1999.

Martus, Steffen. "Die Geistesgeschichte der Gegenwartsliteratur: Wissenschaftliche Aufmerksamkeit für Thomas Mann zwischen 1900 und 1933." In Ansel, Friedrich, and Lauer, *Die Erfindung des Schriftstellers Thomas Mann*, 47–84.

Marx, Friedhelm. "Heilige Autorschaft? *Self-Fashioning*-Strategien in der Literatur der Moderne." In *Autorschaft: Positionen und Revisionen*, edited by Heinrich Detering, 107–20. Stuttgart: Verlag J. B. Metzler, 2002.

——. "'Lauter Professoren und Docenten': Thomas Manns Verhältnis zur Literaturwissenschaft." In Ansel, Friedrich, and Lauer, *Die Erfindung des Schriftstellers Thomas Mann*, 85–96.

Marx, Olga. "German Literature of Today." *Saturday Review of Literature*, February 6, 1926, 545.

"Masterpiece." *Time*, July 3, 1944, 90–91.

Mencken, H. L., and George Jean Nathan. "Répétition Générale." *Smart Set* 63, no. 1 (1920): 45–53.

Mendelsohn, Peter de. *Von deutscher Repräsentanz: Thomas und Heinrich Mann, Hermann Hesse, Gerhart Hauptmann*. Munich: Prestel Verlag, 1984.

——. "Vorbemerkungen des Herausgebers." In *Thomas Mann: Tagebücher 1933–1934*, edited by Peter de Mendelsohn, v–xxii. Frankfurt am Main: S. Fischer, 1977.

M. E. S. *Thomas Mann, Nobel Prize Winner of 1929: A Critical Estimate*. New York: Alfred A. Knopf, 1930.

Meyer, Agnes. E. "A New Novel by Thomas Mann: *The Beloved Returns*." *New York Times Book Review*, August 25, 1940, 1, 22, 23.

Meyer, Martin. "American Literature in Germany and Its Reception in the Political Context of the Postwar Years." Translated by Sally E. Robertson. In *The United States and Germany in the Era of the Cold War: A Handbook*. Vol. 1, *1945–1968*, edited by Detlef Junker, 425–31. Cambridge: Cambridge University Press, 2004.

Moreland, Marc M. "Conversation Piece." *Arkansas State Press*, January 8, 1943, 6.

Moretti, Franco. *Modern Epic: The World System from Goethe to García Márquez*. Translated by Quintin Hoare. London: Verso, 1996.

Mumford, Lewis. "The Magic Mountain." In *The Stature of Thomas Mann*, edited by Charles Neider, 150–55. New York: New Directions, 1947.

——. *My Works and Days: A Personal Chronicle*. New York: Harcourt Brace Jovanovic, 1979.

——. "Opening Address." In *Artists against War and Fascism: Papers of the First American Artists' Congress*, edited by Matthew Baigell and Julia Williams, 62–64. New Brunswick, NJ: Rutgers University Press, 1986.

M. W. S. "Reunion in Weimar." *Christian Science Monitor*, September 7, 1940, 18.

National Conference of Christians and Jews. *Toward Brotherhood: Annual Report 1942 of the President of the National Conference of Christians and Jews*. New York: NCCJ, 1942.

Nawrocka, Irene. "'Verlagssitz: Wien, Stockholm, New York, Amsterdam. Der Bermann-Fischer Verlag im Exil (1933–1950)." *Archiv für Geschichte des Buchwesens* 53 (2000): 1–216.

Neider, Charles. "Thomas Mann's Joseph Myth." *New Mexico Quarterly* 14, no. 3 (1944): 286–98.

Nemerov, Howard. "The Quester Hero: Myth as Universal Symbol in the Works of Thomas Mann." Undergraduate thesis, Harvard University, 1939.

Neumann, Helga, and Manfred Neumann. *Maximilian Harden (1861–1927): Ein unerschrockener deutsch-jüdischer Publizist*. Würzburg: Königshausen & Neumann, 2003.

Niebuhr, Reinhold. "Mann Speaks to Germany." *Nation*, February 13, 1943, 244.

——. "Mann's Political Essays." *Nation*, November 28, 1942, 582–84.

Nied, Marius. *Der Weg zu "Geist und Kunst": Thomas Mann und sein Frühwerk unter dem Blickwinkel der Feldtheorie Pierre Bourdieus*. Darmstadt: Büchner-Verlag, 2010.

Norwood, Stephen H. *The Third Reich in the Ivory Tower: Complicity and Conflict on American Campuses*. New York: Cambridge University Press, 2009.

"Notes on Contributors." *Dial* 73, December 1922, back cover.

"Nymph." *Saturday Review of Literature*, May 8, 1937, 8.

Panizzo, Paolo. "Künstler, Genie und Demagoge: Thomas Manns Essay 'Bruder Hitler.'" In Lörke and Müller, *Thomas Manns kulturelle Zeitgenossenschaft*, 13–27.

Parks, Tim. "The Dull New Global Novel." *New York Review of Books Daily*, February 9, 2010. https://www.nybooks.com/daily/2010/02/09/the-dull-new-global-novel/.

Pendleton, Gene R., and Linda L. Williams. "Themes of Exile in Thomas Mann's 'Voyage with Don Quixote.'" *Cervantes* 21, no. 2 (2001): 73–85.

Pentlin, Susan L. "German Teachers' Reaction to the Third Reich, 1933–1939." In Benseler, Lohnes, and Nollendorfs, *Teaching German in America*, 228–52.

Peter, Niklaus, and Thomas Sprecher, eds. *Der Ungläubige Thomas: Zur Religion in Thomas Manns Romanen*. Frankfurt am Main: Vittorio Klostermann, 2012.

Petersen, Julius. "The Contemporary Short Story." Translated by William Guild Howard. In *The German Classics of the Nineteenth and Twentieth Centuries*, edited by Kuno Francke, vol. 19, edited by Julius Petersen, xi–xlviii. New York: German Publication Society, 1914 [1915].

Pfäfflin, Friedrich, and Ingrid Kussmaul. *S. Fischer, Verlag: Von der Gründung bis zur Rückkehr aus dem Exil.* Stuttgart: Deutsche Schillergesellschaft, 1985.

Phelps, Reginald. "Thomas Mann, LLD, Harvard, and the Third Reich." *Harvard Magazine,* July/August 1986, 65–68.

Phillips, William. "The One and the Many." *Nation,* July 22, 1944, 47–48.

——. "Thomas Mann: Humanism in Exile." *Partisan Review* 4, May 1938, 3–10.

Platen, August von. *The Sonnets of Karl August Georg Max Graf von Platen-Hallermünde.* Translated by Reginald Bancroft Cooke. Boston: Richard G. Badger, 1923.

Poore, Charles. "Books of the Times." *New York Times,* July 2, 1939, 11.

Prater, Donald. *Thomas Mann: A Life.* New York: Oxford University Press, 1995.

Preston, John Hyde. "Searching for Roots in America." *Harper's,* October 1937, 486–96.

Püttner, Conrad. *Rundfunk gegen das "Dritte Reich": Ein Handbuch.* Munich: KG Saur, 1986.

Radway, Janice. *A Feeling for Books: The Book-of-the-Month Club, Literary Taste, and Middle-Class Desire.* Chapel Hill: University of North Carolina Press, 1999.

Rampersad, Arnold. *Ralph Ellison: A Biography.* New York: Vintage, 2007.

Randall, Alec W. G. "Main Currents in Contemporary German Literature." *Dial* 70 (April 1921): 422–27.

Rauschning, Hermann. "Preface: A Conversation with Hitler." In *The Ten Commandments: Ten Short Novels of Hitler's War against the Moral Code,* edited by Arnim L. Robinson, ix–xiii. New York: Simon and Schuster, 1943.

——. *The Revolution of Nihilism.* Translated by E. W. Dickes. New York: Alliance Book Corporation, 1939.

Reed, T. J. *Thomas Mann: The Uses of Tradition.* Oxford: Oxford University Press, 1973.

Rehm, Stefan. "'Könnte das Massenhafte, das Massengerechte nicht einmal gut sein?': Thomas Mann und die Massenkultur des Literaturmarktes der Weimarer Republik." *Düsseldorfer Beiträge zur Thomas Mann Forschung* 2 (2011): 199–209.

Reinhold, Ursula, Dieter Schlenstedt, and Horst Tanneberger. *Erster Deutscher Schriftstellerkongreß, 4.–8. Oktober 1947: Protokoll und Doumente.* Berlin: Aufbau-Verlag, 1997.

Robb, Ines. "Mrs. Roosevelt Holds Peace Hope." *Cleveland Plain Dealer,* September 28, 1939, 8.

Robertson, Ritchie, ed. *The Cambridge Companion to Thomas Mann.* Cambridge: Cambridge University Press, 2001.

——. "Classicism and Its Pitfalls: *Death in Venice.*" In Robertson, *Cambridge Companion to Thomas Mann,* 95–106.

Robin, Ron. *The Barbed-Wire College: Reeducating German POWs in the United States during World War II.* Princeton, NJ: Princeton University Press, 1995.

Robinson, Gladys Lloyd. "Thomas Mann in Hollywood." *Script,* April 9, 1938, 6.

"Roosevelt Bars the Hyphenated." *New York Times,* October 13, 1915, 1, 5.

Roosevelt, Franklin D. "Fireside Chat: September 3, 1939." The American Presidency Project. https://www.presidency.ucsb.edu/node/209990.

Rosenberg, Jane. *The Nation's Great Library: Herbert Putnam and the Library of Congress.* Champaign: University of Illinois Press, 1993.

Ross, Alex. *The Rest is Noise: Listening to the Twentieth Century.* New York: Farrar, Straus and Giroux, 2008.

——. "Will Thomas Mann's House Be Demolished?" *New Yorker,* August 18, 2016. http://www.newyorker.com/culture/cultural-comment/will-thomas-manns-house-be-demolished.

Ross, Harold. "From Captain to Private." *New Yorker,* October 17, 1942, 17–18.

Rubin, Joan Shelley. *The Making of Middlebrow Culture.* Chapel Hill: University of North Carolina Press, 1992.

Rychner, Max. "Literarischer Nobelpreis 1929." *Neue Schweizer Rundschau* (1929). Reprinted in *Thomas Mann im Urteil seiner Zeit: Dokumente 1891–1955,* edited by Klaus Schröter, 170–71. Hamburg: Christian Wegner Verlag, 1969.

Salamanca, Lucy. *Fortress of Freedom: The Story of the Library of Congress.* Philadelphia: J. B. Lippincott, 1942.

Sammons, Jeffrey L. *Kuno Francke's Edition of "The German Classics" (1913–15): A Critical and Historical Overview.* New York: Peter Lang, 2009.

Schiller, Friedrich. "On Naïve and Sentimental Poetry." Translated by Daniel O. Dahlstrohm. In *Essays,* edited by Walter Hinderer and Daniel O. Dahlstrohm, 179–260. New York: Continuum, 1993.

Schivelbusch, Wolfgang. *Three New Deals: Reflections on Roosevelt's America, Mussolini's Italy, and Hitler's Germany, 1933–1939.* New York: Picador, 2007.

Schmidt, Henry J. "Interview with Hermann J. Weigand (1892–1985)." In Benseler, Lohnes, and Nollendorfs, *Teaching German in America,* 285–92.

Schoenberg, Arnold, and Thomas Mann. "'Doctor Faustus' Schoenberg?" Letters to the editor. *Saturday Review of Literature,* January 1, 1949, 22–23.

Schoolfield, George C. "Thomas Mann und Fredrik Böök." In *Deutsche Weltliteratur: Von Goethe bis Ingeborg Bachmann. Festgabe für J. Allan Pfeffer,* edited by Klaus W. Jonas, 158–88. Tübingen: Max Niemeyer Verlag, 1972.

Schröter, Klaus, ed. *Thomas Mann im Urteil seiner Zeit: Dokumente 1891–1955.* Hamburg: Christian Wegner Verlag, 1969.

Schwarz, Karl. "Thomas Mann: Ein Wächter deutscher Kultur?" *Völkischer Beobachter,* October 25, 1935. Reprinted in Schröter, *Thomas Mann im Urteil seiner Zeit,* 256–58.

Schwöbel, Christoph. *Die Religion des Zauberers: Theologisches in den großen Romanen Thomas Manns.* Tübingen: Mohr Siebeck, 2008.

Scott, Donald M. "The Popular Lecture and the Creation of a Public in Mid-Nineteenth-Century America." *Journal of American History* 66, no. 4 (1980): 791–809.

"Scottsboro Protest by Russia, Germany." *Negro World,* July 11, 1931, 8.

Scott-Smith, Giles. *The Politics of Apolitical Culture: The Congress for Cultural Freedom, the CIA and Post-war American Hegemony.* London: Routledge, 2002.

——. "'A Radical Democratic Political Offensive': Melvin J. Lasky, *Der Monat,* and the Congress for Cultural Freedom." *Journal of Contemporary History* 35, no. 2 (April 2000): 263–80.

Siehoff, John-Thomas. "Josephs 'New Deal': Franklin Delano Roosevelts Politik in Thomas Manns *Joseph der Ernährer,*" *New German Review* 11 (1995): 74–88.

Sina, Kai. *Susan Sontag und Thomas Mann.* Göttingen: Wallstein Verlag, 2017.

Slattery, J. F. "Erika Mann und die BBC 1940–1943." *Thomas Mann Jahrbuch* 12 (1999): 309–47.

——. "'Oskar Zuversichtlich': A German Response to British Radio Propaganda during World War II." *Historical Journal of Film, Radio and Television* 12, no. 1 (1992): 69–85.

——. "Thomas Mann und die B.B.C.: Die Bedingungen ihrer Zusammenarbeit 1940–1945." *Thomas Mann Jahrbuch* 5 (1992): 142–70.

Slochower, Harry. "An Open Letter to Thomas Mann." *New Republic*, June 27, 1934, 185.

——. *Three Ways of Modern Man.* New York: International Publishers, 1937.

Smith, Henry. "Thomas Mann Says Democracy Will Win." *Dallas Morning News*, August 7, 1938, 9.

"Some Personal Choices." *Saturday Review of Literature*, December 3, 1927, 410.

Sontag, Susan. "Against Interpretation." In *Against Interpretation and Other Essays.* New York: Picador, 1966.

——. "Pilgrimage." *New Yorker*, December 21, 1987, 38–54.

Sorani, Aldo. "A Letter from Italy." *Saturday Review of Literature*, August 1, 1925, 13.

Sprengel, Peter. *Gerhart Hauptmann: Epoche—Werk—Wirkung.* Munich: C. H. Beck, 1984.

"SRL Reader Poll: From the Subscribing Santas." *Saturday Review of Literature*, December 2, 1950, 48.

Stephan, Alexander. *Im Visier des FBI: Deutsche Exilschriftsteller in den Akten amerikanischer Geheimdienste.* Stuttgart: Verlag J. B. Metzler, 1995.

Stevens, George. "Foothills of the *Magic Mountain.*" *Saturday Review of Literature*, November 11, 1933, 257.

Stonor Saunders, Frances. *Who Paid the Piper? The CIA and the Cultural Cold War.* London: Granta Books, 1999.

"Striking Scenes and Personalities at Brilliant Harvard Commencement." *Boston Post*, June 21, 1935, 14–15.

Strobel, Jochen. *Entzauberung der Nation: Die Repräsentation Deutschlands im Werk Thomas Manns.* Dresden: Thelem Verlag, 2000.

Takayoshi, Ichiro. *American Writers and the Approach of World War II, 1935–1941: A Literary History.* New York: Cambridge University Press, 2015.

Tebbel, John William. *A History of Book Publishing in the United States.* Vol. 3, *The Golden Age between Two Wars 1920–1940.* New York: R. R. Bowker, 1978.

Ter Braak, Menno. "Emigranten-Literatur." *Das Neue Tage-Buch* 2, no. 52 (December 1934): 1244–45.

Thieß, Frank. "Der Fall Thomas Mann." In Grosser, *Die grosse Kontroverse*, 24–26.

——. "German Literature of Today." *Saturday Review of Literature*, May 9, 1925, 745.

——. "Die innere Emigration." In Grosser, *Die grosse Kontroverse*, 22–25.

Thirlwall, John C., ed. *In Another Language: A Record of the Thirty-Year Relationship between Thomas Mann and His English Translator, Helen Tracy Lowe-Porter.* New York: Alfred A. Knopf, 1966.

——. "In Another Language." In Thirlwall, *In Another Language*, 1–147.

"Thomas Mann Charts Course for New German Magazine." *Washington Post*, August 15, 1937, B1.

"Thomas Manns *J'accuse.*" *Basler Arbeiter-Zeitung*, February 6, 1937, 3.

"Thomas Mann's New Novel." *Times Literary Supplement*, March 12, 1925, 170.

"Thomas Mann Will Be Phi Beta Kappa Speaker for Graduates." *Hobart Herald*, May 4, 1939, 1.

Thompson, Dorothy. "The Most Eminent Living Man of Letters." *New York Herald Tribune*, June 10, 1934, G1–2.

——. "To Thomas Mann: An Appreciation." *New York Herald Tribune*, April 14, 1937, 21.

Tillinger, Eugene. "The Moral Eclipse of Thomas Mann." *Plain Talk* 4, no. 3 (December 1949): 53–58.

"Training Leaders: A Test for Colleges." *New York Times Magazine*, June 16, 1935, 3, 15.

Trial of the Major War Criminals before the International Military Tribunal, Nuremberg, 14 November 1945—1 October 1946. 42 vols. Nuremberg: International Military Tribunal, 1947.

Trilling, Lionel. *The Liberal Imagination: Essays on Literature and Society*. New York: Viking Press, 1950.

Trotter, David. *Literature in the First Media Age: Britain between the Wars*. Cambridge, MA: Harvard University Press, 2013.

Troy, William. "Thomas Mann." *Partisan Review*, June 1938, 24–32.

"Turkish Novelists Orhan Pamuk and Elif Shafak Accused of Being Western Stooges by Pro-government Press." *Guardian*, December 12, 2014. http://www.theguardian.com/books/2014/dec/12/pamuk-shafak-turkish-press-campaign.

Turner, Catherine. *Marketing Modernism between the Two World Wars*. Amherst: University of Massachusetts Press, 2003.

United States Holocaust Museum. "Fighting the Fires of Hate: America and the Nazi Book Burnings." Accessed March 20, 2019. https://www.ushmm.org/exhibition/book-burning/burning.php.

Vaget, Hans Rudolf. "'The Best of Worlds': Thomas Mann in Princeton." *Princeton University Library Chronicle* 75, no. 1 (2013): 9–37.

——. "Deutsche Einheit und Nationale Identität: Zur Genealogie der gegenwärtigen Deutschland-Debatte am Beispiel von Thomas Mann." *Literaturwissenschaftliches Jahrbuch der Görres-Gesellschaft* 33 (1992): 277–98.

——. "Erich Kahler, Thomas Mann und Deutschland: Eine Miszelle zum *Doktor Faustus*." In *Ethik und Ästhetik: Werke und Werte in der Literatur vom 18. Bis zum 20. Jahrhundert*, edited by Richard Fisher, 509–18. Frankfurt am Main: Peter Lang, 1995.

——. "Introduction." In *Thomas Mann's "The Magic Mountain": A Casebook*, edited by Hans Rudolf Vaget, 3–11. New York: Oxford University Press, 2008.

——. "Mann, Joyce, and the Question of Modernism in *Doctor Faustus*." In Lehnert and Pfeiffer, *Thomas Mann's "Doctor Faustus*," 167–92.

——. *Seelenzauber: Thomas Mann und die Musik*. Frankfurt am Main: S. Fischer Verlag, 2011.

——. *Thomas Mann, der Amerikaner: Leben und Werk im amerikanischen Exil 1938–1952*. Frankfurt am Main: S. Fischer Verlag, 2011.

——. *Thomas Mann: Kommentar zu sämtlichen Erzählungen*. Munich: Winkler, 1984.

——. "Thomas Mann, Schiller, and the Politics of Literary Self-Fashioning." *Monatshefte* 97, no. 3 (2005): 494–510.

——. "Vorzeitiger Antifaschismus und andere unamerikanische Umtriebe." In *Horizonte: Festschrift für Herbert Lehnert, zum 65. Geburtstag*, edited by Hannelore Mundt, Egon Schwarz, and William J. Lillyman, 173–204. Tübingen: Max Niemeyer Verlag, 1990.

——. "Wehvolles Erbe": Richard Wagner in Deutschland. Hitler, Knappertsbusch, Mann. Frankfurt am Main: S. Fischer Verlag, 2017.

Valentin, Sonja. "Steine in Hitlers Fenster": Thomas Manns Radiosendungen "Deutsche Hörer!" 1940–1945. Göttingen: Wallstein Verlag, 2015.

Viereck, Peter. Metapolitics: From the Romantics to Hitler. New York: Alfred A. Knopf, 1941.

"Vladimir Nabokov." USA: The Novel. NET National Educational Television, February 3, 1965.

Voit, Friedrich. Karl Wolfskehl: Leben und Werk im Exil. Göttingen: Wallstein Verlag, 2005.

Walkowitz, Rebecca. Born Translated: The Contemporary Novel in an Age of World Literature. New York: Columbia University Press, 2015.

Walter, Hans-Albert. Deutsche Exilliteratur 1933–1950. Vol. 4, Exilpresse. Stuttgart: J. B. Metzlersche Verlagsbuchhandlung, 1978.

Warner, Michael. "Origins of the Congress of Cultural Freedom, 1949–50." Studies in Intelligence 38, no. 5 (1995): 89–98.

Weigand, Hermann. Thomas Mann's Novel "Der Zauberberg": A Study. New York: D. Appleton–Century Company, 1933.

Weiss, Andrea. In the Shadow of the Magic Mountain: The Erika and Klaus Mann Story. Chicago: University of Chicago Press, 2008.

Weitz, Hans-J., ed. Johann Wolfgang von Goethe: Die Deutschen. Konstanz: Südverlag, 1949.

Werckmeister, O. K. "Hitler the Artist." Critical Inquiry 23, no. 3 (Winter 1997): 270–97.

West, Rebecca. "Books for Liberated Europe." English-Speaking World: Journal of the English-Speaking Union 26 (December 1943–January 1944): 3–6.

——. "Notes on Three Novels." Saturday Review of Literature, October 17, 1925, 207–8.

White, John Franklin. Thomas Mann in America: The Rhetorical and Political Experiences of an Exiled Artist. Ann Arbor: University of Michigan Doctoral Dissertation Series, 1971.

Whitney, Paul V. C. "Distinguished Exile Speaks Here Tonight." Deseret News, March 21, 1938, 1.

"Why Nabokov Detests Freud." New York Times, January 30, 1966, 346.

Winston, Richard. "On Translating Thomas Mann." American Pen: An International Quarterly of Writing 7, no. 3 (1975): 15–22.

Wißkirchen, Hans. "Gegen Hitler: Thomas Manns mediale Strategien auf dem Weg zum Repräsentanten des anderen Deutschland." Thomas Mann Jahrbuch 23 (2011): 77–90.

Wittek, Bernhard. Der britische Ätherkrieg gegen das Dritte Reich: Die deutschsprachigen Kriegssendungen der British Broadcasting Corporation. Münster: Verlag C. J. Fahle, 1962.

Woodress, James. Willa Cather: A Literary Life. Lincoln: University of Nebraska Press, 1987.

Wright, Tom F. "Introduction." In The Cosmopolitan Lyceum: Lecture Culture and the Globe in Nineteenth-Century America, edited by Tom F. Wright. Amherst: University of Massachusetts Press, 2013.

Wysling, Hans. "'German Letters': Thomas Manns Briefe an *The Dial* (1922–28)." In *Dokumente und Untersuchungen: Beiträge zur Thomas-Mann-Forschung*, edited by Hans Wysling, 13–62. Bern: Francke Verlag, 1974.

Zerner, Marianne. "Thomas Mann in Standard English Anthologies." *German Quarterly* 18, no. 4 (November 1945): 178–88.

Ziolkowski, Theodore. *Uses and Abuses of Moses: Literary Representations since the Enlightenment*. Notre Dame, IN: University of Notre Dame Press, 2016.

Zola, Émile. "J'accuse." Translated by Eleanor Levieux. In *The Dreyfus Affair: "J'accuse" and Other Writings*, edited by Alain Pagès, 43–52. New Haven, CT: Yale University Press, 1996.

Zühlsdorff, Volkmar. *Hitler's Exiles: The German Cultural Resistance in America and Europe*. Translated by Martin H. Bott. London: Continuum, 2004.

INDEX

Page numbers in *italics* refer to figures.